Lecture Notes in Computer Scien

T0237953

Commenced Publication in 1973
Founding and Former Series Editors:
Gerhard Goos, Juris Hartmanis, and Jan van Leeuwen

Ian Goldberg   Mikhail J. Atallah (Eds.)

Privacy Enhancing Technologies

9th International Symposium, PETS 2009
Seattle, WA, USA, August 5-7, 2009
Proceedings

 Springer

Volume Editors

Ian Goldberg
University of Waterloo, David R. Cheriton School of Computer Science
200 University Avenue West, Waterloo, ON, N2L 3G1, Canada
E-mail: iang@cs.uwaterloo.ca

Mikhail J. Atallah
Purdue University, Department of Computer Science
305 North University Street, West Lafayete, IN 47907-2107, USA
E-mail: mja@cs.purdue.edu

Library of Congress Control Number: 2009930653

CR Subject Classification (1998): H.5, H.4, H.3, I.2, I.3, I.7, J.5

LNCS Sublibrary: SL 4 – Security and Cryptology

ISSN 0302-9743

ISBN 978-3-642-03167-0 Springer Berlin Heidelberg New York

springer.com

Typesetting: Camera-ready by author, data conversion by Scientific Publishing Services, Chennai, India
Printed on acid-free paper   SPIN: 12719389   06/3180   5 4 3 2 1 0

Message from the Program Chairs

The 2009 Privacy Enhancing Technologies Symposium was held at the University of Washington in Seattle during August 5–7, 2009. This was the ninth in this series of meetings, and the second after the transition from workshop to symposium. PETS remains a premier forum for publishing research on both the theory and the practice of privacy-enhancing technologies, and has a broad scope that includes all facets of the field.

The PETS program this year included a diverse set of 14 peer-reviewed papers, selected from 44 submissions. Each submission was reviewed by at least four members of the Program Committee. This was the second year of the popular HotPETs session, designed as a venue to present exciting but still preliminary and evolving ideas, rather than formal and rigorous completed research results. HotPETs this year included a program of 14 presentations of 10–20 minutes each; as was the case last year, there were no published proceedings for HotPETs. PETS also included the traditional "rump session," with brief presentations on a variety of topics.

We are grateful to all of the authors who submitted, to the PETS and Hot-PETs speakers who presented their work selected for the program, and to the rump session participants. We are also grateful to the Program Committee members, and to the external reviewers who assisted them, for their thorough reviews and participation in discussions — they were central to the resulting high-quality program. The following subset of these reviewers gracefully volunteered to continue their work as shepherds helping the authors improve their papers and address the reviewer comments and suggestions: Alastair Beresford, Lorrie Cranor, Claudia Diaz, Steven Murdoch, and Carmela Troncoso. It is a also a pleasure to acknowledge the contribution of our General Chair, Adam Shostack, who worked tirelessly on the local arrangements and logistical aspects of the symposium. The University of Washington helped to host the symposium, and our webmaster since 2007, Jeremy Clark, did his usual outstanding job at evolving and maintaining the symposium's website. Our gratitude also goes to the Hot-PETs Chairs, Andrei Serjantov and Thomas Heydt-Benjamin, who put together an outstanding HotPETs program, as well as to Vitaly Shmatikov, who chaired the PET Award Selection Committee, and Roger Dingledine, for handling the stipends. Finally, in these tight economic times, we are particularly grateful to Microsoft for its sponsorship and support; it played a central role in helping attendees—especially students—meet registration and travel costs.

May 2009

Ian Goldberg
Mikhail Atallah

Organization

Organizers

General Chair   Adam Shostack (Microsoft, USA)
Program Chairs   Ian Goldberg (University of Waterloo, Canada)
    Mikhail Atallah (Purdue University, USA)
PET Award Chair   Vitaly Shmatikov (University of Texas, USA)
Stipends Chair   Roger Dingledine (The Tor Project, USA)
HotPETs Chairs   Thomas Heydt-Benjamin (IBM Research
    Zurich, Switzerland)
    Andrei Serjantov (The Free Haven Project,
    UK)

Program Committee

Alessandro Acquisti	Carnegie Mellon University, USA
Michael Backes	Saarland University and Max Planck Institute for Software Systems, Germany
Mira Belenkiy	Microsoft, USA
Alastair Beresford	University of Cambridge, UK
Nikita Borisov	University of Illinois at Urbana-Champaign, USA
Lorrie Cranor	Carnegie Mellon University, USA
George Danezis	Microsoft Research Cambridge, UK
Sabrina De Capitani di Vimercati	Università degli Studi di Milano, Italy
Claudia Diaz	K.U. Leuven, Belgium
Roger Dingledine	The Tor Project, USA
Alexandre Evfimievski	IBM Almaden Research Center, USA
Philippe Golle	Palo Alto Research Center, USA
Rachel Greenstadt	Drexel University, USA
Thomas Heydt-Benjamin	IBM Research Zurich, Switzerland
Apu Kapadia	MIT Lincoln Laboratory, USA
Bradley Malin	Vanderbilt University, USA
Tal Malkin	Columbia University, USA
Nick Mathewson	The Tor Project, USA
David Molnar	University of California, Berkeley, USA
Steven Murdoch	University of Cambridge, UK
Andreas Pfitzmann	Dresden University of Technology, Germany
Len Sassaman	K.U. Leuven, Belgium
Andrei Serjantov	The Free Haven Project, UK
Paul Syverson	Naval Research Laboratory, USA

Marianne Winslett   University of Illinois at Urbana-Champaign,
                                       USA
Matthew Wright   University of Texas at Arlington, USA
Ting Yu   North Carolina State University, USA

External Reviewers

Titus Abraham
Sadia Afroz
Elli Androulaki
Claudio Agostino Ardagna
Sruthi Bandhakavi
Stefan Berthold
John Bethencourt
Rainer Boehme
Katrin Borcea-Pfitzmann
Seung Geol Choi
Sebastian Clauß
Ariel Elbaz
David Evans
Michael Gagnon
Aris Gkoulalas-Divanis
Ragib Hasan
Keith Irwin
Peter Johnson
Zach Jorgensen
Hahna Kane
Benjamin Kellermann
Matthias Kirchner
Kush Kothari
Robert Lass
Grigorios Loukides
Homin Lee
Karsten Loesing

Grigorios Loukides
Nayantara Mallesh
Aaron Massey
Kazuhiro Minami
Esfandiar Mohammadi
Meredith L. Patterson
John Paulett
Stefanie Poetzsch
Sören Preibusch
Mariana Raykova
Sasha Romanosky
Aakash Shah
Entong Shen
Alex Simma
Robin Snader
Sandra Steinbrecher
Evan Sultanik
Evimaria Terzi
Carmela Troncoso
Patrick Tsang
Binh Vo
Wei Wei
Jan Werner
Charles Wright
Seung Yi
Charles Zhang

Table of Contents

Ninth Privacy Enhancing Technologies Symposium

Capturing Social Networking Privacy Preferences:

Can Default Policies Help Alleviate Tradeoffs between Expressiveness and User Burden?

Ramprasad Ravichandran, Michael Benisch,
Patrick Gage Kelley, and Norman M. Sadeh

School of Computer Science,
Carnegie Mellon University,
Pittsburgh PA 15217, USA
{rravicha,mbenisch,pkelley,sadeh}@cs.cmu.edu

Abstract. Social networking sites such as Facebook and MySpace thrive on the exchange of personal content such as pictures and activities. These sites are discovering that people's privacy preferences are very rich and diverse. In theory, providing users with more expressive settings to specify their privacy policies would not only enable them to better articulate their preferences, but could also lead to greater user burden. In this article, we evaluate to what extent providing users with default policies can help alleviate some of this burden. Our research is conducted in the context of location-sharing applications, where users are expected to specify conditions under which they are willing to let others see their locations. We define canonical policies that attempt to abstract away user-specific elements such as a user's default schedule, or canonical places, such as "work" and "home." We learn a set of default policies from this data using decision-tree and clustering algorithms. We examine trade-offs between the complexity / understandability of default policies made available to users, and the accuracy with which they capture the ground truth preferences of our user population. Specifically, we present results obtained using data collected from 30 users of location-enabled phones over a period of one week. They suggest that providing users with a small number of canonical default policies to choose from can help reduce user burden when it comes to customizing the rich privacy settings they seem to require.

Keywords: User modeling, Privacy, Mining default policies.

1 Introduction

Social networking sites such as Facebook and MySpace thrive on the exchange of personal content such as pictures and activities. These sites are discovering that people's privacy preferences are very rich and diverse. While in theory, providing users with more expressive settings to specify their privacy policies

I. Goldberg and M. Atallah (Eds.): PETS 2009, LNCS 5672, pp. 1–18, 2009.

gives them the ability to accurately specify their preferences [7], it can also lead to significant increases in user burden. In this paper, we investigate the extent to which generated default policies can alleviate user burden. The use of default policies has proven to be practical in other domains such as the configuration of compact P3P policies in web browsers (e.g. Internet Explorer, Firefox). Here we explore an extension of this approach by introducing the concept of canonical default policies. These policies abstract away idiosyncratic elements of a user context, making it possible to expose and discover common elements across otherwise seemingly disparate user policies.

Specifically, we explore how we can learn default policies using machine learning techniques, and evaluate their effect in alleviating some of the user's burden in defining their privacy policies. Our objective is to minimize the number of edits the user has to make to the default policy to arrive at a policy which she is willing to use. In this work, we use accuracy as a metric to approximate the user's burden to reach an acceptable policy starting from some initial policy (e.g. a blank policy or a default policy). We assume that a user is more likely to be comfortable using default policies of higher accuracy, and requires less editing to arrive at an acceptable final policy. As reported in previous studies (e.g. [22]), users generally do not require policies that are 100% accurate to start using an application. An example is a user with a policy that allows for less sharing than she ideally would like to have.

In this study, we consider the scenario of helping a new user identify suitable default privacy settings. We present her with a choice of default privacy settings that have been learned from our current set of users' privacy settings that she can easily understand and modify to specify her desired initial policy. This work is complementary to research efforts that make it easier to edit policies to converge to desirable final policies (e.g. user controllable learning [16], example-critiquing [10]).

We conduct this study in the context of location-sharing applications, where users are expected to specify conditions under which they are willing to let others (e.g. friends, colleagues, family members) see their locations based on different contexts (e.g. based on day of the week, time of the day, or where they are).

Prior work [22,7] has shown that users' privacy policies can be very rich. For example, a user may have a policy that only allows her colleagues to access her location information when she is at work, and during regular business hours. Trying to derive default policies through direct application of machine learning techniques does not yield intuitive or usable polices. We show that one can abstract away individual elements of a user's schedule and the set of locations she visits, to arrive at what we call canonical policies, such as 'allow access while at work', or 'deny access while at home in the evening'. We further show that canonical policies lend themselves to identification of more meaningful and intuitive default policies that users are more likely to be able to customize.

We evaluate the accuracy with which a combination of canonical default policies can cover the final privacy policies for a population of 30 users whose privacy preferences were collected during the course of a week-long study. We learn users' individual policies using a decision tree algorithm, and cluster the individual policies into a set of more general default policies. We further discuss tradeoffs between intuitiveness of the default canonical policies and the number of such policies. The main contribution of the work is to show that canonical default polices seem to offer a practical solution where traditional application of machine learning techniques yield unintuitive and unusable policies. Our results further suggest that in the case of location-sharing preferences considered in this study, aiming for about 3 default policies is the "sweet-spot", though additional studies may be needed to further validate this result.

2   Related Work

To the best of our knowledge, there hasn't been any prior work on learning default policies in location-sharing services. However, we briefly summarize some of the work from the location-sharing services and user preference learning literature in general.

2.1   Preference Learning

There has been much prior work in applying machine learning techniques to learn users' preferences. In the recommendation systems literature ([8] is an excellent survey), many successful systems have been proposed and built in both—industry (e.g. Amazon.com, Netflix.com), and academia (e.g. [20],[1]). Recommendation systems can usually be classified into content-based (where the recommendation is based on past behavior), collaborative-filtering (where recommendations are based on preferences of other people with similar taste), or a mixture of both. There are basically two categories of collaborative-filtering: nearest neighbor methods (e.g. [11],[24]), and latent factor modeling (e.g. [12],[23]). Although latent-variable models are closest to our line of work, contrary to their approach, our focus is not in arriving at more efficient representations, but in reducing the amount of user burden in further customizing their policies.

In [16], the authors look at user-controllable learning, which is most related to the field of example-critiquing. Unlike their approach where the user and system tweak a common policy model, our work is geared towards helping users bootstrap their privacy policy.

2.2   Location-Sharing Services

There are many commercial location-sharing services such as Loopt [2], Mobimii [4] and Mobikade [3]. Significant academic work has been done in this area (e.g. [25],[21]), where the focus has been on deployment, accurate location detection and implementation of user's privacy policies. A fair amount of work has been done in looking at the types of information that people are willing to share, and the conditions under which they are willing to share, in the form of diary studies [6], interviews [15,13,14], surveys [18], and experience sampling techniques [22,9,17]. Lederer et. al. suggest that the nature of the requester is the primary factor in choosing whether to disclose information or not [18], while Consolvo et al. determined that along with requester information, the reason for the request and the level of detail were important factors as well [9]. In [7], the authors determined that along with the requester type, time of the request and location of the person during the request were important factors in determining whether to disclose their location information.

3   Experimental Setting

Our experimental data comes from a study conducted over the course of two weeks in October 2008. We supplied 30 human subjects with Nokia N95 cell phones for one week at a time (15 subjects per week).

Subjects were recruited through flyers posted around the university campus. Our 30 subjects were all students from our university. The sample was composed of 74% males and 26% females, with an average age of about 21 years old. Undergraduates made up 44% and graduate students made up 56% of the sample.

Our only requirement for entry into the study, was that they must already have an AT&T or T-mobile phone plan, allowing them to transfer their SIM card, into the phone we provided. We required that for the duration of the study the participants use the phone as their primary phone. This requirement ensured that the subjects kept their phones on their person and charged as much as possible. Each of the phones was equipped with our location tracking program, which ran at all times in the background, recording the phone's location using a combination of GPS and Wi-Fi-based positioning to an easily locatable text file on the phone.

Each day, subjects were required to visit our web site and upload this file, from their phone, containing their location information. We processed this file immediately and then presented the participants with a series of questions based on the locations they had been since they last uploaded (allowing flexibility in case they had missed a day).

Every question pertained to a specific location that the participant had been during that day, with a map showing the location and the duration they remained there. For example, a question may have asked "Would you have been comfortable sharing your location between Tuesday October 28th, 8:48pm and Wednesday October 29th, 10:39am with:"

The users were then presented with four groups, to assess whether or not they would have been comfortable sharing their location with each of these groups. The four different groups of individuals were: i) close friends, ii) immediate family, iii) anyone associated with Carnegie Mellon, and iv) the general population, or anyone.

In each of these assessments, or audits, the participants tagged the information gathered with one of the following four classes

1. *Allow* - The participant would allow the requester to share her location.
2. *Deny* - The participant would prefer to not share her location with the requester.

3. *Part of the time* - The participants would like more granularity so that she can allow requester to access her location part of the time.
4. *Part of the group* - The participant would like more granularity so that she can allow only a part (one or several members) of the requester group to access her location information. The main purpose of this designation was to ensure that we did not over-simplify the types of groups we made available in the study.

An additional option was provided for participants to designate the displayed location as inaccurate. When this designation was made the participant was not required to audit for each group, however in practice this was used very infrequently (less than 1%).

The data collection process, specifics of the software implementation, and survey details from pre- and post- questionnaires are explained in more detail in the study [7], and are not repeated here. Although we use the same physical location and auditing data, our focus is different from that study. [7] examines the impact of different levels of expressiveness for privacy mechanisms. On the contrary, we are interested in learning a few default policies that captures the users' privacy policies as accurately as possible while ensuring the policies are both simple and intuitive.

4 Data Exploration

In all, we collected a little more than 3800 hours of location information. Less than 1% of the audits were marked as inaccurate. We would like to determine which attributes are useful in specifying default policies. We first only focus on two of the features: time of day, and day of the week. Figure 1 shows a typical sample of a user's access policies – we can see a particular user's audit, with time of day (in hours) on the Y-axis, and day of the week on the X-axis. We have used different colors to indicate the different audit statuses as follows: allow (*green*), deny (*red*), inaccurate location information (*white*), and finally missing information (*dark blue*). An audit is marked missing if the user did not provide information for that time period, or if the user had tagged that audit as 'part of the group'.

4.1 Data Cleanup

To learn users' default policies from these data, we first handle the audits with missing information and inaccurate location information; and classify them as 'allow' or 'deny'. The main reason for classifying all data is that we would like to consider duration as a feature in our classifier, and we want to make sure that missing information for a few minutes doesn't affect our classifier. We could inadvertently introduce two types of errors: we classify a deny as allow (false positive), or we classify an allow as a deny (false negative). Different users may face different levels of unhappiness depending on the type of classification error.

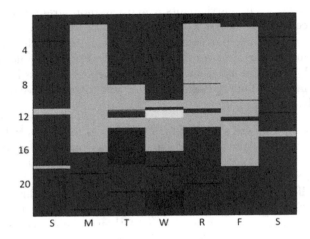

Fig. 1. A typical un-sanitized audit. The requester type is 'university community'. The x-axis in each figure is the day of the week, while the y-axis is time of the day (in hours).

We try to account for this uneven level of happiness by considering the *conservativeness* of a user, as explained below. The conservativeness ratio, κ is defined as the ratio of the user's unhappiness when the system wrongly allows access, to the user's unhappiness when the system wrongly denies access, i.e.

$$\kappa = \frac{Unhappiness\ of\ instance\ wrongly\ classified\ as\ allow}{Unhappiness\ of\ instance\ wrongly\ classified\ as\ deny} \qquad (1)$$

Our definition of the conservativeness ratio assumes that this ratio is fixed for a user across all mistakes that the system makes. For instance, in a real life situation, a user may be more lenient when a university associate is wrongly denied access to her location, than when the requester is a family member, but we do not consider such scenarios here.

We would like to point out that unlike in [7], we assume that the cost of the system making a mistake is equal to the reward when the system gets a correct prediction. In other words, we assume that for every correct prediction, the user's unhappiness reduces by a unit, while for every wrong prediction, the user's unhappiness increases by a unit.

We may have missing information in our data due to many reasons - the data/location may not have been recorded because the cell-phone was turned off; the GPS/Wi-Fi may not have reported an accurate position; or the specifications (with respect to the number and type of groups, and resolution of time during events) may not have had enough expressiveness. The final classification of audits for these missing period depends on a number of factors – source of the error, duration of the error, classification of the encapsulating period, and the conservativeness factor, κ. We found that there is very little correlation between the classification for the same time frame across days, and so we could not use that information to classify missing periods.

If the information is missing for just a couple of minutes (we used a threshold of 5 minutes in this work), or if the source of the missing information is in the data collection process, we classify the audit based on a linear combination of the permissions of the previous and next periods weighted by the conservativeness of the user. In other words, if the missing period is in between two periods with same access types (e.g. both allow), then we classify the period with a similar access type (e.g. allow). The trickier case is when the missing period is in between periods of different access types. For example, if a user allowed access in the period leading to the missing period, and denied access in the period following, and has a conservativeness ratio greater than 1, we deny access during the missing period. Specifically,

$$\delta(period) = \begin{cases} 0 \text{ if } period \text{ is } allow; \\ \kappa \text{ if } period \text{ is } deny. \end{cases} \tag{2}$$

$$class(missing) = \begin{cases} allow \text{ if } \delta(prev.\ period) + \delta(next\ period) < 0.5; \\ deny \ \text{ otherwise.} \end{cases} \tag{3}$$

4.2   Some Observations

The sanitized data (time of day, and day of the week dimensions) for the 30 users when the requester is a member of the University is shown in Figure 2. It has only two possible states: allow (*green*) and deny (*red*). The missing audits and inaccurate audits have also been classified albeit with zero penalty weight, which is not shown in this figure. We assign zero penalty weight to make sure we are not penalized for classifications for which we did not have ground truth.

Preferences collected on weekdays were similar, as were those collected on weekends. We can see this trend in Figure 2, where in each of the 30 cells, the access pattern during most of the day on Sunday and Saturday are correlated while access patterns during nights on Friday and Saturday are similar. Thus, we combined the days of the week into a feature (that we use in our algorithms) with just two values: *weekdays*, and *weekends*. We would also like to note that this grouping would lead to a bias in our learning samples since we have more weekday training samples than weekend training samples. However, assuming that the user cares about the average performance of the system, this should not be a problem since this reflects the actual proportion of weekdays to weekend days in a week.

Another trend that we noticed in our data was that, taking all users' audits into account, variance within a requester type was much lower than between requester types. For instance, when the requester type is 'family', there is a higher tendency for the access to be 'allow', than when the requester type is 'anyone'. This prompted us to learn rules conditioned on the requester type. Thus, much of the analysis in the rest of the paper will look at each requester type separately, and we will explicitly mention when we do not do so.

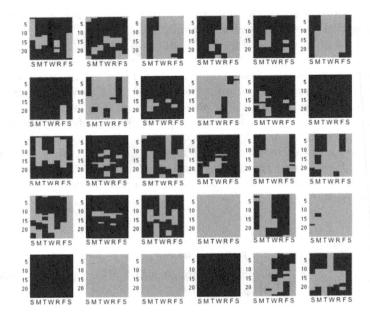

Fig. 2. Sanitized audits of the 30 users (Location shared with University members). The x-axis in each figure is the day of the week, while the y-axis is time of the day (0 - 24 hours).

We also noticed (as may be expected), that there is a tendency for access permissions to switch from 'allow' to 'deny' as we move from family / close friend requester types to the 'anyone' requester type. For instance, if someone denied their close friends from seeing their location during a particular period, it is highly likely that requesters in the 'university members', and 'anyone' categories would also be denied access. We do not take advantage of this observation in our algorithms currently, but we may use this in the future.

5   Methodology

As mentioned earlier, we would like to examine the extent to which we can identify groups of users with similar privacy policies, and ascertain good default policies for them. In addition to the policies being accurate, our aim is to ensure that these policies are both intuitive and understandable, so that our users can customize them to fit their specific needs. While direct application of machine learning algorithms may achieve high accuracy, a naive application of learning may not guarantee understandable and customizable policies. To illustrate this point, in Figure 3, we show the result of applying K-means directly on the input data. Here we cluster the privacy profiles of our users when the requester is a

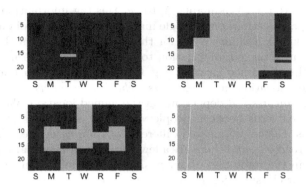

Fig. 3. Base case: Non-canonical and unintuitive policy clusters for Family obtained from direct application of clustering (red = *deny*, green = *allow*)

family member, based on the time of day, and day of the week. We set the number of clusters to 4. Each cluster corresponds to a characteristic privacy profile.

As we can see from Figure 3, using actual times to determine privacy policies yielded rules that were not generalizable and unintuitive. The main reason could be that our user's demographics (students) have schedules that are more event-based (e.g. after work), rather than time based (e.g. after 5:00 PM). In order to capture this, we incorporate a coarser notion of time by dividing a day into coarser intervals of different granularity. We experimented with different intervals of 1, 2, 3, 4, 6, 8, and 12 hours. Every 'activity' is then tagged with the periods during which it occurred. For example, let us consider the case of 3 hour intervals. If a user allowed access from 2:00 PM - 11:30 PM, then we tag that event with three time tags - periods 6, 7 and 8, corresponding to the intervals (3:00 PM - 6:00PM, 6:00 - 9:00 PM, and 9:00 PM to 12:00 AM). We include all the periods where the event occured at least $\gamma\%$ of the time. We determine γ as follows

$$\gamma = \begin{cases} 80 \text{ if } period \ is \ allow; \\ \frac{80}{\kappa} \text{ if } period \ is \ deny. \end{cases} \tag{4}$$

where, κ is the conservativeness ratio defined earlier. The reasoning behind this is that if a user was very conservative (say $\kappa = 5$), and denied access during a portion (say around 40% of the time) of a particular period, we would make sure that the classification of the period in the mined rule lowers the expected unhappiness of the user (and classifies it as deny). We chose 80% as the cutoff (Equation 4) after experimenting with different values for the cutoff. Also, as noted in our data exploration step, we incorporated a coarser notion of day of the week (as weekday or weekend).

Next, we incorporated 'canonical' location information in our study. As mentioned earlier, our location measurement devices (GPS and Wi-fi positioning on the phone) returned location in terms of latitude and longitude observations. We wanted to get a tag for this location, so that we can group locations that have similar context. We used Wikimapia [5] to get this tag information. Wikimapia allows users to tag locations on a google map. Users of Wikimapia mark an area on the map provided, and give a tag for that area such as 'Kiva Han Cafe'. We used this previously tagged information to reverse-geocode the users' latitudes and longitudes into a named location (e.g. Carnegie Mellon, Starbucks etc.). We then tagged these locations as *off-campus, school, on-campus residence, restaurant, mall,* and, *unclassified* depending on the named location. We also noticed different access patterns between people who lived on-campus and those who lived off-campus. Hence, we created different location categories for them. Our University is spread out, and there are a few restaurants very near campus buildings - closer than the resolution of our positioning estimates. In cases where we don't have a clear classification for a particular location, we have two entries in our data - one for campus, and the other for restaurants.

The last attribute we incorporated was the duration of the event. We wanted to see whether the duration of the event would have an impact on the privacy profiles. For instance, a user might want to allow her family to know her location if she was working longer than usual.

As mentioned in the Introduction, the aim of this paper is to present the new user with a choice of default policies learned from existing users. In the first part of this section, we deal with helping users learn a suitable policy using their own audits using a supervised learning approach. We identify a few features, and show how these features can be used to learn an individual privacy policy for the user. In the latter part, we describe how to mine suitable default policies from these individual policies.

5.1 Learning Individual User's Policies: An Empirical Approach to Approximating Accuracy Limits

Along with the fact that we needed to learn policies for new users from their first set of audits, the main reason for this step is also operational — in the data that we collected, we did not collect policies from users in the form of rules. Hence, we need to use this step to determine rules from the audits to determine default policies for our users too.

In order to learn rules from the user's audits, we use a decision tree to generate them based on the attributes that were dicussed earlier. We used the C4.5 decision tree algorithm [19] to mine rules automatically from each of the users' audits separately. We used 10-fold cross validation to ensure that there was no overfitting. We trained various combinations of features (requester type, time in 4 hour intervals, day of the week, tagged location and duration of the event) to understand which of the features were instrumental in reducing the test error. In addition to lower test error, we prefer simpler rules trading off a slightly higher test error. We achieve this by ensuring that the depth of the tree was small. In all, save 1 of the 30 users, the type of requester was the first feature based on which the tree was branched - thus confirming our previous notion that requester type is the most important feature.

We studied the accuracy of our classifier by considering an exhaustive combination of all the features. We observed that using 'duration' as a feature increases both the error and the complexity of the policies (with $p < 0.05$). So, in the rest of the paper, we only use 'canonical' location, day of the week (weekday / weekend) and a coarse representation of time as the relevant features for our classification.

In Figure 9, we give a sample individual policy learned by the decision tree for a specific requester group. In this case, the learned simple policy specifies that the user allows access to her location to anyone from the university only when she is not at home[1]. Hence, this policy does not depend on the day of the week (w.r.t. weekday / weekend) or the time of the day.

In the next set of results, we represent the error in estimation as accuracy loss. Accuracy loss is the error rate in classification weighted by the conservativeness ratio (Equation 5). For instance, if the policy generated has 10% of the periods wrongly classified as allow, and 5% of the periods wrongly classified as deny, and the conservativeness ratio (κ) of the user is 2, the accuracy loss is calculated to be 0.25.

$$\text{accuracy loss} = \frac{Period\ wrongly\ classified\ as\ allow}{Total\ period\ classified} \cdot \kappa + \frac{Period\ wrongly\ classified\ as\ deny}{Total\ period\ classified} \tag{5}$$

We first compare the effect of the granularity of the time information. In Figure 5, we plot a histogram of the test error for various intervals of time, arranged by requester type. We have only included a few of the time intervals in this plot. As we see in Figure 5, we got the best accuracy when we used time intervals of 1 hour. This is useful when learning individualized policies, but often leads to very fractured and possibly unintuitive policies when trying to identify default policies for an entire population of users (Figure 4).

Next, we wanted to see the effect of conservative policies. As mentioned before, the conservativeness ratio (κ) is the ratio between a misclassified allow (i.e. the system decides to deny when the user actually wanted to allow) and a misclassified deny. We plot a histogram of the test error in Figure 6, for various ratios. The ratios are represented as 1:κ in the figure. We see that as a user gets more conservative, the mean error increases (i.e. the distribution spreads out).

5.2   Identifying Promising Default Policies

At the end of the previous step, we have a set of individual policies. Each policy has a set of rules mined for each user based on their audits. Now, we intend

---

[1] Since, the requester cannot differentiate between 'offline' mode and 'deny' mode, having a deny policy for a specific canonical place may not necessarily reveal one's location.

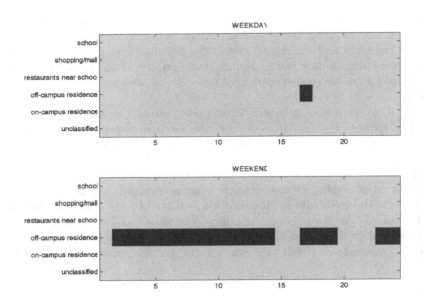

Fig. 4. An example of a less intuitive policy that was learned with time period of 1. Area shaded in green is allow, while area shaded in red is deny.

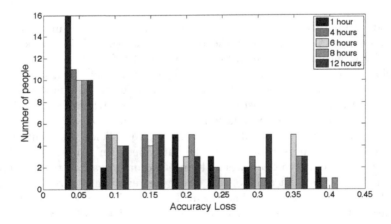

Fig. 5. Histogram of accuracy loss for different time granularity for the University group. Here, each instance is a user, and the accuracy loss is calculated across all audits by that user. We see that as granularity increases, error increases too.

to cluster people into groups such that the ideal policies of the people in each cluster have very little variance, and we can thus ensure that a default policy that is very similar to one person's ideal policy is likely to be very similar to others in the group.

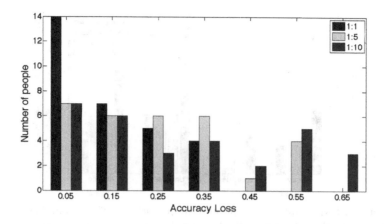

Fig. 6. Histogram of accuracy loss for different conservative ratios for people from the University group. Here, each instance is a user, and the accuracy loss is calculated across all audits by that user. We see that error increases for more conservative users.

We use the K-means clustering algorithm to cluster users into groups. As input to the clustering algorithm, we use the individual policies - either, learned from the users' decision trees (as shown in the previous section), or taken as input directly from an existing user of the system. More specifically, each of the feature vectors is an individual user's decision tree applied to the entire state-space weighted by the frequency of occurence of the various rules in the users training set. This step is required since the learned tree uniformly weighs all rules as equally likely. Once the users are grouped into various clusters, the final rules can be learned again by concatenating the users' rules into a single list of rules, and using a decision tree on this concatenated list. It may seem intuitive to learn directly from the individual policies, instead of using the users' rules. But, learning directly from the individual policies does not take into account the fact that decision tree outputs uniformly weigh all instances – including instances where the tree has never seen a single training point.

We experimented with different values for k (the number of clusters). The number of clusters corresponds to the number of default policies that the new user gets to choose from. We show a comparison of accuracies achieved by different values of k, varying them from 1 to 4 in Figure 7. We see that as the number of default policies increase, the overall classfication error reduces. There is a marked decrease in error when going from 1 default policy to 2 default policies. In contrast, [7] suggests that the users had 6 time rules, 19 location based rules and 24 location / time rules to describe their privacy policy completely, without restricting the rules to be intuitive. While our policies are specified in a slightly different fashion, we see that we are able to get within 90% accuracy with as little as 3 intuitive rules for each requester group type.

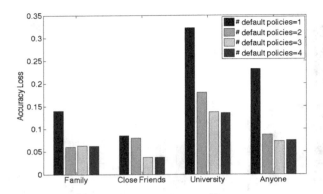

Fig. 7. Accuracy loss for different requester groups and for different number of default policies per group when the day is divided into 6 intervals of 4 hours each

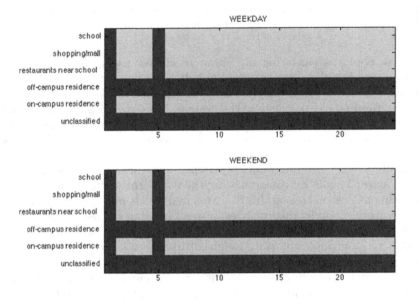

Fig. 8. An example of a less intuitive default policy that was learned (One of the four default policies learned for the friends requester type). It's classified as less intuitive since the policy generated is very fractured.

Using more clusters leads to some policies that are highly specific to a small set of users, and are less intuitive for a general new user (Figure 8). In constrast, Figure 9 shows an example of an intuitive default policy when the requester is a university friend, and we have three default policies. We use the duration of each rule of the policy (i.e. the size of the contiguous block in the figure) as a simple measure of 'intuitiveness' of the policy. Rules with very short durations

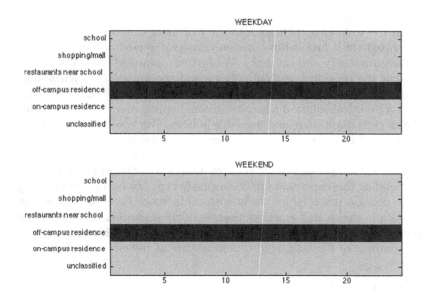

Fig. 9. An example of an intuitive default policy that was learned (One of the three default policies learned for the University member requester type)

are classified as less intuitive. We also see a marginal increase in error, as we increase the time resolution from 1 hour to 6 hours in most cases, although as we saw in Figure 4, the intuitiveness of the resulting policy decreases with 1 hour resolution.

6   Conclusions and Future Work

In this work, we considered the scenario of helping a new user identify suitable default privacy settings. We presented her with a choice of default privacy settings that have been learned from our current set of users' privacy settings that she can easily understand and modify to specify her desired initial policy. We conducted this study in the context of location-sharing applications, where users specified conditions under which they were willing to let others see their locations based on different contexts.

We demonstrated that deriving default policies through direct application of machine learning techniques did not yield intuitive or usable polices. We then showed that one could abstract away individual elements of a user's schedule and the set of locations they visit, to arrive at what we call canonical policies, that lent themselves to identification of more meaningful and intuitive default policies that users were more likely to be able to customize.

We evaluated the accuracy of default canonical policies for a population of 30 users whose privacy preferences were collected during the course of a week-long study. We learned the users' individual policies using a decision tree algorithm, and clustered the individual policies into a set of more general default policies. We demonstrated the relationship between conservativeness and accuracy, and between time granularity and accuracy. We further discussed tradeoffs between intuitiveness of the default canonical policies and the number of such policies. The main contribution of the work was to show that canonical default polices seem to offer a practical solution where traditional application of machine learning techniques yield unintuitive and unusable policies. Our results further suggest that in the case of location-sharing preferences considered in this study, there was a sweet-spot of around 3 default canonical policies per requester group. We have included the final set of default policies obtained in the Appendix.

We are extending this experiment in Locaccino (http://www.locaccino.org), where we are doing a much larger study with many more Facebook users spanning over multiple weeks. In Locaccino, users actively share their locations based on their specified privacy policies. We hope to utilize the more diverse set of users to study the impact of the suggested canonical default policies.

Acknowledgements

This work is supported by NSF Cyber Trust grant CNS-0627513 and ARO research grant DAAD19-02-1-0389 to Carnegie Mellon Universitys CyLab. Additional support has been provided by Microsoft through the Carnegie Mellon Center for Computational Thinking, FCT through the CMU/Portugal Information and Communication Technologies Institute, and through grants from FranceTelecom and Nokia. Our WiFi-based location tracking functionality runs on top of technology developed by Skyhook Wireless. We would also like to thank the members of the User-Controllable Security and Privacy for Pervasive Computing project at Carnegie Mellon University for their advice and assistance with our study.

References

1. Duine project, http://www.telin.nl/project/Home.cfm?id=387&language=en
2. Loopt, http://www.loopt.com
3. Mobikade, http://www.mkade.com
4. Mobimii, http://www.mobimii.com
5. Wikimapia, http://www.wikimapia.com
6. Barkhuus, L., Dey, A.K.: Location-based services for mobile telephony: a study of users' privacy concerns. In: Rauterberg, M., Menozzi, M., Wesson, J. (eds.) INTERACT. IOS Press, Amsterdam (2003)
7. Benisch, M., Kelley, P.G., Sadeh, N., Sandholm, T., Cranor, L.F., Drielsma, P.H., Tsai, J.: The impact of expressiveness on the effectiveness of privacy mechanisms for location sharing. Technical Report CMU-ISR-08-141, Carnegie Mellon University (2008)
8. Breese, J.S., Heckerman, D., Kadie, C.: In: Empirical Analysis of Predictive Algorithms for Collaborative Filtering (1998)

9. Consolvo, S., Smith, I.E., Matthews, T., LaMarca, A., Tabert, J., Powledge, P.: Location disclosure to social relations: why, when, & what people want to share. In: CHI 2005: Proceedings of the SIGCHI conference on Human factors in computing systems, pp. 81–90. ACM, New York (2005)

10. Faltings, B., Pu, P., Torrens, M., Viappiani, P.: Designing example-critiquing interaction. In: Vanderdonckt, J., Nunes, N.J., Rich, C. (eds.) Intelligent User Interfaces, pp. 22–29. ACM, New York (2004)

11. Herlocker, J.L., Konstan, J.A., Borchers, A., Riedl, J.: An algorithmic framework for performing collaborative filtering. In: SIGIR 1999: Proceedings of the 22nd annual international ACM SIGIR conference on Research and development in information retrieval, pp. 230–237. ACM, New York (1999)

12. Hofmann, T.: Latent semantic models for collaborative filtering. ACM Trans. Inf. Syst. 22(1), 89–115 (2004)

13. Hong, J.I., Landay, J.A.: An architecture for privacy-sensitive ubiquitous computing. In: MobiSys 2004: Proceedings of the 2nd international conference on Mobile systems, applications, and services, pp. 177–189. ACM, New York (2004)

14. Kaasinen, E.: User needs for location-aware mobile services. Personal Ubiquitous Comput 7(1), 70–79 (2003)

15. Kawsar, F., Nakajima, T.: Persona: a portable tool for augmenting proactive applications with multimodal personalization support. In: MUM 2007: Proceedings of the 6th international conference on Mobile and ubiquitous multimedia, pp. 160–168. ACM, New York (2007)

16. Kelley, P.G., Drielsma, P.H., Sadeh, N.M., Cranor, L.F.: User-controllable learning of security and privacy policies. In: Balfanz, D., Staddon, J. (eds.) AISec, pp. 11–18. ACM, New York (2008)

17. Ashraf, K., Kay, C.: Context-aware telephony: privacy preferences and sharing patterns. In: CSCW 2006: Proceedings of the 2006 20th anniversary conference on Computer supported cooperative work, pp. 469–478. ACM, New York (2006)

18. Scott, L., Jennifer, M., Dey, A.K.: Who wants to know what when? privacy preference determinants in ubiquitous computing. In: CHI 2003: CHI 2003 extended abstracts on Human factors in computing systems, pp. 724–725. ACM, New York (2003)

19. Quinlan, R.J.: C4.5: Programs for Machine Learning. Morgan Kaufmann Series in Machine Learning. Morgan Kaufmann, San Francisco (1993)

20. Resnick, P., Iacovou, N., Suchak, M., Bergstrom, P., Riedl, J.: Grouplens: An open architecture for collaborative filtering of netnews. In: Proceedings of the ACM 1994 Conference on Computer Supported Cooperative Work, pp. 175–186. ACM Press, New York (1994)

21. Sadeh, N., Gandon, F., Kwon, O.B.: Ambient intelligence: The mycampus experience. Technical Report CMU-ISRI-05-123, Carnegie Mellon University (2005)

22. Sadeh, N., Hong, J., Cranor, L., Fette, I., Kelley, P., Prabaker, M., Rao, J.: Understanding and capturing peoples privacy policies in a mobile social networking application. Personal and Ubiquitous Computing

23. Salakhutdinov, R., Mnih, A., Hinton, G.: Restricted boltzmann machines for collaborative filtering. In: ICML 2007: Proceedings of the 24th international conference on Machine learning, pp. 791–798. ACM, New York (2007)

24. Sarwar, B., Karypis, G., Konstan, J., Riedl, J.: Item-based collaborative filtering recommendation algorithms (2001)

25. Want, R., Hopper, A., Falcao, V., Gibbons, J.: The active badge location system. ACM Trans. Inf. Syst. 10(1), 91–102 (1992)

Appendix

In Table 1, we present the set of default canonical policies that were mined from our experiment. The policies are presented by type of requester. These results are based on a conservativeness ratio of 1, and the days were divided into 6 time periods — morning, mid-day, afternoon, evening, night and late-night.

Table 1. Default policy options arranged by requester types. A user selects a default policy by choosing one default rule for each category of requesters.

Default Canonical Policies Learned	
Requester Type	**Default Rules**
Family Members	1. Allow always 2. Deny if in an unlabeled location
Close Friends	1. Allow Always 2. Deny if in off-campus residence in the mornings 3. Deny if at school during late-nights
University Colleagues	1. Allow Always 2. Deny on weekends and weeknights 3. Deny if at off-campus residence
Anyone	1. Deny Always 2. Allow if in school during morning-to-afternoon on weekdays 3. Allow if in school

Regulating Privacy in Wireless Advertising Messaging: FIPP Compliance by Policy vs. by Design

Heng Xu, John W. Bagby, and Terence Ryan Melonas

College of Information Sciences and Technology
Pennsylvania State University, University Park, PA 16802
{hxx4,jwb7,trm917}@psu.edu

Abstract. This research analyzes consumer privacy issues pertaining to the newly developing wireless marketing context, specifically, wireless advertising messaging (WAM). We develop a conceptual framework named as DIGs (Design innovation/Industry self-regulation/Government regulation/Standards) to assess the efficacy of industry self-regulation, government regulation, and technological solutions in ensuring consumer privacy in WAM. In addition to enhancing our theoretical understanding of WAM privacy, these findings have important implications for WAM service providers, mobile consumers, as well as for regulatory bodies and technology developers.

Keywords: Fair Information Practice Principles (FIPP), industry self-regulation, government regulation, privacy enhancing technologies (PETs), architecture design, wireless advertising messaging (WAM).

1 Introduction

The ubiquity of computing and the miniaturization of mobile devices have generated unique opportunities for wireless marketing that could be customized to an individual's preferences, geographical location, and time of day. Unsurprisingly, the commercial potential and growth of wireless marketing have been accompanied by concerns over the potential privacy intrusion that consumers experience, such as wireless spam messages or intrusive location referencing. This research analyzes privacy issues pertaining to wireless advertising messaging (WAM). In this article, WAM is provisionally defined as advertising messages sent to wireless devices such as cellular telephones, personal data assistants (PDAs) and smart phones.

Fair information practice principles (FIPP), the global standards for the ethical use of personal information, are generally recognized as a standard that addresses consumer privacy risk perceptions. Prior privacy literature describes three approaches to implement FIPP: industry self-regulation, government regulation and privacy-enhancing technologies [15, 19]. Industry self-regulation is a commonly used approach that mainly consists of industry codes of conduct and self-policing trade groups and associations as a means of regulating privacy practices. Seals of approval from trusted third-parties (such as TRUSTe) are one example of the mechanism that was created to provide third-party assurances to consumers based on a voluntary

I. Goldberg and M. Atallah (Eds.): PETS 2009, LNCS 5672, pp. 19–36, 2009.

contractual relationship between firms and the seal provider. Government regulation is another commonly used approach for assuring information privacy, which relies on the judicial and legislative branches of a government for protecting personal information [37]. Finally, PETs, also known as privacy-enhancing or privacy-enabling technologies, are broadly defined as any type of technology that is designed to guard or promote the privacy interests of individuals [9]. PET designers often argue that perhaps technological solutions to privacy, although widely implicated for enabling companies to employ privacy invasive practices, could play a significant role in protecting privacy, particularly because of its ability to cross international political, regulatory, and business boundaries, much like the Internet itself [41].

In general, the public has been skeptical about the efficacy of privacy-enhancing technology and industry self-regulation for protecting information privacy [19, 24, 42]. Privacy advocates and individual activists continue to demand stronger government regulation to restrain abuses of personal information by merchants [13, 37]. We seek to contribute to this debate by discussing whether privacy assurance should be better addressed by policy (through industry self-regulation or government regulation) or by design (through privacy enhancing technologies). Toward this end, we develop a conceptual framework named as DIGs (Design innovation/Industry self-regulation/Government regulation/Standards) to assess the relative effectiveness of industry self-regulation versus government regulation versus technological solutions in ensuring consumer privacy in WAM. Figure 1 depicts the DIGs framework.

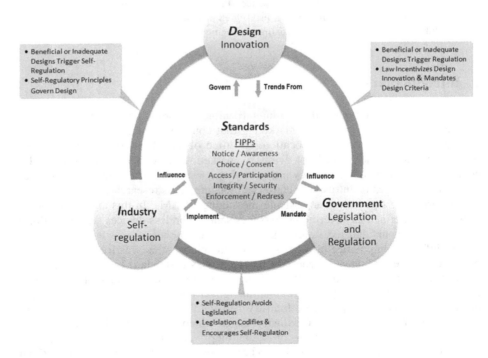

Fig. 1. Conceptual Framework: WAM Privacy by Policy vs. by Design

2 Privacy Standards: The Fair Information Practice Principles

Privacy practices in WAM are subject to a range of standards that purport to protect the privacy of individuals. Among the most notable of these are the "privacy standards" embodied in the Fair Information Practice Principles (FIPP), which originated from a study commissioned by the U.S. Department of Health, Education and Welfare in 1973[30]. FIPP is arguably the first comprehensive treatment of privacy standards that was sufficiently influential to propagate governmental, private-sector and self-regulatory approaches to privacy policy-making. It has been argued that the FIPP have become the de facto global standards for ethical use of personally identifiable information (PII) [29]. However, FIPP are informal, de jure standards that have repeatedly inspired particular mechanisms, rights and procedures in privacy policies including many privacy statutes, regulations and self-regulatory policies that appear in U.S. governmental privacy regulations, in private-sector self-regulatory programs and many other nations privacy public policies (e.g., EU) [3]. Five FIPP are relevant to WAM privacy whether imposed through government regulation, through industry or individual organization/firm self-regulation, arise under contract or result from particular architecture designs. The FIPP include: (1) notice or awareness, (2) choice or consent, (3) access or participation (4) integrity or security and (5) enforcement or redress.

2.1 FIPP Standard No. 1: Notice/Awareness

When applied to WAM, the notice or awareness FIPP standard would alert individuals of the potential for capture, processing and use of their PII. Furthermore, notice could be designed to inform individuals of the purpose intended for the use of their PII. Notice preceding collection of PII would prevent data collection from uninformed individuals. Individuals would be enabled by notice to take counter-measures for protection of their PII before participating in WAM. Furthermore, notice would inform the individual's choice, including: (i) PII data collector identity, (ii) PII recipient identity, (iii) PII use summary, (iv) PII description if targeted for collection, (v) means and methods expected for collection of PII, (vi) notice when PII collection is pre-condition to subject individual's participation (e.g., online access, initiating contractual or other relationship with PII collector) and (vii) summary of the information security controls deployed.

2.2 FIPP Standard No. 2: Choice/Consent

The choice or consent FIPP standard would permit individuals to make the final decision to participate in WAM before the collection and use of their PII. This FIPP standard would require the manifestation of consent to be clear and intentional and this consent would need to precede any use of PII in the immediate transaction. Furthermore, consent is necessary before secondary uses of PII, including future "transfers onward" of PII, such as by sale or barter to third parties, an essential design component to most WAM business models. The manifestation of consent ranges through various methods, most notably with either an opt-out or an opt-in. Forthright and full compliance with this FIPP standard is accomplished when the choice is clear and unequivocal. For example, some WAM architectures would rely on geolocation-based informaiton. This area more strongly suggests the need for clear and unequivocal consent because individuals are subject to more immediate risks if the geolocation PII used in WAM becomes insecure.

2.3   FIPP Standard No. 3: Access/Participation

The third FIPP would enable individuals to review the PII files used in WAM business models in a timely, accurate and inexpensive manner. This standard of access encourages individuals to participate in the assurance of PII accuracy. Without simple and effective means to challenge and correct inaccurate PII individuals' have fewer opportunities to improve PII accuracy that would likely make WAM business models effective. This FIPP standard also illustrates the links among all FIPP: access improves the integrity of PII through personal incentives to audit PII accuracy, thereby enabling security management.

2.4   FIPP Standard No. 4: Integrity/Security

Over a decade of experience now strongly suggests that custodial responsibility over PII has very limited value without close adherence to the fourth FIPP standard: integrity and security. Various government imposed regulation, in the form of statutes, agency regulations, caselaw and standards impose custodial duties on PII database suppliers, owners, customers and operators. These would require WAM participants to assure data quality, assure quality control of data processing methods and thereby safeguard PII from unauthorized access, alteration or deletion. Preventive security under the 4th FIPP deters intrusion. Reactive security under the 4th FIPP must quickly respond to discovered intrusion and effectively remediate the vulnerabilities. Thus, the 4th FIPP requires an adaptive management of continuous improvement of controls that diagnose vulnerabilities as discovered.

2.5   FIPP Standard No. 5: Enforcement/Redress

Many Western societies recognize that rights are hollow without redress. The threat of remedial action against data custodians who are indifferent to the vulnerabilities of subject individual is a powerful incentive towards professionalism. The 5th FIPP standard of enforcement and redress recognizes that duties without correlative rights provide sub-optimal incentives. Therefore, public policy in many Western cultures increasingly relies on some form of enforcement to provide disincentive that closes some of the gaps to shirking by encouraging persistent and quality performance of security-oriented custodial control. Public support is apparently broadening, particularly among victims, to the imposition of enforcement mechanisms that grant remedies for failure of security-related PII custodial duties [20]. The imposition of private rights of action imposing duties enforceable as civil actions for money damages will predictably stimulate opposition from the tort reform movement.

3 FIPP Compliance by Policy: Industry Self-regulation vs. Government Regulation?

As discussed earlier, FIPP are global standards for the ethical use of personal information and are at the heart of U.S. industry guidelines and privacy laws and European Union privacy directives [14]. Complying with FIPP can diminish consumers' privacy risk perceptions through signals that the firm will treat consumers' personal information fairly by addressing procedural, interactional and distributive justice [15]. However, an unresolved issue in this context is *onus* – whether it should be government regulation or industry self-regulation that ensures a firm's implementation of FIPP, and that consumers are accorded legitimate choices about how their personal information is subsequently used [8, 15].

3.1 Industry Self-Regulation or Government Regulation: Privacy as a Commodity or Human Right

The approach for protecting privacy most heavily promoted by industry is self-regulation, which ensures consumers that when they disclose personal information, it will be held in a protective domain wherein a firm becomes a co-owner of the information and accepts responsibility for keeping the information safe and private. The result is that the firm is responsible for managing and protecting the private information by voluntarily implementing privacy policy based on FIPP [15]. Frequently, industry self-regulatory initiatives are reinforced by third party intervention, which involves the setting of standards by an industry group or certifying agency and the voluntary adherence to the set standards by members or associates [15]. An examples of an industry self-regulator is the Direct Marketing Association (DMA) that made compliance with its privacy principles as a condition of membership [17]. Other examples include groups such as TRUSTe have been active as third-party entities certifying that participating firms conform to the FIPP they purport to, and acting as a facilitator for resolving any conflicts that may arise [5, 15].

The legislation approach that embodies the strong institutional structural assurances provided by government agencies [44], has been proposed to have a strong impact on protecting consumer privacy [13]. Some scholars have even suggested that the legal system is the most powerful mechanism for addressing privacy issues because it requires that offenders be punished in order to maintain its deterrent effectiveness [35]. With the legal structures in place, illegal behavior can be deterred through the threat of punishment [39]. Thus, recognizing the deterrent value of a legal system, consumers tend to believe that firms would conform to the FIPP as regulated by legislation, and would therefore collect and use personal information appropriately.

The debate between industry self-regulation versus government regulation of FIPP compliance highlights two camps of privacy researchers: those who hold an idealistic interpretation of privacy cannot logically accept that privacy is a pragmatic concept subject to cost/benefit calculus. It is useful to distinguish these two camps by calling the first a fundamental right view of privacy (i.e., "privacy as a human right") and the second an instrumentalist view of privacy (i.e., "privacy as a commodity"). The first camp views privacy as a fundamental human right, like the right to liberty or life [33, 43]. Such fundamentalist position holds that privacy is tied to a cluster of rights, such as autonomy and dignity [4]. The second camp holds privacy to be of instrumental value rather than fundamental right; that is, the value of privacy comes because it sustains, promotes, and protects other things that we value. In this view, privacy can be traded off because doing so will promote other values (e.g., personalization).

The common theme emerging from current privacy literature is that the distinction between these two camps undergirds much of the dissonance between U.S. and European privacy laws, which is related to (often unstated) assumptions about the validity of "opt in" versus "opt out" information management schema. At the societal level, several studies pointed out that "human right" societies long approached privacy in an "omnibus" fashion by passing sweeping privacy bills that address all the instances of data collection, use and sharing [6, 16, 31]. Some examples of countries in this category include Australia, Canada, New Zealand and countries in European Union [32]. Assigning fundamental rights to personal information would result largely in an opt-in market for information sharing, whereby firms would have access to the information only of those consumers who chose to make it available [31]. In contrast, in "commodity" societies, there are no "omnibus" laws governing collection, use, and sharing of personal information that transcend all types of data in all sectors of the economy [31]. Some countries in this category have "patchwork" of sector-specific privacy laws that apply to certain forms of data or specific industry sectors [6, 16, 31]. For instance, in the U.S., there are sector-specific laws for specific types of records such as credit reports, and video rental records, or for classes of sensitive information such as health information [32]. The "commodity" societies largely see opt-in as an undue burden, thus many would advocate opt-out regimes for protecting consumers' privacy in which firms collect information unless the consumer explicitly takes steps to disallow it.

3.2   Current State of WAM Industry Self-regulation

The debate between fundamental right versus commodity view of privacy corresponds to the question on the relative effectiveness of industry self-regulation versus government regulation in ensuring WAM privacy. Tang et al. [38] indicates that although overarching government regulations can enhance consumer trust, regulation may not be socially optimal in all environments because of lower profit margins for firms and higher prices for consumers. Nevertheless, skepticism about the effectiveness of industry self-regulation in protecting consumer privacy [e.g., 18, 23] has resulted in privacy advocates and consumers clamoring for strong and effective legislation to curtail rampant abuses of information by firms.

In this section, we describe the current state of WAM industry self-regulation. A number of self-regulatory organizations have developed privacy guidelines that are specifically aimed at wireless advertisers and WAM service providers. While the FTC has encouraged all such regulatory frameworks to abide by FIPP, advertisers who abide by these guidelines may lack comprehensive FIPP coverage. This "a la cart" view of FIPP compliance results in inconsistent regulation across the mobile advertising industry.

The Wireless Advertising Association's (WAA) guidelines for privacy [42] require compliance with all of the FIPP with the exception of enforcement/redress. Advertisers are urged to provide notice of their privacy practices and policy changes to mobile consumers through the use of a privacy policy. In addition, users should be given the ability to decide the types and amount of information that is collected and how that information is used. Wireless advertisers must also obtain opt-in consent before transmitting advertisements or providing a user's PII to third parties. Mobile consumers should be given the ability to opt-out of receiving additional advertisements at any time, and should retain the ability to delete their PII. The guidelines require that advertisers take appropriate steps to ensure that all stored data remains secure [7, 28].

The Direct Marketing Association (DMA), American Association of Advertising Agencies (AAAA), and Association of National Advertisers (ANA), have collaborated to develop a set of email guidelines [17]. It is unclear whether these guidelines apply only to emails sent to mobile devices, or to all advertisements, including those sent using SMS text messages. These guidelines satisfy only the first two FIPP: notice/awareness and choice/consent. Under these principles, email advertisements are required to contain an honest subject line, valid return email address, clear identification of sender and subject matter, and a link to the advertiser's privacy policy. Users should be given clear notice of their right to opt-out of receiving additional advertisements. Opt-in consent must be obtained before an unsolicited commercial email can be sent to a user. A reliable opt-out mechanism should also be included. Email lists should never be sold to third parties without obtaining opt-in consent [28]. These guidelines neglect the remaining three FIPPs.

The Cellular Telecommunications and Internet Association (CTIA) privacy standards [12], known as the "Best Practices and Guidelines for Location Based Services," govern location-based services (LBS). Under these guidelines, LBS providers must supply users with notice of how their location information will be used, disclosed, and protected. Users must be informed of the duration their information will be retained, as well as how third parties may use it. When LBS providers utilize sensitive information, additional periodic notice should be provided. Additionally, LBS providers must obtain opt-in consent before collecting or disclosing location information, and users should be given the ability to revoke this consent at any time. Providers should also employ reasonable safeguards in order to maintain the security of all stored information. Finally, LBS providers should allow users to report abuse or non-compliance with the above principles. These guidelines fail to address two FIPPs, access/participation and enforcement/redress. Users are not given the right to view, alter, or delete their location information.

TRUSTe, a popular privacy certification-granting agency, has developed a set of standards known as the "Wireless Privacy Principles and Implementation Guidelines" [40]. Currently, this is the only set of principles that integrates all five of FIPP's provisions. First, advertisers are required to implement a privacy policy that, if possible, should be displayed every time PII is collected. Mobile users should be notified if the content of this policy is altered. In addition, opt-in consent must be obtained before a user's PII may be shared with third parties or before location-based information may be used. Advertisers should implement a reasonable mechanism to allow for the correction of inaccurate data. Providers should also take appropriate steps to ensure that all PII is accurate. Under these guidelines, reasonable security measures should be implemented. Finally, an efficient reporting and complaint mechanism should be implemented. While the FTC has struggled to convince private entities to adopt the all of the requirements outlined by FIPP, TRUSTe's guidelines illustrate that FIPP can act as an effective framework.

3.3 Government Regulation

WAM is not clearly and directly regulated under any U.S. federal or state law protecting privacy. Indeed, WAM ostensibly poses a regulatory vacuum with unclear authorities among various state and federal agencies in the U.S. Similarly, the type of optimal enforcement remains unclear so that there are threats but unclear exposures for WAM participants from civil liability, criminal liability and government regulatory agency enforcement (e.g., FTC). The self-regulatory organization (SRO) enforcement efforts are somewhat clearer but generally lack enforcement authority. The precise boundaries of regulatory jurisdiction remain unclear but may hinge on restrictions of the regulatory authority over telecommunications services, such as that of the U.S. Federal Communications Commission (FCC). Furthermore, WAM could be regulated as SPAM or as telemarketing calls [27]. In the U.S. it is important to note that such ambiguity is not fatal to the adaptation of existing government regulations by analogy to various forms of WAM design. For example, the U.S. Federal Trade Commission (FTC) is actively working on WAM regulation but has taken a slow and deliberate pace that has been decidedly laissez-faire. The FTC's position explicitly promotes self-regulation, most recently reinforced in the FTC's Behavioral Advertising staff report [21]. Finally, there are proposals to unequivocally regulate WAM and this approach might gain traction if individuals are exposed by WAM to annoyance, injury, identity theft or the like.

4 FIPP Compliance by Design

Proof of FIPP's success or failure as a regulatory framework may be inferred from the existence of FIPP in actual WAM system architectures. It is predictable that WAM service providers will oppose stricter government regulation. Particularly given the FTC's encouragement of the self-regulatory approach, an architecture compliant with FIPP as embodied in self-regulation may preempt government regulation. As a result, system architectures that include effective and innovative FIPP integration are arguably an important component of WAM business models.

FIPP itself may directly influence system design. Lawrence Lessig [25] argues that the hardware, software, and system design that comprises the Internet has a strong regulatory effect. This invisible hand creates a system of governance that can be more effective than traditional forms of regulation. Similarly, much of the regulation that governs WAM may be directly integrated into its architecture. In the U.S., wireless

advertising is still in an embryonic state. In order to take advantage of this new opportunity, many companies are innovating with various business models for delivery of
advertisements to mobile users. FIPP is a potentially useful guide for WAM designers
who are intent on implementing privacy-compliant solutions. However, if FIPP is not
integrated during their initial development, then retroactive compliance will be difficult, and FIPP may never be codified in these architectures.

In a recent statement, Rod Beckstrom, former director of the National Cybersecu-
rity Center expressed his belief that security standards should be directly "baked in"
to future network infrastructures rather than being "layered in" after their deployment.
Similarly, as various WAM system architectures become entrenched in the market, it
is important that they implement the appropriate FIPP compliant privacy provisions
up front, rather than as an afterthought or in response to consumer dissatisfaction.

4.1 FIPP Compliance by Design: WAM Patents

Examination of modern WAM architectures reveals the state of FIPP compliance
through design. WAM service providers are predictably hesitant to reveal their business models, but alternate design descriptions are available such as through the publication of U.S. utility patents. The U.S. Patent and Trademark Office (USPTO) and
other patent services maintain publicly accessible, searchable databases of all issued
patents and some patent applications.

Five WAM Patents (see Table 1) are described to examine the FIPP compliance.
WAM patents are explored because they proxy major elements of a WAM design and
thus are ostensibly good exemplars. These WAM patents were identified using key
word in context search methods from among issued U.S. patents. This is clearly a subset of all possible designs for WAM. WAM architectures may include existing designs
deployed or announced outside the U.S. Furthermore, the population of WAM patents
issued in the U.S. does not include published provisional U.S. patent applications,
published full U.S. patent applications, nor any non-U.S. patent or application. A complete WAM architecture may include a combination of elements from WAM patents,
existing non-WAM patents, non-patented design elements (e.g., trade secrets) and
other public domain elements.

Of the various WAM-related patent documents identified in this survey, the following seven were selected for analysis due to the clarity and relevancy of their architectural descriptions. These patents have elements classified in various USPC classes
involving telecommunications, computer communications, business methods, data
processing and multiplexing.[1] However, many additional classes and subclasses are
likely also relevant to the broader WAM architectures generally envisioned.

---

[1] This survey largely examines patents classified in various subclasses of one major USPC
class: Class 455 Telecommunications. Among the selected WAM patents these additional
patent classes are variously claimed: Class 340 Communications: Electrical; Class 370 Multiplex Communications; Class 379 Telephonic Communications; Class 705 Data Processing:
Financial, Business Practice, Management, or Cost/Price Determination; Class 707 Data
Processing: Database and File Management or Data Structures; and Class 709 Electrical
Computers and Digital Processing Systems: Multicomputer Data Transferring.

Table 1. WAM Patents

U.S. Patent No.	Title	Brief Descriptions
6,381,465 (465 patent)	System and Method for Attaching an Advertisement to an SMS Message for Wireless Transmission	A system in which an advertising message is appended to an alert message that a mobile device user registers to receive. Such advertisements would be targeted based on the information that the user entered at the time they registered for the alert, the contextual content of the alert message itself, and the user's location [10].
6,889,054 (054 patent)	Method and System for Schedule Based Advertising on a Mobile Phone	A system for transmitting wireless advertisements to mobile users based on a user defined schedule and personal preferences. Users may also be provided with a reward, such as free "minutes," as an incentive to accept additional advertisements [22].
6,925,307 (307 patent)	Mixed Mode Interaction	A system in which verbal and non-verbal commands are used in conjunction with a mobile device in order to submit search queries and other instructions. Under this system, users have complete control over when and how responses and advertising messages are transmitted. The system also offers a service called a "Voice Wallet," which allows for the storage of sensitive purchasing information, including credit card numbers and expiration dates [26].
7,162,221 (221 patent)	Systems, Method, and Computer Program Products for Registering Wireless Device Users in Direct Marketing Campaigns	A system that allows users to register for targeted, direct marketing campaigns on their mobile devices. After an initial unsolicited advertisement is transmitted, users have the ability to opt-in to participating in the advertising campaign, or opt-out of receiving additional advertising messages [36].
7,251,476 (476 patent)	Method for Advertising on Digital Cellular Telephones and Reducing Cost to the End User	A system in which advertisements are transmitted to cellular phones in a way that does not interfere with the normal operation of the mobile device. The system utilizes a "reverse subscription" model in which advertisers pay users in order to gain permission to send advertisements [11].

4.2 Analysis of FIPP Compliance Using WAM Patents

FIPP is a robust framework that permits analysis of self-regulation or government regulation as well as WAM design. FIPP promotes "Privacy by Policy" and permits the FTC to encourage websites, data collectors, and data processors to integrate FIPP into their privacy policies. This interpretation of FIPP has evolved into a set of standards that influenced the creation and implementation of all forms of privacy regulation, ranging from federal statutes to private self-regulatory frameworks. Spiekermann and Cranor [34] argue, however, that FIPP's "notice" and "choice" principles, arguably two of the most important principles, may not unnecessary if sufficient privacy control is integrated into a WAM system design. Their "Privacy by Architecture" refers to the integration of privacy controls and provisions directly into a system's design. They argue that system engineers fail to account for privacy when prototyping and developing systems [34]. Nevertheless, technology and system design may be the most effective setting for enforcing privacy regulation.

If FIPP compliance truly adds value to WAM architectures, then those who devise systems that directly integrate FIPP should seek out protection by obtaining a patent. Such protection should further incentivize the development of innovative FIPP implementation strategies. Furthermore, the temporary monopoly granted by patents may facilitate the promotion and universal adoption of a given system. If, on the other hand, such privacy provisions are absent, then FIPP compliance and patent incentives may not have the strength required in order to promote the integration of "Privacy by Architecture."

FIPP #1: Notice/Awareness. None of the WAM-related patents examined contain any design provisions that satisfy the notice/awareness principle. However, WAM patents openly admit that PII can be collected from users, either with or without their permission. For example, the '307 patent [26] describes an advertising system in which all transmitted messages and notifications are based on a user's personal preferences. Preference information would only be used internally by the WAM service provider. However, the patent fails to describe a method to inform the end user of how this information would be used to provide targeted advertising or how the provider could use the user's PII in the future. Under the '307 patent, users may not be aware that the system maintains a "user profiles database."

Under the '054 patent [22], a large "profile/history" database is maintained. Users may initially assume use of their PII would be limited to their WAM service provider in order to enable the delivery of targeted advertisements. However, without a strict privacy policy or notice provision, this information could potentially be sold or transmitted to third parties without the data owner's knowledge. Developing unique methods to notify users of the provider's current privacy practices is especially important within the WAM context. The small screen size of many wireless devices severely limits the amount of space available to effectively communicate a detailed notice statement [24]. Innovative methods to deliver a notification document would likely be rewarded, especially if they were directly integrated into the overall WAM architecture.

FIPP #2: Choice/Consent. Several WAM patents contain opt-in and opt-out provisions for the receipt of advertisements. For example, the '476 patent [11] describes a system that is permission-based and only transmits wireless advertisements to users who explicitly opt-in to receiving them. Additionally, under the '221 patent [36], advertisers may transmit an initial unsolicited advertising message that allows opt-in to a particular ad campaign, or opt-out of receiving additional advertisements. This system strikes a balance between the privacy interests of the user and the business interests of the advertiser. The '307 [26] and the '054 [22] patents allow users to determine when, how, and what type of advertisements are received.

Other patents describe wireless advertising systems that do not allow choice. For example, the '465 patent [10] automatically attaches advertisements to subscription-based alert messages. Unless the external subscription agreement imposes separate choice for WAM, the '465 patent does not envision a permission-based system.

Thus, users registered for specific alerts may be unexpectedly exposed to wireless advertisements. Retroactive imposition of an opt-in or opt-out mechanisms could be imposed when the alert service is registered.

FIPP #3: Access/Participation. None of the patents examined explicitly give users any ability to view, modify, or delete PII stored by the WAM service provider. For example, both the '054 [22] and the '307 [26] patents maintain PII databases based on information that wireless users actively supply to WAM service provides. Nevertheless, neither patent clearly articulates whether this information can be retrieved, altered, or deleted by its owners. Like the discussion above, access might be retroactively supplied, perhaps in an improvement patent.

Even in the patents that do not specifically solicit user preference information, the lack of FIPP #3 access/participation compliance is clear. For example, the '465 patent [10] may use the information that the user inputs when registering for an alert in order to append targeted advertisements to these alert messages. Because such information may be obtained without the user's knowledge, this design fails to provide functionality to view or modify this information once collected. Location information is a key feature of many WAM patents, including the '476 [11], '054 [22], and '307 [26] patents. None of the systems are clearly designed to permit users access to revise or delete their PII.

FIPP #4: Integrity/Security: None of the patents examined in this study contain any security provisions obligating WAM service providers to collect, store, and utilize PII in a secure way. For example, the "Voice Wallet" maintained by the '307 patent [26] may contain critical data, such as a users credit card number, expiration dates, and pin number. Although the "voice authentication" itself is claimed to be secure, there are no patent claims illustrating actual protection of user PII. Moreover, users' preference information may be sent via SMS text message, WML, or voice message, all of which are insecure formats. The '054 [22] system also maintains numerous pieces of critical information, including a "profile/history" database, purchasing information, and shipping information. None of the patent provisions address security maintenance. Many systems, including the '476 [11], '054 [22], and 307 [26] patents, collect and utilize location data, but fail to address the integrity or security of this highly sensitive PII.

Information systems often rely on a series of "standard" information security practices, including data encryption and firewalls, in order to protect the information that they store and process. While these techniques are effective, they are not particularly new or innovative. Such standard security controls might be retroactively applied to business models based on these patents.

FIPP #5: Enforcement/Redress. None of the examined WAM-related patents included any enforcement or redress provision. Enforcement may be viewed as a policy provision rather than a technical constraint exogenous to the design. Here, it is unlikely that the consequences of violating one of the aforementioned self-regulatory principles would be included in a technical system architecture discussion, such as those that are contained in patent documents. Similarly, any possible remedies that may be imposed for such a violation could be included in the subscription agreement, made part of self-regulatory guidelines, or imposed by government regulation. Nevertheless, future WAM system designs could include technical provisions to satisfy the enforcement FIPP such as automatic recall of PII distributed to third parties or destruction of PII if its collection was unauthorized. Many other alternatives are conceivable, but unexplored in the WAM patents examined for this study.

The WAM-related patents examined here universally fail to comprehensively integrate FIPP. This "al a cart" view of FIPP results in severe privacy inadequacies. Despite these shortcomings, many WAM patents examined here exhibit some form of privacy awareness. As unique and innovative privacy protecting measures are developed, inventors may be incentivized by self-regulation and government regulation to design PII privacy compliant with FIPP. WAM is in its infancy in the U.S., so FIPP privacy compliance is still possible without regulation. The patents examined appear to focus more on providing unique delivery systems rather than FIPP compliance. Once a set of standardized WAM transmission techniques achieve critical mass in the market, developers may seek new methods to differentiate their products. This could include innovative privacy enhancement methods that might better ensure FIPP compliance. The temporary monopolies provided by patents will likely further incentivize these developments if FIPP compliance becomes mandatory.

Unfortunately, under the recent decision of the court in in re Bilski, business methods and abstract ideas that are not directly tied to a specific piece of hardware or which do not transform physical matter may no longer be eligible for patent protection. This is the "machine or transformation" test of the Bilski case that raises validity questions for most business methods and software patents that operate on general use computers or on standardized platforms. Bilski could extend to the WAM-related patents examined here. Thus, the economic incentives to develop innovative FIPP compliance may undermine WAM patents as a major form of system architecture design.

5 Discussion and Conclusion

5.1 Tentative Findings

This research has focused on the following propositions: First, the WAM industry and potential entrants into WAM argue that government regulation would suppress innovation and competition considered socially useful. Second, WAM patents initially appear to provide significant financial reward for WAM innovation. Third, the Bilski case and the more general patent reform movement that seeks to limit the impact of business methods patents (BMP) and even software patents more generally, if successful mill also suppress WAM innovation.

Several tentative findings from the initial stages of this research lead to the following assertions. Self-regulation and BMP encourage innovation in WAM designs and WAM system architectures. WAM is not directly regulated under any federal privacy, spam or other similar regulatory scheme. The FTC's current work on location-based services and behavioral marketing has not been clearly merged to adequately address WAM through regulation. The FTC's deliberate pace has a decidedly laissez-faire character that continues to incentivize the development of WAM architectures without close or costly regulation. Indeed, the clear promotion of self-regulation illustrates the nascent WAM industry has some remaining time to address privacy concerns before the threatened imposition of enforcement or corrective legislation might diminish innovation in WAM architectures.[2]

WAM poses a regulatory vacuum with unclear authorities among the FTC, FCC, the states, the Justice Department (DoJ). Regulatory uncertainty is exacerbated by ambiguity in the optimal types of enforcement: civil, criminal, regulatory agency, self-regulatory organization (SRO). Regulatory jurisdiction may hinge on boundaries of telecommunications services.[3]

FIPP is a powerful de jure and de facto privacy standard and it should continue to inspire any and all government or self-regulation of WAM, however, there is evidence that FIPP is all too often mere rationalization. Opting in vs. opting out, as the satisfaction of the FIPP #1 notice and FIPP#2 choice standards, offer significantly different economic outcomes and costs. The impact of opting form on the size and value of consumer PII databases is also significant clearly incentivizing industries that control the opting scope and method to prefer opt-out over opt-in.

5.2 Future Research Directions

The DIGs framework was proposed in this research to examine FIPP compliance of a few WAM designs as found in WAM patents and the FIPP compliance of various self-regulatory frameworks. This type of analysis should be extended in various ways. First, the patent analysis should be expanded from the current sample of five WAM patents with empirical validation approach. For example, Allison and his colleagues [1, 2] provided some promising methods by working on some large patent datasets, performing patent validity comparisons, analyzing demographic and industrial organization data about inventors, and focusing on particular technology sectors. Second, FIPP compliance is amenable to doctrinal legal and regulatory analysis from various authoritative sources, including inter alia: civil litigation among private parties, regulatory enforcement proceedings of various federal agencies engaged in regulation of various WAM components, and criminal violations of various state and federal law. This analysis should address each FIPP separately and then collectively: notice, consent, participation, security enforcement. Results of such analyses are likely discrete given the broad differences between regulatory foci of the agencies in their development of guidelines and rules/regulations, their undertaking of investigations and enforcement and the level of their activity in engagement in "jawboning" with the emerging WAM industry.

The institutional structure of a regulatory domain is of recurring interest to many scholars. For example, the financial crisis of 2008 was marked by very broad public interest in the fragmented regulatory program oversight of the financial services industry. Many of these were the legacy result of Depression-era Glass-Steagall separations of enforcement powers that were specifically intended to spread regulatory powers to avoid regulatory capture, regulatory arbitrage and the financial services monopolization that was experienced during the roaring 20s. Therefore, institutional structural analysis, comparison and prediction are potentially fruitful research avenues.

---

[2] FTC Online Behavioral Ad Self-Regulatory Principles at 47.
[3] See e.g., 47 U.S.C. §153 (2003).

The sectoral nature of privacy regulation has similar potential for the examination of institutional structure where regulation is fragmented. Consider how WAM architectures immediately implicate telecommunications regulations traditionally within the jurisdiction of the Federal Communications Commission (FCC) but which has been the subject of FTC scrutiny. Additional privacy regulation of the financial transaction components of possible WAM transactions (e.g., automatic crediting of electronic coupons to credit cards, bank accounts or non-bank financial service provider such as PayPal) could be within the regulatory jurisdiction of financial services regulators. Health related advertisements could implicate health needs profiles regulated under HIPAA. Many other WAM architectures and component services could implicate other regulatory programs and other regulators (e.g., children). Research into the optimal regulatory structure is feasible and quite likely to be of interest to various journal readerships.

Finally, a content and stakeholder analysis of the FTC's various dockets in WAM-related areas may be useful. For example, there are sometimes very considerable comment databases accessible online in areas such as behavioral marketing, location-based services, spam, identity theft, data-mining, RFID technology deployments and tracking consumer preferences would be informed by content analysis and of the considerable FTC comment databases.

5.3 Conclusion

Innovation in WAM privacy is incentivized from three major sources: government regulation, industry self-regulation, and privacy enhancing technologies that enable particular WAM market models. Balancing these incentives to improve the security of PII for consumers of WAM services is uncertain because WAM platforms in the U.S. are still under development. WAM is not clearly and directly regulated under any current U.S. law. The prospects for adapting federal privacy law to regulate WAM as a form of spam or telecommunications privacy matter still remains unclear. The FTC's focus on behavioral marketing and location referencing holds the greatest promise for the application of government regulation to WAM. However, the FTC's deliberate pace and laissez-faire approach promotes self-regulation providing there is compliance with FIPP. FIPP has inspired government regulation and industry self-regulation of privacy in various contexts. Furthermore, WAM patents reveal at least some FIPP compliance. However, there is mounting evidence that FIPP is not comprehensively represented in industry self-regulatory programs or in WAM patents. Despite the promise for competitively-inspired innovation to provide privacy-enhancing WAM designs, our examination of industry self-regulation programs as well as WAM patents clearly illustrates that FIPP is not fully implemented. Indeed, the enforcement remedial FIPP is seldom represented and the participation/access of FIPP is lacking in many programs and in issued WAM patents.

It may be useful to examine FIPP compliance in other nations to gain insights. For example, WAM privacy is better established in EU nations so FIPP privacy compliance in the U.S. remains feasible. Other nations' experience can be interpreted to assist WAM policymaking as well as WAM design innovation. WAM privacy resulting from design innovation could be weakened by the invalidity of WAM-related patents, if they are undermined by intellectual property reform such as that in the recent Bilski case. Nevertheless, great insights into the design architecture of WAM services are evident from analysis of WAM patents and such analysis in this article helps pinpoint FIPP non-compliance in design architecture.

Acknowledgments. The authors gratefully acknowledge the financial support of the National Science Foundation under grant CNS-0716646. Any opinions, findings, and conclusions or recommendations expressed herein are those of the researchers and do not necessarily reflect the views of the National Science Foundation.

References

1. Allison, J.R., Lemley, M.A.: Who's Patenting What-An Empirical Exploration of Patent Prosecution. Vanderbilt Law Review 53(6), 2099–2174 (2000)
2. Allison, J.R., Lemley, M.A., Moore, K.A., Trunkey, R.D.: Valuable patents. Georgetown Law Journal 92(3), 435–480 (2004)
3. Bagby, J.W.: The Public Policy Environment of the Privacy-Security Conundrum/ Complement. In: Park, S. (ed.) Strategies and Policies in Digital Convergence, pp. 195–213. Idea Group Reference, Hershey (2007)
4. Beaney, W.M.: Right to Privacy and American Law. The Law and Contemporary Problems 31, 253–271 (1966)
5. Benassi, P.: TRUSTe: An Online Privacy Seal Program. Communications of the Acm 42(2), 56–59 (1999)
6. Bennett, C.J., Raab, C.D.: The adequacy of privacy: The European Union data protection directive and the North American response. Information Society 13(3), 245–263 (1997)
7. Brantley, A.S., Farmer, S.T., Jackson, B.L., Krupoff, J., List, S.S., Ray, E.G.: The Legal Web of Wireless Transactions. Rutgers Computer and Technology Law Journal 29(1), 53–88 (2003)
8. Caudill, M.E., Murphy, E.P.: Consumer Online Privacy: Legal and Ethical Issues. Journal of Public Policy & Marketing 19(1), 7–19 (2000)
9. Cavoukian, A.H., Hamilton, T.J.: The Privacy Payoff: How Successful Businesses Build Customer Trust. McGraw-Hill Ryerson, Toronto (2002)
10. Chern, V., Thorton, K.: System and Method for Attaching an Advertisement to an SMS Message for Wireless Transmission. In: U.S. (ed.) (2002)
11. Cortegiano, M.L.: Method for Advertising on Digital Cellular Telephones and Reducing Cost to the End User. In: U.S. (ed.) (2007)
12. CTIA. Best Practices and Guidelines for Location Based Services the Cellular Telecommunications and Internet Association (CTIA) (2008)
13. Culnan, M.J.: Protecting Privacy Online: Is Self-Regulation Working? Journal of Public Policy & Marketing 19(1), 20–26 (2000)
14. Culnan, M.J., Armstrong, P.K.: Information Privacy Concerns, Procedural Fairness and Impersonal Trust: An Empirical Investigation. Organization Science 10(1), 104–115 (1999)
15. Culnan, M.J., Bies, J.R.: Consumer Privacy: Balancing Economic and Justice Considerations. Journal of Social Issues 59(2), 323–342 (2003)
16. Dholakia, N., Zwick, D.: Contrasting European and American approaches to privacy in electronic markets: a philosophical perspective. Electronic Markets 11(2) (2001)
17. DMA. Privacy Promise Member Compliance Guide. Direct Marketing Association (2003)

18. Edelman, B.: Adverse Selection in Online "Trust" Certifications. Working paper, Harvard University (2006)
19. Fischer-Hüber, S.: IT-Security and Privacy. Springer, Heidelberg (2000)
20. FTC. Federal Trade Commission Report. National and State Trends in Fraud & Identity Theft: January - December 2003 (2004)
21. FTC. FTC Staff Report: Self-Regulatory Principles For Online Behavioral Advertising (2009)
22. Himmel, M.A., Rodriguez, H., Smith, N.J., Spinac, C.J.: Method and System for Schedule Based Advertising on a Mobile Phone. In: U.S. (ed.) (2005)
23. Hui, K.-L., Teo, H.-H., Lee, T.S.Y.: The Value of Privacy Assurance: An Exploratory Field Experiment. MIS Quarterly 31(1), 19–33 (2007)
24. King, N.J.: Direct Marketing, Mobile Phones, and Consumer Privacy: Ensuring Adequate Disclosure and Consent Mechanisms for Emerging Mobile Advertising Practices. Federal Communications Law Journal 60(2), 229–324 (2008)
25. Lessig, L.: Code: And Other Laws of Cyberspace, Version 2.0. Basic Books, New York (2006)
26. Mamdani, M., Johnson, P., Bomar, K., Whatley, T., Grant, C.: Mixed Mode Interaction. In: U.S. (ed.) (2005)
27. Noonan, J., Goodman, M.: Third-Party Liability for Federal Law Violations in Direct-to-Consumer Marketing: Telemarketing, Fax, and E-mail. The Bus. Lawyer 63, 585–596 (2008)
28. Petty, R.D.: Wireless advertising messaging: legal analysis and public policy issues. Journal of Public Policy & Marketing 22(1), 71–82 (2003)
29. Reidenberg, J.R.: Setting Standards for Fair Information Practice in the U.S. Private Sector. Iowa Law Review 80, 497–551 (1994)
30. Secretary. Records, Computers and the Rights of Citizens - Report of the Secretary's Advisory Committee on Automated Personal Data Systems. Secretary of Health, Education, and Welfare (1973)
31. Smith, H.J.: Information privacy and marketing: What the US should (and shouldn't) learn from Europe. California Management Review 43(2), 8 (2001)
32. Smith, H.J.: Information Privacy and Its Management. MIS Quaterley Executive 3(4) (2004)
33. Sopinka, J.: Freedom of speech and privacy in the information age. Information Society 13(2), 171–184 (1997)
34. Spiekermann, S., Cranor, L.F.: Engineering Privacy. IEEE Transactions on Software Engineering 25(1), 67–82 (2009)
35. Spiro, W.G., Houghteling, L.J.: The Dynamics of Law. Harcourt Brace Jovanovich, New York (1981)
36. Spitz, D., Watkins, D., Cox, S., Thrash, J., Squire, M., Borger, D.: Systems, Method, and Computer Program Products for Registering Wireless Device Users in Direct Marketing Campaigns. In: U.S. (ed.) (2007)
37. Swire, P.P.: Markets, Self-Regulation, and Government Enforcement in the Protection of Personal Information. In: Daley, W.M., Irving, L. (eds.) Privacy and Self-Regulation in the Information Age, pp. 3–19. Department of Commerce, Washington (1997)
38. Tang, Z., Hu, Y.J., Smith, M.D.: Gaining Trust Through Online Privacy Protection: Self-Regulation, Mandatory Standards, or Caveat Emptor. Journal of Management Information Systems 24(4), 153–173 (2008)
39. Tittle, C.R.: Sanctions and Social Deviance: The Question of Deterrence. Praeger, New York (1980)

40. TRUSTe. TRUSTe Plugs into Wireless: TRUSTe's Wireless Advisory Committee Announces First Wireless Privacy Standards (2004)
41. Turner, C.E., Dasgupta, S.: Privacy on the Web: An Examination of User Concerns, Technology, and Implications for Business Organizations and Individuals. Information Systems Management, 8–18 (Winter 2003)
42. WAA. Wireless Advertising Association Guidelines on Privacy and Spam (2000)
43. Walczuch, R.M., Lizette, S.: Implications of the new EU Directive on data protection for multinational corporations. Information Technology & People 14(2), 142 (2001)
44. Zucker, L.G.: Production of trust: Institutional sources of economic structure, 1840-1920. In: Staw, B.M., Cummings, L.L. (eds.) Research in Organizational Behavior, pp. 53–111. JAI Press, Greenwich (1986)

A Comparative Study of Online Privacy Policies and Formats⋆

Aleecia M. McDonald[1], Robert W. Reeder[2], Patrick Gage Kelley[1],
and Lorrie Faith Cranor[1]

[1] Carnegie Mellon, Pittsburgh, PA
[2] Microsoft, Redmond, WA

Abstract. Online privacy policies are difficult to understand. Most privacy policies require a college reading level and an ability to decode legalistic, confusing, or jargon-laden phrases. Privacy researchers and industry groups have devised several standardized privacy policy formats to address these issues and help people compare policies. We evaluated three formats in this paper: layered policies, which present a short form with standardized components in addition to a full policy; the Privacy Finder privacy report, which standardizes the text descriptions of privacy practices in a brief bulleted format; and conventional non-standardized human-readable policies. We contrasted six companies' policies, deliberately selected to span the range from unusually readable to challenging. Based on the results of our online study of 749 Internet users, we found participants were not able to reliably understand companies' privacy practices with any of the formats. Compared to natural language, participants were faster with standardized formats but at the expense of accuracy for layered policies. Privacy Finder formats supported accuracy more than natural language for harder questions. Improved readability scores did not translate to improved performance. All formats and policies were similarly disliked. We discuss our findings as well as public policy implications.

1 Introduction

The United States relies on a self-regulation approach to Internet privacy. There are some Internet privacy laws, for example the Children's Online Privacy Protection Act of 1998 (COPPA), which protects children's privacy [6], and the Gramm-Leach-Bliley Act (GLB), which applies to financial data [11]. But by and large the theory of Internet privacy hinges on two assumptions:

⋆ Funded by NSF Cyber Trust grant CNS-0627513, Microsoft through the Carnegie Mellon Center for Computational Thinking, Army Research Office grant number DAAD19-02-1-0389 to Carnegie Mellon CyLab, and FCT through the CMU/Portugal Information and Communication Technologies Institute. Thanks to Robert McGuire and Keisha How for programming assistance.

I. Goldberg and M. Atallah (Eds.): PETS 2009, LNCS 5672, pp. 37–55, 2009.

- Consumers will choose companies with acceptable privacy policies.
- Companies will not violate their privacy policies because the Federal Trade Commission (FTC) can bring action for unfair and deceptive practices.

In both cases privacy policies play a vital role in Internet privacy. Self-reports show three quarters of Internet users take active measures to protect their privacy, ranging from installing privacy protective technology to providing false information to web sites [1]. Yet only 26% read privacy policies during a recent study and readership outside of laboratory conditions is believed to be far lower [14]. To study the effectiveness of various approaches to improving the readability of privacy policies, we investigated the performance of three different formats for privacy policies and compared policies from six different companies.

In section two we describe related work and the formats we contrasted. We describe our methods in section three. We present accuracy and time to answer results in section four, and psychological acceptability results in section five. We discuss implications from these results and conclude in section six.

2   Related Work

Several studies frame willingness to read privacy policies as an economic proposition and conclude that asymmetric information is one reason why people find it not worth their time to read privacy policies [28,1]. Other studies show that privacy policies and financial disclosures require a college reading level to understand [12,24,10,2]. A study of ambiguities in privacy policies shows they contain language that downplays privacy issues [20]. The 2006 Kleimann report on GLB financial privacy notices found that subheadings and standard formats dramatically improved readability [22]. In response to these issues, privacy researchers and industry groups devised several standardized formats for privacy policies based on the expectation that standardized formats would improve comprehension. Our study is a comparative analysis to analyze how well standardized policies work in practice.

While not in the realm of privacy policies, Kay and Terry's research on open source license agreements includes testing multiple formats. Early work found modest improvements in likelihood to read well designed agreements but no improvement in retention of the material [15]. Tsai found when study participants searched for products to purchase and saw a single icon view that evaluated the privacy practices for each site, they were willing to pay a small premium for more privacy-protective sites [27,8]. On the other hand, translating an entire privacy policy into a grid that conveyed information by icons and colors did not improve comprehension [21]. Attempts at visualizing privacy are ongoing, including a set of icons modeled after Creative Commons [3]. This study, in contrast, examines three text-based formats as described below.

2.1   Privacy Finder

Privacy Finder (PF) is a privacy-enhanced front end to Yahoo! and Google search that was developed by AT&T and refined at the Cylab Usable Privacy and Security (CUPS) Laboratory. Privacy Finder includes a privacy report that displays standardized text generated automatically from Platform for Privacy Preferences (P3P) policies. P3P is a standardized format for privacy policies, and is formally recommended by the World Wide Web Consortium (W3C) [29]. P3P policies are encoded in XML (eXtended Markup Language), which is computer readable and thus allows software tools to help people manage their privacy preferences.

Because Privacy Finder generates text from P3P tags, the Privacy Finder report avoids emotionally charged language and ensures uniform presentation. However, Privacy Finder reports allow a free-form text description of the highest level of policy statements. This can improve readability by providing context for readers, but also means that companies with identical practices may have different Privacy Finder reports.

2.2   Layered Notices

The law firm Hunton & Williams popularized the notion of layered notices [25] which include a short one-screen overview with standardized headings which then links to the full natural language policy. Although the headings for the first layer are standardized the text within each section is free form.

By 2005, several large companies deployed layered policies including Microsoft (MSN), Procter & Gamble, IBM, and JP Morgan [17]. European Union Information Commissioner Richard Thomas called for the use of layered policies in response to research showing nearly 75% of participants said they would read privacy policies if they were better designed [19]. Article 29 of European Union Directive created the "Working Party on the Protection of Individuals with regard to the processing of Personal Data," which issued guidance on how to create layered policies [4]. Privacy commissioners in EU countries supported layered policies. In Australia, the Privacy Commissioner released a layered policy for their own office, intending it "as a model for other agencies and organisations" [26].

2.3   Natural Language

Most privacy policies are in natural language format: companies explain their practices in prose. One noted disadvantage to current natural language policies is that companies can choose which information to present, which does not necessarily solve the problem of information asymmetry between companies and consumers. Further, companies use what have been termed "weasel words" — legalistic, ambiguous, or slanted phrases — to describe their practices [20]. Natural language policies are often long and require college-level reading skills. Furthermore, there are no standards for which information is disclosed, no standard place to find particular information, and data practices are not described using consistent language.

3   Methods

We conducted an online study from August to December 2008 in which we presented a privacy policy to participants and asked them to answer questions about it. We posted advertisements on craigslist and used personal networks to recruit participants. We offered a lottery for a chance to win one of several $75 Amazon gift certificates as incentive for participating in the study.

We used a between subjects design and assigned each participant to one of 15 privacy policy representations. We used a between subjects design rather than within group design because in this context it is unrealistic to eliminate learning effects simply by reordering policies. Reading the questions could affect how participants read subsequent policies. It is also unrealistic to expect participants to spend more than 20 minutes completing an online survey. Questions remained constant over all conditions; only the policy differed.

3.1   Study Conditions

We contrasted six different companies' conventional natural language (NL) policies and their corresponding Privacy Finder privacy report format (PF) plus three layered policies. We refer to these companies as A through F. We analyzed 749 participants across 15 conditions, for an average of 50 participants per condition. The study conditions are listed in Table 1.

Table 1. Participants per Condition

Company	Designation	NL	PF	Layered
Disney	A	41	50	N/A
Microsoft	B	47	46	52
Nextag	C	46	41	N/A
IBM	D	47	47	49
Walmart	E	52	51	N/A
O'Reilly	F	62	55	63

We replaced all companies' names with "Acme" to avoid bias from brand effects. For natural language polices we used black text on white backgrounds regardless of the original graphic design. We left other formatting that might aide comprehension (for example, bulleted lists) intact.

Note that we did not study layered policies for companies A, C, and E. Of the six companies, only B and D had layered policies. We followed the directions from the Center for Information Policy Leadership [5] to create a third layered policy for company F as part of a prior study [21] and used it here to facilitate comparisons between studies.

As deployed in practice, Privacy Finder highlights the most important information at the top of the report and provides links to expand details. We discovered in earlier testing that people rarely expanded the Privacy Finder report.

We were interested in testing how well people are able to use the information in the Privacy Finder report, not how well they are able to navigate the user interface, so in our research we presented all information in a single flat file.

We selected privacy policies from six popular websites that engage in e-commerce, and thus must collect a variety of personal information as part of their business. We chose what we believe to be a comparatively easy to read and a comparatively difficult to read policy with several typical policies. We selected policies guided by several measurements of readability summarized in Table 2. For each company, we noted the length of the natural language policy. We calculated the Flesch-Kincaid Reading Ease Score, which ranges from a low of 1 to a high of 100 based on syllable count and line lengths. High Flesch-Kincaid scores are more readable than low scores. In general, experts suggest a score of at least 60—70, which is considered easily understandable by 8th and 9th graders [18]. *Reader's Digest* has a readability index in the mid 60s, *Time* is in the low 50s, and *Harvard Law Review* in the low 30s [13]. Note that while the policies we selected span a range from 32 to 46, even the most readable policy is more challenging than is normally recommended for a general audience.

We calculated the percentage of sentences written in the passive voice, which is both more difficult for readers to understand and an indicator the company may not be comfortable taking full responsibility for their privacy practices. We counted the number of cross references within each policy; the more times readers are asked to refer to other parts of the document the more difficult it is to understand. Finally, we note that the standardized Privacy Finder format also has a range of lengths due to differing numbers of statements, how much information they collect, and how much text the policy authors elected to supply.

Table 2. Attributes of six companies' privacy policies

Co.	NL Words	NL Pages	Flesch	% Passive	Cross ref.s	PF Words
A	6329	13	31.8	11%	27	880
B	3725	7	35.5	22%	0	1964
C	2920	6	36.3	17%	7	2011
D	2586	8	42.8	18%	2	554
E	2550	8	44.9	11%	0	1373
F	928	3	46.3	9%	1	1843

3.2   Study Questions

Study questions comprised several groups:

- *Comprehension.* Participants answered a series of multiple choice questions to determine how well they were able to understand the policy. These questions are realistic information retrieval tasks based on typical privacy concerns, and are similar to questions used in an earlier study by Cranor et al [7]. In the study, we conducted three rounds of pilot tests with over two dozen people to ensure the questions were well-worded and understandable.

We randomized the order of these questions to mitigate learning effects and captured both accuracy and time to respond. We also included a warm-up task which we did not score.

- *Psychological Acceptability.* Saltzer and Schroeder coined the term psychological acceptability to convey that if people do not like a system they will not use it. They wrote, "It is essential that the human interface be designed for ease of use, so that users routinely and automatically apply the protection mechanisms correctly." [23] Participants answered subjective questions on a seven-point Likert scale.
- *Demographics.* We collected basic information like gender, educational attainment, and income so we could understand how closely our study population resembles Internet users as a whole.

We also measured the time it took for participants to answer each one of the comprehension questions. When not engaged in a research study, few people even skim privacy policies let alone read them to find answers to their concerns [15]. The times we measured do not reflect normal practices, but they do allow us to compare performance between formats, which is our goal.

3.3   Research Questions

Standardized formats were designed with care to help readers make sense of online privacy policies. With all of the resources invested in standardized policies we expected they would help people understand privacy policies. We held multiple hypotheses:

- Participants will have (a) higher accuracy scores, (b) shorter times to answer, and (c) greater psychological acceptability with both of the standardized formats than with their natural language counterparts.
- Participants will have (a) higher accuracy scores, (b) shorter times to answer, and (c) greater psychological acceptability with highly readable natural language than they will on natural language policies with low readability metrics.

Understanding these issues contributes to determining the most effective ways to present policies to end users. This is particularly relevant given Gramm-Leach-Bliley regulations on paper-based financial privacy policies; similar legislation could apply to online privacy policies in the future. The FTC's most recent report on behavioral advertising was described by the FTC Chairman Leibowitz as the last chance to make industry self-regulation work [9]. If we move away from industry self-regulated content, what should we do instead? Do any of the standardized approaches help enough to warrant considering regulation of policy formats?

3.4   Analysis

We performed a comparative analysis across all three formats (Natural Language, Privacy Finder, and Layered) and from all six companies to see if there were statistically significant differences in the mean scores for accuracy, time to completion, and psychological acceptability questions.

After we removed outliers[1] we performed ANOVA analysis for both time data and psychological acceptability, which we recorded on a seven point Likert scale and treated as continuous variables. We performed all tests of statistical significance at the $\alpha = 5\%$ confidence level. For the sake of readability, all details of statistical significance tests are in the Appendix.

4   Accuracy and Speed Results

Accuracy scores are all reported as the percentage of people who answered the question correctly.[2] As compared to natural language, we found that layered policies led to lower accuracy scores for topics not in the short layer. Privacy Finder was indistinguishable from natural language until questions became harder, at which point Privacy Finder was slightly superior to natural language.

Accuracy spanned a wide range. An average of 91% of participants answered correctly when asked about cookies, 61% answered correctly about opt out links, 60% understood when their email address would be "shared" with a third party, and only 46% answered correctly regarding telemarketing. With only three possible answers, if participants guessed randomly we would expect 33% accuracy.

All other things being equal, lower times are better because they reflect participants were better able to comprehend the policy. Participants answered more

---

[1] We only included results from participants who completed all of the accuracy questions. Because this was an online study to enter a drawing for a gift certificate, a few people just "clicked through" answers without engaging with the material. We picked a fixed lower threshold of 1.5 seconds per question and removed participants entirely if they had two or more questions they answered in under 1.5 seconds (7 participants removed out of an original 756 for a total of 749.) For participants with only one time under 1.5 seconds, it is possible they accidently double-clicked once but answered other questions properly. We removed the time and accuracy data for just the affected question (3 question/time pairs out of 3000.) At the other extreme, sometimes people were diverted by other tasks while answering questions and we recorded unduly long times to answer. We discarded question times in excess of 2.5 times the mean for their condition along with their corresponding answers. This resulted in $N = 723$ for cookies, 728 for opt out, 726 for share email, and 723 for the telemarketing questions.

[2] Interpreting results is complicated by potential confusion of how participants answered when answers are inferred. For example, we asked about opt out practices for policies where there is no opt out link. The straight-forward answer we envisioned is "No." However, participants may also have replied that the policy "Does Not Say," intending to convey the same information since there is no opt out link within the policy. Arguably, in that case the correct way to score responses is to combine the correct answer with "Does Not Say." We analyzed the combined percentage for each question and found in all but one case there was no difference in the threshold for statistical significance. Further, the relative ranking of formats and companies remained stable.

quickly with both layered and Privacy Finder formats. Times to answer increased with question difficulty, with an average of 2.3 minutes to answer the question about cookies, 4.7 minutes to answer about opt out links, 5.3 minutes for email sharing, and 6.7 minutes for telemarketing.

4.1 Cookies

We asked: Does the Acme website use cookies?

Answer: Yes for all policies.

Most participants got the cookie question right (91%). This was an easy question to answer because our question is phrased with the same term the policies use. All policies, in all formats, call out cookies use explicitly. For example, one policy has a heading of "Cookies and Other Computer Information" with a paragraph that begins: "When you visit Acme.com, you will be assigned a permanent 'cookie' (a small text file) to be stored on your computer's hard drive." There is no ambiguity. Even someone who has no idea what a cookie is, or what the implications for privacy are, can skim through any of the natural language policies to find the word "cookie" and answer correctly.

Table 3. Percentage correct and minutes to answer, cookies question

Policy	% correct	Time
A NL	87%	3.6
A PF	96%	1.5
B NL	96%	2.0
B PF	98%	1.6
B Layered	86%	2.3
C NL	93%	2.4
C PF	98%	3.5
D NL	86%	2.6
D PF	91%	1.9
D Layered	69%	2.2
E NL	96%	2.6
E PF	96%	1.8
F NL	100%	2.3
F PF	94%	2.7
F Layered	80%	2.3

We found significant differences in accuracy for company and format. The six companies have a relatively small span between the worst performance (D, 82%) and best performance (E, 96%.) See Table 3 for a summary of results.

Layered policies gave participants a little more trouble (78%) than other formats. Cookie information was under the heading "Personal Information" in F Layered (80%,) which may not be where people expected to look. In D Layered (69%,) the policy mentions in passing that "You may also turn off cookies in your browser," without explicitly saying they use cookies. People must deduce that information or go to the full policy for a direct statement that the site uses cookies. This highlights two results we will see again: first, when participants needed to think about an answer rather than just perform a search for information, accuracy dropped. Second, it appears few people ventured beyond the first page of the layered policies. Kay and Terry found similar issues with layered policies [15].

In another sign that this was an easy question for most participants, times to answer were shorter than the other questions (2.3 minutes.) We found no significance for time based on company but format was significant. Privacy Finder (2.1 minutes) and Layered (2.3 minutes) supported faster responses than Natural Language, but the Layered condition was also more likely to result in incorrect answers.

4.2   Opt Out Link

We asked: Does the company provide a link to a webform that allows you to remove yourself from Acme's email marketing list?
Answer: Yes for all policies except: B NL, D NL, D Layered, E NL, which are No.[3]

This question is a little more difficult than the question about cookies. Policies refer to this concept as "opting out." For example, company C's natural language policy phrases it as "To opt out of receiving all other Acme mailings after you have registered, click here or click the appropriate unsubscribe link contained within the email that you receive." Participants need to map the concept of removing themselves from an email marketing list to the technical jargon of opting out. However, this question is again fairly straight forward. Either there is an opt out link or there is not. See Table 4 for a summary of results.

We found significant differences for company and format. Natural language policy accuracy rates are dissimilar, with averages ranging from 93% (F) to 33% (A). Finding the opt out link in the A NL policy was looking for a needle in a haystack: there is one link halfway through the policy in the middle of a paragraph without any headings or other cues—and the policy runs to 13 pages when printed.

Table 4. Percentage correct and minutes to answer for the opt out question

Policy	% correct	Time
A NL	33%	5.7
A PF	85%	3.7
B NL	33%	9.3
B PF	91%	4.6
B Layered	18%	4.8
C NL	80%	3.2
C PF	73%	5.1
D NL	29%	6.1
D PF	71%	3.8
D Layered	19%	5.5
E NL	55%	5.4
E PF	51%	4.6
F NL	93%	3.4
F PF	79%	3.7
F Layered	92%	2.2

It would seem Privacy Finder should have consistent results across all six policies, since an opt out link is a standard part of Privacy Finder reports. However, companies with an opt out default have additional links for each category of opt out data. As a result, policies with opt out practices fared better, ranging from 85% correct (A PF) with less privacy protective practices and many prominent opt out links, to 51% correct (E PF) which required opt out for all data collection and had only one opt out link. Interestingly, the F PF policy (79%) has identical practices as E PF (51%) yet different accuracy scores. The author of the F PF policy included an additional opt out link in the text at the very end of the policy, which is prime real estate for readers' attention. Policy authors choices affect outcomes, even within the PF standardized presentation.

Since there is no requirement to discuss opt out choices within the layered format, once again we see dissimilar results across a standardized format. B layered policy (18%) required clicking the opt out link to see what it did, phrased

---

[3] Answers are not the same across a given company because the companies elected to provide different information in different formats. P3P requires an opt out link, which is then included in Privacy Finder.

as "For more information about our privacy practices, go to the full Acme Online Privacy Statement. Or use our Web form," with a link from "Web form" to the opt out page. In contrast, results were quite good with F layered (92%), which contained the same opt out text as at the end of the F PF (79%) policy.

We found significant differences in time to answer for company as well as format. We would expect longer times for longer policies since this is in many ways an information search task. Instead, time appears to be based on the underlying practices: policies without opt out links took longer. Since some of the policies with opt out links mentioned them at the end, it is unlikely the difference in times is based on reading through the entire policy to determine the absence of a link. Instead, participants likely reread to satisfy themselves that they had not missed anything. Once again participants completed the task more quickly with layered (4.0 minutes) and Privacy Finder (4.2 minutes) than Natural Language (5.4 minutes,) but the wide variance and sometimes poor performance for standardized policies reduces the strength of this result.

Table 5. Percentage correct and minutes to answer for the email sharing question

Policy	% correct	Time
A NL	76%	3.2
A PF	53%	5.4
B NL	49%	5.9
B PF	64%	5.9
B Layered	52%	4.8
C NL	80%	4.7
C PF	72%	6.9
D NL	67%	4.6
D PF	78%	4.0
D Layered	56%	4.7
E NL	53%	6.9
E PF	44%	6.2
F NL	50%	6.0
F PF	54%	4.4
F Layered	62%	5.0

4.3　Share Email

We asked: Does this privacy policy allow Acme to share your email address with a company that might put you on their email marketing list (with or without your consent)?

Answer. Yes for all policies except: companies E and F (all formats) which are No.

We tested the wording of this question in multiple pilot studies to ensure people understood it without asking something pejorative or jargon-laden like "will Acme sell your email address to spammers." This question requires participants to understand the question, read the policy carefully, and make inferences for most policies. For example, C NL reads: "We may provide your contact information and other personal data to trusted third parties to provide information on products and services that may be of interest to you." Participants need to understand that "contact information" includes email, that "trusted third parties" are companies other than Acme, and that "provide information on products and services" means marketing messages, in order to correctly answer "Yes." See Table 5 for a summary of results.

Overall accuracy was only 60%. We found significant differences for company but not format. Times to answer averaged 5.3 minutes, which indicates people had a harder time completing this task. We found no significant results for time based on company or format.

As the answers to our questions become more nuanced we would expect the more readable policies to shine, yet that is not the case. Company A, with the hardest to read policy, had a higher accuracy score (64%) than F (55%) with the most readable policy and there was no overall discernible pattern based on readability. Similarly, we would expect standardized policies to convey information better, especially the Privacy Finder format which avoids the emotion-rich wording of "trusted third parties" and "valuable offers," yet we did not find significant differences between formats. Privacy Finder summarizes "With whom this site may share your information" as "Companies that have privacy policies similar to this site's" which again requires participants to refer to a separate section to determine if the parent company may engage in email marketing.

4.4   Telemarketing

We asked: Does this privacy policy allow Acme to use your phone number for telemarketing?

Answer. Yes for all policies except companies A, E and F (all formats) which are No.

Participants struggled with this question as shown in Table 6. Except in the Privacy Finder version where companies are required to provide information about their telemarketing practices, policies typically do not highlight telemarketing practices. The way to answer this question correctly was typically to read through the entire policy for all mentions of when the company collects phone numbers, then see what policies they have around that data. For example, B NL discloses telemarketing as: "You may also have the option of proactively making choices about the receipt of promotional e-mail, telephone calls, and postal mail from particular Acme sites or services." Sometimes policies were even more vague, for example D NL, "The information you provide to Acme on certain Acme Web sites may also be used by Acme and selected third parties for marketing purposes. Before we use it, however, we will offer you the opportunity to choose whether or not to have your information used in this way." Not only is telemarketing swept under the phrase "marketing purposes," telephone numbers are not

Table 6. Percentage correct and minutes to answer for the telemarketing question

Policy	% correct	Time
A NL	23%	8.7
A PF	43%	5.9
B NL	41%	6.7
B PF	67%	5.9
B Layered	16%	6.2
C NL	42%	9.2
C PF	68%	5.5
D NL	42%	7.6
D PF	82%	3.2
D Layered	33%	5.5
E NL	65%	10.2
E PF	56%	5.4
F NL	26%	7.1
F PF	55%	7.4
F Layered	34%	5.9

mentioned explicitly either. It was necessary to deduce practices from a very careful and nuanced reading, frequently referring to multiple sections of the policy and then putting pieces together like a jigsaw puzzle. One could even make the case that answering "The policy does not say" is correct in cases as above where "information you provide" may be used for "marketing purposes" is by no means an explicit statement about telemarketing. However, we think it is important to note that the company likely does believe they have conveyed their practices: privacy policies are vetted by lawyers and are generally expected to be able to withstand a court or FTC challenge. If necessary, companies can point to the language in their policy and show that they did not violate the text by telemarketing.

We found significant differences in accuracy scores for company and format.[4] We found no significant results for time based on company but format does have significant differences. Once again layered (5.7 minutes) and Privacy Finder (5.5 minutes) are an improvement over natural language (8.2 minutes) but with the caveat that layered does not do as well for accuracy.

Even though we called out D NL as particularly indirect, it falls solidly in the middle of the accuracy scores (42%.) When participants cannot find information in layered policies, by design they should continue to the full policy for more details. In practice this appears not to happen, with a very low accuracy of 28%.

Privacy Finder does support more accurate answers (61%) even in contrast to natural language (39%.) Privacy Finder is the only format that requires a company to disclose, yes or no, if they telemarket. For example, under the heading "The ways your information may be used" D PF includes "To contact you by telephone to market services or products – unless you opt-out." Again there is a lot of variation between Privacy Finder policies based on the supplemental text they provide. For example B PF, is particularly confusing by stating in free form text "While Acme does not currently support telemarketing, it is possible that in the future Acme properties may contact you by voice telephone," directly above an automatically generated statement that they may use information for telemarketing.

5   Psychological Acceptability Results

After completing the initial accuracy questions, participants answered a series of questions designed to elicit their emotional reactions. Participants responded on a scale from 1 = strongly disagree to 7 = strongly agree. Most answers hovered right around 4, which is a neutral reaction. Higher numbers are always better.

5.1   Ease of Finding Information

We asked four questions about how easy it was to find information. We expected responses to these questions to reflect how well participants were able to understand a particular policy, and thus be related to the accuracy questions and times. However, we found few significant results. Participants found layered easier to understand even though they were less accurate with the layered format.

---

[4] Accuracy scores for telemarketing are the single exception where including "Does Not Say" as a correct answer changes whether we find significance between formats.

- "I feel that Acme's privacy practices are explained thoroughly in the privacy policy I read" (M = 4.7, s.d. = 1.5.) We found significant effects for company but not format. A, B, and F (M = 4.8 for all) scored better than C, D, and E (M=4.4 for C and D; M=4.5 for E.)
- "I feel confident in my understanding of what I read of Acme's privacy policy" (M = 4.7, s.d. = 1.6.) We found no significant differences between companies or formats.
- "This privacy policy was easier to understand than most policies" (M = 4.5, s.d. = 1.5.) We found no significant differences between companies but did find significant results for formats. Layered (M=4.8) scored better than natural language (M=4.4) or Privacy Finder (M=4.4.)
- "It was hard to find information in Acme's policy" (M = 3.8, s.d. = 1.6.) We found no significant differences between companies or formats. (Note that based on the wording for this question we had to report the inverse of responses to keep higher numbers as better.)

5.2 Trust

If a format conveys information well but results in lack of trust of the company, it is unlikely that corporations will adopt the format. Participants trusted Privacy Finder formats slightly more than other formats.

- "I feel secure about sharing my personal information with Acme after viewing their privacy practices" (M = 4.0, s.d = 1.7.) We found significant effects for both company and format.
- "I believe Acme will protect my personal information more than other companies" (M = 4.0, s.d = 1.6.) We found significant effects for both company and format.

5.3 Enjoyment

We asked two questions to gauge how much participants liked reading the privacy policy. If people are unwilling to read policies then improving them does not provide much benefit. We found no significant differences between formats.

- "Finding information in Acme's privacy policy was a pleasurable experience" (M = 3.7, s.d. = 1.7.) We found no significant differences between companies or formats. This was the lowest score of all eight psychological acceptability questions.
- "If all privacy policies looked just like this I would be more likely to read them" (M = 4.2, s.d. = 1.7.) We found significant effects for format but not company.

6 Discussion

Our hypotheses were not fully supported and in some cases were refuted. Both layered and Privacy Finder formats did improve times to answer, but not by much, and at the expense of accuracy for layered policies. Privacy Finder policies showed modest improvement in accuracy for complex questions but no improvement for easy questions. While the accuracy scores for Privacy Finder were low in some cases, the format does represent a step forward from the status quo. Readability did not determine outcomes for natural language policies. For natural language, in some cases it appears the practices of the company were greater determinants than the words they used to describe those practices. We found few statistically significant differences in psychological acceptability.

Many researchers start from the observation that privacy policies are not usable in their current format and suggest ways to fix the problem. All of the formats were tested were unsatisfactory with a low rate of comprehension on questions that required synthesis of information. Participants did not like privacy policies of any type, and the highest mean score on the psychological acceptability questions was barely above neutral.

Privacy researchers tend to talk about policies as being uniformly bad. We expected that more readable natural language policies would have higher accuracy scores, lower times, and improved psychological acceptability than less readable policies, but that was not the case. These results could suggest that readability metrics are not a good way to differentiate between policies. This seems unlikely because the Flesch index has proven robust in many contexts and we do not immediately see any reason why privacy policies should be dramatically different from other types of textual analysis. It seems more likely that the range from 32 to 46 on the Flesch index is too similar to see major variations in outcome: even the most readable policies are too difficult for most people to understand and even the best policies are confusing.

Our results are robust across a variety of different policies, but our study does not concretely identify what makes a given policy comprehensible. However, we can offer three observations. First, results from the layered format suggest participants did not continue to the full policy when the information they sought was not available on the short notice. Unless it is possible to identify all of the topics users care about and summarize to one page, the layered notice effectively hides information and reduces transparency. Second, participants struggled to map concepts in the questions to the terms used in policies. It may prove fruitful to research how people internally represent privacy concepts: which terms do they currently use and which industry terms do they understand? As suggested in the Kleimann report for printed financial statements, online privacy policies may need an educational component so readers understand what it means for a site to engage in a given practice [22]. Third, the standardized formats we studied still offer policy authors quite a bit of leeway. Companies with identical practices conveyed different information, and these differences were reflected in participants' ability to understand the policies. The flexibility of the standardized formats may undermine their expected benefits to consumers.

Our study used a between subjects rather than within subjects structure. We expect that we would see larger differences, particularly in psychological acceptability, if we were to place policies side-by-side. Prior work[7] found that when participants have both the natural language and the Privacy Finder versions available, Privacy Finder fares well. If people are reading multiple companies' policies to compare them, Privacy Finder may be advantageous. However, for just understanding a single policy, we find differences between formats are not as pronounced. By only showing one policy, our study did not capture one of the potential advantages to standardized formats. Standardized formats should be more useful once readers understand where to find information. Learning effects may play a role over time when people can take greater advantage of standardized formats as they become more familiar with their layout.

At this time, we do not recommend regulating the format of online privacy policies. While we did not find substantial benefit from the standardized formats we tested, that is not an inditement of the concept of standardized formats. Early results testing a new format for privacy policies based around a nutrition label concept are encouraging [16]. Ideally, future formats will identify problems with existing approaches and attempt to improve upon what has come before. In the future, we encourage rigorous testing for new formats before their supporters encourage wide-spread adoption.

References

1. Acquisti, A., Grossklags, J.: Privacy and rationality in individual decision making. IEEE Security & Privacy Magazine 3, 26–33 (2005)
2. Anton, A., Earp, J.B., Qingfeng, H., Stufflebeam, W., Bolchini, D., Jensen, C.: Financial privacy policies and the need for standardization. IEEE Security & Privacy 2(2), 36–45 (2004)
3. Bendrath, R.: Icons of privacy (2007),
   http://bendrath.blogspot.com/2007/05/icons-of-privacy.html
   (accessed Feburary 22, 2009)
4. Business Wire: European union issues guidance on privacy notices; new notices make it easier for consumers to understand, compare policies (January 2005), http://www.tmcnet.com/usubmit/2005/jan/1104731.htm (accessed May 19, 2009)
5. Center for Information Policy Leadership: Ten steps to develop a multilayered privacy policy (2007), www.hunton.com/files/tbl_s47Details (July 2007)
6. Children's Online Privacy Protection Act of 1998 (COPPA), Public Law No. 104–191 (October 1998), www.cdt.org/legislation/105th/privacy/coppa.html (accessed March 27, 2007)
7. Cranor, L.F., Guduru, P., Arjula, M.: User interfaces for privacy agents. ACM Transactions on Computer-Human Interaction (TOCHI) (2006)
8. Egelman, S., Tsai, J., Cranor, L.F., Acquisti, A.: Timing is everything? the effects of timing and placement of online privacy indicators. In: CHI 2009, Boston, MA, USA (2009)
9. Federal Trade Commission: FTC staff revises online behavioral advertising principles (February 2009), http://www.ftc.gov/opa/2009/02/behavad.shtm (accessed May 15, 2009)

10. Graber, M.A., D'Alessandro, D.M., Johnson-West, J.: Reading level of privacy policies on internet health web sites. Journal of Family Practice (July 2002)
11. U.S. Gramm-Leach-Bliley Financial Modernization Act of 1999, Public Law no. 106–102 (1999)
12. Hochhauser, M.: Lost in the fine print: Readability of financial privacy notices (July 2001), http://www.privacyrights.org/ar/GLB-Reading.htm (accessed March 27, 2007)
13. Huang, H.J.: Language-focus instruction in EFL writing: Constructing relative clauses in definition paragraphs. In: 2008 International Conference on English Instruction and Assessment (2008),
    http://www.ccu.edu.tw/fllcccu/2008EIA/English/C16.pdf (accessed Feburary 22, 2009)
14. Jensen, C., Potts, C., Jensen, C.: Privacy practices of Internet users: Self-reports versus observed behavior. International Journal of Human-Computer Studies 63, 203–227 (2005)
15. Kay, M., Terry, M.: Textured agreements: Re-envisioning electronic consent. Technical report cs-2009-19, David R. Cheriton School of Computer Science, University of Waterloo (2009)
16. Kelley, P.G., Bresee, J., Reeder, R.W., Cranor, L.F.: A "nutrition label" for privacy. In: Symposium on Usable Privacy and Security (SOUPS) (2009)
17. Lemos, R.: MSN sites get easy-to-read privacy label. CNET News.com (2005), http://news.com.com/2100-1038_3-5611894.html (accessed May 30, 2007)
18. My Byline Media. The Flesch reading ease readability formula,
    http://www.readabilityformulas.com/flesch-reading-ease-readability-formula.php (accessed March 9, 2009)
19. OUT-LAW News: Drop the jargon from privacy policies, says privacy chief (September 2005), http://www.out-law.com/page-5791 (accessed March 23, 2007)
20. Pollach, I.: What's wrong with online privacy policies? Communications of the ACM 30(5), 103–108 (2007)
21. Reeder, R.W., Kelley, P.G., McDonald, A.M., Cranor, L.F.: A user study of the expandable grid applied to P3P privacy policy visualization. In: WPES 2008: Proceedings of the 7th ACM workshop on Privacy in the electronic society, pp. 45–54. ACM Press, New York (2008)
22. Report by Kleimann Communication Group for the FTC: Evolution of a prototype financial privacy notice (2006),
    http://www.ftc.gov/privacy/privacyinitiatives/ftcfinalreport060228.pdf (accessed March 2, 2007)
23. Saltzer, J.H., Schroeder, M.D.: The protection of information in computer systems. Proceedings of the IEEE 63, 1278–1308 (1975)
24. Sheng, X., Cranor, L.F.: An evaluation of the effect of US financial privacy legislation through the analysis of privacy policies. I/S - A Journal of Law and Policy for the Information Society 2, 943–980 (2006)
25. The Center for Information Policy Leadership, H.. W. L. Multi-layered notices, http://www.hunton.com/Resources/Sites/general.aspx?id=328 (accessed March 23, 2007)
26. The Office of the Privacy Commissioner: Release of privacy impact assessment guide and layered privacy policy (August 2006),
    http://www.privacy.gov.au/news/06_17.html (accessed Feburary 22, 2009)

27. Tsai, J., Egelman, S., Cranor, L.F., Acquisti, A.: The effect of online privacy information on purchasing behavior: An experimental study. In: The 6th Workshop on the Economics of Information Security (WEIS) (2008), http://weis2007.econinfosec.org/papers/57.pdf (accessed Feburary 22, 2009)
28. Vila, T., Greenstadt, R., Molnar, D.: Why we can't be bothered to read privacy policies: models of privacy economics as a lemons market. In: ACM International Conference Proceeding Series, vol. 5, pp. 403–407 (2003)
29. W3C Working Group: The platform for privacy preferences 1.1 (P3P1.1) specification (2006), http://www.w3.org/TR/P3P11/ (accessed March 28, 2007)

A Appendix

This appendix includes supporting statistical details. We performed all tests of statistical significance at the $\alpha = 5\%$ confidence level. We performed ANOVA analysis for both time data and psychological acceptability, which we recorded on a seven point Likert scale and treated as continuous variables. Accuracy questions were categorical data (either accurate or inaccurate) so we used Chi Squared tests. Details of that analysis follows.

A.1 Accuracy

Accuracy scores are all reported as the percentage of people who answered the question correctly. Answers are always either Yes, No, or the policy Does Not Say. We tested for statistically significant differences in mean accuracy rates by company (Table 7) and by format (Table 8).

Table 7. Statistical Significance Tests for Accuracy Questions by Company

Question	d.f.	χ^2 value	p	Significant?
Cookies	5	12.16	.033	✓
Opt Out Link	5	108.31	< .001	✓
Share Email	5	22.43	< .001	✓
Telemarketing	5	24.99	< .001	✓

Table 8. Statistical Significance Tests for Accuracy Questions by Format

Question	d.f.	χ^2 value	p	Significant?
Cookies	2	28.95	< .001	✓
Opt Out Link	2	40.80	< .001	✓
Share Email	2	1.90	.387	
Telemarketing	2	50.08	< .001	✓

Table 9. Statistical Significance Tests for Time to Answer by Company

Question	d.f.	F value	p	Significant?
Cookies	5	1.18	.320	
Opt Out Link	5	5.58	$< .001$	✓
Share Email	5	1.81	.109	
Telemarketing	5	1.75	.122	

Table 10. Statistical Significance Tests for Time to Answer by Format

Question	d.f.	F value	p	Significant?
Cookies	2	4.50	$< .012$	✓
Opt Out Link	2	3.59	.028	✓
Share Email	2	0.15	.864	
Telemarketing	2	8.59	$< .001$	✓

A.2 Time

We recorded time in milliseconds though we reported it in minutes to assist readability. With such a fine grain unit of measure time is nearly continuous and we used ANOVA for analysis. We tested for statistically significant differences in mean times to answer by company (Table 9) and by format (Table 10).

A.3 Psychological Acceptability

We asked a series of questions to capture subjective impressions of the privacy policies. Responses were on a seven point Likert scale which is sufficient granularity to treat them as continuous variables. We performed ANOVA analysis to test for statistically significant differences in mean Likert scores by company (Table 11) and by format (Table 12).

Table 11. Statistical Significance Tests for Psychological Acceptability by Company

Topic	Question	d.f.	F value	p	Significant?
Finding Info.	Explained thoroughly	5	1.9	.038	✓
Finding Info.	Confident understood	5	1.9	.099	
Finding Info.	Easier to understand	5	1.6	.148	
Finding Info.	Hard to find	5	.75	.589	
Trust	Feel secure	5	7.0	$< .001$	✓
Trust	Protect more	5	3.9	.020	✓
Enjoyment	Pleasurable	5	1.7	.135	
Enjoyment	Likely to read	5	2.4	.096	

Table 12. Statistical Significance Tests for Psychological Acceptability by Format

Topic	Question	d.f.	F value	p	Significant?
Finding Info.	Explained thoroughly	2	1.6	.203	
Finding Info.	Confident understood	2	.33	.722	
Finding Info.	Easier to understand	2	2.89	.051	
Finding Info.	Hard to find	2	.60	.549	
Trust	Feel secure	2	14.4	< .001	✓
Trust	Protect more	2	8.0	< .001	✓
Enjoyment	Pleasurable	2	.62	.539	
Enjoyment	Likely to read	2	2.4	.032	✓

Vida: How to Use Bayesian Inference to De-anonymize Persistent Communications

George Danezis[1] and Carmela Troncoso[2]

[1] Microsoft Research Cambridge
gdane@microsoft.com
[2] K.U. Leuven/IBBT, ESAT/SCD-COSIC
Carmela.Troncoso@esat.kuleuven.be

Abstract. We present the *Vida* family of abstractions of anonymous communication systems, model them probabilistically and apply Bayesian inference to extract patterns of communications and user profiles. The first is a very generic Vida Black-box model that can be used to analyse information about all users in a system simultaneously, while the second is a simpler Vida Red-Blue model, that is very efficient when used to gain information about particular target senders and receivers. We evaluate the Red-Blue model to find that it is competitive with other established long-term traffic analysis attacks, while additionally providing reliable error estimates, and being more flexible and expressive.

1 Introduction

Anonymous communications allow conversing parties on a network to exchange messages without revealing their network identifiers to each other or to third party observers. Anonymity is of special importance to ensure privacy, support protocols such as on-line polls, or enable high-security government or military communications over commodity network infrastructures.

The most practical proposal for engineering anonymous communications is the *mix*, proposed by David Chaum [3] in 1981. A mix is a network router offering a special security property: it hides the correspondences between its input and output messages, thus providing some degree of anonymity. A large body of research, surveyed in [6], is concerned with extending and refining mix based protocols.

In parallel with advances in anonymity, techniques have been developed to uncover persistent and repeated patterns of communication through mix networks. Such attacks were first named "intersection attacks" [17] since they were based on the idea that when a target user systematically communicates with a single friend it is possible to uncover the identity of the latter by intersecting the anonymity sets of the sent messages. Kesdogan *et al.* [1,12,13] introduced a family of disclosure and hitting set attacks that generalises this idea to users with multiple friends. These attacks' result is the set of friends of each sender being uncovered, after a number of messages communicated. Statistical

I. Goldberg and M. Atallah (Eds.): PETS 2009, LNCS 5672, pp. 56–72, 2009.

variants of these attacks were also developed, known as statistical disclosure attacks [5], and applied to pool mixes [8], traffic containing replies [7], and evaluated against complex models [15]. The state of the art in statistical disclosure is the Perfect Matching Disclosure Attack introduced by Troncoso *et al.* [21]. The PMDA allows to guess who are communication partners in a round of mixing with higher accuracy than its predecessors. Further the authors show how this information can be in turn used to improve the estimation of users' sending profiles.

This work re-examines the problem of extracting profiles and, in parallel, uncover who is talking with whom, from traffic traces of anonymous communications. We offer a generalisation of the disclosure attack model of an anonymity system [1,12,13], and analyse it using modern Bayesian statistics. We note that at the heart of long term traffic analysis lies an inference problem: from a set of public observations the adversary tries to infer a "hidden state relating" to who is talking to whom, as well as their long term contacts. Applying Bayesian techniques provides a sound framework on which to build attacks, standard well studied algorithms to co-estimate multiple quantities, as well as accurate estimates of error.

Our key contributions are first *the very generic* Vida *models to represent long term attacks against any anonymity system*, and second *the application of Bayesian inference techniques to traffic analysis*. Throughout this work we show that our models and techniques lead to effective de-anonymization algorithms, and produce accurate error estimates. Furthermore they are far more flexible and reliable than previous ad-hoc techniques.

This paper is organised as follows: Sect. 2 offers an overview of Bayesian inference techniques, their relevance to traffic analysis, as well as an overview of the Gibbs sampling algorithm; Sect. 3 presents the Vida generic model for anonymous communications, that can be used to model any system. In Sect. 4 we present a simplification of the model, the Vida Red-Blue model, that allows an adversary to perform inference on selected targets, as it would be operationally the case, along with an evaluation of the effectiveness of the inference technique. Finally we discuss the future directions of inference and traffic analysis in Sect. 5 and conclude in Sect. 6.

2   Bayesian Inference and Monte Carlo Methods

Bayesian inference is a branch of statistics with applications to machine learning and estimation [14]. Its key methodology consists of constructing a full probabilistic model of all variables in a system under study. Given observations of some of the variables, the model can be used to extract the probability distributions over the remaining, hidden, variables.

To be more formal lets assume that an abstract system consists of a set of hidden state variables $\mathcal{HS}$ and observations $\mathcal{O}$. We assign to each possible set of these variables a joint probability $\Pr[\mathcal{HS}, \mathcal{O}|\mathcal{C}]$ given a particular model $\mathcal{C}$.

By applying Bayes rule we can find the distribution of the hidden state given the observations as:

$$\Pr[\mathcal{HS}, \mathcal{O}|\mathcal{C}] = \Pr[\mathcal{HS}|\mathcal{O}, \mathcal{C}] \cdot \Pr[\mathcal{O}|\mathcal{C}] \Rightarrow \Pr[\mathcal{HS}|\mathcal{O}, \mathcal{C}] = \frac{\Pr[\mathcal{HS}, \mathcal{O}|\mathcal{C}]}{\Pr[\mathcal{O}|\mathcal{C}]} \Rightarrow$$

$$\Pr[\mathcal{HS}|\mathcal{O}, \mathcal{C}] = \frac{\Pr[\mathcal{HS}, \mathcal{O}|\mathcal{C}]}{\sum_{\forall \mathcal{HS}} \Pr[\mathcal{HS}, \mathcal{O}|\mathcal{C}] \equiv \mathcal{Z}} = \frac{\Pr[\mathcal{O}|\mathcal{HS}, \mathcal{C}] \cdot \Pr[\mathcal{HS}|\mathcal{C}]}{\mathcal{Z}}$$

The joint probability $\Pr[\mathcal{HS}, \mathcal{O}|\mathcal{C}]$ is decomposed into the equivalent $\Pr[\mathcal{O}|\mathcal{HS}, \mathcal{C}] \cdot \Pr[\mathcal{HS}|\mathcal{C}]$, describing the model and the a-prior distribution over the hidden state. The quantity $\mathcal{Z}$ is simply a normalising factor.

There are key advantages in using a Bayesian approach to inference that make it very suitable for traffic analysis applications:

– The problem of traffic analysis is reduced to building a generative model of the system under analysis. Knowing how the system functions is sufficient to encode and perform the attacks, and the inference steps are, in theory, easily derived from this forward model. In practice computational limitations require careful crafting of the models and the inference techniques to be able to handle large systems.
– The Bayesian approach allows to infer as many characteristics of the system as needed by introducing them in the probabilistic model. This permits to infer several hidden variables jointly as we show for users' sending profiles and their recipient choices for each message.
– A Bayesian treatment results in probability distributions over all possible hidden states, not only the most probable one as many current traffic analysis methods do. The marginal distributions over different aspects of the hidden state can be used to measure the certainty of the attacker, and provide good estimates of her probability of error.

The last point is the most important one: the probability distribution over hidden states given an observation, $\Pr[\mathcal{HS}|\mathcal{O}, \mathcal{C}]$, contains a lot of information about all possible states. When traffic analysis is used operationally the probability of error of particular aspects of the hidden state can be calculated to inform decision making. It is very different to assert that, in both cases, the most likely correspondent of Alice is Bob, with certainty 99% versus with certainty 5%. Extracting probability distributions over the hidden state allows us to compute such error estimates directly, without the need for an ad-hoc analysis of false positives and false negatives. Furthermore, the analyst can use the inferred probability distribution to calculate directly anonymity metrics [9,19].

Despite their power Bayesian techniques come at a considerable computational cost. It is often not possible to compute or characterise directly the distribution $\Pr[\mathcal{HS}|\mathcal{O}, \mathcal{C}]$ due to its complexities. In those cases sampling based methods are available to extract some of its characteristics. The key idea is that a set of samples $\mathcal{HS}_0, \ldots, \mathcal{HS}_\iota \sim \Pr[\mathcal{HS}|\mathcal{O}, \mathcal{C}]$ are drawn from the a-posterior distribution, and used to estimate particular marginal probability distributions of interest. For this purpose, Markov Chain Monte Carlo methods have been proposed. These are stochastic techniques that perform a long random walk on a state space representing the hidden information, using specially crafted transition probabilities that make the walk converge to the target stationary distribution, namely $\Pr[\mathcal{HS}|\mathcal{O}, \mathcal{C}]$. Once the Markov Chain has been built, samples of the hidden states of the system can be obtained by taking the current state of the simulation after a certain number of iterations.

2.1 Gibbs Sampler

The Gibbs sampler [11] is a Markov Chain Monte Carlo method to sample from joint distributions that have easy to sample marginal distributions. These joint distributions are often the a-posterior distribution resulting from the application of Bayes theorem, and thus Gibbs sampling has been extensively used to solve Bayesian inference problems. The operation of the Gibbs sampler is often referred to as *simulation*, but we must stress that it is unrelated to simulating the operation of the system under attack.

For illustration purposes we assume an a-posterior distribution $\Pr[\mathcal{HS}|\mathcal{O}, \mathcal{C}]$ can be written as a joint probability distribution $\Pr[X, Y|\mathcal{O}, \mathcal{C}]$ that is difficult to sample directly. If, on the other hand, there is an efficient way of sampling from the marginal distributions $\Pr[X|Y, \mathcal{O}, \mathcal{C}]$ and $\Pr[Y|X, \mathcal{O}, \mathcal{C}]$, then Gibbs sampling is an iterative technique to draw samples from the joint distribution $\Pr[X, Y|\mathcal{O}, \mathcal{C}]$. The algorithm starts at an arbitrary state (x_0, y_0). Then it iteratively updates each of the components through sampling from their respective distributions, i.e. $x_i \sim \Pr[X|Y = y_{i-1}, \mathcal{O}, \mathcal{C}]$, and $y_i \sim \Pr[Y|X = x_i, \mathcal{O}, \mathcal{C}]$. After a sufficient number of iterations, the sample (x_i, y_i) is distributed according to the target distribution, and the procedure can be repeated to draw more samples. We note that in this process the computation of the normalising factor $\mathcal{Z}$ is not needed.

The other parameters of the Gibbs algorithm, namely the number of iterations necessary per sample, as well as the number of samples are also of some importance. The number of iterations has to be high enough to ensure the output samples are statistically independent. Calculating it exactly is difficult so we use conservative estimates to ensure we get good samples. The number of samples to be extracted, on the other hand, depends on the necessary accuracy when estimating the marginal distributions, which can be increased by running the sampler longer.

3 The Vida General Black-Box Model for Anonymity Systems

Long term attacks traditionally abstract the internal functioning of any anonymity system and represent it as an opaque router, effectively operating as a very large threshold mix. This model has its limitations, and some studies have attempted to extend it. In this section we first propose the Vida Black-box model, the most flexible abstraction of an anonymity system so far, and base our Bayesian analysis on this model.

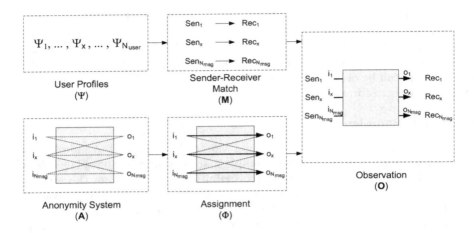

Fig. 1. The generative model used for Bayesian inference in anonymous communications

We start by proposing a 'forward' generative model describing how messages are generated and sent through the anonymity system. We then use Bayes rule to 'invert' the problem and perform inference on the unknown quantities. The broad outline of the generative model is depicted in Figure 1.

An anonymity system is abstracted as containing N_{user} users that send N_{msg} messages to each other. Each user is associated with a sending profile Ψ_x describing how they select their correspondents when sending a message. We assume, in this work, that those profiles are simple multinomial distributions, that are sampled independently when a message is to be sent to determine the receiver. We denote the collection of all sending profiles by $\Psi = \{\Psi_x | x = 1 \ldots N_{\text{user}}\}$.

A given sequence of N_{msg} senders out of the N_{user} users of the system, denoted by $\text{Sen}_1, \ldots, \text{Sen}_{N_{\text{msg}}}$, send a message while we observe the system. Using their sending profiles a corresponding sequence of receivers $\text{Rec}_1, \ldots, \text{Rec}_{N_{\text{msg}}}$ is selected to receive their messages. The probability of any receiver sequence is easy to compute. We denote this matching between senders and receivers as $\mathcal{M}$:

$$\Pr[\mathcal{M}|\Psi] = \prod_{x \in [1, N_{\text{msg}}]} \Pr[\text{Sen}_x \to \text{Rec}_x | \Psi_x].$$

In parallel with the matching process where users choose their communication partners, an anonymity system $\mathcal{A}$ is used. This anonymity system is abstracted as a bipartite graph linking input messages i_x with potential output messages o_y, regardless of the identity of their senders and receivers. We note that completeness of the bipartite graph is not required by the model. The edges of the bipartite graph are weighted with w_{xy} that is simply the probability of the input message i_x being output as o_y: $w_{xy} = \Pr[i_x \to o_y | \mathcal{A}]$.

This anonymity system $\mathcal{A}$ is used to determine a particular assignment of messages according to the weights w_{xy}. A single perfect matching on the bipartite graph described by $\mathcal{A}$ is selected to be the correspondence between inputs and outputs of the anonymity system for a particular run of the anonymity protocol. We call it the assignment of inputs to outputs and denote it by Φ. Contrary to previous work [20] on probabilistic modelling, and following the tendency started by Troncoso *et al.* [21], we consider all inputs simultaneously. In this case the probability of the assignment Φ is easy to calculate, given the set of all individual assignments $(i_x \rightarrow o_x)$:

$$\Pr[\Phi|\mathcal{A}] = \prod_x \frac{\Pr[i_x \rightarrow o_x|\mathcal{A}]}{\sum_{\text{free } i_y} \Pr[i_y \rightarrow o_x|\mathcal{A}]}.$$

This is simply the probability of the matching given the anonymity system weights. By free i_y we denote the set of sent messages i that has not yet been assigned an output message o as part of the match.

The assignment Φ of the anonymity system and the matching $\mathcal{M}$ of senders and receivers are composed to make up the observation of the adversary, that we denote as $\mathcal{O}$. An adversary observes messages from particular senders Sen_x entering the anonymity as messages i_x, and on the other side messages o_y exiting the network on their way to receivers Rec_y. No stochastic process takes place in this deterministic composition and therefore $\Pr[\mathcal{O}|\mathcal{M}, \Phi, \Psi, \mathcal{A}] = 1$.

Now that we have defined a full generative model for all the quantities of interest in the system, we turn our attention to the inference problem: the adversary observes $\mathcal{O}$ and knows about the anonymity system $\mathcal{A}$, but is ignorant about the profiles Ψ, the matching $\mathcal{M}$ and the assignment Φ. We use Bayes theorem to calculate the probability $\Pr[\mathcal{M}, \Phi, \Psi|\mathcal{O}, \mathcal{A}]$. We start with the joint distribution and solve for it:

$$\Pr[\mathcal{O}, \mathcal{M}, \Phi, \Psi|\mathcal{A}] = \Pr[\mathcal{M}, \Phi, \Psi|\mathcal{O}, \mathcal{A}] \cdot \Pr[\mathcal{O}|\mathcal{A}]$$

$$\Pr[\mathcal{O}, \mathcal{M}, \Phi, \Psi|\mathcal{A}] = \Pr[\mathcal{O}|\mathcal{M}, \Phi, \Psi, \mathcal{A}] \qquad (\equiv 1)$$
$$\cdot \Pr[\mathcal{M}|\Phi, \Psi, \mathcal{A}] \qquad (\equiv \Pr[\mathcal{M}|\Psi])$$
$$\cdot \Pr[\Phi|\Psi, \mathcal{A}] \qquad (\equiv \Pr[\Phi|\mathcal{A}])$$
$$\cdot \Pr[\Psi|\mathcal{A}]$$

$$\Rightarrow \Pr[\mathcal{M}, \Phi, \Psi|\mathcal{O}, \mathcal{A}] = \frac{\Pr[\mathcal{M}|\Psi]\Pr[\Phi|\mathcal{A}]}{\Pr[\mathcal{O}|\mathcal{A}] \equiv \mathcal{Z}} \Pr[\Psi|\mathcal{A}]$$

We have discussed how to calculate the probabilities $\Pr[\mathcal{M}|\Psi]$ and $\Pr[\Phi|\mathcal{A}]$. The quantity $\Pr[\Psi|\mathcal{A}] \equiv \Pr[\Psi]$ is the a-prior belief the attacker has about user profiles and it is independent from the chosen anonymity system $\mathcal{A}$. We consider throughout our analysis that all profiles are a-priori equally probable and reduce it to a constant $\Pr[\Psi] = c$. Taking into account those observations we conclude that the posterior probability sought is,

$$\Pr[\mathcal{M}, \Phi, \Psi|\mathcal{O}, \mathcal{A}] \sim \prod_{x \in [1, N_{\text{msg}}]} \Pr[\text{Sen}_x \rightarrow \text{Rec}_x|\Psi_x] \cdot \prod_x \frac{\Pr[i_x \rightarrow o_x|\mathcal{A}]}{\sum_{\text{free } i_y} \Pr[i_y \rightarrow o_x|\mathcal{A}]}$$

where we omit the constant normalising factor $\Pr[\mathcal{O}|\mathcal{A}]$ as it is very hard to calculate, which restricts the methods we can use to manipulate the a-posterior distribution.

It is computationally unfeasible to exhaustively enumerating the states of this distribution. Hence to calculate the marginals of interest such as profiles of users, or likely recipients of specific messages, we have to resort to sampling states from that distribution. Sampling directly is very hard (due to the interrelation between the profiles, the matches and the assignments) hence Markov Chain Monte Carlo methods are used.

3.1   A Gibbs Sampler for the Vida Black-Box Model

Sampling states $(\mathcal{M}_j, \Phi_j, \Psi_j) \sim \Pr[\mathcal{M}, \Phi, \Psi | \mathcal{O}, \mathcal{A}]$ directly is hard, due to the complex interactions between the random variables. A Gibbs sampler significantly simplifies this process by only requiring us to sample from the marginal distributions of the random variables sought. Given an arbitrary initial state (Φ_0, Ψ_0) we can perform ι iterations of the Gibbs algorithm as follows:

$$\text{for } j := 1 \ldots \iota :$$
$$\Phi_j, \mathcal{M}_j \sim \Pr[\Phi, \mathcal{M} | \Psi_{j-1}, \mathcal{O}, \mathcal{A}]$$
$$\Psi_j \sim \Pr[\Psi | \Phi_j, \mathcal{M}_j, \mathcal{O}, \mathcal{A}] \ .$$

Each of these marginal probabilities distributions is easy to sample:

- The distribution of assignments $\Pr[\Phi, \mathcal{M} | \Psi_{j-1}, \mathcal{O}, \mathcal{A}]$ is subtle to sample directly. Each message assignment $i_x \rightarrow o_x$ has to be sampled, taking into account that some message assignments are already taken by the time input message i_x is considered. For each input message i_x we sample an assignment o_y according to the distribution:

$$i_x \rightarrow o_y \sim \Pr[i_x \rightarrow o_y | \text{free } o_y, \forall_{\text{assigned } o_v} i_v \rightarrow o_v, \mathcal{A}, \Psi]$$
$$= \frac{\Pr[i_x \rightarrow o_y | \mathcal{A}] \cdot \Pr[\text{Sen}_x \rightarrow \text{Rec}_y | \Psi_x]}{\sum_{\text{free } o_y} \Pr[i_x \rightarrow o_y | \mathcal{A}] \cdot \Pr[\text{Sen}_x \rightarrow \text{Rec}_y | \Psi_x]} \ .$$

For complex anonymity systems $\mathcal{A}$, this algorithm might return only partial matches, when at some point an input message i_x has no unassigned candidate output message o_y left. Since we are only interested in perfect matchings, where all input messages are matched with different output messages, we reject such partial states and re-start the sampling of the assignment until a valid perfect matching is returned. This is effectively a variant of rejection sampling, to sample valid assignments.

The matchings between senders and receivers are uniquely determined by the assignments and the observations, so we can update them directly without any need for sampling, and regardless of the profiles (i.e. $\mathcal{M}_j = f(\Psi_j, \mathcal{O})$).

- The distribution of profiles $\Pr[\Psi | \Phi_j, \mathcal{M}_j, \mathcal{O}, \mathcal{A}]$ is straightforward to sample given the matching $\mathcal{M}_j$ and assuming that individual profiles Ψ_x are multinomial distributions.

We note that the Dirichlet distribution is a conjugate prior of the multinomial distribution, and we use it to sample profiles for each user. We denote as

$\Psi_x = (\Pr[\mathrm{Sen}_x \to \mathrm{Rec}_1], \ldots, \Pr[\mathrm{Sen}_x \to \mathrm{Rec}_{N_{\mathrm{user}}}])$ the multinomial profile of user Sen_x. We also define a function that counts the number of times a user Sen_x is observed sending a message to user Rec_y in the match $\mathcal{M}$, and denote it as $\mathrm{Ct}_{\mathcal{M}}(\mathrm{Sen}_x \to \mathrm{Rec}_y)$. Sampling profiles $(\Psi_1, \ldots, \Psi_{N_{\mathrm{user}}}) \sim \Pr[\Psi|\mathcal{M}]$ involves sampling independently each sender's profile Ψ_x separately from a Dirichlet distribution with the following parameters:

$$\Psi_x \sim \mathrm{Dirichlet}(\mathrm{Ct}_{\mathcal{M}}(\mathrm{Sen}_x \to \mathrm{Rec}_1) + 1, \ldots, \mathrm{Ct}_{\mathcal{M}}(\mathrm{Sen}_x \to \mathrm{Rec}_{N_{\mathrm{user}}}) + 1) \quad .$$

If the anonymity system $\mathcal{A}$ describes a simple bipartite graph, the rejection sampling algorithm described can be applied to sample assignments $i_x \to o_x$ for all messages. When this variant of rejection sampling becomes expensive, due to a large number of rejections, a Metropolis-Hastings [4] based algorithm can be used to sample perfect matchings on the bipartite graph according to the distribution $\Pr[\Phi, \mathcal{M}|\Psi_{j-1}, \mathcal{O}, \mathcal{A}]$. Our implementation was tested against mix-based anonymity systems, with bipartite graphs representing the anonymity system that do not lead to any rejections.

The Gibbs sampler can be run multiple times to extract multiple samples from the a-posterior distribution $\Pr[\mathcal{M}, \Phi, \Psi|\mathcal{O}, \mathcal{A}]$. Instead of restarting the algorithm at an arbitrary state $(\mathcal{M}_0, \Phi_0, \Psi_0)$, it is best to set the starting state to the last extracted sample, that is likely to be within the typical set of the distribution. This speeds up convergence to the target distribution.

4   A Computationally Simple Vida Red-Blue Model

After the PMDA [21] it has become dogma that sender profiles have to be co-estimated simultaneously with the assignments, and our Bayesian analysis so far reflects this approach. Senders are associated with multinomial profiles with which they choose specific correspondents. We sample these profiles using the Dirichlet distribution, and use them to directly sample weighted perfect assignments in the anonymity system. The output of the algorithm is a set of samples of the hidden state, that allows the adversary to estimate the marginal distributions of specific senders sending to specific receivers.

We note that this approach is very generic, and might go beyond the day to day needs of a real-world adversary. An adversary is likely to be interested in particular target senders or receivers, and might want to answer the question: "who has sent this message to Bob?" or "who is friends with receiver Bob?". We present the Vida Red-Blue model to answer such questions, which is much simpler, both mathematically and computationally, than the generic Vida model presented so far.

Consider that the adversary chooses a target receiver Bob (that we call "Red"), while ignoring the exact identity of all other receivers and simply tagging them as "Blue". The profiles Ψ_x of each sender can be collapsed into a simple binomial distribution describing the probability sender x sends to Red or to Blue. It holds that:

$$\Pr[\mathrm{Sen}_x \to \mathrm{Red}|\Psi_x] + \Pr[\mathrm{Sen}_x \to \mathrm{Blue}|\Psi_x] = 1. \tag{1}$$

Matchings $\mathcal{M}$ map each observed sender of a message to a receiver class, either Red or Blue. Given the profiles Ψ the probability of a particular match $\mathcal{M}$ is:

$$\Pr[\mathcal{M}|\Psi] = \prod \Pr[\text{Sen}_x \rightarrow \text{Red} \;/\; \text{Blue}|\Psi_x]$$

The real advantage of the Vida Red-Blue model is that different assignments Φ now belong to equivalence classes, since all Red or Blue receivers are considered indistinguishable from each other. In this model the assignment bipartite graph can be divided into two sub-graphs: the sub-graph Φ_R contains all edges ending on the Red receiver (as she can receive more than one message in a mixing round), while the sub-graph Φ_B contains all edges ending on a Blue receiver. We note that these sub-graphs are complementary and any of them uniquely defines the other. The probability of each Φ can then be calculated as:

$$\Pr[\Phi|\mathcal{A}] = \sum_{\forall \Phi_B} \Pr[\Phi_B, \Phi_R|\mathcal{A}] =$$

$$= \sum_{\forall \Phi_B} \Pr[\Phi_B|\Phi_R, \mathcal{A}] \cdot \Pr[\Phi_R|\mathcal{A}] =$$

$$= \Pr[\Phi_R|\mathcal{A}] \cdot \sum_{\forall \Phi_B} \Pr[\Phi_B|\Phi_R, \mathcal{A}] =$$

$$= \Pr[\Phi_R|\mathcal{A}]$$

The probability of an assignment in an equivalence class defined by the assignment to Red receivers, only depends on Φ_R describing this assignment. The probability of assignment Φ_R can be calculated analytically as:

$$\Pr[\Phi_R|\mathcal{A}] = \prod_{x \in \Phi_R} \frac{\Pr[i_x \rightarrow o_x]}{\sum_{\text{free } i_j} \Pr[i_j \rightarrow o_x]}.$$

The assignment Φ_R must be a sub-graph of at least one perfect matching on the anonymity system $\mathcal{A}$, otherwise the probability becomes $\Pr[\Phi|\mathcal{A}] = 0$. As for the full model the probability of all the hidden quantities given the observation is:

$$\Pr[\mathcal{M}, \Phi, \Psi|\mathcal{O}, \mathcal{A}] = \frac{\Pr[\mathcal{M}|\Psi]\Pr[\Phi_R|\mathcal{A}]}{\Pr[\mathcal{O}|\mathcal{A}] \equiv \mathcal{Z}} \Pr[\Psi|\mathcal{A}] \tag{2}$$

The a-prior probability over profiles $\Pr[\Psi|\mathcal{A}]$ is simply a prior probability over parameters of a binomial distribution. Each profile can be distributed as $\Pr[\Psi_x|\mathcal{A}] = \text{Beta}(1,1)$ if nothing is to be assumed about the sender's x relationship with the Red receiver.

In practice a prior distribution $\Pr[\Psi_x|\mathcal{A}] = \text{Beta}(1,1)$ is too general, and best results are achieved by using a prior supporting skewed distributions, such as $\text{Beta}(1/100, 1/100)$. This reflects the fact that social ties are a-prior either strong or non existent. Given enough evidence the impact of this choice of prior fades quickly away.

4.1 A Gibbs Sampler for the Vida Red-Blue Model

Implementing a Gibbs sampler for the Vida Red-Blue model is very simple. The objective of the algorithms is, as for the general model, to produce samples of profiles (Ψ_j), assignments and matches $(\Phi_j, \mathcal{M}_j)$ distributed according to the Bayesian a-posterior distribution $\Pr[\mathcal{M}, \Phi, \Psi | \mathcal{O}, \mathcal{A}]$ described by eq. 2.

The Gibbs algorithm starts from an arbitrary state (Ψ_0, Φ_0) and iteratively samples new marginal values for the profiles $(\Phi_j, \mathcal{M}_j \sim \Pr[\Phi, \mathcal{M} | \Psi_{j-1}, \mathcal{O}, \mathcal{A}])$ and the valid assignments $(\Psi_j \sim \Pr[\Psi | \mathcal{M}_j, \Phi_j, \mathcal{O}, \mathcal{A}])$. The full matchings are a deterministic function of the assignments and the observations, so we can update them directly without any need for sampling (i.e. $\mathcal{M}_j = f(\Psi_j, \mathcal{O})$).

As for the general Gibbs sampler, sampling from the desired marginal distributions can be done directly. Furthermore the Vida Red-Blue model introduces some simplifications that speed up inference:

- **Sampling assignments.** Sampling assignments of senders to Red nodes (i.e. $\Phi_{Rj}, \mathcal{M}_j \sim \Pr[\Phi, \mathcal{M} | \Psi_{j-1}, \mathcal{O}, \mathcal{A}]$) can be performed by adapting the rejection sampling algorithm presented for the general model. The key modification is that only assignments to Red receivers are of interest, and only an arbitrary assignment to blue receivers is required (to ensure such an assignment exists). This time for each Red output messages o_x we sample an input message i_x according to the distribution:

$$i_x \to o_y \sim \Pr[i_x \to o_y | \text{free } i_x, \forall_{\text{assigned } i_v} i_v \to o_v, \mathcal{A}, \Psi]$$

$$= \frac{\Pr[i_x \to o_y | \mathcal{A}] \cdot \Pr[\text{Sen}_x \to \text{Red} | \Psi_x]}{\sum_{\text{free } i_j} \Pr[i_j \to o_y | \mathcal{A}] \cdot \Pr[\text{Sen}_j \to \text{Red} | \Psi_x]}$$

- **Sampling profiles.** Sampling a profile $\Psi_j \sim \Pr[\Psi | \mathcal{M}_j, \Phi_j, \mathcal{O}, \mathcal{A}]$ for every user x simply involves drawing a sample from a Beta distribution with parameters related to the number of links to Blue and Red receivers. To be formal we define a function $\text{Ct}_{\mathcal{M}}(\text{Sen}_x \to \text{Red}, \text{Blue})$ that counts the number of messages in a match that a user x sends to a Red or Blue receiver. The profile of user x is then sampled as:

$$\Psi_x \sim \text{Beta}(\text{Ct}_{\mathcal{M}}(\text{Sen}_x \to \text{Blue}) + 1, \text{Ct}_{\mathcal{M}}(\text{Sen}_x \to \text{Red}) + 1)$$

This yields a binomial parameter that is the profile of user x, describing the probability they send a message to a Red target user.

The cost of each iteration is proportional to sampling N_{user} Beta distributions, and sample from the distribution of senders of each of the Red messages. Both the sampling of profiles, and the sampling of assignments can be performed in parallel, depending on the topology. In case a large number of samples are needed multiple Gibbs samplers can be run on different cores or different computers to produce them.

4.2   Evaluation

The Vida Red-Blue model for inferring user profiles and assignments was evaluated against synthetic anonymized communication traces, to test its effectiveness. The communication traces include messages sent by up to 1000 senders to up to 1000 receivers. Each sender is assigned 5 contacts at random, to whom they send messages with equal probability. Messages are anonymized in discrete rounds using a threshold mix that gathers 100 messages before sending them to their receivers as a batch.

The generation of communication patterns was peculiar to ensure a balance between inferring the communications of a target user (as in the traditional disclosure, hitting set and statistical disclosure attacks) to a designated Red receiver, as well as to gain enough information about other users to build helpful profiles for them. A target sender was included in 20% of the rounds, and the Red node was chosen to be one of their friends. A sequence of experiments were performed to assess the accuracy of the attack after observing an increasing number of rounds of communication.

The aim of each experiment is to use the samples returned by a Gibbs sampler implementing the Vida Red-Blue model to guess the sender of each message that arrives at a designated Red receiver. The optimal Bayes criterion [2] is used to select the candidate sender of each Red message: the sender with the highest a-posterior probability is chosen as the best candidate. This probability is estimated by counting the number of times each user were the sender of a target Red message in the samples returned by the Gibbs algorithm. The Bayesian probability of error, i.e. the probability another sender is responsible for the Red message, is also extracted, as a measure of the certainty of each of these "best guesses". For each experiment the Gibbs sampler was used to extract 200 samples, using 100 iterations of the Gibbs algorithm each. The first 5 samples were discarded, to ensure stability is reached before drawing any inferences.

A summary of the results for each experiment is presented in Figure 2. The top graph illustrates the fraction of correct guesses per experiment (on the x axis – we selected 20 random experiments to display per round number) grouped by the number of rounds of communication observed (16, 32, 64, 128, 256, 512 and 1024). For each experiment the fraction of correctly identified senders is marked by a circle, along with its 90% confidence interval. The dashed line of the same graph represents the prediction of success we get from the Bayesian probability of error. The bottom graph on Figure 2 illustrates on a logarithmic scale the inferred probability assigned to the Red node for the target sender, for each of the experiments. The experiments for which a high value of this probability are inferred (median greater than 1%) are marked by a solid red circle on both graphs. The 50% confidence interval over the profile parameter is also plotted.

Some key conclusions emerge from the experiments illustrated on Figure 2:

- The key trend we observe is, as expected, that the longer the observation in terms of rounds, the better the attack. Within 1024 rounds we expect the target sender to have sent about 40 messages to the designated red target. Yet, the communication is traced to them on average 80% of the cases

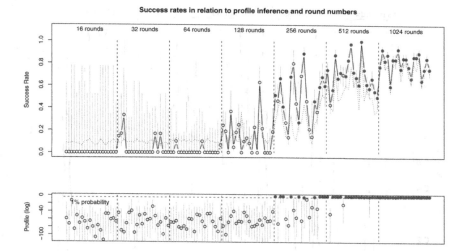

Fig. 2. Performance of the Vida Red-Blue model in assigning senders to the target red receiver, as a function of the number of rounds observed. Twenty sample experiments are used per round number.

with high certainty. Even when only 256 rounds are observed the correct assignment is guessed in about 50% of the time.

- The quality of the inference when it comes to the correspondence between messages, senders and receivers, is intimately linked to the quality of the profile inference. The solid red circles mark experiments that concluded that the median value for the probability the target sender is friends with the target Red receiver is high (greater than 1%). We observe that these experiments are linked to high success rates when it comes to linking individual messages to the target sender. We also observe the converse: insufficient data leads to poor profiles, that in turn lead to poor predictions about communication relationships.

- The probability of success estimates (represented on the top graph by a dotted line) predict well the success rate of the experiments. Our prediction systematically falls within the 90% confidence interval of the estimated error rate. This shows that the Vida Red-Blue model is a good representation of the process that generated the traces and thus the estimates coincide with the actual observed error rate, on average. This is due to the very generic model for Vida Red-Blue profiles that represent reality accurately after a few rounds. Yet, when few rounds are observed the a-prior distribution of profiles dominates the inference, and affects the error estimates.

A key question is how the results from the Vida Red-Blue model compare with traditional traffic analysis attacks, like the SDA [15], the NSDA [21] or the PMDA [21]. The SDA attack simply uses first order frequencies to guess the profiles of senders. It is fast but inaccurate. The normalised SDA (NSDA) constructs

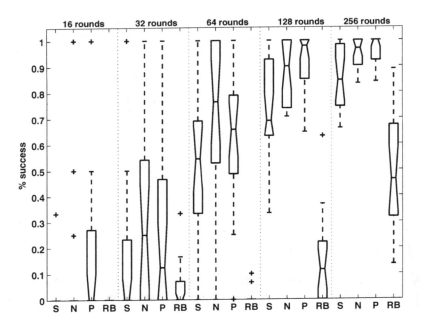

Fig. 3. Performance of the Vida Red-Blue inference model (RB) compared to the SDA (S), NSDA (N) and PMDA (P)

a traffic matrix from senders to receivers, that is normalised to be doubly stochastic. The operation is as fast as matrix multiplication, and yields very good results. The PMDA finds perfect matchings between senders and receivers based on a rough profile extraction step – it is quite accurate but slow.

Figure 3 illustrates the relative performances of the different attacks compared with the Vida Red-Blue model proposed. We observe that the inference based technique is quite competitive, against the SDA, but performs worse than the NSDA and PMDA in most settings. This is due to our strategy for extracting best estimates for the senders: we use the output samples to chose the sender with highest marginal probability instead of extracting a full match with the maximal marginal probability. In that sense applying an algorithm to find the maximal perfect matching based on the marginal probabilities output by the RB attacks should produce much better results.

Despite the lower success rate inference based techniques can be advantageous. Their key strength is the certainty that no systematic bias has been introduced by reusing data twice, as reported in [10,21], and the tangible and reliable error estimate they output. A traffic analyst is thus able to judge the quality of the inference to guide them operationally.

A second important advantage is the ability to infer who is the "second most likely" receiver, compute anonymity metrics, or other arbitrary statements on the a-posterior probability distribution of profiles and assignments. This can be done efficiently simply using the samples output by the Gibbs algorithm. Furthermore the correct probabilities of error can be associated with those probabilistic statements.

5   Discussion and Future Directions

The Bayesian treatment of long term attacks against anonymity systems is promising, but still at its infancy. We foresee some key theoretical as well as implementation steps to move the state of the art forward.

- **Bipartite weighted anonymity set.** The Vida Black-box model as well as the Vida Red-Blue model proposed represent an observation from an anonymity system as a generic weighted bipartite graph, linking senders with receivers. Our experiments, on the other hand, only considered anonymity systems working in discrete rounds, forming full bipartite sub-graphs with a number of senders equal to the batch size. This is a limitation of our sampler implementation, that could be extended to deal with the general case of any bipartite weighted network.

  While in theory this modification is straightforward, in practice it is harder to sample directly matchings from arbitrary bipartite graphs. The rejection sampling algorithm suggested can be inefficient, since it might use links that are not part of a perfect matching, forcing multiple aborts. It might be wise to first prune the assignment graph from such edges using techniques from the constrain satisfaction literature such as Regin's algorithm [18].

- **Profile models.** The a-prior model for user profiles is very generic, meaning that it can represent, and thus learn, any multinomial distribution of receivers per sender. While being generic more information could be incorporated if it is established that the profile belongs to a social network (with some standard characteristics like degree, clustering etc). Traditional hitting set as well as disclosure attacks make extensive use of the number of friends of a target sender to be applicable at all, whereas the presented approaches do not require such information. Yet, adding related constraints would yield better results.

- **Learning social networks.** It has been an open problem in the literature how to incorporate known information about communication patterns to help the inference of unknown communication patterns, and some ad-hoc techniques were presented to combine social network information to de-anonymize traces, along with a discussion of systematic errors introduced [10]. The sampling techniques presented in this work can be straightforwardly modified to incorporate known correspondences between senders and receivers: the Gibbs sampler is modified to only sample valid assignments that contain the known matches. These known assignments, far from being useless, drive the sampling of profiles (as part of the Gibbs sampling) leading to higher quality profiles, which in turn become higher quality assignments for the unknown messages.

- **Beyond communications.** Both models presented are very generic and apply to attempts to anonymize traces that are not communications. As long as a system has users with multinomial preferences, that are expressed and anonymized in an arbitrary manner (as long as there is one expressed preference per observed action), our algorithms are applicable to de-anonymize the preferences and extract user profiles. This problem has recently received considerable attention though de-anonymization algorithms applied to the NetFlix database [16].

6   Conclusions

The contribution of this work is two-fold: First it presents Vida, the first truly general model for abstracting any anonymity system, in the long term, to perform de-anonymization attacks. Users and their preferences are modelled in the most generic way, using multinomial profile, eliminating the need to know the number of contacts each sender has. Instead of abstracting an anonymity system as a single threshold mix, or even pool mix, an arbitrary weighted mapping of input to output messages can be used. We show that the model performs well when it comes to guessing who is talking to whom, as well as guessing the profiles of senders. The Vida Red-Blue model focuses on the need the working traffic analyst has to infer patterns of communications to specific targets – it has the potential to be implemented efficiently and parallelized aggressively.

The second contribution is methodological, and might be even more significant than the specific Vida models. We demonstrate that probabilistic modelling, Bayesian inference, and the associated conceptual toolkit relating to Monte Carlo Markov chain sampling is an appropriate framework upon which to build traffic analysis attacks. It ensures that information is used properly avoiding over fitting or systematic biases; it provides a clear framework to perform the analysis starting with the definition of a probabilistic model, that is inverted and sampled to estimate quantities of interest; it provides good and clear estimates of error, as well as the ability to answer arbitrary questions about the hidden state with a clear probability statement. These qualities are in sharp contrast with the state of the art in traffic analysis, that provides ad-hoc best guesses of very specific quantities, with a separate analysis to establish their accuracy based on labeled data – something that the traffic analyst does not have on the ground.

We hope this work is the start of an exploration of the applicability of inference techniques to problems in traffic analysis – that will eventually outperform established techniques. Some clear future directions include the definition of better user models, the analysis of the internals of anonymity systems, as well as a better integration of prior information and learning. The inference approach leans itself well to be extended to encompass these problems, that have in the past been a thorn on the side of traffic analysis techniques.

Acknowledgements. The authors would like to thank the participants of the second UK anonymity meet-up in 2008, and in particular Andrei Serjantov, Ben Laurie, and Tom Chothia for their valuable comments on this research. While this work was developed its direction benefited considerably by our discussions with Steven Murdoch, who also provided significant logistical support. C. Troncoso is a research assistant of the Fund for Scientific Research in Flanders (FWO) and this work was partly performed while C. Troncoso was an intern at Microsoft Research Cambridge, between September and December 2008. This work was supported in part by the IAP Programme P6/26 BCRYPT of the Belgian State.

References

1. Agrawal, D., Kesdogan, D., Penz, S.: Probabilistic Treatment of MIXes to Hamper Traffic Analysis. In: Proceedings of the 2003 IEEE Symposium on Security and Privacy, May 2003, pp. 16–27 (2003)
2. Chatzikokolakis, K., Palamidessi, C., Panangaden, P.: Probability of error in information-hiding protocols. In: Proceedings of the 20th IEEE Computer Security Foundations Symposium (CSF20) (2007)
3. Chaum, D.: Untraceable electronic mail, return addresses, and digital pseudonyms. Communications of the ACM 4(2) (February 1981)
4. Chib, S., Greenberg, E.: Understanding the metropolis-hastings algorithm. The American Statistician 49(4), 327–335 (1995)
5. Danezis, G.: Statistical disclosure attacks: Traffic confirmation in open environments. In: Gritzalis, Vimercati, Samarati, Katsikas (eds.) Proceedings of Security and Privacy in the Age of Uncertainty (SEC 2003), Athens, IFIP TC11, May 2003, pp. 421–426. Kluwer, Dordrecht (2003)
6. Danezis, G., Diaz, C.: A survey of anonymous communication channels. Technical Report MSR-TR-2008-35, Microsoft Research (January 2008)
7. Danezis, G., Diaz, C., Troncoso, C.: Two-sided statistical disclosure attack. In: Borisov, N., Golle, P. (eds.) PET 2007. LNCS, vol. 4776, pp. 30–44. Springer, Heidelberg (2007)
8. Danezis, G., Serjantov, A.: Statistical disclosure or intersection attacks on anonymity systems. In: Fridrich, J. (ed.) IH 2004. LNCS, vol. 3200, pp. 293–308. Springer, Heidelberg (2004)
9. Díaz, C., Seys, S., Claessens, J., Preneel, B.: Towards measuring anonymity. In: Dingledine, R., Syverson, P.F. (eds.) PET 2002. LNCS, vol. 2482, pp. 54–68. Springer, Heidelberg (2003)
10. Diaz, C., Troncoso, C., Serjantov, A.: On the impact of social network profiling on anonymity. In: Borisov, N., Goldberg, I. (eds.) PETS 2008. LNCS, vol. 5134, pp. 44–62. Springer, Heidelberg (2008)
11. Gelman, A., Carlin, J.B., Stern, H.S., Rubin, D.B.: Bayesian Data Analysis, 2nd edn. Chapman and Hall, Boca Raton (2003)
12. Kesdogan, D., Agrawal, D., Penz, S.: Limits of anonymity in open environments. In: Petitcolas, F.A.P. (ed.) IH 2002. LNCS, vol. 2578, pp. 53–69. Springer, Heidelberg (2003)
13. Kesdogan, D., Pimenidis, L.: The hitting set attack on anonymity protocols. In: Fridrich, J. (ed.) IH 2004. LNCS, vol. 3200, pp. 326–339. Springer, Heidelberg (2004)
14. Mackay, D.J.C.: Information Theory, Inference, and Learning Algorithms. Cambridge University Press, Cambridge (2003)
15. Mathewson, N., Dingledine, R.: Practical traffic analysis: Extending and resisting statistical disclosure. In: Martin, D., Serjantov, A. (eds.) PET 2004. LNCS, vol. 3424, pp. 17–34. Springer, Heidelberg (2005)

16. Narayanan, A., Shmatikov, V.: Robust de-anonymization of large sparse datasets. In: IEEE Symposium on Security and Privacy, pp. 111–125. IEEE Computer Society Press, Los Alamitos (2008)
17. Raymond, J.-F.: Traffic Analysis: Protocols, Attacks, Design Issues, and Open Problems. In: Federrath, H. (ed.) Designing Privacy Enhancing Technologies. LNCS, vol. 2009, pp. 10–29. Springer, Heidelberg (2001)
18. Régin, J.-C.: A filtering algorithm for constraints of difference in csps. In: AAAI, pp. 362–367 (1994)
19. Serjantov, A., Danezis, G.: Towards an information theoretic metric for anonymity. In: Dingledine, R., Syverson, P.F. (eds.) PET 2002. LNCS, vol. 2482, pp. 41–53. Springer, Heidelberg (2003)
20. Shmatikov, V.: Probabilistic analysis of an anonymity system. Journal of Computer Security 12(3-4), 355–377 (2004)
21. Troncoso, C., Gierlichs, B., Preneel, B., Verbauwhede, I.: Perfect matching disclosure attacks. In: Borisov, N., Goldberg, I. (eds.) PETS 2008. LNCS, vol. 5134, pp. 2–23. Springer, Heidelberg (2008)

Scalable Link-Based Relay Selection
for Anonymous Routing

Micah Sherr, Matt Blaze, and Boon Thau Loo

University of Pennsylvania
{msherr,blaze,boonloo}@cis.upenn.edu

Abstract. The performance of an anonymous path can be described using many network metrics – e.g., bandwidth, latency, jitter, loss, etc. However, existing relay selection algorithms have focused exclusively on producing paths with high bandwidth. In contrast to traditional *node-based* path techniques in which relay selection is biased by relays' node-characteristics (i.e., bandwidth), this paper presents the case for *link-based* path generation in which relay selection is weighted in favor of the highest performing links. Link-based relay selection supports more flexible routing, enabling anonymous paths with low latency, jitter, and loss, in addition to high bandwidth. Link-based approaches are also more secure than node-based techniques, eliminating "hotspots" in the network that attract a disproportionate amount of traffic. For example, misbehaving relays cannot advertise themselves as "low-latency" nodes to attract traffic, since latency has meaning only when measured between two endpoints. We argue that link-based path selection is practical for certain anonymity networks, and describe mechanisms for efficiently storing and disseminating link information.

1   Introduction

Anonymous communication networks have been gaining in popularity in recent years. As they scale to support large user bases and diverse applications, there is an increasing need not only for these networks to ensure that high performance routes are selected, but also to provide flexibility to tradeoff between performance and anonymity in order to meet the requirements of different applications.

In response to these challenges, there have been a variety of proposals [6,22,35] that are aimed at improving the performance of anonymous routes. These proposals have primarily used *node characteristics* such as self-advertised bandwidth [6,3] as the main criteria for selecting intermediate relay nodes.

In this paper, we argue that an alternative – one that offers strong security guarantees and flexibility – is to utilize *link-based* path selection strategies. In link-based selection, the sender (also called the *initiator*) selects high performing links to construct her anonymous paths. The initiator ranks randomly generated (but not instantiated) paths according to their predicted end-to-end (e2e) performance, estimated by aggregating the costs of their constituent links. From its set of candidate paths, the initiator selects (and subsequently constructs) a path using a probability distribution weighted by the e2e cost estimates. As

I. Goldberg and M. Atallah (Eds.): PETS 2009, LNCS 5672, pp. 73–93, 2009.

with recently proposed node-based strategies [35], our link-based algorithm allows the sender to bias her paths towards either anonymity or performance. Link-based routing is appropriate for anonymity networks in which the performance of anonymous paths is determined by the network topology rather than local effects at end nodes (e.g., congestion, queuing delay, etc.).

Link-based path selection offers several advantages over node-based techniques. First, link-based path selection supports various metrics such as latency, bandwidth, jitter, and loss. The flexibility provided by link-based solutions enables anonymity networks to support a wide variety of network applications that have previously been considered incompatible with these networks. For example, real-time applications (in particular, VoIP clients) require connections with specific latency, jitter, and loss properties. Existing node-based path selection algorithms cannot accurately predict the link properties of their generated routes and are therefore unfit for particular classes of network communication.

Second, link-based strategies are less susceptible to manipulation. In a node-based scheme, a malicious node can easily advertise favorable node characteristics in order to increase the likelihood of being selected as a relay node [3]. Given that *link* metrics are defined only with respect to a pair of relays, the same attack strategy is harder to succeed without the infiltration of a large number of attackers. For instance, a host cannot truthfully promote itself as a "low-latency node", as such a claim may be accurate only for its nearby peers.

The contributions of this paper are as follows:

The case for link-based strategies: Using realistic network traces [14,38,40], we demonstrate that link-based selection not only achieves a high degree of flexibility by supporting a variety of metrics, it is also significantly more resilient to manipulation as compared to node-based strategies. To quantify the anonymity properties of relay selection, we introduce *node prevalence*, a metric that measures the probability that a relay participates in an anonymous path. For example, using a snapshot of available bandwidths from the Tor [7] network's directory servers, we note that the highest bandwidth Tor relay is expected to participate in nearly 40% of anonymous paths when Tor's default relay selection algorithm is used. In comparison, the most popular node using our link-based selection strategy on a comparable dataset (in which bandwidth is described as a link characteristic) is present in just 2.5% of paths. We show that our techniques leak little information about the communicating parties, protecting their anonymity even against powerful and colluding adversaries.

Practical link-based selection implementation: A potential disadvantage of link-based path selection is the need to maintain pairwise link information. We demonstrate that network *coordinate embedding systems* [4,5,23] provide a lightweight and scalable mechanism for maintaining link-based metrics while requiring only minimal communication overhead at each node. In coordinate systems, each node is mapped to n-dimensional coordinates such that the Cartesian distance between two nodes' coordinates corresponds to the network distance (e.g., latency, bandwidth, jitter, or loss) between them. Participants of coordinate embedding systems update their coordinate by periodically conducting measurements between themselves and randomly selected peers. Each node maintains a single coordinate for each link metric and updates a directory service whenever its coordinates change. Coordinate embedding systems effectively *linearize* the amount of information required to represent pairwise link characteristics, since the coordinates of N nodes are sufficient to estimate pairwise distances.

2 Assumptions and Limitations

The link-based path selection strategies presented in this paper estimate the e2e performance of potential anonymous routes by aggregating the costs of their constituent hops. For example, the e2e latency of a possible anonymous path is estimated by summing the latencies between adjacent nodes in the path. To be effective, link-based routing requires that path performance (whether it be measured by bandwidth, latency, jitter, etc.) be due to network effects.

If, however, local effects at end nodes (e.g., congestion or queuing delay) dominate performance, then link-based path selection is less effective (since the savings gained from optimizing link costs is overshadowed by node effects). At the extreme, link-based selection becomes equivalent to node-based selection when the communication cost of routing between two nodes is determined solely by properties of the receiving host.

The performance and anonymity results in the remainder of this paper assume path performance is dictated by the network rather than end-host effects. Although we leave the determination of the dominant factors that influence performance in various anonymity networks as a future research direction, we briefly note that link-based relay selection is likely better suited for P2P anonymity networks rather than networks in which the client to relay ratio is very high (e.g., in the case of Tor), causing congestion to determine path performance.

3 Related Work

Previously proposed relay selection techniques have focused on improving the bandwidth of generated paths [6,35]. To produce high bandwidth routes, the Tor [7] path selection algorithm sorts relays in increasing order of bandwidth and computes the sum $B = \sum_{i=0}^{|N|-1} b_i$, where b_i is the bandwidth of node i. The initiator chooses r uniformly at random from $[0, B)$ and selects the node with index k as a relay, where k is the largest integer such that $\sum_{i=0}^{k-1} b_i \leq r$. The initiator repeats this procedure to select each relay in the anonymous circuit [6].[1]

Øverlier and Syverson first identified that Tor's path selection algorithm is susceptible to manipulation [24]. By falsely advertising high bandwidths, nodes under an adversary's control can exploit the weighted probability distribution and increase their chances of being selected. If multiple nodes under the attacker's control are selected as relays, the adversary can apply a circuit-linking

---

[1] In practice, Tor may apply different weights for entry and exit nodes. For simplicity, we assume that all nodes may function as entry or exit relays.

algorithm [3] or perform timing analysis [21] to discern whether two of its relays reside on the same path. (Tor is designed to restrict each relay to knowing only the previous and next hop [7].) If the attacker controls the first and last relays in an anonymous path, he defeats anonymity since the first and last relays respectively know the identities of the initiator and responder. Bauer *et al.* demonstrate that when an adversary controlled just six of 66 nodes in a Tor deployment on PlanetLab [25], the attacker compromised more than 46% of all anonymous paths [3].

Snader and Borisov [35] propose two modifications to Tor to defend against Øverlier *et al.*'s attack. First, to prevent nodes from reporting false bandwidths, relays report the observed bandwidths of peer relays to the directory server. When queried for a node's bandwidth, the directory server reports the median of the node's observed measurements. Second, Snader and Borisov introduce a more tunable weighting system in which the initiator can tradeoff between anonymity and performance. They define the family of functions

$$f_s(x) = \begin{cases} \frac{1-2^{sx}}{1-2^s} & \text{if } s \neq 0 \\ x & \text{if } s = 0 \end{cases} \tag{1}$$

where s is a parameter chosen by the initiator that allows it to tradeoff between anonymity and performance. After having ranked the relays by bandwidth, the initiator chooses the relay with index $\lfloor n \cdot f_s(x) \rfloor$, where n is chosen uniformly at random from $[0, 1)$. By applying higher values of s, the initiator is able to more heavily bias her selections towards bandwidth. If $s = 0$, a relay is chosen uniformly at random [35]. Each relay is selected independently and without replacement according to the distribution imposed by Eq. 1.

Snader and Borisov's defense relies on *opportunistic measurements* – relays report the observed bandwidths of their peers [35]. There are unfortunately disadvantages of such an approach. First, a relay can report opportunistic measurements only when it participates in an anonymous circuit with a peer. Transmitting the observation to a directory server effectively informs the server of the existence of the circuit as well as the identities of the two relays that constitute one of its hops. Given that directory servers may be malicious, revealing segments of the path is undesirable. Second, the directory cannot discern whether reported measurements are truthful. Colluding malicious relays may (falsely) report that members of their coalition have high bandwidth. If there are a sufficient number of attackers to influence the median of a relay's measurements, then Øverlier *et al.*'s attack becomes feasible. Finally, as noted in Murdoch and Watson's recent work [22], attackers may have access to large botnets and may therefore join the anonymity network with relays that have sufficient bandwidth to attract peers. The use of opportunistic measurements attempts to protect against false self-reported measurements, but does not prevent an attacker from acquiring high performing nodes to attract traffic. As we show below, link-based measurements inherently reduce the attacker's ability to influence path selection, as each node is restricted to advertising a single coordinate, which, in turn, is perceived as favorable only to its nearby peers.

Table 1. Link concatenation operators. The distance between successive links is denoted as $d_1, d_2, ..., d_n$.

Metric	Path cost
Latency / RTT	$\sum_{i=1}^{h} d_i$
Bandwidth	$\min(d_1, d_2, ..., d_h)$
Loss rate	$1 - \prod_{i=1}^{h}(1 - d_i)$
Jitter (variance) (assumes jitter of two successive links is independent)	$\sum_{i=1}^{h} d_i$
Autonomous System (AS) Traversals	$\sum_{i=1}^{h} d_i$

The use of coordinate systems to estimate e2e path performance was first proposed in our earlier position paper [33]. This paper presents novel path selection algorithms, and is the first work of which we are aware that analyzes the performance and anonymity properties of link-based relay selection.

4   Link-Based Path Selection

Existing approaches [6,7,35] to producing high performance anonymous paths have focused exclusively on *node characteristics* – performance metrics (i.e., bandwidth) that may be attributed to individual relays. Node-based relay selection strategies randomly select relays according to a nonuniform probability distribution biased by the relays' node characteristics.

In link-based path selection, the e2e performance of a path is computed by aggregating the cost of all links that comprise the path, where cost is defined in terms of *link characteristics* such as latency, loss, and jitter. (While bandwidth is a node-based characteristic, it can also be represented as a link characteristic by considering the measured available bandwidth on a link connecting two nodes.) The use of link rather than node characteristics enables more flexible routing, as initiators can construct anonymous routes that meet more specific communication requirements.

WEIGHTED *Path Selection* Our link-based path selection algorithm, WEIGHTED, operates in two phases. In the first phase, the initiator rapidly generates (but does not instantiate) candidate paths consisting of three relays chosen uniformly at random without replacement. The initiator computes the e2e cost of each generated candidate path using a *link concatenation operator* (see Table 1).[2] For example, the e2e bandwidth of a path is the minimum of the bandwidths of its links, whereas the latency of the route may be estimated by summing the latencies of its hops.

In the second phase, the initiator sorts the candidate paths by their cost estimates. Using the family of functions introduced by Snader and Borisov [35] (see Eq. 1), the initiator instantiates the candidate path with index $\lfloor n \cdot f_s(x) \rfloor$, where

---

[2] Our approach may be extended to define the performance of a path in terms of *multiple metrics* by assigning weights to each metric in a manner that reflects its importance as determined by the initiator. The e2e path cost estimate is then calculated as the weighted average over the cost estimates for each individual metric.

n is chosen uniformly at random from $[0, 1)$. As with Snader's and Borisov's algorithm, a larger value of s more heavily weighs path selection in favor of performance. When $s = 0$, each randomly generated path is equally likely to be chosen. For clarity, we will refer to the case in which $s = 0$ as using the UNIFORM selection strategy.

5   The Case for Link-Based Selection

In this section, we present the case for link-based path selection. We demonstrate that link-based anonymous routing is flexible, enabling high performance paths, whether performance be quantified in terms of bandwidth, latency, or jitter. Additionally, we show that our selection strategy is more resilient to manipulation than previously established techniques, providing greater anonymity to the communication endpoints.

We first consider an *oracular* model in which all measurements (node or link) in the network are known to the initiator. This enables us to compare node- and link-based path selection strategies irrespectively of their measurement techniques. We revisit actual implementation strategies in Section 6.

5.1   Performance Analysis

Our performance analysis highlights two main benefits of link-based path selection over existing node-based techniques. First, link-based techniques support a variety of performance metrics, hence offering greater flexibility. In particular, the WEIGHTED selection strategy produces paths with low latency and jitter, few autonomous system (AS) traversals, and high bandwidth. Second, as with recently proposed node-based approaches [35], our link-based relay strategy enables the initiator to carefully tradeoff between anonymity and performance.

Our performance analysis is carried out using a trace-driven path simulator that takes as input an $N \times N$ matrix describing the pairwise network distances (i.e., latency, bandwidth, etc.) between relays. The pairwise link distances used as input to the simulator are obtained from actual network traces [14,40] as well as our own measurements carried out on the PlanetLab testbed [25]. Since the performance and security of link-based path selection is influenced by the underlying topology, we analyze the results of generating 150 anonymous paths between each of the $N(N-1)$ pairs of relays. That is, for each pair of relays, we generate anonymous paths between the pair using the remaining $N - 2$ nodes in the dataset as potential relays. The simulator models a single pair of communicants at any given time; i.e., we assume node congestion does not impact path performance. To produce each path, WEIGHTED generates (but does not instantiate) 150 candidate paths before randomly selecting the chosen path according to the weighted (e.g., by bandwidth) probability distribution.

Table 2 describes the trace-driven datasets used as input to our simulator. The King [14] and S^3-BW [40] datasets are based on measurements obtained from prior publications and are commonly used in the networking research community; PL-ASes and PL-Jitter represent newer metrics that are novel to this work. Due

Table 2. Network datasets used to evaluate link-based relay selection

Dataset	Metric	Nodes	Description
King [14]	Latency	500	Pairwise latencies captured using the King method [12]
S³-BW [40]	Available Bandwidth	365	Pairwise bandwidths from PlanetLab measured using PathChirp [29]
PL-ASes	AS Traversals	156	Pairwise number of AS crossings on PlanetLab measured using traceroute
PL-Jitter	Jitter (variance)	153	Pairwise jitter (variance of interarrival times of 30 pings) on PlanetLab
Tor-BW	Available Bandwidth	500	Available (also called "observed") bandwidth of 500 Tor nodes, obtained from Tor directory servers

to the lack of existing published traces on these metrics, we conducted our own measurements using geographically distributed PlanetLab nodes.

Since simulation time grows geometrically with network size, only the pairwise measurements for the first 500 relays from the King and Tor-BW datasets are used as input to the simulator. The remaining datasets contained fewer than 500 nodes, and are used in their entirety.

Bandwidth metric: Fig. 1 shows the bandwidth improvement resulting from using WEIGHTED on the S³-BW dataset. When $s = 9$, WEIGHTED more than doubles the median available bandwidth over all pairwise paths to 42.3 Mbps, compared to 20.1 Mbps when relays are selected uniformly at random (UNIFORM). (Recall that relay selection is weighted more heavily towards performance when s is increased.) The ability to provide high performance bandwidth paths using link-based relay selection is particularly interesting, given that bandwidth is often perceived as a node characteristic [2,15]. Bandwidth may, of course, be represented as a link characteristic (as is the case in the S³-BW dataset). This latter characterization enables more flexible routing, as bandwidth bottlenecks may result from Internet routing policies rather than node capacities.

Non-bandwidth metrics: Fig. 2-4 demonstrates WEIGHTED's ability to produce high performance paths for non-bandwidth metrics. The median e2e latency of the anonymous paths formed using Uniform is 277.2ms (Fig. 2). The median latency decreases by 20.6% to 220.1ms when $s = 3$ and by 52.7% to 131.2ms when $s = 15$. Additionally, WEIGHTED decreases the percentage of high latency paths: 93.0% of paths produced via UNIFORM have latencies of 250ms or greater compared to just 22.5% of routes generated using WEIGHTED with $s = 3$.

Jitter, defined as the variance in interarrival times (measured in ms) of 30 ping messages, significantly decreased using WEIGHTED. As shown in Fig. 3 (log scale), the median jitter decreased by 72% when $s = 3$ and by 97% when $s = 9$.

It may also be advantageous to minimize the number of AS crossings in an anonymous path, both to decrease the probability that a given AS can observe multiple hops in the path [8] and also to potentially achieve greater path performance (since routing within an AS is typically low-latency and high-bandwidth). Although analyzing the relationships between AS traversals, anonymity, and performance is beyond the scope of this paper, we include the metric here to emphasize the flexibility of link-based routing. Fig. 4 shows the cumulative distribution of AS traversals for anonymous paths. Using Uniform, 66% of anonymous paths

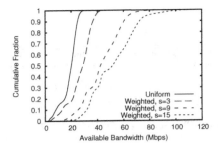

Fig. 1. E2e available bandwidth using the S^3-BW dataset

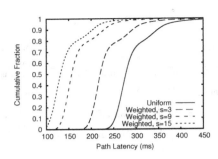

Fig. 2. E2e path latencies using the King dataset

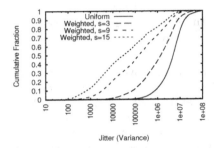

Fig. 3. E2e jitter using the PL-Jitter dataset

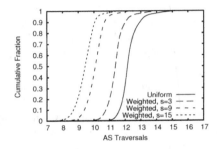

Fig. 4. E2e AS traversals using the PL-ASes dataset

traversed 12 or more ASes. When $s = 3$ and $s = 9$, only 10% and 0.3% of their respective paths crossed 12 or more ASes.

5.2 Anonymity Analysis

Our anonymity analysis aims to compare the anonymity properties of link-based and node-based relay selection under various attacker strategies. As with the existing literature, we consider an anonymous route to be compromised if the attacker controls its first and last relay [35]. (Resiliency to the *predecessor attack* [28,39] is discussed in Appendix B.)

We model an attacker that controls or monitors $f \cdot N$ of a N-node network, where $0 \leq f < 1$. We further assume that the adversary has complete network information and may select *a priori* which of the $f \cdot N$ nodes it controls (e.g., those with highest bandwidth). While this is a particularly strong threat model, it enables us to explore the limitations of our techniques by allowing the attacker to select the most "attractive" relays in a realistic network topology.[3] Due to the

---

[3] Prior work utilizes attacker models in which the adversary may supplement the network with additional malicious relays [22]. Link-based path selection is difficult to accurately assess using such models, as the performance and anonymity of anonymous paths depend upon the precise locations of all relays.

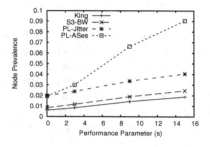

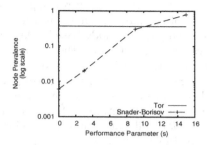

Fig. 5. The maximum of relays' node prevalences in the King, S^3-BW, PL-Jitter, and PL-ASes datasets using WEIGHTED

Fig. 6. Maximum node prevalences of relays in the Tor-BW dataset using the default Tor routing algorithm and the Snader-Borisov refinement

ease at which an adversary may acquire high performance nodes using a botnet, we view our threat model as conservative, but realistic.

Node Prevalence. To quantitatively compare link- and node-based relay selection, we introduce a new measure of anonymity, *node prevalence*, defined as the probability that a relay is selected as a participant in an anonymous path. Since link-based routing selects relays based on e2e performance estimations (including links containing the initiator or responder), we compute the node prevalence of a relay as the average probability of selection over all combinations of initiators and responders.[4] Intuitively, relays with high node prevalences are valuable to attackers since, by definition, they have a greater chance of being selected in anonymous paths.

In node-based techniques, high-bandwidth nodes are consistently perceived as attractive to all initiators, leading to relays with high node prevalences. In contrast, the likelihood that a node will be attractive for all paths using link-based approaches is fairly small, since a node's attractiveness is a function of the locations of the initiator, responder, and already chosen relays in the path. The ability of link-based relay selection to prevent "hotspots" leads to increased anonymity since a small coalition of malicious relays cannot easily attract a disproportionate amount of traffic.

Fig. 5 plots the *maximum* of all relays' node prevalences – the frequency at which the most popularly chosen node is present in anonymous paths. Even when WEIGHTED is tuned for high performance ($s = 15$), the most popular relay is present in less than 5% of paths in the King, S^3-BW, and PL-Jitter datasets,

---

[4] Snader *et al.* [35] propose the use of the Gini Coefficient [11] as a summary statistic of the inequality of relay selection. In contrast, node prevalence measures the popularity of a particular node. By calculating the node prevalence of each relay, we can study the worst-case anonymity of a particular path selection technique, which happens when the adversary has under its control the relays with highest node prevalences (i.e., those used most often in anonymous paths).

and less than 10% of routes using the PL-ASes trace. The corresponding performance of the paths is shown in Fig. 1 through 4.

In comparison, node-based relay selection yields substantially higher node prevalences. Fig. 6 shows the maximum node prevalence for the default Tor path selection strategy [6] and Snader and Borisov's proposed refinement [35] using the Tor-BW dataset. (Tor's routing algorithm takes no performance parameter and is shown as a straight line.) For both strategies, high bandwidth relays are attractive to all initiators. In particular, the highest bandwidth node is present in 36.9% of all paths produced using the default Tor algorithm. The tunable Snader-Borisov strategy has a modest maximum node prevalence of 2.0% when $s = 3$, but results in much poorer anonymity for greater values of s. When $s = 15$, 79.2% of paths contain the node with the greatest bandwidth. Although Fig. 5 and Fig. 6 cannot be directly compared since they use different underlying topologies and metrics, it is apparent from the figures that while there are no statically-attractive relays as perceived by WEIGHTED, node-based techniques result in hotspots that are present in a large fraction of paths.

Attack Strategies. We next consider various strategies available to the attacker. As described above, we utilize a conservative attacker model in which the adversary can choose *a priori* which relays he will compromise (up to some fraction f of the network). We further assume that the attacker has complete network knowledge (i.e., pairwise distances) to which to base his decision.

BestLinks: *Compromising Attractive Links.* In the BestLinks strategy, the attacker compromises the endpoints of the most attractive links. Mirroring the behavior of the initiator, the attacker ranks smaller distances more favorably if the metric is latency, jitter, loss, or AS traversals, and views larger distances as more advantageous for bandwidth. Given an ordering of links, the two endpoints of each link are assigned to the attacker until he controls $f \cdot N$ relays.

The effectiveness of the BestLinks strategy is depicted in Fig. 7. The x-axis denotes the fraction of nodes controlled by the attacker (f), while the y-axis plots the resultant percentage of paths that are compromised. As can be observed from the Fig., WEIGHTED successfully protects most anonymous paths even when the attacker controls 50% of the network. When paths are weighted heavily in favor of performance ($s = 15$) and 30% of the network is controlled by the attacker, only 12.4% of the anonymous paths in the King dataset become compromised (Fig. 7(a)). Similarly, for bandwidth (Fig. 7(b)), 16.4% of paths are compromised when 30% of the network is malicious. Results for the PL-ASes and PL-Jitter datasets are comparable, and are omitted for brevity.

For comparison, Fig. 8 shows the percentage of compromised paths for node-based selection strategies when the attacker uses the BestNodes attacker strategy on the Tor-BW dataset. Analogous to BestLinks, BestNodes ranks nodes according to their advertised bandwidths, with the attacker controlling the $f \cdot N$ nodes with greatest bandwidth. BestNodes is particularly successful against the default Tor algorithm. When the attacker controls the top 10% of relays, he is able to compromise 54.7% of anonymous paths. The Snader-Borisov ("SB") algorithm fares better for low values of s. However, the strategy becomes vulnerable

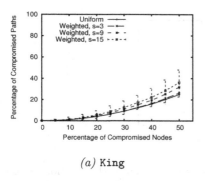
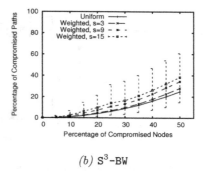

(a) `King`   *(b)* S^3-`BW`

Fig. 7. The percentage of compromised paths as a function of the fraction of compromised nodes when the attacker uses the `BestLinks` strategy and the initiator uses WEIGHTED with the *(a)* `King` and *(b)* S^3-`BW` datasets. Points represent the mean value with error bars (for $s = 15$) indicating the 5th and 95th percentiles. Error bars are omitted for $s \neq 15$ for readability. In all cases, the 5th-95th percentile ranges for $s \neq 15$ were less than that for $s = 15$.

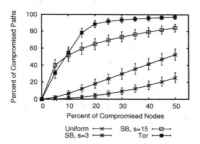
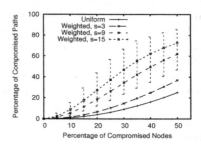

Fig. 8. The percentage of compromised paths when the attacker uses `BestNodes` and the initiator uses node-based strategies with the `Tor-BW` dataset

Fig. 9. The percentage of compromised paths when the attacker uses the `Confirmation` strategy and the initiator uses WEIGHTED with the `King` dataset

when performance is more highly valued. An adversary who operates the top 30% of high bandwidth nodes controls 73.1% of paths when $s = 15$.

`MedianDist`: *Compromising Nodes with Shortest Median Distances.* Alternatively, the attacker may choose the $f \cdot N$ nodes that have the smallest median distance between itself and all other nodes. Intuitively, `MedianDist` locates relays that are likely to be chosen due to their proximity to other relays. Fig. 10 plots the effectiveness of such a strategy when used with the `King` dataset. When weighted most heavily in favor of performance ($s = 15$), only 13.1% of paths are compromised when the attacker controls 30% of the network. Results for the remaining link-based topologies are consistent with `King` and are omitted for brevity. Although `MedianDist` is more effective than `BestLinks`, link-based relay selection significantly limits the ability to compromise paths, even against our powerful attacker.

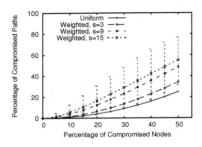

Fig. 10. The percentage of compromised paths as a function of the fraction of compromised nodes when the attacker uses the `MedianDist` strategy and the initiator uses WEIGHTED with the `King` dataset

`Confirmation`: *Determining whether Alice is Communicating with Bob.* The previous attacks attempt to compromise arbitrary paths in the anonymous network. In contrast, an attacker may apply the `Confirmation` attack to test whether a fixed pair of nodes (Alice and Bob) is anonymously communicating. Here, the attacker compromises the nearest node (e.g., having smallest RTT) to Alice that has not yet been compromised, and does the same with respect to Bob, and continues compromising nodes in this manner until he has controls $f \cdot N$ nodes. That is, the attacker compromises the nodes that are nearest to Alice and Bob to maximize the probability that he controls the first and last relays in their anonymous path (assuming such a path exists).

The results of using the `Confirmation` strategy against the `King` dataset are shown in Fig. 9. The figure plots the results of experiments between all pairwise initiators and responders. In each experiment, the attacker compromises the $f \cdot N$ nodes in the manner described above to target the particular initiator and responder pair. When routes are weighted heavily in favor of performance ($s = 9$), an attacker who controls 30% of the network and who can target particular initiator and responder pairs, can discern 34.4% of anonymous paths. As discussed in Appendix A, a slightly modified WEIGHTED strategy better protects against the `Confirmation` attack at the cost of a small degree of performance.

`Relay-in-the-Middle`: *Deducing Communication Endpoints.* If the adversary controls the middle relay (R2) in a three-relay anonymous path, she trivially knows the first (R1) and last (R3) relays as well. Since WEIGHTED ranks candidate paths based on e2e path estimates (i.e., the cost of Alice→R1→R2→R3→Bob), the attacker can estimate the cost of α →R1→R2→R3→ β for all possible initiator and responder pairs $\alpha, \beta \in N \setminus \{R1, R2, R3\}$, $\alpha \neq \beta$. By applying Eq. 1, she can compute the probability that a given candidate initiator/responder pair selected the subsequence R1→R2→R3 in its anonymous path. Although the size of the anonymity network and the performance parameter s may reduce the practicality and usefulness of this attack, we describe a countermeasure in Appendix A.

Cluster: *Joining the Network with a Cluster of Nodes.* An attacker may attempt to attract anonymous paths by joining the network with a large cluster of nodes that share a local network, offering low latency and high bandwidth connections between malicious peers. The efficacy of **Cluster** is described in Appendix D.

6   Practical Link-Based Path Selection

In this section, we explore the practical considerations of scalably deploying link-based anonymous path selection over the Internet.

6.1   Link Cost Estimation

Our analysis in Section 5 assumes that the initiator has knowledge of pairwise distances between potential relays. In practice, maintaining pairwise distances will require $O(N^2)$ in communication and network state, hence imposing a significant overhead on the anonymity network.

One practical solution to the above challenge is via the use of *network coordinate systems* that enable the pairwise distances between all participating nodes to be estimated to high accuracy with low overhead. Network coordinate systems, such as Vivaldi [5], PIC [4], NPS [23], and Big Bang Simulation [31] map each relay to n-dimensional coordinates such that the Euclidean distance between two relays' coordinates corresponds to the actual network distance between the pair. Although their individual implementations differ, coordinate systems use distributed algorithms in which each participant periodically measures the distance between itself and a randomly selected peer. By comparing the empirical measurement with the Euclidean distance between the two nodes' coordinates, the relay can adjust its coordinate either towards (in the case of over-estimation) or away from (for under-estimation) the neighbor's coordinate.

Network coordinate systems are well-suited for link-based relay selection, effectively linearizing the quantity of information that must be stored and communicated. By downloading the coordinates of N relays, an initiator can estimate the pairwise distances between them. These systems are lightweight, requiring little bandwidth overhead, and adapt quickly to changes in the network [5]. Additionally, these systems have proved to operate efficiently at Internet scale. For example, the Vuze BitTorrent client [36] currently operates a coordinate system consisting of more than one million nodes [16]. Finally, as we describe below, there exist well-established techniques for securing these systems to ensure the accuracy of advertised coordinates, preventing misbehaving relays from falsifying their coordinates to attract traffic.

Performance Impact of Coordinate Systems. To quantify the accuracy of coordinate systems, a well established metric is the *median error ratio* of each node – the median of the percentage differences between the estimated and actual distances between itself and all other relays in the network. Note that these errors are due to the presence of network triangle inequality violations (TIVs) that cannot be accurately modeled using Euclidean geometry.

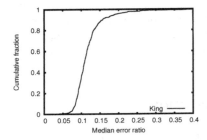 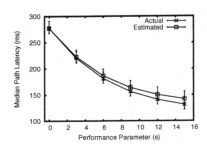

Fig. 11. *Left:* CDF of median error ratios for the King dataset. *Right:* Path performance for the King dataset using actual network distances ("Actual") and coordinate-based distance estimations ("Estimated"). Points denote median values with errorbars representing the standard deviation.

Fig. 11 *(left)* plots the CDF of the median error ratios of all relays after stabilization for the King dataset. Coordinates were calculated using Vivaldi [5] with a 5 dimensional coordinate system. The median of the relays' median error ratios (the median error in link estimation) is just 10.9% (6.1ms). The use of coordinate systems for non-latency metrics is considered later in this section.

Using the King dataset, Fig. 11 *(right)* shows the resulting impact these estimation errors have on the actual e2e performance of anonymous paths. The figure compares the e2e performance obtained using actual distances ("Actual") against the performance that results from using coordinate-based estimations ("Estimated"). The use of the coordinate system to estimate distances produces paths with low-latency. For example, when $s = 15$, the median e2e path latency is 131.2ms using actual network distances; the use of virtual coordinates incurs a modest 8% increase in latency, resulting in paths with a median e2e latency of 141.9ms (still far below the 277.1ms median obtained by UNIFORM).

In addition to performance, the use of coordinate systems has implications to anonymity. We investigate the relationship between coordinate-based link estimation and anonymity in Appendix C. To summarize the results, the use of coordinate systems does not decrease anonymity relative to using actual distances. For example, an attacker who controls 30% of the network is able to compromise 29.0% of anonymous paths when he uses the MedianDist attack and the initiator uses actual distances with $s = 15$. Using coordinate-based distance estimations and keeping all other parameters fixed, the attack compromises 28.5% of paths.

6.2   Other Practical Considerations

We briefly outline other practical considerations of link-based relay selection.

Securing coordinate systems. The distributed nature of coordinate systems make them vulnerable to manipulation if not properly defended. Malicious relays may advertise false coordinates or delay measurement probes, either to make themselves appear more favorable or to cause disorder in the system. Fortunately, practical techniques exist that mitigate such attacks. For example, the Veracity system protects the accuracy of coordinate systems when up to 40% of the network is malicious [34,32]. Given the large number of available coordinate protection schemes [4,30,13,41,34,32], we consider the challenge of securing coordinate systems to be orthogonal and out-of-scope of this paper.

Pairwise bandwidth estimation. Coordinate systems have been known to estimate with high accuracy (i.e. low error ratios) link metrics that tend to be additive in nature when used to compute metrics across multiple links. Examples of metrics that work well include latency and AS traversal. However, these systems have been shown to be inaccurate at estimating pairwise bandwidth between any two nodes, due to the high incidence of TIVs in bandwidth measurements.

However, we note that there have been a number of recent promising proposals that enable one to estimate pairwise bandwidth accurately and scalably. For example, there have been several attempts to identify links that cause severe network TIVs [37,18,17], enabling initiators to avoid them when forming paths. Separate work [26,27] has directly addressed the problem of bandwidth embeddings, introducing techniques for embedding bandwidth distances in tree structures. Their results show that pairwise PlanetLab bandwidths can be embedded with a median error ratio of approximately 0.25 [26]. Finally, as a third alternative, rather than rely on coordinate embedding systems, initiators can anonymously query network measurement services such as IDMaps [9] or iPlane [19] to estimate the bandwidth of network links.

Locating the Responder. To estimate e2e path performance, the initiator must predict the distance between the exit relay and the responder. The initiator cannot estimate the cost of this final hop if the responder does not participate in the coordinate system. Instead, the initiator can locate the closest relay to the responder using publicly available network information services. For example, OASIS [10], ClosestNode [1], and iPlane [19] all provide interfaces for resolving the closest server to any given IP address. The initiator can anonymously query such services to locate the relay that is nearest to the responder. The closest relay can then proxy requests between the exit relay and the responder.

Alternatively, initiators can disregard the link between the exit relay and the responder when selecting anonymous paths. As discussed in Appendix A, such an approach incurs only a modest decrease in performance.

7   Conclusion

This paper makes the case for link-based relay selection for flexibly tuning the performance and anonymity properties of anonymous paths. In comparison to node-based techniques in which performance may be quantified only in terms of node properties (i.e., bandwidth), link-based selection enables the generation of high performance paths across multiple metrics: latency, jitter, loss, and bandwidth. Using realistic network traces, we validate that our link-based WEIGHTED strategy reduced by 71% the number of paths with end-to-end latencies greater than 250ms (in comparison to selecting relays uniformly at random), and doubled the median available bandwidths of anonymous paths.

We also show that link-based relay selection is also significantly more resilient to manipulation than traditional node-based techniques. For example, when applying the default Tor path selection algorithm to a subset of bandwidth data obtained from the Tor network, an adversary who controls the top 30% of highest bandwidth relays is able to compromise 93.5% of anonymous paths. In comparison, using WEIGHTED on a network trace in which bandwidth is measured as a link characteristic, an attacker who controls the same percentage of anonymizing relays compromises less than a third of anonymous paths.

Acknowledgments

The authors are grateful to Roger Dingledine for his many helpful suggestions. We would like to thank the anonymous reviewers for their insightful feedback, and Steven Murdoch who shepherded the paper. This work is partially supported by NSF Grants CNS-0831376, CNS-0524047, CNS-0627579, and CNS-0721845 and ONR MURI N00014-07-1-0907.

References

1. ClosestNode.com, http://www.closestnode.com/
2. Akella, A., Seshan, S., Shaikh, A.: An Empirical Evaluation of Wide-area Internet Bottlenecks. In: Conference on Internet Measurement (IMC) (2003)
3. Bauer, K., McCoy, D., Grunwald, D., Kohno, T., Sicker, D.: Low-Resource Routing Attacks against Tor. In: Proceedings of the 2007 ACM Workshop on Privacy in Electronic Society, pp. 11–20 (2007)
4. Costa, M., Castro, M., Rowstron, R., Key, P.: PIC: Practical Internet Coordinates for Distance Estimation. In: International Conference on Distributed Computing Systems (2004)
5. Dabek, F., Cox, R., Kaashoek, F., Morris, R.: Vivaldi: a Decentralized Network Coordinate System. SIGCOMM Comput. Commun. Rev. 34(4), 15–26 (2004)
6. Dingledine, R., Mathewson, N.: Tor Path Specification (January 2008), http://www.torproject.org/svn/trunk/doc/spec/path-spec.txt
7. Dingledine, R., Mathewson, N., Syverson, P.: Tor: The Second-Generation Onion Router. In: Proc. of the 13th USENIX Security Symposium, pp. 303–320 (2004)
8. Feamster, N., Dingledine, R.: Location Diversity in Anonymity Networks. In: WPES 20: Proceedings of the 2004 ACM workshop on Privacy in the electronic society, pp. 66–76 (2004)
9. Francis, P., Jamin, S., Jin, C., Jin, Y., Raz, D., Shavitt, Y., Zhang, L.: IDMaps: A Global Internet Host Distance Estimation Service. IEEE/ACM Trans. Netw. 9(5), 525–540 (2001)
10. Freedman, M.J., Lakshminarayanan, K., Mazières, D.: OASIS: Anycast for Any Service. In: Proc. 3rd USENIX/ACM Symposium on Networked Systems Design and Implementation (NSDI 2006) (2006)
11. Gini, C.: Measurement of Inequality of Incomes. The Economic Journal 31(121), 124–126 (1921)
12. Gummadi, K.P., Saroiu, S., Gribble, S.D.: King: Estimating Latency Between Arbitrary Internet End Hosts. In: ACM SIGCOMM Workshop on Internet Measurment (IMW) (2002)

13. Kaafar, M.A., Mathy, L., Barakat, C., Salamatian, K., Turletti, T., Dabbous, W.: Securing Internet Coordinate Embedding Systems. In: ACM SIGCOMM (August 2007)
14. "king" data set, http://pdos.csail.mit.edu/p2psim/kingdata/
15. Lakshminarayanan, K., Padmanabhan, V.N.: Some Findings on the Network Performance of Broadband Hosts. In: IMC 2003: Proceedings of the 3rd ACM SIGCOMM conference on Internet measurement, pp. 45–50 (2003)
16. Ledlie, J.T.: A Locality-Aware Approach to Distributed Systems. PhD thesis, Harvard University (September 2007)
17. Lee, S., Zhang, Z.-L., Sahu, S., Saha, D.: On Suitability of Euclidean Embedding of Internet Hosts. In: SIGMETRICS 2006/Performance 2006: Proceedings of the joint international conference on Measurement and modeling of computer systems, pp. 157–168 (2006)
18. Lumezanu, C., Levin, D., Spring, N.: PeerWise Discovery and Negotiation of Shorter Paths. In: Workshop on Hot Topics in Networks (HotNets) (2007)
19. Madhyastha, H.V., Isdal, T., Piatek, M., Dixon, C., Anderson, T., Krishnamurthy, A., Venkataramani, A.: IPlane: An Information Plane for Distributed Services. In: Symposium on Operating Systems Design and Implementation (OSDI 2006) (2006)
20. Muller, M.E.: A Note on a Method for Generating Points Uniformly on N-Dimensional Spheres. Communications of the ACM 2(4), 19–20 (1959)
21. Murdoch, S.J.: Hot or Not: Revealing Hidden Services by Their Clock Skew. In: CCS 2006: Proceedings of the 13th ACM Conference on Computer and Communications Security, pp. 27–36 (2006)
22. Murdoch, S.J., Watson, R.N.M.: Metrics for Security and Performance in Low-Latency Anonymity Systems. In: Borisov, N., Goldberg, I. (eds.) PETS 2008. LNCS, vol. 5134, pp. 115–132. Springer, Heidelberg (2008)
23. Ng, T.S.E., Zhang, H.: A Network Positioning System for the Internet. In: Proceedings of the 2004 USENIX Annual Technical Conference (June 2004)
24. Øverlier, L., Syverson, P.: Locating Hidden Servers. In: IEEE Symposium on Security and Privacy (2006)
25. PlanetLab, http://www.planet-lab.org
26. Ramasubramanian, V., Malkhi, D., Kuhn, F., Abraham, I., Balakrishnan, M., Gupta, A., Akella, A.: A Unified Network Coordinate System for Bandwidth and Latency. Technical Report MSR-TR-2008-124, Microsoft Research (Sept. 2008)
27. Ramasubramanian, V., Malkhi, D., Kuhn, F., Balakrishnan, M., Gupta, A., Akella, A.: On the Treeness of Internet Latency and Bandwidth. In: SIGMETRICS/Performance (June 2009)
28. Reiter, M.K., Rubin, A.D.: Crowds: Anonymity for Web Transactions. In: ACM Transactions on Information and System Security (1998)
29. Ribeiro, V., Riedi, R., Baraniuk, R., Navratil, J., Cottrell, L.: pathChirp: Efficient Available Bandwidth Estimation for Network Paths. In: Passive and Active Measurement Workshop (2003)
30. Saucez, D., Donnet, B., Bonaventure, O.: A Reputation-Based Approach for Securing Vivaldi Embedding System. In: Dependable and Adaptable Networks and Services (2007)
31. Shavitt, Y., Tankel, T.: Big-bang Simulation for Embedding Network Distances in Euclidean Space. In: IEEE Infocom (April 2003)
32. Sherr, M., Blaze, M., Loo, B.T.: Veracity: Practical Secure Network Coordinates via Vote-based Agreements. In: USENIX Annual Technical Conference (USENIX 2009) (June 2009)

33. Sherr, M., Loo, B.T., Blaze, M.: Towards Application-Aware Anonymous Routing. In: USENIX Workshop on Hot Topics in Security (HotSec) (August 2007)
34. Sherr, M., Loo, B.T., Blaze, M.: Veracity: A Fully Decentralized Service for Securing Network Coordinate Systems. In: IPTPS (February 2008)
35. Snader, R., Borisov, N.: A Tune-up for Tor: Improving Security and Performance in the Tor Network. In: 15th Annual Network and Distributed System Security Symposium (NDSS) (February 2008)
36. Vuze bittorrent client, http://azureus.sourceforge.net/
37. Wang, G., Zhang, B., Ng, T.S.E.: Towards Network Triangle Inequality Violation Aware Distributed Systems. In: ACM SIGCOMM Conference on Internet Measurement (IMC 2007), pp. 175–188 (2007)
38. Wong, B., Slivkins, A., Sirer, E.G.: Meridian: a Lightweight Network Location Service without Virtual Coordinates. In: SIGCOMM (2005)
39. Wright, M., Adler, M., Levine, B., Shields, C.: The Predecessor Attack: An Analysis of a Threat to Anonymous Communications Systems. ACM Transactions on Information and System Security (TISSEC) 4(7), 489–522 (2004)
40. Yalagandula, P., Sharma, P., Banerjee, S., Basu, S., Lee, S.: S^3: A scalable Sensing Service for Monitoring Large Networked Systems. In: SIGCOMM Internet Network Management Workshop (2006)
41. Zage, D.J., Nita-Rotaru, C.: On the Accuracy of Decentralized Virtual Coordinate Systems in Adversarial Networks. In: CCS (2007)

Appendix A: A Revised WEIGHTED Algorithm

The WEIGHTED algorithm introduced in Section 4 ranks candidate paths by the expected e2e path cost. Unlike node-based relay selection strategies, the e2e path cost includes the links from the initiator to the first relay and from the last relay to the responder, potentially leaking information about the communication participants.

To prevent the `Relay-in-the-Middle` attack (see Section 5.2), an alternative strategy is to exclude the first (from the initiator) and last (to the responder) links when ranking paths. That is, the initiator ranks paths by the cost of the subsequence R1→R2→R3, where R1, R2, and R3 are the relays in a candidate path.

The revised WEIGHTED strategy has two advantages. First, it disassociates the communication endpoints from path selection. An adversary who knows the identities of R1, R2, and R3 cannot infer any information about the initiator and responder. Second, it does not require the responder to participate in the coordinate system (see Section 6.2) since the distance from the exit relay to the responder does not influence router selection.

The obvious cost of using the revised WEIGHTED strategy is that the first and last hops may be expensive, incurring poor performance even though the subsequence R1→R2→R3 may be efficient.

Our experimental evaluation indicates that the performance penalty due to the revised WEIGHTED strategy is minimal. Fig. 12 shows the performance of the vanilla and revised WEIGHTED strategies with $s = 9$. For comparison, the performance achieved using UNIFORM is also plotted. Although the unmodified

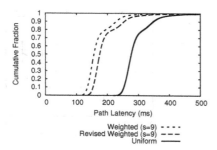

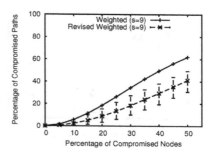

Fig. 12. The cumulative distribution of e2e path latencies when using variants of the WEIGHTED strategy on the King dataset. The performance achieved using Uniform is provided for comparison.

Fig. 13. The percentage of compromised paths as a function of the fraction of compromised nodes when the attacker users the Confirmation strategy and the initiator uses variants of WEIGHTED with the King dataset

WEIGHTED algorithm achieves the lowest median e2e path latency (156.3ms), the modified version also achieves significantly lower latencies (174.9ms) than UNIFORM (277.2ms).

Fig. 13 compares the resilience to the Confirmation attack using the vanilla and modified versions of WEIGHTED. Since the positions of the initiator and responder do not influence relay selection when revised WEIGHTED is used, the attacker's strategy is less effective. For example, when 30% of nodes are malicious, the attacker compromises 34.4% of paths when the initiator uses the unmodified WEIGHTED technique and only 18.5% against revised WEIGHTED.

Appendix B: Preventing the Predecessor Attack

An anonymized connection between an initiator and responder is often reset due to node churn, requiring it to be reconstructed using different relays [39]. The adversary can conduct a *predecessor attack* to discover the initiator by counting the number of times each relay precedes the attackers' relays in the anonymous path [28,39]. Since the initiator is always present in such circuits, it will have a higher count than the relays that are chosen randomly whenever the circuit is rebuilt.

Tor mitigates the predecessor attack by using a small number of fixed entry nodes called *guards* [6]. Link-based path selection is equally vulnerable to the predecessor attack, but may also be defended using guards. Guards must be chosen carefully since their locations affect the performance of a path. However, as described in Appendix A (see, in particular, Fig. 12), link-based routing produces high performance paths even if the first hop (connecting the initiator to the guard node) is not considered by the path selection algorithm. Link-based

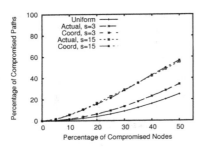

Fig. 14. The percentage of compromised paths on the King dataset when the attacker uses the MedianDist strategy. "Actual" denotes results obtained using actual network distances. "Coord" reflects performance when initiators estimate distances using the coordinate embedding system.

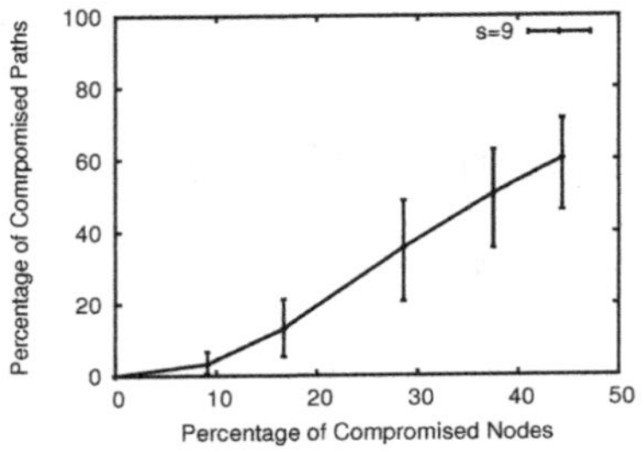

Fig. 15. The percentage of compromised paths as a function of the fraction of compromised nodes when the attacker uses the Cluster strategy and the initiator uses WEIGHTED with the King dataset using $s = 9$

routing may therefore adopt the same mitigation strategy as Tor [7]; namely, the initiator selects a relay (having a long uptime) to act as its entry guard for all anonymous paths.

Appendix C: The Impact of Coordinate Systems on Anonymity

Coordinate systems linearize pairwise distances by mapping each node to n-dimensional coordinates. Due to network triangle inequality violations that cannot be represented in Euclidean space, coordinate systems do not perfectly predict distances. As shown in Fig. 11 *(right)*, the use of coordinate systems imposes a modest decrease in path performance. In this Appendix, we consider the effects of using coordinate systems on anonymity.

Fig. 14 shows the percentage of compromised paths using the King dataset when the attacker applies the MedianDist strategy. The figure compares performance results obtained using network distances ("Actual") to estimations based on the coordinate system ("Coord"). As can be observed from the Fig., the effectiveness of the attack does not substantially differ when actual and coordinate distances are used. For example, when $s = 15$ and actual distances are used, an attacker who controls 30% of the network can compromise 29.0% of paths. In comparison, the same attacker can compromise 28.5% of paths when virtual coordinates are used in place of actual distances.

Appendix D: The Cluster Attack

An attacker may attempt to compromise a large fraction of anonymous paths by joining the anonymity network using multiple nodes from the same LAN. Due to the high bandwidths and low latencies within the LAN, paths composed entirely of malicious nodes from the LAN will have low e2e cost estimates and will be favored by the WEIGHTED algorithm.

Since our experimental datasets do not contain large clusters of similarly located nodes, it was necessary to adapt the attacker model to permit the attacker to insert nodes. To determine the location for the new nodes, we first use the Vivaldi [5] virtual embedding system to assign n-dimensional coordinates to each node in the existing topology such that the Cartesian distance between two nodes' coordinates corresponds to the network distance (e.g., latency) between them. To provide the attacker with a desirable location in the topology, we assign each malicious node a coordinate that is at most 5ms from the centroid of the network. Hence, any two malicious nodes are separated by at most 10ms. Locations from the centroid are randomly chosen according to Muller's uniform hypersphere point generation technique [20]. Network distances between a malicious node and another peer are estimated using the Cartesian distance between the nodes' coordinates.

Fig. 15 illustrates the efficacy of the Cluster attack when the initiator uses the WEIGHTED algorithm with $s = 9$ on the King dataset. When the attacker controls 28.6% of the network (i.e., he adds 200 nodes to the existing 500 node topology), he compromises just 35.6% of anonymous paths.

It is worth noting that the Cluster attack may be further mitigated by requiring that adjacent nodes in anonymous paths reside in separate autonomous systems or have a minimum latency between them.

Using Linkability Information to Attack Mix-Based Anonymity Services⋆

Stefan Schiffner[1] and Sebastian Clauß[2]

[1] K.U.Leuven, ESAT/SCD/COSIC and IBBT
Kasteelpark Arenberg 10
B-3001 Leuven-Heverlee, Belgium
Stefan.Schiffner@esat.kuleuven.be
[2] Technische Universität Dresden
Institute of Systems Architecture
D-01062 Dresden, Germany
Sebastian.Clauss@tu-dresden.de

Abstract. There exist well established models for anonymity focusing on traffic analysis, i. e., analysing properties of single messages as, e. g., timing. However there is only little work done that use linkability information, that is information about the probability that two messages have been sent by the same sender.

In this paper we model information about linkability between messages as a weighted graph. We show lower and upper bounds with regards to the usefulness of linkability information for matching messages to senders. In addition to that we present simulation results, showing to which extent a matching of messages to senders is possible by using linkability information with different grades of noise.

1 Introduction

The number of applications and services on the Internet that enable or even require the user to create a user account increases rapidly. By offering user accounts, services try to achieve customer retention in a positive as well as in a negative sense. More precisely, providers are able to offer user-specific services, but they might also trace users, in order to place customized advertisements or even to deploy a discriminatory pricing model. Also, with regard to recent privacy scandals, service providers might aim for less personal data in their databases to avoid recourse receivables from customers in the case of data loss.

Privacy-enhancing identity management (see e. g. [1]) is being developed in order to protect users from overly greedy data collectors, but many services need

---

⋆ This work was supported by the Integrated Projects IST-015964 AEOLUS on Algorithmic Principles for Building Efficient Overlay Computers and ICT-2007-216483 PrimeLife on Privacy and Identity Management in Europe for Life.The information in this document reflects only the authors' views, is provided as is, and no guarantee or warranty is given that the information is fit for any particular purpose. The user thereof uses the information at its sole risk and liability.

I. Goldberg and M. Atallah (Eds.): PETS 2009, LNCS 5672, pp. 94–107, 2009.

a minimal amount of data to actually serve their customers. This leads to the problem that users actually do reveal personal data, which might be analyzed by the service provider. An identity management system needs to estimate how much a service provider can learn from a user's messages in order to assist the user in choosing the least privacy compromising data for a given purpose.

Recently several attempts have been made to define and formalize the notions of anonymity [2,3] and unlinkability [4,5]. Most of the models are only formulated for communication scenarios.

In this paper we show how information about linkability between messages (gathered, e. g., by a service provider from knowledge of the content of messages) can be used to reduce sender anonymity beyond what is possible by traffic analysis alone. We present a model where prior knowledge learned from network traffic can be integrated in a "layer-combining model". We simulate such a model and show analytical lower and upper bounds for the attacker's success rate, and we show under which conditions the attacker can breach the user's privacy.

In the next section we summarize related work on this topic. We describe our model in the section thereafter. In Sect. 4 we present our attack. Finally, in Sect. 5 we provide a conclusion on the results of this paper and briefly discuss issues open to further research.

2   Related Work

In this paper we discuss how noisy linkability information can be utilized to attack sender anonymity. Therefore, we focus on specifying a *connection* between information gathered by traffic analysis and linkability information gathered elsewhere.

First we need to model an anonymity system at the network layer, so that we can model the information an attacker obtains by observing this system. Over the past couple of years, much research has been done on aspects of anonymity with regards to network layer anonymity systems. Basic concepts of anonymity systems have been proposed [6,7] and enhanced in various ways. Systems, which proved to be practically usable on the Internet, e. g., Web mixes [8] or Tor [9] are based more or less on Chaum's Mixes [6]. Various attacks on such systems have been discussed, e. g. [10]. Since we focus on specifying a *connection* between anonymity properties on the network layer and linkability information gathered elsewhere, we do not emphasize a sophisticated traffic analysis model here. However, we want to keep close to well established models. Hence, the network-layer part of the model we describe in Sect. 3 is based on Chaum's Mixes [6].

Linkability aspects with regards to user profiles have been discussed not only in the course of privacy-enhancing identity management systems, e. g. [11,12], but as well with regards to statistical databases, e. g. [13,14]. In this paper we abstract from the derivation of linkability information. Similar to [4], we just assume that there *is* information about the fact whether pairs of messages have been sent by the same sender or not, which, e. g., might be derived from the contents of the messages sent over the network-layer anonymity system.

Recently, some aspects regarding the *connection* between information gathered from observing an anonymity system on the network layer and linkability information have been researched. In [11,12], Clauß and Schiffner focus on modelling knowledge gained from attributes of user profiles, but information gained by traffic analysis is not explicitly incorporated in this model. In [15], Díaz et al. calculate an example for combining information from network layer and application layer. Finally, in [16], Díaz et al. simulate a social network setting. In this setting, they calculate anonymity of users of the social network based on a combination of information gained by observations of the network layer and information gained from the known social network graph. From their simulations, they derive conclusions about relations between profiles, the size of network etc. to the anonymity of users. They especially focused on how much one can learn from these profiles depending on their quality, i. e., their expressiveness. In contrast to this work, we abstract from the source of profile information and model this information as a weighted graph where every node is a message and every edge is a score representing the probability that the two messages are from the same user.

Furthermore, attacks have been presented that gain from longterm traffic analysis, especially from evaluating the natural behavior of users with regards to leaving and joining the system. Such attacks are, e. g., intersection attacks, like the attack recently presented by Berthold et al. with regards to data retention [17], and the hitting-set attack [10] by Kesdogan and Pimenidis. In contrast to these we focus on a single round of a batch mix where we can assume that the user set stays the same during the whole attack.

3   Model Description

When Internet users communicate with service providers, they often reveal personal information. A service provider can use this information to build user profiles, that is all kinds of data a service provider can collect about a user. Some of these profiles might be linkable with a certain probability, i. e., the service provider can guess that these profiles belong to the same user. In this section we first explain our model, which is later on formalized.

We assume a set of users who send their messages to a single service provider, while a batch mix is obfuscating the relation between senders and messages. The service provider is considered as the attacker, who wants to de-anonymize his users, i. e., he aims at a complete mapping of messages to users[1]. Naturally, he has access to the content of the messages. We further assume that he gains

---

[1] In our model, a user is an entity which can send messages. The attacker can distinguish users by observing senders on the network layer. With regards to information about linkability between messages on the application layer, we do not explicitly model users by their profiles. We just assume that there exists information about the fact whether pairs of messages have been sent by the same sender or not, which, e. g., might be derived from the contents of the messages sent over the network-layer anonymity system.

additional information by observing all links in the network, but he is not able to observe the mixing process of the messages. Furthermore the system is assumed to be *closed*, i. e., all messages are transmitted between nodes within the system, and there are no messages sent to or received from outside of the system. Fig. 1 illustrates our model.

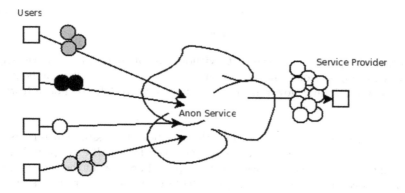

Fig. 1. The attacker's view on the system. Users (squares on the left) send messages (circles) to an anonymity service. The service provider on the right hand side receives these anonymized messages and may analyze the content of the messages.

In the following paragraphs we formalize our model. It contains a set of users $U = \{u_1, \ldots, u_m\}, m \in \mathbb{N}, m \geq 1$, and sets of messages $c_{u_1}, \ldots, c_{u_m}$, where c_u consists of the messages user u has sent. Furthermore, in our model we assume a perfect anonymizer that obfuscates the relation between senders and messages. Finally, we assume a service provider which receives all messages sent by the users.

With respect to the (anonymized) network layer, the service provider can observe the number of messages that a user u has sent, cardinality $|c_u|$. This is the type of information an attacker can learn from observing the network traffic of a perfect batch mix implementation, where all messages sent within the system form one single batch.

Clusterings and Number of Clusterings. With slight abuse of notation we will use clusterings of the set of messages to describe intermediate results of the attack, where a cluster c_i is not necessarily assigned to a user u_i, since the attacker can often assume that messages are from the same sender but not from which. A *clustering* is defined as follows:

Definition 1 (clustering). *A set of sets $C = \{c_1, \ldots, c_m\}, m \in \mathbb{N}$, is called clustering of a set S if and only if $S = \bigcup_{i=1}^{m} c_i$ and $\forall c_i, c_j$ with $i \neq j : c_i \cap c_j = \emptyset$.*

Informally speaking, that is, sorting all elements of a set in different classes, where every element can only be member of exactly one class.

For our aims, we are interested in the number of different clusterings of a set S, $n = |S| = \sum_{i=1}^{m} |c_i|$, under the condition that the clusters' cardinalities are given. This number can be calculated as follows:

$$
\begin{aligned}
& \binom{n}{|c_1|} \cdot \binom{n-|c_1|}{|c_2|} \cdot \ldots \cdot \binom{n-\sum_{i=1}^{n-1} |c_i|}{|c_m|} \\
= \; & \prod_{k=1}^{m} \binom{n-\sum_{i=1}^{k-1} |c_i|}{|c_k|} \\
= \; & \frac{n!}{\prod_{i=1}^{m} |c_i|!}
\end{aligned}
\tag{1}
$$

Figuratively speaking, for the first (without loss of generality) partitioning we start by choosing the elements of the first cluster (c_1) from all n elements. For the second partitioning now only $n - |c_1|$ elements are left to choose from and so on.

Complexity. As one can see from (1), the number of possible clusterings with regard of the order of clusters becomes huge even for small examples. Without additional knowledge, each of these clusterings could represent the correct system state. Thus, even if we can in principle calculate the probability of a state, it is extremely time-consuming, and therefore practically not feasible, to iterate over all states to find the most likely. Therefore, in Sect. 4 we present a simulation that uses simulated annealing in order to find a good, i. e., a likely system state.

The Random Attacker (Lower Bound). The random attacker is an attacker that randomly maps messages to senders, but only takes the known cluster sizes into account. Given a set of messages $S = \{s_1, \ldots, s_n\}$, a clustering $C = \{c_1, \ldots, c_m\}$ of S, a hidden function $f : S \mapsto C$ that maps every message to its actual cluster, and $f' : S \mapsto C$ which describes the random guess of the attacker for f, we can calculate the expected number of messages the attacker guesses correctly. Given an urn filled with coloured balls where the number of balls of each colour is known, then the number of balls of a certain colour in a snap sample of a given size follows a multivariante hypergeometric distribution. If all messages of the same sender are seen as balls of the same colour, the number of messages allocated to a certain cluster c_i, that is messages that are actually sent by user u_i in a snap sample follows this distribution. The mean of the number of messages belonging to cluster c_i in a sample a of size $|a|$ is then $\frac{|a|*|c_i|}{n}$.

Without loss of generality, we assume that the attacker first draws a sample of size $|c_1|$, then $|c_2|$ and so on in order to construct f'. The expected number of correctly guessed mappings for c_1, i. e., the mean of the number of guessed messages which really belong to c_1, is thus $\frac{|c_1|*|c_1|}{n}$. For the second sample, the choice has narrowed down to $|c_2|$ out of $n - |c_1|$ and we have to take into account that on average $\frac{|c_1|*|c_2|}{n}$ messages of cluster c_2 are mapped to c_1 in f'. That is, the expected number of correctly mapped messages in f' for c_2 is $\frac{|c_2|*(|c_2|-\frac{|c_1|*|c_2|}{n})}{n-|c_1|}$. Analogous, the number of correctly guessed messages can be described for c_3 to c_n.

More generally, the expected number of correctly guessed messages in f' for c_i is $E(c_i) = \dfrac{|c_i| * \left(|c_i| - \frac{(\sum_{j=1}^{i-1} |c_j|) * c_i}{n}\right)}{n - (\sum_{j=1}^{i-1} |c_j|) * |c_i|}$. By factoring $|c_i|$ out of the numerator and n out of the denominator we derive $E(c_i) = \frac{|c_i|^2}{n}$.

The sum of all $E(c_i)$ is the expected number of correctly guessed messages for a random attacker:

$$E_{\text{Random}} = \sum_{(C)} \frac{|c_i|^2}{n}$$

Beyond these network layer observations, the service provider can analyze the message content in order to "link" messages, i. e., to estimate whether pairs of messages have been sent by the same user or not. Without such content analysis, any clustering with the correct cardinalities is possible and equally likely.

The Perfect Attacker (Upper Bound). A perfect attacker, that is an attacker that knows exactly which messages are from the *same* sender, might even not be able to map all messages to the *right* sender. Even though he has a perfect clustering, he can not distinguish between two clusters of the same size and thus he can only randomly map the clusters of the same size to the senders that sent the corresponding number of messages.

The multiplicity of a cluster size is the number of clusters of this size. Formally, given the multiplicity mult_i of the size of cluster $|c_i|$ and the cluster sizes $|c_i|$, we can calculate the expected number of correctly assigned messages of a perfect attacker E_{perf}.

$$E_{\text{perf}} = \sum_{(C)} \frac{|c_i|}{\text{mult}_i}$$

Soundness of Lower and Upper Bound. Since the random attacker should never be more successful than the perfect attacker, we need to show that the lower bound is always smaller or equal to the upper bound. The multiplicity mult_i of the cluster size c_i is always smaller or equal to $\frac{n}{|c_i|}$, since the sum of all cluster sizes is n. Thus, $E_{\text{Random}} = \sum_{(C)} \frac{|c_i|^2}{n} = \sum_{(C)} \frac{|c_i|}{n/|c_i|} \leq \sum_{(C)} \frac{|c_i|}{\text{mult}_i}$. Since equality holds only for $\text{mult}_i = \frac{n}{|c_i|}$, a random attacker can achieve as much as a perfect attacker iff all clusters are of equal size. Otherwise, he is less successful. Note that the perfect attacker indeed has the choice between less states than the random attacker, since he will never assign messages sent from one single sender to different senders. Nevertheless, in case of equal cluster sizes the perfect attacker either assigns all messages sent by a given user correctly to this user, or he assigns all messages of this user to another user. This leads to the same expected number of correctly assigned messages as for a random attacker, even though the number of possible states is much smaller for the perfect attacker.

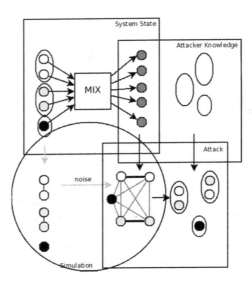

Fig. 2. Overview of the experimental setting (gray arrows: simulation, black arrows: attacker's behavior)

4 Simulation and Results

In this section we present our simulation method and our attacker model. In Fig. 2 our experimental setting is sketched. From the knowledge gained from observation of the network layer, the attacker derives the cluster sizes. Furthermore, by analyzing the message content, he derives a weighted graph that represents the knowledge about which messages were probably sent by the same sender. Since we want to abstract from the concrete process of gaining this knowledge by content analysis, we run the attack with the original graph plus noise (circle). The following pseudocode shows the steps for one simulation round.

```
SystemState sys = generate(message number n, cluster sizes
min,max,dist)
SystemState noisy = addNoise(s,d)
Clusters c = cluster(noisy)
for SystemState i = allPossibleStates(c) do
    compare i and sys
end for
```

Initialization. The system state (see Fig. 2) is a random mapping of messages to senders with a given total number of messages n, given minimal and maximal number of messages per sender. Two senders might have sent either the same number of messages, or the number of messages differs in at least a given distance dist. Furthermore the messages are organized in a graph where a message s_i is connected to another message s_j with a weight 1 iff the two messages have been sent by the same sender, otherwise with the weight 0^2.

In the next step we add noise in order to model the uncertainty of the attacker. Therefore, for every edge of the graph a random number r is chosen from a zero-mean Gaussian distribution. If the edge's weight was zero, it is replaced by r. If the edge's weight was 1, is is replaced by $r + d$, where d is a *noise distance*[3]. Hence the resulting distribution for the former zero-weighted edges becomes a zero-mean Gaussian distribution. For the former one-weighted edges the resulting distribution becomes a Gaussian distribution with its mean at the noise distance.

Clustering. In this step an optimal clustering is needed, i. e., a clustering where messages that are strongly connected in the graph are assigned to the same clusters. As fitness function we use the average fitness of all clusters, where the fitness of a cluster is the sum of all edges within the cluster. In order to cluster the graph we use *simulated annealing* [18], since we can guess a good starting solution and the change of the fitness function can be calculated quickly. Furthermore the algorithm is easy to adapt to fixed cluster sizes. The following algorithm sketches simulated annealing. Note that $c_i[s_j/s_k]$ denotes that within cluster c_i message s_j is replaced by s_k.

```
Clustering c choseStartSolution(graph)
temp = startTemp
repeat
    time = maxTime
    repeat
        chose 2 different clusters c₁ and c₂
        chose s₁ from c₁, and s₂ from c₂
        if fit(c₁, c₂) < fit(c₁[s₁/s₂], c₂[s₂/s₁]) then
            c₁ ⇐ c₁[s₁/s₂]
            c₂ ⇐ c₂[s₂/s₁]
        else
            if temp < rnd(temp) then
                c₁ ⇐ c₁[s₁/s₂]
                c₂ ⇐ c₂[s₂/s₁]
            else
                s = s − 1
            end if
        end if
    until time == 0
    temp = temp − 1
until temp == 0
```

---

[2] Thereby, the weight can be interpreted as an (inverse) distance measure.

[3] The higher the value of the noise distance, the better it is possible to distinguish between former zero-weighted and one-weighted edges.

The general idea of simulated annealing is that the algorithm starts with a guessed solution, then randomly picks two elements and swaps these two. If the new solution is better than the old one, it repeats the loop with the newly found solution. Otherwise it continues with a certain probability with either the old or the new solution. The probability that it continues with a worse solution decreases over the running time and depends on how much the average fitness decreases by using the worse solution.

For our problem, we search for the clustering where all messages that are in the same cluster have been sent by the same sender. Edges between messages from the same sender have more likely a higher weight than others, thus the average of the sums of the edges' weights between messages in the same cluster should be maximal for the clustering where all messages from the same sender are in the same cluster.

In order to calculate the change of quality of the solution in one optimization step it is sufficient to calculate the fitness of each of the two clusters that are chosen in that step. Thereby, a cluster's fitness is the sum of all edges among the messages within the cluster. If after swapping the sum of these two fitnesses is higher than before, then the average fitness over all clusters increases as well, thus the new solution is better than the old one. Otherwise, the old solution was better.

In order to speed up the clustering we also take into account that the cluster size is proportional to the *degree* of the nodes, which should be in this cluster. Thereby, the degree of a node is the sum of the weights of all edges of this node. We deploy this in two ways. At the beginning of the simulation, we need to guess a first solution. This is done by putting higher degree messages in larger clusters. Furthermore, the fitness function is adapted in a way that the quality of the solution is lower if messages are in clusters that are of a very different size than their degree would let expect. This prevents that messages that are actually members of small clusters are grouped in large ones, since this would lead to high local maxima, that is a solution to which the algorithm is likely to converge to, although it is not globally optimal.

However, if clusters are of similar size it still might happen that messages end up in cluster of the wrong size as Fig. 3 illustrates. Since with simulated annealing it is impossible to estimate the quality of a final solution, the algorithm is then very likely to end up in the wrong maxima. In the following paragraph we describe what the attacker does with this solution and which effect wrong clustered messages have on the result of the attack.

System States and Success Rate. The attacker uses this optimal clustering to enumerate all remaining possible system states. The number of remaining possible states depends on the number of clusters of equal size, since two states where clusters of the same size are mapped to different senders are indistinguishable for the attacker (cf. Sect. 3). In order to determine the quality of the attack we compare every possible system state with the original state and count the number

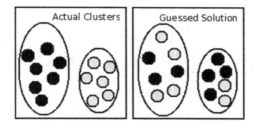

Fig. 3. Guessed solution with messages mapped to clusters of the wrong size

of correctly allocated messages. The average number of correctly allocated messages in relation to the total number of messages in the system is the success rate of the attacker in the given experiment.

Since we average over all possible system states the success rate never goes beyond its upper bound. However it might fall below the expectation since if the clustering is in fact not the right clustering (because of noise) it might make the correct state unlikely as illustrated in Fig. 3. Assume that most of the messages of cluster c_i are in cluster c_j with $|c_i| \neq |c_j|$. If now a message pair from these two clusters, which is actually correctly assigned to these clusters, is chosen to be switched, the resulting fitness of the solution will be considered better by the algorithm, since then both messages are among more messages from the same sender.

Simulation Results

In this section we present simulation results that illustrate how an attacker could use knowledge about the linkability of messages.

In Fig. 4, a typical result of our attack is shown. 100 messages were sent by 11 senders. On the x-axis the distance between the two Gaussian distributions which were used to add noise is displayed, while on the y-axis the (min, max and average) success rate is displayed. For this example, a random attacker would have a success rate of about 0.1. Note that our attack is already for very small noise distances, i.e., below 1, slightly better. However, for higher noise distances our simulation reaches the theoretical upper bound (cf. Sect. 3) of 0.81. Furthermore, one can see that the errors are quite large. This is because the noise affects also the local maxima, which might become global maxima by analogous reasons as shown in Fig. 3 in the section before.

In cases where every sender sent a different number of messages our attack can totally deanonymize the systems' users as shown in Fig. 5. Furthermore, one can see that with rising distance between the weights for messages belonging to the same cluster and messages not belonging into the same cluster also the errors start to diminish and therefore the average converges to the actual optimal solution.

In Fig. 6 one can see that the larger the distances between the number of messages different senders have sent are, the faster our attack converges to its

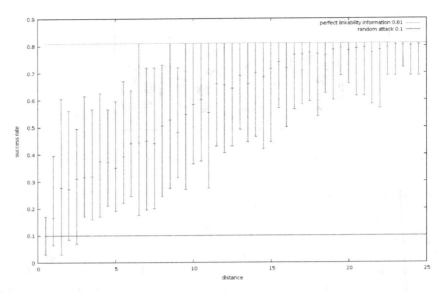

Fig. 4. Simulation results for 100 messages, distribution of cardinalities $|c_i|$: [4,5,7,8,9,9,10,10,11,12,15]. For each noise distance displayed, 25 experiments have been made. For each noise distance, the minimum, maximum and average success rate is displayed.

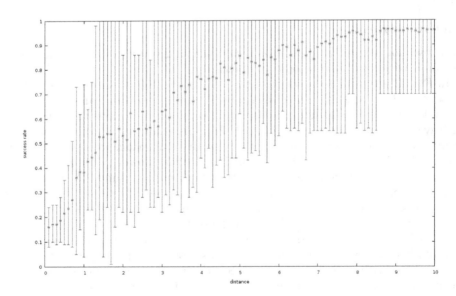

Fig. 5. Simulation results for 100 messages, distribution of cardinalities $|c_i|$: [4,7,8,12,14,15,18,22], i. e. all clusters have different sizes. In this case we reach total deanonymization.

individual maximum. Thereby the red pluses represent results from a system where the number of messages sent by each two senders is either equal or differs by at least 5. As we can see, already for small noise distances our simulation reaches its maximum. In contrast to that, the blue stars represent results from a system where the number of messages per sender is much closer to each other. Hence, noise has much more influence on the simulation results since already a small change of the degree of a message might lead to a different clustering.

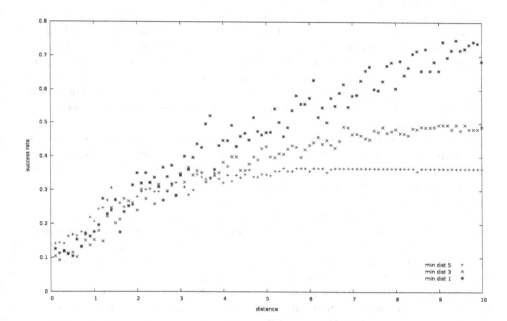

Fig. 6. Faster convergence with larger distances between clusters. Red pluses: each two senders sent either the same number of messages or the number of messages differs by at least 5. Green crosses: same number of messages or at least 3 messages difference for each two senders. Blue stars: same number of messages or at least 1 message difference for each two senders.

5   Conclusion

In this paper we show how information about linkability between messages (gathered, e.g., by a service provider from knowledge of the content of messages) can be used to reduce sender anonymity beyond what is possible by traffic analysis alone. Therefore, we present a model which integrates information gathered from the network layer with information about linkability between messages.

In order to show the usefulness of incorporating such linkability information for deanonymizing users, we present an appropriate attack using both information from observing the network and linkability information. Thereby, we consider an abstract service provider that receives all messages. This models many realistic attackers, such as coalitions of service providers or attackers that observe the exit node of a mix cascade.[4] However, even if the service provider does not receive all messages he can assume for every unknown message that it was sent equally likely by the same user as any other message, that is, it has an edge to any other message with the same wight. This would introduce more noise the more unknown messages are introduced, i.e., the less observations the attacker had made. The assumption hereby is that users which heavily use the attacker's service also use the other services often.

The information we consider from the network layer consists of the number of messages sent by different senders. From the application layer we regard information about linkability between messages. We show upper and lower bounds for the success rate of the attack. We simulate our attack in order to show that messages belonging to the same sender are grouped together even in case of rather noisy linkability information. Further, the attack is the more successful in assigning messages to actual senders the more different amounts of messages the senders have sent.

However, in further research we will deal with better clustering algorithms especially with regards to proven quality bounds (e. g. branch and bound). Furthermore we will extend our model to more comprehensive network as well as application layer models. With regards to network layer models we will combine our attack with more sophisticated traffic analysis attacks.

We expect that our attack is generalizable to pool mixes, since the incoming message stream can be used to count the number of messages sent by the users. Furthermore the attacker can exploit the expected delay of the messages (which depends on the pool size) to determine which part of the outgoing message stream should match the ingoing message stream.

Another interesting field of research will be to show how we can use our model to directly derive sender anonymity measures in terms of Shannon entropy as metric, that is calculating the probability distribution that a given user has sent a given message.

References

1. Clauß, S., Pfitzmann, A., Hansen, M., Van Herreweghen, E.: Privacy-enhancing identity management. The IPTS Report. Special Issue: Identity and Privacy, 8–16 (2002)
2. Serjantov, A., Danezis, G.: Towards an information theoretic metric for anonymity. In: Dingledine, R., Syverson, P.F. (eds.) PET 2002. LNCS, vol. 2482, pp. 41–53. Springer, Heidelberg (2003)
3. Díaz, C., Seys, S., Claessens, J., Preneel, B.: Towards measuring anonymity. In: Dingledine, R., Syverson, P.F. (eds.) PET 2002. LNCS, vol. 2482, pp. 54–68. Springer, Heidelberg (2003)
4. Steinbrecher, S., Köpsell, S.: Modelling unlinkability. In: Dingledine, R. (ed.) PET 2003. LNCS, vol. 2760, pp. 32–47. Springer, Heidelberg (2003)

---

[4] Note, that most of the traffic is sent to service providers that do not support end to end encryption.

5. Franz, M., Meyer, B., Pashalidis, A.: Attacking unlinkability: The importance of context. In: Borisov, N., Golle, P. (eds.) PET 2007. LNCS, vol. 4776, pp. 1–16. Springer, Heidelberg (2007)
6. Chaum, D.: Untraceable electronic mail, return addresses, and digital pseudonyms. Communications of the ACM 24(2), 84–88 (1981)
7. Chaum, D.: The dining cryptographers problem: Unconditional sender and recipient untraceability. Journal of Cryptology 1, 65–75 (1988)
8. Berthold, O., Federrath, H., Köpsell, S.: Web MIXes: A system for anonymous and unobservable Internet access. In: Federrath, H. (ed.) Designing Privacy Enhancing Technologies. LNCS, vol. 2009, pp. 115–129. Springer, Heidelberg (2001)
9. Dingledine, R., Mathewson, N., Syverson, P.: Tor: The second-generation onion router. In: Proceedings of the 13th USENIX Security Symposium (2004)
10. Kesdogan, D., Pimenidis, L.: The hitting set attack on anonymity protocols. In: Fridrich, J. (ed.) IH 2004. LNCS, vol. 3200, pp. 326–339. Springer, Heidelberg (2004)
11. Clauß, S.: A framework for quantification of linkability within a privacy-enhancing identity management system. In: Müller, G. (ed.) ETRICS 2006. LNCS, vol. 3995, pp. 191–205. Springer, Heidelberg (2006)
12. Clauß, S., Schiffner, S.: Structuring anonymity metrics. In: Goto, A. (ed.) DIM 2006, Proceedings of the 2006 ACM Workshop on Digital Identity Management, Fairfax, Virgina, USA, pp. 55–62. ACM, New York (2006)
13. Sweeney, L.: Guaranteeing anonymity when sharing medical data, the datafly system. Journal of the American Medical Informatics Association (1997)
14. Fischer-Hübner, S.: IT-Security and Privacy. LNCS, vol. 1958. Springer, Heidelberg (2001)
15. Díaz, C., Troncoso, C., Danezis, G.: Does additional information always reduce anonymity? In: Yu, T. (ed.) Proceedings of the Workshop on Privacy in the Electronic Society 2007, Alexandria,VA,USA, pp. 72–75. ACM, New York (2007)
16. Díaz, C., Troncoso, C., Serjantov, A.: On the impact of social network profiling on anonymity. In: Borisov, N., Goldberg, I. (eds.) PETS 2008. LNCS, vol. 5134, pp. 44–62. Springer, Heidelberg (2008)
17. Berthold, S., Böhme, R., Köpsell, S.: Data retention and anonymity services – introducing a new class of realistic adversary models. In: Švenda, P. (ed.) The Future of Identity in the Information Society – Challenges for Privacy and Security. Springer, Heidelberg (2008) (to appear)
18. Kirkpatrick, S., Gelatt Jr., C.D., Vecchi, M.P.: Optimization by simulated annealing. Science (1983)

Physical Layer Attacks on Unlinkability in Wireless LANs

Kevin Bauer[1], Damon McCoy[1], Ben Greenstein[2],
Dirk Grunwald[1], and Douglas Sicker[1]

[1] University of Colorado
{bauerk,mccoyd,grunwald,sicker}@colorado.edu
[2] Intel Research Seattle
benjamin.m.greenstein@intel.com

Abstract. Recent work has focused on hiding explicit network identifiers such as hardware addresses from the link layer to enable anonymous communications in wireless LANs. These protocols encrypt entire
wireless packets, thereby providing unlinkability. However, we find that
these protocols neglect to hide identifying information that is preserved
within the wireless physical layer. We propose a technique using commodity wireless hardware whereby packets can be linked to their respective transmitters using signal strength information, thus degrading
users' anonymity. We discuss possible countermeasures, but ultimately
we argue that controlling information leakage at the physical layer is
inherently difficult.

1 Introduction

The inherent broadcast nature of wireless communications coupled with the
widespread availability of commodity receivers poses a significant privacy concern for users of wireless technology. The threat that third parties who eavesdrop
on communications may profile users and track their movements is well understood [1,2]. Even when message confidentiality is provided by standards such as
WPA for 802.11, only the payload is protected and every user's identifying MAC
address is revealed. This enables any third party within signal range to monitor
and track other users in the network.

To eliminate the transmission of identifying information at the link layer,
recent work has focused on providing identifier-free link layer protocols that encrypt all transmitted bits to increase privacy with respect to third party eavesdroppers [3,4,5]. By obfuscating all bits of the frames including the addresses,
these protocols attempt to provide *unlinkability*, since it is difficult for unin-
tended recipients to associate sequences of packets to their source transmitters.

Despite these protocols, we demonstrate that information derived from the
physical layer can be applied to classify packets by their respective transmitters,
thereby violating this unlinkability property. While we focus our study on a variant of 802.11, we believe that the fundamental problem of information leakage

I. Goldberg and M. Atallah (Eds.): PETS 2009, LNCS 5672, pp. 108–127, 2009.

at the physical layer exists in a wide variety of other wireless protocols including WiMax, 3G, 4G, and future protocols that do not protect the physical layer.

Our approach is based on recording the strength of received signals from devices at several locations and applying a clustering algorithm to perform packet source classification. The method is practical, since it utilizes commodity hardware instead of expensive signal analyzers (as in previous work [6,7]) and requires no training or cooperation from the wireless devices in the network.

While this approach can determine which packets originated at the same source, it won't identify sources by name. However, we demonstrate that the packet source classification is accurate enough to enable complex traffic analysis attacks which use features such as packet size to reveal more about who the user is and what he/she is doing. Examples of the types of information that can be inferred through traffic analysis attacks include videos watched [8], passwords typed [9], web pages viewed [10,11], languages and phrases spoken [12,13], and applications run [14]. These traffic analysis attacks become more dangerous when coupled with additional information such as visual identification of users.

Results. In order to demonstrate the efficacy of this method, we evaluate the technique by conducting experiments in a real indoor office building environment. We apply the packet clustering technique, which uses well-known statistical methods, and the results show that packets are correctly linked to their transmitting devices with 77–85% accuracy, depending on the number of transmitters in the network. As more sophisticated techniques may be applied in the future, we consider these results as a lower bound on attainable accuracy.

Since the clustering method is often imprecise, we evaluate how the reconstructed sequences of packets can be used to perform a previously described website fingerprinting traffic analysis attack [10,11]. While any number of traffic analysis tasks could be performed, we chose website fingerprinting because web browsing is among the most common on-line activities. Our results indicate that a website can be identified 40–55% of the time from source classified packets, depending on the number of devices in the network.

Toward Solutions. Finally, we explore methods to mitigate the effectiveness of source classification using information derived from the physical layer. We evaluate solutions based on transmit power control and directional antennas and show that these techniques make source classification more difficult. However, we observe that altering the properties of the wireless physical layer is fundamentally challenging and we recognize that additional research attention should be focused on addressing information leaks at the physical layer.

Contributions. This paper has three primary contributions:

1. We explore a source of identifying information contained within the wireless physical layer and show that it can be used to violate the unlinkability property of anonymous link layer protocols.
2. We present and experimentally validate an unsupervised statistical technique to perform packet source classification that is robust to the inherent noise

of the RF space and is accurate enough to enable complex traffic analysis tasks to be performed.

3. We experimentally investigate methods to mitigate source classification by altering signal strength properties. While these techniques mitigate the accuracy of packet source classification and subsequent traffic analysis to some extent, we argue that information leakage at the wireless physical layer presents a particularly challenging privacy threat.

2 Background

Traditional anonymity. Anonymous communications have historically been facilitated by mix networks [15] and onion routing networks [16]. Fundamentally, these networks attempt to hide a message's sender and receiver from an adversary residing within the network. This requires that network layer identifiers such as source and destination IP addresses and other transport and application layer identifiers be hidden.

However, due to the inherent broadcast nature of wireless, there is a significant threat that an eavesdropper within range of a wireless signal may use persistent explicit identifiers found at the link layer (such as a MAC address) to uniquely identify users, and subsequently track their movements and profile their activity. This threat presents a serious privacy concern for users of wireless technology such as the ubiquitous 802.11 standard and an even greater threat to users of wide area networking devices, such as WiMax and 4G. These long range protocols allow an attacker potentially up to one mile away from the transmitting device the ability to eavesdrop. While mix network and onion routing techniques hide identifiers at the network layer and above, they were not designed to provide anonymity at the link layer. Thus, additional anonymity mechanisms are necessary to obscure these identifiers found at the link layer.

Anonymity in wireless networks. Several strategies have been proposed to address the leakage of identifying information within wireless networks. Gruteser and Grunwald suggest that disposable interface identifiers replace explicit identifiers such as the MAC address to mitigate location tracking and user profiling [17]. Arkko et al. propose a generic technique that replaces identifiers such as the MAC address with pseudo-random values drawn from a random number generator seeded with a shared secret [18]. This approach may also be used to obfuscate other identifiers at higher layers of the protocol stack such as IP addresses and TCP sequence numbers. During the session initiation, a mutually agreed-upon seed value is derived by the wireless client and access point. However, it is necessary to share seed values for every potential identifier and this general approach does not hide identifying information revealed by the application layer. A similar approach has been proposed using protocol stack virtualization [19]. This general approach enables the identifiers to change for each packet sent, thereby increasing the size of a wireless client's anonymity set to the number of clients participating in the wireless LAN.

To address the limitations of this general approach, link layer encryption has been proposed to obfuscate all bits transmitted in the wireless frames [3,4,5]. This hides any identifying information contained in the transmission, including explicit identifiers. At the link layer and above, these packets are unlinkable to their senders. However, we show that these protocols that hide explicit identifiers are limited since they do not address the physical layer.

Physical device fingerprinting. Recent advances in physical device finger-printing technology have introduced the possibility of identifying specific devices. Kohno *et al.* demonstrate that minute, yet distinguishable variations in a device's clock skew persist over time and can be detected remotely without any cooperation from the targeted device [20]. This technique has also been extended for the purpose of locating hidden services within the Tor network. [21,22].

Beyond the identifying characteristics of clock skew, RF-based device identification techniques have been previously proposed. Gerdes *et al.* show that Ethernet interface cards can be uniquely fingerprinted by their varying RF properties [23]. In the wireless context, techniques have emerged for fingerprinting distinct 802.11 interface cards based on the observation that minor flaws in device manufacturing are often manifested as modulation errors [6,7]. Both works propose a machine learning-based identification framework to detect specific modulation errors and empirically demonstrate that the techniques can identify distinct 802.11 cards with over 99% accuracy. While these techniques require expensive signal analyzer hardware, they represent a significant privacy risk to wireless users, especially if the required hardware becomes inexpensive.

Device driver, OS, and user fingerprinting. In addition to physical device fingerprinting, techniques have been developed to remotely identify device drivers of wireless network interface cards, a device's operating system, and even specific users. Probing tools such as Nmap [24] and p0f [25] are widely available to remotely scan ports, determine what operating system (and version) is running, and obtain information about packet filters and firewalls. Such information could potentially be used to aid in identifying and profiling devices. Franklin *et al.* present a passive device driver fingerprinting technique based on the wireless device driver's active probing behavior that can identify specific drivers with high accuracy [26]. Device driver information could also contribute to identifying and profiling wireless devices. Pang *et al.* and Aura *et al.* show that implicitly identifying information can inadvertently leak during wireless communication sessions [1,2]. Examples of such information include service discovery for specific wireless networks, file shares, and networked printers. Even more latent information sources can be uniquely identifying, such as websites viewed or applications used.

Physical device localization. Localization systems such as Place Lab allow wireless devices to passively localize themselves in physical space [27]. A wireless device can identify its location by comparing their beacon observations that identify the nearby stationary wireless infrastructure to a database of prior beacon observations tagged with physical location information. Widely deployed commercial services such as Skyhook [28] use this technique to help wireless devices perform self-localization.

There also exist a variety of techniques that enable the wireless infrastructure to localize wireless devices based on the physical layer properties of their transmitted signals. The most common approach to infrastructure-based wireless localization applies a supervised learning approach and uses commodity wireless cards. During the training phase, signal strength measurements are collected from several positions throughout a target environment (such as an office space) to train a machine learning algorithm. RADAR uses the k-nearest neighbors classifier to compute the wireless signal's physical position [29]. Other methods use a naïve Bayes classifier for location estimation [30]. While the training procedure can be expensive and time consuming, they are relatively accurate in practice. Other approaches often require specialized non-commodity hardware. Such approaches include estimating a signal's angle of arrival and applying triangulation [31], calculating time of arrival (*i.e.*, the global positioning system) [32], and applying time difference of arrival techniques [33].

The ease with which a device's location can be estimated from its signal properties presents significant privacy risks. Gruteser and Grunwald present algorithms and middleware that enable anonymous usage of location-based services [34]. Their approach is based on manipulating the resolution of location information along space and time dimensions. However, this solution assumes that the wireless client provides its own location information to a location server that implements the location privacy middleware. It does not address the scenario in which an adversary uses signal strength information to locate and track other users. Jiang *et al.* propose a solution to enhance location privacy based on randomized MAC address pseudonyms and silent periods to help decouple pseudonyms from devices [35]. In addition, this work explores the application of transmit power control to reduce the precision of localization algorithms by reducing devices' transmit power levels such that a only minimal number of listening access points can hear and localize the signals.

Inferring identity from the physical layer. Physical layer information has previously been used to detect identity-based attacks (such as MAC address spoofing) in wireless networks [36]. Since signal strength varies with physical location, a rogue device has distinct signal strength readings from the expected device, assuming that they are transmitting at different locations. Therefore, a device's identity is linked to its physical location. This observation can be useful for determining whether an identity-based attack is taking place. We rely on this fact in the design of our packet source classification technique.

3   Packet Source Classification

In this section, we first provide the necessary background and intuition behind the packet source classification techniques. Next, we describe the design of the

RSS-Localization based technique that can be used to perform packet source classification. However, it requires an expensive training process to learn the relationship between signal strength and physical location. To address this limitation, we present RSS-Clustering, a packet source classification method that does not require training.

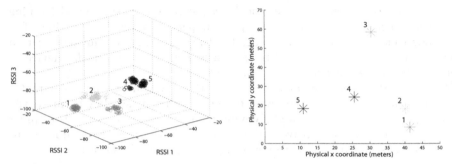

(a) RSSI values (in dB) from three sensors for five different devices

(b) The corresponding physical locations of the five devices

Fig. 1. A visualization of the RSSI values from transmitters at five different locations

3.1   Background and Intuition

When a commodity 802.11 wireless card receives a packet, it records the signal strength of the received packet as a received signal strength indication (RSSI) value. The RSSI value reported by standard 802.11 hardware is measured only during the reception of a message's preamble, which is transmitted at the lowest rate (1 Mb/s). In a simplified signal propagation model, wireless signals fade with distance as they propagate over physical space. Thus, the RSSI values are (roughly) inversely proportional with the distance between the transmitter and receiver. This means that the same transmission will be received at different RSSI values depending on the distance between the transmitter and receiver. Using these RSSI values, we show that it is possible to passively associate a set of packets to their source device.

However, several factors affect a packet's RSSI value in real world environments, which makes accurately associating packets to their transmitting devices using physical layer information a very challenging task. At one receiver, the RSSI values of different packets from the same transmitter often vary over time due to noise factors such as multipath interference and unpredictable fading [37]. Figure 1(a) shows the RSSI values recorded from multiple packets sent over time from five distinct transmitting devices whose corresponding physical locations are given in Figure 1(b). While the values are similar for each device, there is some unpredictable, but small fluctuation due to the inherent noise in the physical environment.

3.2 RSS-Based Localization

RF-based localization is a well-studied problem in which wireless devices are physically located using the signal strengths of their transmitted packets. Therefore, it is reasonable to try this localization strategy to perform packet source classification, since these methods have been shown to provide accurate device localization to within about three meters of the device's true location [29].

The localization technique uses the k-nearest neighbors supervised learning framework, as in previous work [29] to perform packet source classification.[1] Beyond source classification, this approach has the ability to add semantic location information, which could be used to associate packets to a particular device or user and thereby reconstruct persistent identities.

However, localization requires that the adversary collect training data for every environment in which they wish to perform this attack. Furthermore, the training process must be repeated if environmental changes occur. This training data collection is very expensive and even unnecessary, since our goal is not to localize packets, but instead is to perform packet source classification.

3.3 RSS-Based Clustering

To address the limitations of the localization approach, we propose RSS-Clustering, an unsupervised technique to perform packet source classification. Since the RSSI values are inherently noisy, we use the k-means clustering algorithm [38] to group packets by their respective transmitting devices. In order to perform source classification, k-means requires the RSSI feature vectors and the number of devices (k), which we assume is known (or can be closely estimated) by the attacker using visual information or one of many techniques to determine the number of clusters in a data set [39,40,41,42]. While k-means is a computationally efficient linear-time algorithm, it is stochastic and therefore, not guaranteed to produce a globally optimal clustering solution. For this reason, it is common to execute k-means several times on a data set to arrive at a stable clustering result.

There exist several classes of cluster analysis algorithms, including hierarchical, partitional, and spectral techniques [38]. We chose k-means for its simplicity and strong performance on our clustering task. However, it is possible that other clustering algorithms may offer better performance or relax the requirement that the number of clusters be known in advance. Consequently, we consider the results obtained with k-means to be a lower bound on attainable performance.

4   Threat Model

In this section, we enumerate our assumptions about the attack, the adversary, and the victims.

---

[1] Since these localization techniques have a certain amount of error, it is necessary to cluster the imprecisely localized packets by estimated location.

Attack. An eavesdropper first performs packet source classification and subsequently uses the sequences of encrypted packets associated with their respective transmitters to perform complex traffic analysis tasks. The attack is completely passive, so users can be subjected to it without their knowledge. In addition, this technique requires only commodity 802.11 hardware.

Adversary. We consider the adversary to be a person or group of people with limited resources and access to only commodity 802.11 hardware. The adversary has the ability to place n passive commodity 802.11 wireless sensors in chosen positions around a target location (such as a building). For each received packet p_i, the RSSI values across all sensors are combined into a feature vector $(RSSI_{i1}, RSSI_{i2}, ..., RSSI_{in})$. Also, the attacker has the ability to estimate how many devices are present in the area.

Victims. It is trivial to classify packets when it is known that only a single device is active at any particular time, *e.g.*, at a public hotspot. However, we assume a more common situation in which several devices may transmit at arbitrary times, possibly with interspersed transmissions. A prior analysis of wireless traces has shown that there are often many simultaneously active devices at tight time scales [4].

The victims use a standard 802.11 wireless device to communicate using an identifier-free link layer protocol and transmit at a constant power level. Also, the victims use a common application such as a web browser. They remain stationary while they transmit, but are free to move when their transmitters are silent.

5   Experimental Validation

To demonstrate the efficacy of the physical layer source classification technique, we present a series of experiments conducted with 802.11 devices in a real indoor office building environment. In this section, we describe the methodology used to collect real RSSI values. To understand how the packet source classification techniques performs in practice, we present metrics with which to evaluate their ability to accurately associate packets to wireless devices. We characterize the clustering technique's performance with respect to how the number of devices effects clustering accuracy and how the number of listening sensors effects accuracy. Our results show that this method is highly accurate even when 25 devices are active at the same time and requires few sensors.

5.1   Experimental Setup

In order to understand how our physical layer packet clustering technique works in practice, we deployed five 802.11 wireless devices to act as sensors in the "Center for Innovation and Creativity" building located on the University of Colorado's Boulder campus. Deploying five sensors ensures that signals can be received when transmitted from nearly any position in the building, and multiple overlapping sensors also increases the accuracy of our method. This single-storey office building measures $75\,m \times 50\,m$. Each sensor, a commodity Linux desktop machine, passively listens for packets on a fixed 802.11 channel. This allows the sensors to record RSSI values from all audible packets on that particular channel. To collect RSSI measurements, we used a laptop computer to transmit 500 packets at a constant power level of 16 dBm at 58 distinct physical locations throughout the office space (see Appendix A for detailed hardware specifications).

In addition, to evaluate the localization approach, we collect RSSI readings from 179 additional training locations at a constant 16 dBm transmit power level. The k-nearest neighbors algorithm is used for localization and we verify that the median localization error is approximately 3.5 meters, which is consistent with prior work [29]. The layout of the office space marked with the positions of the passive sensors, training locations, and device locations is provided in Appendix B.

To evaluate how the number of devices effects the accuracy, we vary the network size from 5, 10, 15, 20, to 25 devices. Since we only used a single wireless device to transmit packets at multiple locations, to construct scenarios with multiple devices we generated traces of packets transmitted at multiple locations. However, during the data collection, there were other wireless devices transmitting which added interference to the RF space. In order to ensure that there is no bias in the selection of the devices' locations that may influence performance, we generate 100 randomly chosen device location configurations for each network size[2]. Next, we perform clustering on these device location configurations. Recall that since k-means is not guaranteed to provide a globally optimal solution, it is necessary to perform the clustering several times to arrive at a stable clustering solution. We observed that the algorithm stabilized after approximately 100 runs, which takes approximately one minute to complete on a 3.6 GHz Pentium computer. Therefore, we perform k-means clustering 100 times on each device location configuration.

To measure clustering accuracy, we apply the standard *F-Measure* metric from information retrieval. The F-Measure is a weighted harmonic mean *precision* and *recall* in which both are weighted equally [43]. Within the context of our clustering problem, precision captures the homogeneity of each cluster. Recall measures the extent to which packets from a given device are clustered together.

5.2 Packet Source Classification Results

We next present the results of the physical layer packet clustering technique in terms of its ability to accurately associate packets with their respective transmitting devices. In particular, we examine two factors that we believe to be significant with respect to clustering accuracy: (1) the number of devices in the observation space, and (2) the number of sensors in the observation space.

---

[2] Although we collected RSSI measurements at 58 distinct positions, we chose to limit the number of devices to 25 in any experiment to allow for variety in the randomly chosen locations of the devices included in the experiments.

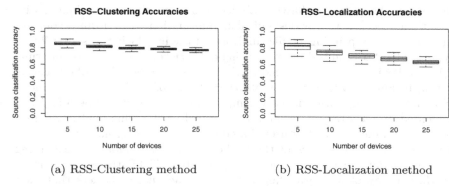

(a) RSS-Clustering method   (b) RSS-Localization method

Fig. 2. Packet source classification accuracies as the number of devices increases

Effect of number of devices on accuracy. The average packet source classification accuracy ranged from 85–77% as the number of devices in the network was varied from 5–25, as shown in Figure 2. In general, the accuracies decrease as the number of devices increases. In other words, the clustering algorithm performs better on a smaller number of devices and produces additional clustering errors as more devices are introduced. However, the 20 and 25 device experiments produced similar clustering accuracies, so there is evidence that the clustering accuracy may, in fact, level off as the number of devices reaches a critical threshold. Additionally, within all device configurations, the RSS-Clustering method provided slightly better accuracy than the RSS-Localization approach.

Effect of number of sensors on accuracy. As shown in Figure 3, the clustering accuracy is surprisingly high, ranging from 75–47%, when just one sensor is used for clustering. However, as more sensors are added, the accuracy for each configuration increases gradually, with diminishing returns: as the number of sensors increases from three to five, the accuracy only improves by at most 3%. This indicates that the resources required—in terms of number of sensors to deploy—are very minimal, making the packet clustering technique practical for a low resource adversary.

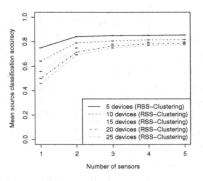

Fig. 3. Mean source classification accuracies (with 95% confidence intervals) for each device configuration as the number of sensors varies

6   Traffic Analysis Application: Website Fingerprinting

Having evaluated the packet source classification techniques in isolation, we now explore how they can be used to perform complex traffic analysis attacks. In particular, we demonstrate that the ability to achieve short-term linking with relatively high accuracy provides sufficient information to perform a sophisticated website fingerprinting traffic analysis attack in which the source of an encrypted HTTP session is discovered using only packet count and size information [10,11]. While we could have chosen to demonstrate the utility of our packet clustering technique with a variety of other classes of traffic analysis attacks, website fingerprinting is a sufficiently complex problem which can be practically implemented by an attacker. In addition, through such traffic analysis, it may be possible to uniquely identify users based on their browsing habits.

In this section, we first present the traffic analysis methodology. Next, using our real RSSI data in combination with encrypted HTTP traces, we demonstrate the efficacy of a website fingerprinting attack using packets that have been classified by their source.

6.1   Traffic Analysis Methodology

In order to apply our real RSSI data to the problem of website fingerprinting, it is necessary to combine the RSSI data with an encrypted HTTP data set. Liberatore and Levine [10] provide a data set consisting of several instances of encrypted connections to many distinct real websites over the course of several months. A website instance consists of the number of packets and their respective sizes.

To perform a simplified website fingerprinting traffic analysis attack after packet source classification, we extract multiple instances of 25 distinct websites from this data set. In general, to perform a website fingerprinting attack it is necessary to partition the website trace data into two disjoint sets, a training set, and a validation (or testing) set, and consider the task of website identification as a classification problem. We construct the website training set by collecting precisely 20 instances of each of the 25 websites that we wish to identify. The validation set is constructed by affixing an RSSI vector onto a packet that is taken from a new instance (*i.e.*, not in the training set) of one of the 25 websites. For the website classification, we apply the naïve Bayes classifier provided by Weka [44], as in Liberatore and Levine [10].

Similar to the experiments presented in Section 5, we construct realistic scenarios by varying the number of wireless devices from 5, 10, 15, 20, to 25 and fix the number of sensors at 5. However, instead of including an equal number of generic packets, we make the assumption that every device downloads a single randomly selected webpage and include all packets with affixed RSSI vectors from a randomly selected position.

6.2   Traffic Analysis Results

We first explore the performance of the clustering algorithm on the website data. A key distinguishing feature of the website data is that each website has an arbitrary number of packets. For some websites, the device transmits several hundred packets, while for others the device transmits less than ten packets.

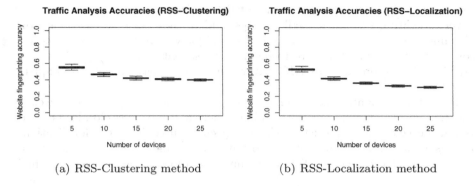

(a) RSS-Clustering method   (b) RSS-Localization method

Fig. 4. Website fingerprinting accuracies as the number of devices increases

Clustering devices that transmit an unequal number of packets does not appear to be a significant factor. The accuracy for the website data is only marginally lower (72–82% accuracy) than for the equal packet data (given in Figure 2).

Given the clustering algorithm's ability to accurately classify encrypted website data, we next perform a website fingerprinting attack on packets that are grouped by wireless device. The website fingerprinting accuracies for each experiment are shown in Figure 4. Using the naïve Bayes classifier, the attack is able to correctly identify the encrypted web page between 40–55% of the time. This accuracy is significantly greater than random chance, in which an adversary guesses the website. In this case, the expected accuracy is $1/25 = 4\%$. For comparison, if packets are perfectly clustered, the website fingerprinting attack achieves 92% accuracy for each device configuration. The accuracy of the website identification is strongly linked to the accuracy of the clustering result. For example, in the 5 device network, both the clustering and website identification accuracies are the highest, and each respective accuracy degrades as the number of devices increases. The website fingerprinting accuracy when the localization approach is applied is slightly worse than the clustering approach.

7   Discussion

In this section, we discuss techniques for reconstructing persistent identifiers, mitigating source classification, the benefits of large crowds for anonymity in the wireless context, and the potential for using jamming and frequency hopping to protect privacy.

7.1   Reconstructing Persistent Identifiers

The packet source classification technique as presented enables short-term linking, but cannot directly reconstruct the persistent identifiers that are necessary to enable user tracking or profiling across sessions. Once short-term linking has been accomplished, it becomes possible to perform a variety of traffic analysis tasks to identify such information about the device including its wireless NIC driver, operating system, firewall settings, and/or more specific user behavior. This information can sometimes be used to uniquely identify devices across session, and thus could be used to reconstruct persistent identifiers. For instance, a device with an obscure OS/NIC driver combination may be easy to uniquely identify.

In addition, semantic location information can augment the packet source classification with a physical location binding. Such information could also be used to link source classified packets back to a specific source. The RSS localization-based source classification technique ostensibly provides the device's location, but it comes at the cost of collecting training data for the target environment.

7.2   Mitigating Packet Source Classification

We next explore techniques using transmit power control and directional antennas to reduce the effectiveness of packet source classification.

Intuition. For a given transmitter's location, the expected received signal strength at each sensor is predictable within some variance. However, if the transmitter's signal strength is reduced or amplified, then it becomes more likely that the received signal strengths observed at each sensor may overlap with those from other wireless devices. The result of a single transmitter varying its power levels often results in a cluster that encompasses a different portion of the signal space. In addition, directional antennas attenuate the wireless signal in certain directions while amplifying the signal in other directions, enabling the packets sent in each direction to form their own distinct clusters.[3] This phenomenon, as we will demonstrate, has an adverse effect on clustering accuracy and therefore reduces an adversary's ability to perform traffic analysis attacks on the source classified packets.

Transmit Power Control. We conduct experiments to understand the extent to which variable transmission power levels can be used to protect devices from short-term linking at the physical layer (see Appendix A for detailed hardware specifications). All other devices in the network transmit their packets at a fixed 16 dBm. Experiments are conducted with 15 total devices in which 1, 3, 6, 9, and 12 devices transmit their packets at a randomly chosen power level. As the number of devices with variable transmit power levels increases, the source classification accuracy using the clustering method varies between 61–72%.[4] The accuracy decreases by 10–15% from the results in Section 5.2. The reduction in clustering accuracy has a negative impact on the website fingerprinting traffic analysis. The traffic analysis accuracy is approximately 30%, an improvement

---

[3] We also conducted informal experiments in which the throughput is measured while manipulating a single transmitter's power levels. We found that the impact on throughput was insignificant. Similarly, pointing a directional antenna in different orientations also had an insignificant impact on throughput.

[4] The localization-based source classification method performed similarly.

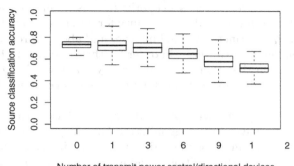

Fig. 5. For a 15 device network, the effect of introducing 0–12 devices using transmit power control in combination with directional antennas is shown

over the results from Section 6. However, devices that do not use this strategy show the same vulnerability to traffic analysis.

Directional Antennas. Low-cost directional antennas, such as sectored or MIMO antennas, are becoming widely deployed with the 802.11n standard. We next explore how directional antennas can be used to alter physical layer information, by repeating the same experiments as above except using directional antenna transmitters in place of variable transmit power level devices. The directional antenna was oriented in four different directions as the device transmitted packets. We found that the clustering accuracy decreases in a similar fashion as the experiments with the variable transmit power levels. The website fingerprinting traffic analysis attack also achieves about 30% accuracy for directional devices while non-directional devices obtain no protection from traffic analysis.

Combined Effect. The most significant reduction in source classification accuracy occurs when devices utilize transmit power control in combination with directional antennas. Figure 5 shows that the mean clustering accuracy decreases to nearly 50% as more devices use the combined strategy. The traffic analysis attack's accuracy also decreases to 26% for devices that utilize this strategy.

Hiding Signal Strength Information is Hard. The relative success of the source classification and subsequent traffic analysis despite these defensive techniques highlights the inherent difficulty of manipulating the properties of the physical layer. Ultimately, intentionally changing RSSI values is a hard problem, since there are many unobservable and environmental factors including multipath fading and attenuation that are difficult to isolate and predict. Furthermore, it is necessary to transmit at a level that is sufficient to reach an access point. Thus, these observations are consistent with prior findings that there are fundamental limitations to the extent to which the signal strength properties of the physical layer can be altered [45,46].

7.3   Anonymity *Still* Loves Company

Anonymity mechanisms for wireless networks (discussed in Section 2) such as link layer encryption achieve sender anonymity for wireless clients by effectively randomizing explicit identifiers. At the link layer and above, wireless packets are unlinkable to their senders. However, in order for this condition to hold, there is an implicit assumption that there are significantly many wireless clients in the network. For instance, if only one client uses the network, it is trivial to link their traffic to a user.

Since signal strength varies with physical distance, devices that are closer to one another typically have similar signal strengths. A group of devices within close physical proximity may be more difficult to distinguish using their signal strengths. Thus, as with traditional anonymity, a larger user base enables stronger anonymity properties than a smaller one [47]. In the wireless case, the caveat is that these users should physically arrange themselves close to each other so their signal strengths are less distinguishable to the source classification method.

7.4   Wireless Cover Traffic

Cover traffic is a well-known strategy to frustrate traffic analysis [15]. In wireless networks, cover traffic may be another tool to mitigate traffic analysis, but there are additional challenges posed by the wireless medium. First, the wireless medium is a shared resource and adding additional traffic may degrade everyone's performance. In addition, wireless devices are often battery powered and, thus try to conserve energy. Contributing cover traffic could have serious implications for power consumption and may reduce a device's lifetime. Cover traffic increases the number of packets on which an adversary could perform source classification, but the subsequent traffic analysis tasks may become more difficult. A complete study of cover traffic in the wireless context is beyond the scope of this work.

7.5   Physical Space Security, Jamming, and Frequency Hopping

Beyond hiding the contents of a communication session with cryptography, other radical approaches have been proposed that aim to reduce the number of packets that can be overhead by an eavesdropper. Lakshmanan *et al.* and Sheth *et al.* demonstrate this by using directional antennas to focus transmissions within a secure physical space that is free of eavesdroppers [48,49].

In addition, jamming has been suggested as another method to mitigate an eavesdropper's ability to overhear wireless packets [50]. An intelligent jamming strategy aimed at the locations of potential eavesdroppers can effectively raise the noise floor at their positions, which makes it difficult to distinguish between wireless signals and normal background noise on the wireless medium. While jamming may be an effective way to neutralize eavesdroppers, it may also interfere with legitimate communications and degrade the network's performance.

Another potential technique to evade eavesdroppers is to use frequency agility to transmit on different channels in a certain pattern [51]. However, the 802.11 standard limits transmissions to the 2.4 GHz and 5 GHz frequency bands, which have a limited number of channels; thus, an eavesdropper could feasibly monitor all channels simultaneously. To mitigate harmful interference among devices, most governments in developed nations regulate the allocation and usage of wireless spectrum for specific wireless devices. Consequently, spectrum is a scarce resource, which impedes the effectiveness of frequency hopping to evade eavesdroppers.

8 Conclusion

In this paper, we demonstrate that even when explicit identifiers are removed from wireless packets at the link layer, a significant amount of information remains preserved within the wireless physical layer. We provide a packet source classification technique that uses this information to achieve short-term linking. The proposed packet source classification approach is unsupervised and requires no specialized hardware.

Through experiments, we show that this approach provides sufficient accuracy to enable complex traffic analysis tasks. As an example, we conduct a website fingerprinting attack on source-classified packets with reasonably high success. To mitigate the effectiveness of the packet source classification, we evaluate methods to alter the transmitted signal strength of packets, thereby introducing additional noise which degrades the accuracy of both the packet source classification and the subsequent traffic analysis. We hope that this work will bring more awareness to the privacy problems that are present at the wireless physical layer and encourage further exploration of methods to mitigate these types of attacks.

Acknowledgments

We thank Jeffrey Pang and the anonymous reviewers for their insightful suggestions and comments, James Martin for granting access to our office building testbed, and Eric Anderson for assisting with the data collection. This research was partially funded by NSF Awards ITR-0430593 and CRI-0454404.

References

1. Pang, J., Greenstein, B., Gummadi, R., Seshan, S., Wetherall, D.: 802.11 user fingerprinting. In: MobiCom (2007)
2. Aura, T., Lindqvist, J., Roe, M., Mohammed, A.: Chattering laptops. In: Borisov, N., Goldberg, I. (eds.) PETS 2008. LNCS, vol. 5134, pp. 167–186. Springer, Heidelberg (2008)

3. Armknecht, F., Girão, J., Matos, A., Aguiar, R.L.: Who said that? Privacy at link layer. In: INFOCOM. IEEE, Los Alamitos (2007)
4. Greenstein, B., McCoy, D., Pang, J., Kohno, T., Seshan, S., Wetherall, D.: Improving wireless privacy with an identifier-free link layer protocol. In: Mobisys (2008)
5. Singelée, D., Preneel, B.: Location privacy in wireless personal area networks. In: WiSe (2006)
6. Brik, V., Banerjee, S., Gruteser, M., Oh, S.: Wireless device identification with radiometric signatures. In: MobiCom (2008)
7. Danev, B., Capkun, S.: Physical-layer identification of wireless sensor nodes. In: Technical Report ETH Zurich System Security Group D-INFK 604 (August 2008)
8. Saponas, T.S., Lester, J., Hartung, C., Agarwal, S., Kohno, T.: Devices that tell on you: Privacy trends in consumer ubiquitous computing. In: Proc. 16th USENIX Security Symposium (2007)
9. Song, D.X., Wagner, D., Tian, X.: Timing analysis of keystrokes and timing attacks on ssh. In: 10th USENIX Security Symposium (2001)
10. Liberatore, M., Levine, B.N.: Inferring the source of encrypted HTTP connections. In: CCS 2006: Proceedings of the 13th ACM conference on Computer and communications security. ACM, New York (2006)
11. Sun, Q., Simon, D.R., Wang, Y.M., Russell, W., Padmanabhan, V.N., Qiu, L.: Statistical identification of encrypted web browsing traffic. In: IEEE Symposium on Security and Privacy (2002)
12. Wright, C., Ballard, L., Monrose, F., Masson, G.: Language identification of encrypted VoIP traffic: Alejandra y roberto or Alice and Bob? In: Proceedings of the 16th USENIX Security Symposium (2007)
13. Wright, C.V., Ballard, L., Coull, S.E., Monrose, F., Masson, G.M.: Spot me if you can: Uncovering spoken phrases in encrypted VoIP conversations (2008)
14. Wright, C., Monrose, F., Masson, G.: On inferring application protocol behaviors in encrypted network traffic. Journal of Machine Learning Research (2006)
15. Chaum, D.: Untraceable electronic mail, return addresses, and digital pseudonyms. Communications of the ACM (February 1981)
16. Goldschlag, D.M., Reed, M.G., Syverson, P.F.: Hiding routing information. In: Anderson, R. (ed.) IH 1996. LNCS, vol. 1174, pp. 137–150. Springer, Heidelberg (1996)
17. Gruteser, M., Grunwald, D.: Enhancing location privacy in wireless LAN through disposable interface identifiers: A quantitative analysis. ACM MONET 10 (2005)
18. Arkko, J., Nikander, P., Nslund, M.: Enhancing privacy with shared pseudo random sequences. In: Christianson, B., Crispo, B., Malcolm, J.A., Roe, M. (eds.) Security Protocols 2005. LNCS, vol. 4631, pp. 197–203. Springer, Heidelberg (2007)
19. Lindqvist, J., Tapio, J.M.: Protecting privacy with protocol stack virtualization. In: WPES 2008: Proceedings of the 7th ACM workshop on Privacy in the electronic society, pp. 65–74. ACM, New York (2008)
20. Kohno, T., Broido, A., Claffy, K.: Remote physical device fingerprinting. In: IEEE Symposium on Security and Privacy, pp. 211–225. IEEE Computer Society, Los Alamitos (2005)
21. Murdoch, S.J.: Hot or not: Revealing hidden services by their clock skew. In: Proceedings of CCS 2006 (October 2006)

22. Zander, S., Murdoch, S.J.: An improved clock-skew measurement technique for re-vealing hidden services. In: Proceedings of the 17th USENIX Security Symposium, San Jose, CA, US (July 2008)
23. Gerdes, R., Daniels, T., Mina, M., Russell, S.: Device identification via analog signal fingerprinting: A matched filter approach. In: NDSS (2006)
24. Fyodor: Nmap network security scanner, http://insecure.org/nmap
25. p0f, http://lcamtuf.coredump.cx/p0f.shtml
26. Franklin, J., McCoy, D., Tabriz, P., Neagoe, V., Randwyk, J.V., Sicker, D.: Passive data link layer 802.11 wireless device driver fingerprinting. In: USENIX Security Symposium, Vancouver, Canada, July-August 2006, pp. 167–178 (2006)
27. Smith, I., Scott, J., Sohn, T., Howard, J., Hughes, J., Potter, F., Tabert, J., Powledge, P., Borriello, G., Schilit, B.: Place lab: Device positioning using radio bea-cons in the wild. In: Gellersen, H.-W., Want, R., Schmidt, A. (eds.) PERVASIVE 2005. LNCS, vol. 3468, pp. 116–133. Springer, Heidelberg (2005)
28. Skyhook Wireless, http://www.skyhookwireless.com
29. Bahl, P., Padmanabhan, V.N.: RADAR: An in-building RF-based user location and tracking system. In: INFOCOM (2), pp. 775–784 (2000)
30. Haeberlen, A., Flannery, E., Ladd, A.M., Rudys, A., Wallach, D.S., Kavraki, L.E.: Practical robust localization over large-scale 802.11 wireless networks. In: Pro-ceedings of the Tenth ACM International Conference on Mobile Computing and Networking (MOBICOM), Philadelphia, PA (September 2002) (to appear)
31. Niculescu, D., Nath, B.: VOR base stations for indoor 802.11 positioning. In: MobiCom 2004: Proceedings of the 10th annual international conference on Mobile computing and networking, pp. 58–69. ACM, New York (2004)
32. Hofmann-Wellenhof, B., Lichtenegger, H., Collins, J.: Global Positioning System: Theory and Practice. Springer, Heidelberg (1997)
33. Yamasaki, R., Ogino, A., Tamaki, T., Uta, T., Matsuzawa, N., Kato, T.: TDOA location system for IEEE 802.11b WLAN. In: IEEE WCNC (2005)
34. Gruteser, M., Grunwald, D.: Anonymous usage of location-based services through spatial and temporal cloaking. In: MobiSys 2003: Proc. 1st international conference on Mobile systems, applications and services, pp. 31–42. ACM Press, New York (2003)
35. Jiang, T., Wang, H., Hu, Y.C.: Preserving location privacy in wireless LANs. In: MobiSys (2007)
36. Faria, D.B., Cheriton, D.R.: Detecting identity-based attacks in wireless networks using signalprints. In: WiSe 2006: Proceedings of the 5th ACM workshop on Wire-less security, pp. 43–52. ACM, New York (2006)
37. Reis, C., Mahajan, R., Rodrig, M., Wetherall, D., Zahorjan, J.: Measurement-based models of delivery and interference in static wireless networks. SIGCOMM Comput. Commun. Rev. 36(4) (2006)
38. Hastie, T., Tibshirani, R., Friedman, J.H.: The Elements of Statistical Learning. Springer, Heidelberg (2001)
39. Hamerly, G., Elkan, C.: Learning the k in k-means. In: Proc. 17th NIPS (2003)
40. Dan Pelleg, A.M.: X-means: Extending k-means with efficient estimation of the number of clusters. In: Proceedings of the Seventeenth International Con-ference on Machine Learning, pp. 727–734. Morgan Kaufmann, San Francisco (2000)
41. Tibshirani, R., Walther, G., Hastie, T.: Estimating the number of clusters in a dataset via the gap statistic. Technical report (2000)

42. Fallah, S., Tritchler, D., Beyene, J.: Estimating number of clusters based on a general similarity matrix with application to microarray data. Statistical applications in genetics and molecular biology 7 (2008)
43. Van Rijsbergen, C.J.: Information Retrieval, 2nd edn. Dept. of Computer Science, University of Glasgow (1979)
44. Witten, I.H., Frank, E.: Data mining: Practical machine learning tools and techniques. Morgan Kaufmann, San Francisco (2005)
45. Shrivastava, V., Agrawal, D., Mishra, A., Banerjee, S., Nadeem, T.: Understanding the limitations of transmit power control for indoor WLANs. In: IMC 2007: Proceedings of the 7th ACM SIGCOMM conference on Internet measurement, pp. 351–364. ACM, New York (2007)
46. Blanco, M., Kokku, R., Ramachandran, K., Rangarajan, S., Sundaresan, K.: On the effectiveness of switched beam antennas in indoor environments. In: Claypool, M., Uhlig, S. (eds.) PAM 2008. LNCS, vol. 4979, pp. 122–131. Springer, Heidelberg (2008)
47. Dingledine, R., Mathewson, N.: Anonymity loves company: Usability and the network effect. In: Anderson, R. (ed.) Proceedings of the Fifth Workshop on the Economics of Information Security (WEIS 2006), Cambridge, UK (June 2006)
48. Lakshmanan, S., Tsao, C.L., Sivakumar, R., Sundaresan, K.: Securing wireless data networks against eavesdropping using smart antennas. In: ICDCS 2006: Proceedings of the 2008 The 28th International Conference on Distributed Computing Systems, Washington, DC, USA, pp. 19–27. IEEE Computer Society, Los Alamitos (2008)
49. Sheth, A., Seshan, S., Wetherall, D.: Geo-fencing: Confining Wi-Fi coverage to physical boundaries. In: Seventh International Conference on Pervasive Computing (2009)
50. Martinovic, I., Pichota, P., Schmitt, J.B.: Jamming for good: Design and analysis of a crypto-less protection for WSNs. In: Proceedings of the Second Conference on Wireless Network Security (WiSec) (March 2009)
51. Xu, W., Wood, T., Trappe, W., Zhang, Y.: Channel surfing and spatial retreats: defenses against wireless denial of service. In: WiSe 2004: Proceedings of the 3rd ACM workshop on Wireless security, pp. 80–89. ACM, New York (2004)

A   Hardware Used in Experiments

Device type	Wireless NIC type	Antenna type
Sensors	D-Link DWL-AG530	Omni directional dipole antenna 2-4 dBi
Transmitters	WNC WLAN Cardbus Adaptor CB9	Omni directional dipole antenna 2-4 dBi
Directional Transmitters	WNC WLAN Cardbus Adaptor CB9	"Super Cantenna" 12 dBi 30 degree beam width directional antenna

B   Building Floorplan for Experiments

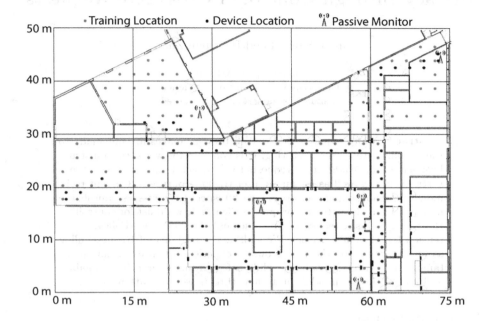

Wireless devices are placed at 58 distinct physical locations in an office building. The training locations for the localization approach are also shown.

RequestPolicy: Increasing Web Browsing Privacy through Control of Cross-Site Requests

Justin Samuel and Beichuan Zhang

University of Arizona
Department of Computer Science
{jsamuel,bzhang}@cs.arizona.edu

Abstract. Many requests that a Web browser makes are not made to the primary site a user is visiting. It is common for websites to instruct browsers to make additional requests to third-party sites for content, advertisements, as well as for purely user-tracking purposes. Current techniques for maintaining user privacy with respect to cross-site requests are limited and inadequate. We propose a client-side whitelist for controlling third-party website requests. We implement this as RequestPolicy, an extension for Mozilla browsers. We look at the usability of RequestPolicy as well its impact on the Web browsing experience. Our extension maintains a high level of usability while safeguarding user privacy against well-known threats in addition to new threats we draw attention to.

1 Introduction

When a browser requests a page from a website, the response sent to the browser frequently includes instructions for the browser to make additional requests for content. These additional requests are often cross-site requests: requests whose hosts are different from the host of original website. Such cross-site requests often result in advertising companies and other websites gaining information about a user's browsing habits, including knowledge about specific pages the user has viewed and when those pages were viewed.

Any website that receives cross-site requests is in a position to collect and use this information. In some cases, this is the intended purpose of the cross-site request, such as with services that provide site traffic analysis. In other cases, the intention is not to provide a third-party site with user data but only to include off-site content in a webpage. In either situation, more information about a user's browsing habits is exposed than many users meant to reveal. This information and the potential for adversaries to link a user's separate website browsing sessions also puts users of anonymizing networks and proxies at risk of de-anonymization.

Other work has also identified specific risks to Tor [1] users due to the lack of a client-side exit policy. In the described attacks, the ability for a malicious party to reveal the identity of a client by means of timing attacks can be greatly increased [2]. This is done by a malicious exit node or destination server responding to the client with a webpage that causes the client to make outgoing requests to nonstandard ports.

I. Goldberg and M. Atallah (Eds.): PETS 2009, LNCS 5672, pp. 128–142, 2009.

More general timing attacks using cross-site requests and differences in completion time for cached and non-cached requests have been known for many years [3]. These methods allow a malicious site to identify URLs of other sites that a client has previously visited. The ability for this information to be discovered by unrelated websites is contrary to the privacy expectations of users.

In this work we identify where existing tools and methods fail to protect users from privacy loss due to cross-site requests. Based on this information, we identify a need for users to have full control over their browser's cross-site request behavior. Other work has recognized the great privacy benefits of cross-site request blocking, but considered the usability of this method to be impractical [4].

We design and implement RequestPolicy, an extension for Mozilla browsers that focuses on usability while providing complete control in the form of a user-maintained cross-site request whitelist [5]. We discuss the user interface challenges in implementing such a tool and the difficulty in maintaining correctness in the face of the need for minimal complexity and high ease-of-use. We also look at the impact our tool has on the functionality of websites and find ways to minimize disruption and avoid user frustration. Within the first few months of its release, RequestPolicy has been downloaded thousands of times.

While implementing RequestPolicy, we encountered new threats to privacy that have not been sufficiently considered elsewhere. DNS prefetching is a new technique used by browsers to decrease page load times by anticipatorily making DNS requests. We draw attention to how DNS prefetching can be abused for user tracking and other purposes. In accordance with our goal of giving users complete control over privacy-damaging requests made by their browser, we add protections against DNS prefetching abuse to RequestPolicy.

A cross-site request whitelist such as that implemented by RequestPolicy offers increased security in addition to privacy benefits. In this work we focus solely on the privacy aspects of RequestPolicy.

The remainder of this paper is organized as follows: In Section 2 we look at related work that provides methods users have available to limit information exposure due to cross-site requests. Looking at where current technologies fail to protect privacy with cross-site requests, in Section 3 we define requirements for a new system. Section 4 looks at the implementation of these requirements as a Mozilla browser extension and Section 5 discusses usability considerations. Future work is discussed in Section 6 and Section 7 concludes.

2   Related Work

Some technologies do exist that allow users to block certain cross-site requests or decrease the amount of information sent in cross-site requests. However, none of these have been developed with the privacy implications of cross-site requests as their primary focus.

Various proxies and browser extensions exist to suppress sending `Referer` headers in cross-site requests [6,7]. The risk of privacy loss from cross-site requests, however, is not only due to `Referer` headers. Information about the user is still contained in cookies, the user's IP address, and most fundamentally in the URL being requested. The requested URL can contain information such as the user's session ID from the originating site; this alone may put the user's privacy at risk.

Similarly, most modern browsers have options to block third-party cookies. Browser extensions also exist [8] that allow control over allowed cookies. As with `Referer` headers, blocking cookies does not eliminate the risk of privacy loss from cross-site requests.

A small number of tools do exist that block some cross-site requests. These include browser extensions that use predictive analysis for cross-site request blocking [9] and others that use blacklist-based advertisements blocking [10]. Predictive analysis has the potential to block many undesirable cross-site requests given the correct rules and history, but privacy cannot be guaranteed with such a system due to the occurrence of false negatives. Advertisement blocking, on the other hand, only targets privacy loss due to advertising companies. Further, advertisement blocking systems are generally blacklist-based and thus will have a delay time between false negatives and updates to the blacklist, which is often updated automatically. Other browser extensions exist that focus on general, manual request blacklisting [11], but these extensions have the same inadequacies as subscription-based advertisement blocking systems in addition to having user interfaces not intended for fine-grained cross-site request control.

The use of proxies that hide a user's true IP address from destination websites is common for users with an interest in maintaining privacy [1,12]. However, as mentioned in Section 1, cross-site requests should be of concern to users of anonymizing proxies due to their potential for de-anonymization.

A solution to cache timing attacks has been proposed through cache partitioning [13]. However, the solution implemented in that work, the Firefox extension SafeCache, has been shown to be easily bypassed [14] and SafeCache is no longer maintained.

Krishnamurthy has added a great amount to the body of knowledge related to privacy and cross-site requests. In [4], various methods and tools for preserving privacy were looked at, concluding that all methods were inferior to blocking cross-site requests. The blocking of cross-site requests, however, was found to have very low usability. Other work by Krishnamurthy has studied metrics for quantifying privacy loss due to cross-site requests, the increase in cross-site requests for user tracking, and the impact of company acquisitions on the centralization of accumulated cross-site request data [15,16].

3   Requirements

The existing tools that mitigate privacy loss due to cross-site request can be categorized as either reducing information sent with cross-site requests or blocking a portion of cross-site requests. Tools that reduce the amount of sent information fail to preserve privacy due to the fact that certain information they allow, such as the cross-site requests' URL, can cause loss of privacy. Tools that use defined or predictive blacklists fail to preserve privacy due to only blocking some privacy-impacting cross-site requests. Additionally, these blacklisting tools have a weak ability to block new cross-site requests that do not trigger existing rules within those tools.

To create a tool that provides privacy-concerned users with the control they need over cross-site requests, neither information-decreasing nor blacklist-based approaches will suffice. These users need to have the ability to block cross-site requests unless they specifically choose to allow them. A whitelist solution rather than a blacklist solution is therefore required in order to ensure that all unwanted requests are blocked.

The use of a whitelist for cross-site requests, though, raises several usability concerns.

3.1   User Understanding

Blacklist-based tools generally require little or no understanding of how the tool works. Users of such tools may not understand what the privacy risks are but only that they want to guard against privacy loss.

With a whitelist solution, it is even more important to recognize that many users desiring a high level of privacy do not have a full understanding of what cross-site requests are. However, other browser extensions have overcome the hurdle of user-understanding and have provided useful services to many who do not grasp the underlying technical issues. An example of such an extension is NoScript, a popular whitelist-based security extension for Mozilla browsers that has been downloaded more than 40 million times [17]. It is highly likely that a large number of NoScript's users do not fully understand the threats NoScript protects against. Despite this lack of understanding, these users are still able to benefit from a highly-secure whitelist solution.

It is worth recognizing, however, that NoScript's user base is not representative of the average Internet user. Such users are in the minority in that most have specifically chosen a browser other than their operating system's default browser. Additionally, their likelihood of higher-than-average technical understanding is evident in that they are aware of the existence of browser extensions and know how to install them.

3.2   User Interface

With respect to user interface, blacklist solutions are generally non-invasive. Many users never have to interact with the interface. This level of automation will not be possible with a whitelist solution. Care will need to be taken to keep the user interface of a cross-site request whitelist tool intuitive.

User intuition is also a key to the usability of NoScript's interface. Users are alerted when the whitelist has restricted components of a website; users then must make whitelisting decisions based on their level of security knowledge, perceived need for a blocked component, and trust in the website the component is from. Similarly, we will rely upon user judgment for our cross-site request whitelist. As discussed above, basing a standard of user intuition off of the users of a popular addon will likely not translate directly to the intuition of an average Internet user.

3.3 Website Functionality

A cross-site request whitelist will undoubtedly impact the appearance as well as the functionality of some websites. Any tool we develop will have very limited ability to compensate for any such breakage. What a whitelist tool should do, however, is enable users to identify as easily as possible what the blocked content is that is causing the breakage. Based on that knowledge, users should be able to quickly whitelist the cross-site requests required for that desired content.

4 Implementation

We implemented RequestPolicy, a Mozilla browser extension that provides a cross-site request whitelist. Browser extensions provide an ideal way to implement changes to the browsing experience. Through a browser extension, software can maintain the user's expectations of appearance and behavior with respect to their existing browser. When a website does not behave as a user expects or requires security decisions to be made by the user, the browser commonly provides users additional information. An example of this is when a user visits a website whose SSL certificate is invalid. Modern browsers will present the user additional information directly in the content pane of the browser. Users do not expect to look to separate windows or applications when there is a problem with their browsing experience.

Browser extensions also provide an ideal way to implement our changes due to the large amount of available information about the user's actions. This same information would not be accessible through, for example, a proxy that can only see and modify requests and responses. This is especially important with cross-site requests. Many cross-site requests are fully intentional by the user. For example, users will often follow links from one site to another. These are not the kinds of cross-site requests we want to block. Rather, we want to be able to selectively allow user-intended cross-site requests while subjecting others to the user's whitelist.

Implementation as an extension for Mozilla browsers as opposed to an extension for other browsers was chosen because of the ease of implementation of Mozilla browser extensions, the extensive API allowing large amounts of access from extensions, as well as the wide reach of Firefox, the most popular Mozilla browser. Additionally, the use of browser extensions is very popular among Firefox users. Firefox even provides a built-in feature that allows users to search for and install extensions hosted by the Mozilla project [18].

4.1   Blocking Cross-Site Requests

All cross-site requests that are not intended by the user should be blocked by default. A partial list of the many ways cross-site requests may be initiated in a browser is shown in Table 1.

Table 1. Methods of initiating cross-site requests within a browser

Method	Execution
Images	`<img>` tag, CSS styles
Script files	`<script>` tag
Stylesheets	`<link rel="stylesheet">` tag
Frames	`<frame>` and `<iframe>` tags
HTML-based redirects	`<meta http-equiv="refresh">` tag
Header-based redirects	`Location` header, `Refresh` header
Prefetched webpages	`<link rel="prefetch">` tag
Cross-site XMLHttpRequest	New feature in Firefox 3.5
Favicons	`<link rel="icon">` tag
Plugin-initiated requests	Flash, QuickTime, Java

In order to attain the most accurate behavior possible, the extension was implemented to block as much as possible without requiring special cases for different types of content. This minimized the chance that an oversight of a type of cross-site request could result in holes in the privacy the extension provides. The Mozilla XPCOM [19] nsIContentPolicy interface provided our extension the ability to make per-request blocking decisions for the majority of requests based on the URL of the originating document and the requested URL.

When URLs use IP addresses rather than domain names as the URL host, IP addresses are treated as distinct from different IP addresses as well as any domain names. The actual classification and comparison of origin and requested URLs is assisted by various XPCOM interfaces, including nsIURI and nsIEffectiveTLD-Service. These comparisons will be discussed in more detail in Section 5.2.

Though it may appear that knowing the origin URL and destination URL for any given request would be enough information to make an accurate decision for that request, our decision algorithm needed more information to avoid false positives. For example, when a user clicks a cross-site link or submits a cross-site form, we do not want to block those requests. In order to not subject link clicks and form submissions to the whitelist rules, a combination of methods were used. For simple link clicks and form submissions, event handlers provided by the browser were sufficient to allow the decision algorithm to allow these requests. More difficult but highly important was to also recognize other actions such as choosing to open a link in a new tab or window through the context menu (the menu the displays when a link is clicked with the alternate mouse button). To detect these cases, the browser functions that are called to open links from the context menu were replaced with modified versions of those functions.

Not all cross-site requests could be handled through the nsIContentPolicy interface. Header-based redirects, for example, were not subjected to this interface and neither were prefetched webpages. Header-based redirects could be caught and acted on through a separate observer interface within Mozilla. Prefetched webpages, unfortunately, could not be. Webpage prefetching occurs when a webpage includes a tag that hints to the browser what it believes is a likely next page the user will visit. Webpage prefetching allows some content to be anticipatorily requested and cached. The only way to disable webpage prefetching in our extension was to globally disable this functionality through the browser preferences system. This means that all prefetched webpages are blocked rather than just those that are blocked according to whitelist rules.

4.2   DNS Prefetching

DNS prefetching is a new feature being added in Firefox 3.1. DNS prefetching is where the browser looks at all links on every page and, during browser idle time, performs DNS resolution on domain names in those links. DNS prefetching is an idea first implemented in the Google Chrome browser [20].

Before DNS prefetching was added to Firefox, a security review was performed by the Firefox developers [21]. The review, unfortunately, only considered privacy in terms of how DNS prefetching related to the Private Browsing mode being added to Firefox [22].

Although no cases of privacy abuse through DNS prefetching are currently known to exist, there is clearly the possibility for abuse. User privacy could be violated by having the authoritative DNS servers for a domain record requests for specially-crafted domain names that are used in links. For example, DNS prefetching could be used for user tracking by embedding links in a page that have subdomain parts which include information about the user session and visited page. Such a domain might look like `page-123.session-456.example.com`. The same tactic could be used to obtain email open-rate data for webmail users. Email open-rate information is useful for email marketers, spammers, and phishers. DNS prefetching could even be used by individuals who want to bypass a recipient's potential refusal to provide read receipts from their webmail client.

No granular method for control over DNS prefetching exists in Firefox's current implementation. In order to protect users against privacy loss due to DNS prefetching, we had to use the same approach as with webpage prefetching. Namely, DNS prefetching is disabled by RequestPolicy through Firefox's preferences system.

4.3   Problematic Requests

Some cross-site requests are difficult to manage. When a user clicks a cross-site link, we want to allow that request. However, non-standard links that are actually triggers for JavaScript which redirect the browser to a different site cannot be detected as user-intended actions. As a result, these types of links are blocked when clicked by a user. Fortunately, while links that trigger JavaScript are common, we have found that the use of such links to trigger cross-site redirection is extremely uncommon. If such a case were to be encountered by a user, the user would be able to follow the link by whitelisting the cross-site request so that it would be allowed.

More difficult are cross-site requests performed by third-party browser plugins (such as Flash and Java) and other browser extensions which can make requests that bypass RequestPolicy's whitelist. In general, there is no way to prevent a separate application installed by a user from bypassing the browser's privacy or security mechanisms. We did find, though, that some plugin-initiated requests do go through the browser's request interface. As a result, these requests are often subjected to the cross-site request whitelist.

4.4 Identifiability of RequestPolicy

For users seeking anonymity on the Web, browser extensions should not be identifiable to websites. Any browser extension that can be identified by analyzing web requests adds to the information an adversary can use to potentially de-anonymize a user. However, it does not seem possible to make RequestPolicy unidentifiable. At best, individual websites may not be able to determine which browser extension is blocking certain requests. Looking at a user's request pattern across multiple websites would likely remove any doubt as to which extension was in use.

5 Usability

The usability of a system is highly dependent on the needs of those using the system. RequestPolicy, fundamentally, does not address a need of all users browsing the Web. Specifically, only users sufficiently concerned about privacy to be willing to make changes to their browsing experience would consider a tool such as RequestPolicy for privacy preservation. Thus, RequestPolicy must meet a level of ease of use that is acceptable to people willing to incur some impact on their browsing. The goal, of course, is to minimize that impact and make RequestPolicy usable to those with the least amount of privacy concern as well as the least patience and technical savvy.

The most important user interface aspects in developing RequestPolicy were how users were to be notified of blocked content and how they would then interact with the extension to control their whitelist. In addition, the aggressiveness of the default cross-site request classification policy needed to be balanced with the privacy concerns of the largest segment of the expected user base.

5.1 User Interface

In order to notify users of blocked content on the current page, some form of notification needed to be added to the browser window. A RequestPolicy icon was added to the browser's status bar, the bar that runs along the bottom of the browser window. When content is blocked, this icon changes to indicate that there is blocked content. When RequestPolicy was first made available as a beta for public testing, immediate feedback from multiple users was received requesting a similar notification icon be made available in the toolbars at the top of the browser window. An optional toolbar button was soon added.

Some types of blocked content are difficult to indicate directly to the user. For example, blocked CSS stylesheets cannot be easily represented to many users because they don't occupy a specific area of a webpage and, more importantly, many users do not understand what stylesheets are. Images, on the other hand, are understood by users and do occupy a specific region of a webpage. Request-Policy therefore indicates blocked images with a special graphic and also displays the image's blocked destination host when the cursor is hovered over the graphic representing the blocked image.

Fig. 1. The RequestPolicy menu while visiting `amazon.com`. The destination `amazon-images.com` has been white whitelisted for requests originating from `amazon.com`.

Once a user becomes aware of blocked cross-site content, in many cases they will want to determine which requests were blocked as well as which were allowed. Further, they will often want to add or remove items from their whitelist at that time. One type of interface for per-site whitelisting has been shown to be popular by the NoScript extension. In NoScript, each domain that provides scripts is listed in the menu users see when clicking on the NoScript icon. RequestPolicy used this interface concept as a starting point and improved upon it for greater clarity, granularity, and ease of use with cross-site request whitelisting.

The RequestPolicy menu groups destination domains by whether requests to those domains were blocked or allowed from the current site (Figure 1). Each destination domain entry has a submenu associated with it which allows adding or removing the destination from the whitelist (Figure 2). Any item added to the whitelist can be added temporarily if the user chooses. Temporarily whitelisted items are removed from the whitelist at the end of the browser session.

Importantly, users have much more granularity than just being able to whitelist destination domains. Users can whitelist by origin, destination, or origin-to-destination. For example, a user can allow all requests originating from bbc.co.uk, but from amazon.com only allow requests to amazon-images.com. Users can also allow requests to a specific destination from any origin, such as allowing all requests to recaptcha.net.

A primary goal with RequestPolicy was to maintain simplicity in the menu while still providing the information a user needs and quick access to the options they are likely to use. A case where this simplicity was jeopardized was when dealing with situations where there are multiple origins within a single Web page a user views. Multiple origins in a page can happen when that page includes frames or iframes whose origin is different from the main page and those frames make cross-site requests of their own. In RequestPolicy, we refer to such frames as *other origins*. It is not very common for a page to have other origins within it, but situations can occur where a user needs to be able to whitelist requests belonging to one of these other origins. Ultimately, we handled this case in RequestPolicy by adding a single menu item for "other origins within this page" when there are other origins. This provides access to a somewhat complex series of submenus that provides the same level of control over these other origins that a user has over the primary origin of a page. There is likely still room for improvement with this part of the user interface.

Fig. 2. The RequestPolicy menu while visiting amazon.com. No requests have been whitelisted.

5.2 •Usability vs. Correctness

Ideally, RequestPolicy should default to the highest level of privacy possible with respect to cross-site request blocking. Link clicks and form submissions are notable exceptions; allowing cross-site requests in these cases is considered to be correct behavior in terms of user intent. However, there is one important case where we decided that the usability impact of the most strict privacy settings was not a good default. This case is the way in which RequestPolicy classifies requests as same-site or cross-site.

It is very common for webpages at a given registered domain to include content from different subdomains. For example, a page may be accessed at example.com but that page includes images from www.example.com. There are also situations where many different subdomains are used to serve images and other static content for a page. This is especially common for the purpose of speeding up page load time. Browsers generally limit the number of simultaneous requests to a single host. This limit can be worked around by providing content from different hosts. The use of many subdomains within the same page is a common method of doing this. Notable sites that serve images this way include `amazon.com` and `yahoo.com`.

This situation results in a marked increase in the number of distinct blocked destinations when classifying URLs by full domain name as opposed to the registered domain name. Therefore, in order to decrease its impact on many websites, RequestPolicy defaults to using the strictness level of only the registered domain name when determining whether a request is cross-site. If a request's origin and destination have the same registered domain, the request is considered to be a same-site request and is allowed. This is also regardless of protocol and port.

There is a privacy risk with this default setting, though. Allowing all requests within a registered domain allows sites to serve ads, for example, through subdomains pointing to advertising company servers (e.g. a website makes `ads.their-domain.com` a CNAME for an advertising network). Though this technique is not commonly used [4], the potential for its increased use does exist. Having a default setting that ignores the destination port also makes RequestPolicy ineffective by default against the attacks on Tor users described in Section 1.

RequestPolicy therefore allows users to choose a stricter site classification method. Rather than using the default of the registered domain name, requests can optionally be classified as cross-site requests by either the full domain name or the combination of the protocol, domain, and port (that is, the criteria used for the "same origin policy"). This gives increased usability for the majority of users while allowing better privacy for those with greater privacy needs.

5.3   Impact on Websites

The impact that blocking cross-site requests would have on the appearance and functionality of websites was a major concern for the overall usability of Request-Policy. With RequestPolicy, we found three major ways to categorized sites according to the impact of blocked cross-site requests: those that are not noticeably impacted, those that remain functional but have moderately or drastically altered appearance, and those that do not function as expected when all cross-site requests are blocked.

Not every blocked destination from a given site generally needs to be whitelisted in order to correct the affected appearance or functionality of the site. In fact, when using RequestPolicy's default of classifying sites by registered domain name, it is often the case that at most one destination for a site needs to be whitelisted. Using the stricter classification policies, both the number of blocked destinations as well as the number of those that need to be whitelisted increases (Table 2).

Additionally, with the stricter classification policies, it can be much more difficult to know which destinations need to be allowed. This is the case even when only one destination may need to be allowed among the many blocked destinations. For example, with `www.yahoo.com`, the following domains are blocked when using the strictness level of the full domain (the specific domains may be dependent on the requesting IP address as well as other factors):

- `l.yimg.com`
- `ads.yimg.com`
- `us.il.yimg.com`
- `us.bc.yahoo.com`

The only one of those which needs to be allowed in order to have the site look and behave as expected is `l.yimg.com`. This isn't obvious, though. The only item which would intuitively be assumed to not be required is `ads.yimg.com`.

Table 2. The impact of RequestPolicy on popular websites. Impact is classified as None, Appearance (missing images, formatting), or Functionality (does not work as intended). For each site, the number of destinations needing to be whitelisted out of the total number of blocked destinations is given. This varies by classification policy: registered domain, full domain, and "same origin" (protocol, host, and port).

	Impact			Required to Whitelist		
Site	None	Appear.	Func.	Reg. domain	Full domain	Same origin
www.google.com	•			0/0	0/1	0/1
www.yahoo.com		•		1/2	1/4	1/4
www.youtube.com		•		1/2	5/6	5/6
www.youtube.com (videos)			•	2/3	2/7	2/7
www.live.com	•			0/1	0/3	0/3
www.facebook.com			•	1/1	2/2	2/2
www.msn.com		•		1/3	2/9	2/9
en.wikipedia.org		•		1/1	1/2	1/2
www.blogger.com			•	1/2	1/2	1/2
www.myspace.com			•	1/3	2/5	2/5
www.amazon.com		•		1/2	3/4	3/4

After releasing RequestPolicy to the public, general feedback indicated that the period requiring the most interaction with the whitelist menu was the initial one to two weeks of using the extension. After this period of time, most users have whitelisted the majority of cross-site requests required for proper functionality of their frequently-visited websites. In order to ease this transition into using RequestPolicy, we added a dialog window that displays after initial installation which gives users the opportunity to add common cross-site but same-organization items to their whitelist. Examples of such optional default whitelist items include requests from `wikipedia.org` to `wikimedia.org` and from `yahoo.com` to `yimg.com`. The default whitelist items are available in region-specific groups and, in total, currently offer around 100 origin-to-destination pairs as well as a single destination from any origin, `recaptcha.net`.

5.4   Policy Creep

There are two major ways a user may experience *policy creep*, where the user whitelists broader requests than they may have wanted in order to decrease the number of times they need to whitelist specific origins-to-destinations. The first of these situations is where a user visits a site and, upon finding the site does not function as desired, the user decides to whitelist all requests from that origin rather than the individual origins-to-destinations needed to make the site work properly. The user may do this, for example, because there are many blocked destinations that may be the cause of the breakage and they do not want to determine the subset of the blocked requests that need to be allowed.

The other cause of policy creep is where users may find they often need to allow requests to a certain destination in order to make sites they visit work properly. As a result, a user may decide to whitelist requests from any origin to that destination in order to avoid having to whitelist the destination from many different origins. Notable cases of many websites being dependent on cross-site requests to a small number of destinations are websites using certain Content Delivery Networks (CDNs) and hosted services. For example, this includes sites that make use of JavaScript libraries hosted by Google [23] and Yahoo [24]. In the case of Google's hosted JavaScript libraries, a RequestPolicy user with the default domain strictness settings could potentially allow requests from any site to google.com.

6   Future Work

One clear area for usability improvements within RequestPolicy involves the large number of cross-site requests that exist between sites run by the same organization. The privacy concerns of these types of cross-site requests are generally low. Blocking these types of cross-site requests is responsible for a significant amount of site breakage. The addition of optional default whitelist items lessened RequestPolicy's impact on website functionality for many popular websites. However, this form of one-time import provides no way for users to stay updated with a list of same-organization cross-site requests in their whitelist. One possible solution for this is to use a subscription model for additional whitelisting. This type of subscription model is used by extensions such as Adblock Plus [10]. However, this may add unnecessary complexity to the interface, especially in cases where users want to override their subscription's whitelist in specific cases. We intend to wait for more user feedback before deciding whether to proceed with a subscription model.

We briefly discussed the privacy risk of cross-site requests for users of anonymizing networks. However, more work needs to be done studying the impact of cross-site requests on anonymity in anonymizing networks such as Tor.

RequestPolicy's most notable privacy deficit is the usability decision to default to using only the registered domain name for determining whether a request is cross-site. Further work needs to be done to determine if the simplicity of the user interface can be maintained while defaulting to a stricter classification policy.

7   Conclusion

In this work, we explored the reasons why existing tools fail to provide a high level of privacy with respect to cross-site requests. We then used that knowledge to define the requirements for a system that does provide users full control over data leakage due to cross-site requests. Fundamentally, users need to be able to block cross-site requests by default and whitelist only those they want to allow.

Designing and implementing such a whitelist-based system brought with it serious usability concerns. We found, however, that with proper attention to user interface issues such as making blocked elements of a webpage easy to identify and whitelist, our browser extension was able to remain easy to use. Our extension, RequestPolicy, has been rapidly adopted since its release and has been downloaded thousands of times.

In the process of implementing RequestPolicy, we also discovered a lack of attention to the privacy ramifications of DNS prefetching. We added privacy protections against abuse of DNS prefetching to RequestPolicy and raised awareness of this issue.

Acknowledgments. We thank Justin Cappos, John Hartman, and Robert Hansen for their feedback and suggestions for RequestPolicy. We also thank the anonymous reviewers for their suggestions and comments. We are grateful to the Mozilla developers for providing the powerful extension architecture they have and to the many RequestPolicy users who have given us feedback.

References

1. Tor: anonymity, http://www.torproject.org/
2. Abbott, T., Lai, K., Lieberman, M., Price, E.: Browser-Based Attacks on Tor. In: Borisov, N., Golle, P. (eds.) PET 2007. LNCS, vol. 4776, pp. 184–199. Springer, Heidelberg (2007)
3. Felten, E., Schneider, M.: Timing attacks on web privacy. In: Proceedings of the 7th ACM conference on Computer and communications security, pp. 25–32. ACM, New York (2000)
4. Krishnamurthy, B., Malandrino, D., Wills, C.: Measuring privacy loss and the impact of privacy protection in web browsing. In: Proceedings of the 3rd symposium on Usable privacy and security, pp. 52–63. ACM Press, New York (2007)
5. RequestPolicy - Firefox addon for privacy and security, http://www.requestpolicy.com/
6. Privoxy, http://www.privoxy.org/
7. RefControl, http://www.stardrifter.org/refcontrol/
8. Extended Cookie Manager, http://www.defector.de/blog/category/firefox-extensions/extended-cookie-manager/
9. Karma Blocker, http://trac.arantius.com/wiki/Extensions/KarmaBlocker
10. Adblock Plus, http://adblockplus.org/
11. BlockSite - Firefox Add-ons, https://addons.mozilla.org/en-US/firefox/addon/3145

12. Psiphon, http://psiphon.ca/
13. Jackson, C., Bortz, A., Boneh, D., Mitchell, J.: Protecting browser state from web privacy attacks. In: Proceedings of the 15th international conference on World Wide Web, pp. 737–744. ACM, New York (2006)
14. Web Security Research - Alex's Corner: Attacking the SafeCache Firefox Extension,
    http://kuza55.blogspot.com/2007/02/attacking-safecache-firefox-extension.html
15. Krishnamurthy, B., Wills, C.: Generating a privacy footprint on the internet. In: Proceedings of the 6th ACM SIGCOMM conference on Internet measurement, pp. 65–70. ACM, New York (2006)
16. Krishnamurthy, B., Wills, C.E.: Privacy Diffusion on the Web: A Longitudinal Perspective. In: Proceedings of the World Wide Web Conference (2009)
17. NoScript - Firefox Add-ons,
    https://addons.mozilla.org/en-US/firefox/addon/722
18. Firefox Add-ons, https://addons.mozilla.org/
19. XPCOM, http://www.mozilla.org/projects/xpcom/
20. Google Chrome, http://www.google.com/chrome
21. Firefox 3.1 / DNS Prefetching Security Review,
    https://wiki.mozilla.org/Firefox3.1/DNS_Prefetching_Security_Review
22. Private Browsing, https://wiki.mozilla.org/PrivateBrowsing
23. Google AJAX Libraries API - Google Code,
    http://code.google.com/apis/ajaxlibs/
24. The Yahoo! User Interface Library (YUI), http://developer.yahoo.com/yui/

Enlisting ISPs to Improve Online Privacy: IP Address Mixing by Default

Barath Raghavan, Tadayoshi Kohno, Alex C. Snoeren, and David Wetherall

University of California, San Diego and University of Washington

Abstract. Today's Internet architecture makes no deliberate attempt to provide identity privacy—IP addresses are, for example, often static and the consistent use of a single IP address can leak private information to a remote party. Existing approaches for rectifying this situation and improving identity privacy fall into one of two broad classes: (1) building a privacy-enhancing overlay layer (like Tor) that can run on top of the existing Internet or (2) research into principled but often fundamentally different new architectures. We suggest a middle-ground: enlisting ISPs to assist in improving the identity privacy of users in a manner compatible with the existing Internet architecture, ISP best practices, and potential legal requirements[1].

1   Introduction

Today's Internet service providers (ISPs) log user behavior for security purposes as a matter of best common practice. Legislators have also ceased to rest on this matter. In February 2009, U.S. House Resolution 1076 was introduced. Though its purported aim is not to monitor users' online behavior, it requires that "A provider of an electronic communication service or remote computing service shall retain for a period of at least two years all records or other information pertaining to the identity of a user of a temporarily assigned network address the service assigns to that user." Combined, these trends—administrative and legislative—indicate that many or most Internet users will soon be indelibly associated with an Internet address. Equally as important are the privacy effects of ordinary Internet use. It is well-known that Internet services provide poor privacy for users. Every time users visit websites or use networked applications, they leave a trail of bread crumbs sprinkled around the Internet. These crumbs can manifest themselves in many ways, such as the IP addresses stored in the logs of a remote web server.

To improve their online privacy, some sophisticated users either choose to avoid certain activities online or choose to use special applications designed to help scramble the remote logs of their activities. As a flagship example of the latter, Tor [7] is a peer-to-peer overlay system that operates on top of the existing Internet and that is very effective at destroying these bread crumbs. Taking an

---

[1] This work was supported in part by NSF awards CNS-0722000, CNS-0722004, CNS-0722031 and the Alfred P. Sloan Foundation.

egalitarian view of the Internet, however, the principal disadvantage of Tor is that it only benefits those knowledgeable enough to know to download and run it. (There are additional barriers to the use of overlay systems like Tor, including usability and performance. For our purposes, however, these issues are important but of secondary concern.)

We propose a new perspective to improving the privacy of Internet users. Extending an observation from Dingledine and Mathewson [6] about usability, security, and privacy, we argue that users would benefit greatly if their ISPs chose to proactively assist in improving users' privacy. ISPs should be able to do this seamlessly and by default for all their users. Moreover, we wish for a privacy-enhancing approach that ISPs can deploy today, not one that must wait for some future "redesign" of the Internet.

We overcome these challenges in this paper. We show not only that it is possible to enlist ISPs to improve the base privacy of Internet users, but also that it is possible to do so efficiently and cheaply, and in a way that ISPs would actually *want* to deploy. The best analogy to our high-level goals (though not our design) is "caller-ID blocking" in traditional telephone networks. Telephone companies provide caller-ID blocking because of the value-add to consumers. Using a combination of cryptographic and systems-oriented techniques, our solution—the Address Hiding Protocol (AHP)—provides an equivalent "IP address blocking" for the Internet. Informally, the effect of IP Address Hiding is that—from the perspective of a third-party service—every flow that a client node initiates will appear to come from a different (random) IP address within the ISP's address block. One might be tempted to refer to our approach as creating a "super NAT" capable of mixing and scrambling all the IP addresses within an ISP so that they are "anonymized" from the perspective of parties within other ISPs. Such terminology, while somewhat accurate from a functionality perspective, ignores architectural complexities and design constraints that we discuss below.

Returning to our goals in the broader context of encouraging deployment, we observe that ISPs can advertise the value-add of Address Hiding for Internet users just as telephone companies advertise the value add of caller-ID blocking. However, we must overcome other challenges associated with the constraints imposed on ISPs. The first—just as for telephone networks—is that even if an ISP provides Address Hiding to external parties, the ISP must be able to associate a given network flow with a network end-point upon legal intervention (such as when presented with a warrant). As noted above, today many ISPs retain DHCP logs, and it is possible that in the near future all ISPs will be compelled to do so by law. As we shall see, this need, coupled with other architectural complexities like support for multiple ingress and egress points for a single flow and minimal space consumption, imposes challenges on our design space and is what makes our technical solutions more complex than simply deploying a large-scale NAT.

Our approach (AHP), Tor, and applications. We do *not* aim to compete with stronger, pure Internet anonymity overlay systems like Tor, but rather aim to improve the base privacy of all Internet users in a way that is compatible with the existing Internet architecture and the incentive structure for ISPs. We believe that our system thus provides the best of both worlds—if an ISP deploys our Address Hiding protocol, then the IP addresses of its users would be meaningless to third-party remote services. Thus, such an ISP will have successfully increased the privacy of all of its users from the vantage of external hosts and services. At the same time, we experimentally show that it is straightforward for Internet users to layer Tor on top of our system. We do, however, share one property with Tor and other anonymity systems: the applications (like an email or IM client) running on top of these systems can still compromise a user's privacy (for example, if the application uses cookies or sends users' login names and passwords in the clear). Providing privacy at the lowest network layer is still fundamentally valuable because it can serve as an enabling technology and is immediately useful if a user's application is also privacy preserving, such as if the user configures his or her browser to not store cookies, as offered by Safari and Firefox with "Private Browsing" mode and Explorer with "InPrivate" mode.

2   Address Hiding Goals

Consider a scenario in which a user, Alice, installs one of the latest versions of a popular browser such as Safari, Explorer, or Firefox. She reads the "new features" list and has learned of the "private browsing modes" for these browsers—modes that will (among other things) not allow cookies to be stored or will always scrub cookies upon exit. While such application-level control will improve Alice's privacy, it is fundamentally limited since the websites Alice visits will still be able to record, recognize, and profile Alice's originating IP address. Anonymity solutions, like Tor [7], can help improve Alice's anonymity but will require Alice to install a separate application package, are less usable than simply clicking a control within the browser like "Private Browsing" or "Reset Safari," may be too heavyweight for all applications, and may bring with them their own risks of surveillance by P2P exit nodes [18].

In contrast, AHP enlists ISPs to assist in improving the privacy of users like Alice by scrubbing their outgoing IP addresses. In order for AHP to have any hope of being deployed in practice, AHP must respect the forensic requirements and existing practices of ISPs—including the need to maintain identity information in compliance with legislative requirements or corporate policies. Thus, AHP strikes a balance: increased privacy in the common case when the average Internet user is interacting with webservers, but not so much privacy as to force ISPs into an awkward state of non-compliance. As we show later, users can still easily layer Tor (and other applications) on top of AHP. We elaborate on these specific goals, requirements, and assumptions below.

System requirements and goals. Informally, we have five requirements and goals: (1) hide the network-layer identity (IP address) of the two parties involved in a network flow from an outsider; (2) prevent the correlation of any two network flows between the same two parties by an outsider through network or transport-layer information; (3) for legal compliance and compatibility with existing practices, enable high-speed, long-term forensic attributability of packets without onerous storage or bandwidth requirements on the part of the ISP; (4) ensure that AHP is compatible with popular network applications and that it composes well with existing anonymity systems (such as Tor); (5) require no modifications to the client applications participating in traditional client-server communications.

Trust. We begin with the assumption that we trust the ISP, as users already do today; i.e., we do not introduce new trust assumptions so users are no worse off than they are today[2]. AHP is a protocol implemented in the network by a trusted provider. The network provider can log all network traffic, and moreover, all address mappings, thereby enabling it to revoke client-side address privacy for network administration. Indeed, once we place trust in the ISP to perform address hiding, there is little incentive for it to *not* hide its customers' addresses to outsiders. Any system that does not concede this ability to network providers is unlikely to be deployed.

Types of attackers. Beyond the trust relationship required with the service provider, our threat model is straightforward. We divide the path a flow traverses into three components, with the end two pieces of the path within the client's and the server's network provider domains respectively. We consider two types of attacker: the insider and the outsider. The insider is an attacker within a trusted network provider's domain that is capable of sniffing and/or injecting packets; for example, an insider (from the perspective of a client) might be a server with which it is communicating or a neighboring host that can sniff packets, provided that the server or host are within the same ISP's network. An outsider is a transit provider between the client and server networks.

Space- and time-efficient forensic support. To comply with deployment constraints, we wish to enable an ISP to recover the true source of any packet that was hidden by one of its AHP gateways, thereby ensuring that all packets are attributable to their sender. A naive solution for attributable address hiding would require the storage of an ever-growing table of source-to-public-flow-identifier mappings on the order of several gigabytes per day per router for a large ISP. Our aim is to support attribution regardless of how far in the past the packet was sent with minimal state stored at the ISP.

Compatibility and composability. ISPs are unlikely to deploy any system that breaks popular network applications in the process; backward-compatibility is crucial. In Appendix A we present a case study of several common user applications—including Firefox, Tor, and BitTorrent—while using our proto-type of AHP. AHP provides network-layer IP address privacy. However, some users will wish to use anonymity systems, which are more heavyweight but also have broader aims and stronger guarantees. We believe it is essential that AHP not decrease the options a user has to protect her privacy, and thus, we design AHP to be composable with existing systems such as Tor.

---

[2] Those users who do not trust their ISP can and do use anonymity systems such as Tor; we aim for defense in depth, so such users can continue using Tor.

Non-goals. While AHP is designed to improve users' privacy, we do not aim to provide "anonymity" in the usual sense. More generally, we enumerate several non-goals that inform our design—that is, goals that we do not seek to achieve: (1) to prevent insider attacks, regardless of outsider cooperation; (2) to prevent attacks that involve application-layer payloads; (3) to prevent timing or other side-channel attacks; (4) to provide data privacy or authenticity; (5) to provide privacy for dedicated server hosts; (6) to support per-flow privacy for non-TCP transport protocols.

Summary. This specific collection of non-goals, as well as the earlier goals, were chosen to be supportive of the example applications such as the one we mentioned earlier, as well as the needs of ISPs. As Dingledine and Mathewson [6] noted, users would benefit greatly if their ISPs chose to proactively assist in improving users' privacy, and our goal is to instantiate their vision. Power users can, however, continue to layer stronger mechanisms like Tor on top of AHP.

3   Measurement Study: Your ISP Is Crowded

Privacy researchers have long held that identity privacy can only be provided by hiding within a "crowd" of other users [26]. When an adversary cannot distinguish between the members of the crowd, each member of the crowd's privacy is preserved. The larger the crowd, the better the privacy. In the past, researchers have designed systems to artificially induce a crowd of privacy-seeking users, typically through an overlay network. Then, by measuring the size and properties of the induced crowd, we can ask "how much privacy does the induced crowd provide?" This approach has yielded many fruitful results in the anonymity research literature.

In this paper, we learn from the crowd-based approach and apply it to the new research area at hand. Specifically, since we aim to raise the privacy bar across the board for users of an ISP, we ask: "how much privacy can we provide by default?" The answer to this question comes in two parts. First, we must determine whether an appropriate crowd exists in the Internet today. Second, we must design a system to leverage this crowd appropriately. In this section we address the first part, and show that **ISPs are already crowds** of sufficient size to provide privacy given an appropriate system design. Our key observation is that each IP address prefix provides a "crowd" of addresses within which we can provide identity privacy[3]. Thus, the requirement is simply that the system multiplex the hosts within that address space across the available addresses in a manner that is opaque to an outside party.

---

[3] The Internet's routing system today is structured hierarchically, with so-called "Tier-1" ISPs at the top of the hierarchy—such ISPs have complete routing information for all valid destinations in the Internet. Other ISPs and networks attach to these Tier-1 ISPs to perform routing. Each ISP or network is assigned one or more IP address blocks or "prefixes" within which it can assign public addresses for its hosts. These prefixes are publicly announced to other networks via the Border Gateway Protocol (BGP).

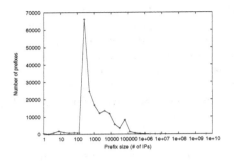 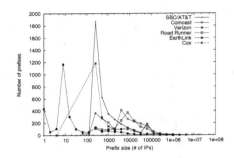

(a) Prefix size distribution for ASes in   (b) Prefix size distribution for 6 largest
the RouteViews BGP feed   ISPs

Fig. 1. Address block sizes in the Internet

Since we wish to understand how much potential for privacy already exists in today's Internet, we first need to look at where the potential crowd comes from. The Internet consists of numerous Autonomous Systems (ASes)—each of which is typically an ISP or large organization—that route traffic to each other. An AS contains thousands or millions of hosts, each of which is typically assigned an IP address. Although routing protocols operate on the level of ASes, packet forwarding operates on the level of IP addresses—each packet must name both a source and a destination IP. As such, each packet identifies a host, which is a crowd of size one. What if we view each AS or ISP as a crowd within which outside parties cannot peek? Each ISP controls some portion of the Internet's address space; an ISP can provide the required opaqueness by obfuscating packets' source addresses as they traverse the network boundary to the outside Internet.

Thus, our challenge is to understand the size of crowds that are possible when hiding hosts within existing ISP address spaces. To this end, we examine the BGP routing advertisements as seen by RouteViews on Sept. 7, 2007 [19][4]. As a baseline, Figure 1(a) shows the size distribution of all advertised IP prefixes; we can see quite clearly that many prefixes are small—on the order of a few thousand addresses at most. The most prevalent prefix size advertised is /24, few prefixes that are advertised are smaller than that. Thus it appears that prefixes as advertised today provide insufficiently large crowd size.

However, the deployment of AHP is of most value in larger ISPs, within which there is both more room to hide and perhaps more commercial incentive for deployment. To explore such a scenario, we examine in Figure 1(b) the sizes of address space advertisements for the six largest consumer ISPs—SBC/AT&T, Comcast, Verizon, Road Runner, EarthLink, and Cox[5]. The results show that many small prefixes are being advertised even in these large ISPs. However,

---

[4] The specific date has no special significance and is simply a snapshot of route advertisements taken at the time of our analysis.

[5] We isolate the advertisements for these ISPs by searching the text identifiers of the IANA AS number allocations for these ISPs' common names.

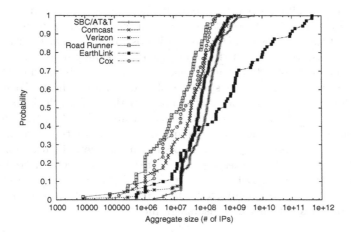

Fig. 2. Size of crowds if ISPs were to aggregate based upon physical location; CDFs of the size of the aggregated crowds (log scale) based upon BGP advertisements from RouteViews

upon aggregation, many of these small prefixes are subsumed. ISPs have an interest in advertising larger address blocks, if for no other reason than to reduce management overhead and reduce routing table sizes. With small prefixes comes greater routing flexibility. These two factors are in tension. However, prefixes can be reasonably aggregated together if they originate from the same geographic region; this is aided by the network structure of large ISPs, which have points of presence (PoPs) in most major cities.

To discover how much potential there is for such geographic aggregation, we used the Oasis [9] and NetGeo [20] geolocation services to map all the IP prefixes of the six ISPs above and aggregated them based upon location. Many IP prefixes map to the same location, likely indicating that they originate from the same PoP. This approach is not perfect, as the services contain necessarily incomplete and inaccurate data; about 15% of the prefixes were unmappable, and we omit them since we are interested in the potential for large aggregates, not small aggregates. Thus, our results represent a lower bound on the aggregation possible within the studied ISPs. Figure 2 shows CDFs of the aggregated address spaces with prefixes aggregated if they mapped to the same physical location irrespective of numerical proximity. We immediately see that address spaces that are geographically close have great potential for aggregation on those grounds. While in the scope of the Internet's address space a million addresses is relatively small, such a space is likely ample for hiding[6]. For example, 50% of Road Runner crowds (that is, 50% of prefixes) would contain over ten million IPs if aggregated by location; 50% of Earthlink crowds would contain over 100 million IPs.

---

[6] We leave open the question of when and where from an ISP traffic engineering perspective it is appropriate to actually perform such aggregation among geographically-proximate IP prefixes.

Since address hiding is a fundamentally different service than mix-net style anonymity systems, direct comparisons of the sizes of IP prefixes to that of anonymity sets is not possible. However, it is possible to look at the raw numbers for other systems, to check that the values are in the same range. Tor is estimated to have on the order of 200,000 active users. Architecturally, each of these users appears the same from the perspective of a destination host. To consider a parallel concept—what level of identifiability in the real world is acceptable— we can look at the Census. The U.S. Census Bureau has long had policies to enable meaningful extraction of demographic data from the decennial census while still maintain a level of privacy for people in the queried data sets. As of last year, different microdata queries with the Census Bureau were limited to return data for population groups of at least 10,000 and, for another dataset, 100,000 individuals. Thus we are comforted that ISPs can easily advertise 1,000,000 address IP prefixes within which users can hide.

4   A Cryptographic Approach to ISP Crowds

AHP's design is realized in two parts, one at the ISP gateway, and an *optional* component on the client. An ISP can unilaterally deploy AHP-capable gateways, thereby enabling its clients to immediately benefit from deployment. Importantly, with AHP, ISPs can provide the benefit of client-side privacy to their users even in the absence of any explicit client support for it. The client-side component of AHP is required only to support peer-to-peer and server applications; it does not affect application-level protocols, and thus supports both legacy clients and servers.

We wish to protect users from having their applications inadvertently reveal their identity. Thus, AHP must be transparent to ordinary client-server applications and must maintain privacy. Some user applications, such as peer-to-peer programs, require the ability to support both outgoing and incoming connections. Because incoming connections generally require an externally routable IP address, AHP allows applications to request a temporary, but fixed inbound identifier at which external hosts can contact them. We denote one-time only addresses as hidden addresses and denote sticky addresses to be those that can be reached by many parties from the outside. Internal to the ISP, we assign each host two addresses, a default hidden one with which to communicate with full privacy, and a sticky one that provides a stable external identifier that can be contacted by multiple hosts via multiple flows. In our design, applications must explicitly request use of the sticky address.

4.1   Design Overview

While there are numerous challenges that we faced in the design of AHP—such as the need to handle multiple ingress and egress points and the need to minimize the amount of data stored for forensic purposes—the high-level design of the AHP gateway is both simple and efficient. Each outgoing packet's IP address

Table 1. A summary of AHP design components and mechanisms

Goal	Mechanism	Description	§
Secure default	hidden and sticky	Each host is assigned two addresses; the default is strictly-hidden (hidden), the other partially-exposed (sticky)	4.2
Address hiding	Tweakable block cipher	Efficient permutation of local IP/port into public IP/port given private key and public destination IP/port	4.3
Long-lived flow support	Collision detection	Prevents two flows of different epochs from mapping to the same public IP/port	4.3
Birthday attack prevention	Key rotation	AHP gateway changes its block cipher key per epoch to prevent repeat flow transformations	4.3
Forensic support	Time-based keys	Epoch keys selected during key rotation are derived from a master key based on the time, and can be regenerated later	4.3
Inbound flow support	sticky mode	Enables hosts behind an AHP gateway to request semi-permanent public addresses to accept inbound connections	4.4
Backward compatibility	expose wrapper	Wraps unmodified applications to enable their use of sticky mode to allow inbound connections from remote hosts	4.4

(host portion only)/port is encrypted. Encryption on short values, such as 16 bits of an address, is non-trivial; these and other challenges lead us to selecting a short-domain tweakable block cipher. The key used in this process is rotated over time, mitigating birthday attacks and ensuring that the permutation can be reproduced at a later time—this is crucial not only for forensic support, but to support multiple ingress and egress routers within an ISP.

Most large ISPs have many routers through which packets can enter and leave the network. Due to asymmetry of routes, a flow's outbound packets may traverse a different router than its inbound packets. A non-keyed, NAT-like solution would require constant, real-time replication of flow-table state between all participating routers in the ISP—clearly an onerous process. While we omit a full concept of multi-ingress/egress support using AHP, our approach is straightforward—all participating routers simply use the same keyed permutation and exchange small amounts of information every few hours to keep their state in sync.

When presented with packets from a hidden address, the gateway performs a full hiding operation, which includes transforming the IP/port into a different public IP/port for every distinct destination. However, when presented with packets from a sticky address, the gateway performs the transformation solely based upon the internal IP/port pair and not the destination IP/port pair, so as to maintain a consistent public IP/port to which remote hosts can connect and communicate[7]. Next we delve deeper into the details of our implementation, both abstractly and as it pertains to our software prototype. Table 1 provides a summary of several AHP design components and mechanisms described below, and hints at some of the challenges that our design overcomes.

---

[7] We must note, however, that providing sticky addresses is not without consequences. Any system that provides pseudo-permanent identifiers like our sticky addresses may inadvertently reveal at the client-side the destination of packets through correlated inbound flows. Most modern NATs enable hosts to register ports to be forwarded, but a NAT's goal is not to ensure identity privacy. In our context, to fully understand the impact sticky addresses and peer to peer applications when used with AHP, we hope to study a real deployment of AHP within a small ISP.

4.2   Address Partitioning

To preserve privilege separation, all hosts within the local routing domain receive two addresses for routing within the ISP: a hidden address and a sticky address. A hidden address can be converted into a sticky address and vice versa by flipping the high order bit of a /8 address. hidden addresses reside in 10.128.0.0/9 and sticky addresses reside in 10.0.0.0/9[8]. The hidden address is assigned to the default network interface on the user's host, thereby ensuring that network communication is private by default. The ISP will scramble hidden and sticky addresses when communicating with hosts outside of the ISP.

4.3   Handling Traditional Client Applications: hidden Mode

In hidden mode, when using client-server applications, there are no perceptible changes required by the client. Since each host's hidden address is its default, all programs that do not explicitly specify an interface will bind to it and use it for outgoing TCP connection requests. sticky addresses are not even needed for such applications, so no changes need to be made on the host. Thus AHP requires no modifications to web applications like Firefox and Safari or even Tor clients.

Address hiding. Similar to a NAT, we aim to translate addresses. However, our fundamental design constraint is that we provide forensic support. Given the large storage requirements to store a NAT's flow tables over a long history, the challenge we face is to translate hidden addresses deterministically by permuting the hidden address and the TCP source port. To improve privacy and ensure that no two flows from the same source can be correlated, we must base the permutation not just on a private key, but on the destination IP and port.

We find that the primitive that meets this challenge is the tweakable block cipher [17]. Given a public "tweak" t and a private key k (known only to the gateway router), we can instantiate a tweakable block cipher $E_{k,t}(M) = F_k(M \oplus H(t)) \oplus H(t)$, where F is an underlying block cipher and H is a cryptographic hash function. In our prototype, we instantiate the block cipher F using 20-round RC5 with a 16-bit word length (producing a 32-bit block length) and instantiate H with SHA-1[9]. In our discussion, we restrict the space of hidden addresses to 10.128.0.0/16; we also discuss address spaces and hiding sets in Appendix B. Used in this manner, $E(\cdot)$ yields a secure PRP keyed on the private key k that is held by the AHP gateway and by the public data t that—in the manner of tweakable block ciphers—selects the particular PRP family that the key operates with. The operation amounts to a single-block encryption, and

---

[8] In our implementation, we assume that all local addresses are assigned from within the 10.0.0.0/8 address block, which is officially reserved as a block of private-network IP addresses. Note that this assumption holds even when the externally advertised prefix is small, e.g., a /24 or smaller.

[9] Cryptanalysis has proved effective against lower-round variants of RC5; in addition, any block cipher with only a 32-bit block width is potentially vulnerable to birthday attacks. We mitigate these potential issues via key rotation, as we discuss later.

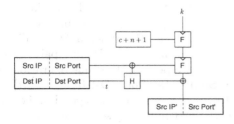

Fig. 3. The concrete instantiation of AHP. The final result, (Src IP', Src Port') replaces the original source IP and Port pair.

Table 2. Summary of findings from trace-based simulation of flow collisions

Quantity	Value
Duration	30000s
Total number of flows	8960585
Largest epoch current flowset	227489
Largest epoch old flowset	3062
Total number of collisions	120511
Total number of old-flow collisions	582

requires no authentication (say, with an appended MAC) because tampering of the packet header will necessarily cause misrouting of the packet by the routing system. We apply the tweakable block cipher $E(\cdot)$ as shown in Figure 3: we refer to this as the Hide operation. We store the host portion of the hidden address in the high-order two bytes of a four-byte block b, and store the TCP source port in the low-order two bytes. We compute the tweak t using the same approach, except that we use the entire destination address and port, yielding a six-byte tweak. We apply $E_{k,t}(b)$ and replace host portion of the hidden address with the two high-order bytes of the result and similarly replace the port with the two low-order bytes. Finally, we replace the network portion of the hidden address with that of the public IP prefix, and forward the packet.

While our description suffices to explain how ordinary data packets are sent, there are several issues that arise with this basic design. First, to ensure long-term security from birthday attacks, the gateway must rotate keys. Second, since each permutation (created by $E(\cdot)$) is independent, collisions in the public IP/port space will occur between flows hidden with different keys. As we describe next, these two issues must be resolved simultaneously. A separate issue is that we must be able to handle multiple ingress and egress points; handling such ingress and egress points is technically straightforward given our solutions to the above two challenges, which is not surpising since we iterated on this goal in combination with the first two issues mentioned above. We do not detail our somewhat involved design for handling multiple ingress/egress points, however it may prove to be a useful extension for a real deployment in a large ISP.

Overcoming challenges of long-lived flows. Key rotation presents a fundamental challenge: since no bits introduced by the AHP gateway can persist solely in packet state over the lifetime of a flow, there is no way to tag packets within a flow with their time of birth (which would indicate which key to use for the flow). Instead, we must associate a flow with a key without packet state or per-flow state at the gateway. We achieve this by maintaining sets that associate packets with the keys that are used for their translation—each key corresponds to its *epoch*. We maintain a set of sets, $(S_1, \ldots, S_n)$ each associated with a counter designating its epoch number, $(c, \ldots, c+n-1)$ for some value c[10]. The last element of each of these sets is $(S_n, c+n-1)$. When a TCP SYN packet arrives, our goal is to ensure that the resulting public IP/port pair are not already in use by another flow. To this end, we perform the Hide operation on the outgoing packet and search for the (Src IP', Src Port', Dst IP, Dst Port) in the sets beginning with S_1 proceeding to S_n. We use the corresponding key to translate the flow and stop the search at the first matching set. If there is no match, we insert it into the "current" set. If there is a match, we send a TCP RST to the client, forcing it to attempt to reconnect. While this solution is somewhat complex, most network applications are designed to be robust to temporary outages; we evaluate the frequency of matches in the next section. When a TCP RST or TCP FIN packet arrives, we perform the same search for the matching set, but perform a set remove operation of the flow. Maintaining sets of each key's associated flows requires flow state within each epoch; in Section 5 we study the memory requirements of these flow sets.

Avoiding birthday attacks. To ensure that two flows with the same flow ID do not translate the same twice, we must rotate keys at the AHP gateway over a fixed time period—an *epoch*. The lifetime of each key is determined based on the privacy guarantees we wish to provide. For each existing set S_i, we create a parallel set S_i' and, for some constant time window (say, five minutes), we insert any active flows that match S_i into S_i'. After the time window expires, we shift all counters and sets down by one, and replace them each with their parallel sets that only contain currently active flows. We add all flows present in the oldest set S_1 into a per-flow table of very long-lived flows, indexed by their destination IP/port. Finally, we clear the newest set and increment its counter, thereby changing the current key.

Epoch key selection. By deriving epoch keys from a master key and the current epoch counter, we avoid having to store all epoch keys. Thus, if needed for forensics, we can easily regenerate the key for any particular epoch. The current key, k_{c+n-1}, is derived from the master key k using AES as a PRF, $k_{c+n-1} \leftarrow F_k(c+n-1)$. ($c$ increments every epoch; n is the number of sets used for collision detection.)

Multiple ingress and egress points. AHP's design extension to support multiple ingress/egress points ensures that large ISPs that have asymmetric routes can still use AHP. We can ensure that each router increments its epoch counter at the same time via ordinary ntp time synchronization. At the end of each epoch, all routers responsible for a given IP prefix merge their parallel sets S_i'. This ensures that the flow state at these routers is synchronized, thereby avoiding collisions upon flow arrival.

---

[10] Here we present the conceptual model; in practice, set of sets is circular, and only requires the low value, c, rather than the entire set of counters.

4.4   Handling Peer-to-Peer Applications: sticky Mode

Moving beyond client-only applications poses a new challenge—enabling applications to reserve public IP/port pairs to receive incoming connections as is necessary to support P2P applications like BitTorrent. Since the available address and port space must be shared with that of hidden mode connections, we must change our mechanism to ensure that the two modes operate harmoniously.

As we have discussed, when in sticky mode, two fundamental changes in behavior occur. First, since sticky mode entails a publicly addressable IP/port pair, the external address for a host does not change based upon the remote IP or port. Second, for the gateway to know to reserve an IP/port pair, the user application must make an explicit request; we provide a wrapper that makes these requests on behalf of unmodified client applications. Since an explicit mapping must be made, the gateway behaves like a NAT. However, to avoid having to store the mappings for forensics, we select the mappings in a manner similar to in hidden mode.

sticky **wrapper library.** Unlike ordinary client applications, peer-to-peer applications require inbound connection support. Thus, we provide a wrapper script, expose, that uses library interposition in Unix (via LD_PRELOAD) to intercept specific system calls that require special handling in sticky mode[11]. Changing the gateway to support reservation of sticky addresses is straightforward. The primary cause for concern is that sticky addresses will collide with hidden addresses. To avoid this, we add a smaller, parallel group of flow sets to pre-test incoming packets: any that match the sticky sets are translated in the same manner as hidden addresses, except that the gateway uses a constant (0) as the tweak value, and in doing so ensures that the sticky address maps to the same sticky address for all incoming flows, regardless of origin IP or port.

---

[11] Specifically, bind() and getsockname() both require modification. With bind(), our main task is to explicitly select the sticky interface on the host in the sin_addr field. However, before returning to the application from the library, but after the local bind() call, we make a request via a single UDP packet to the gateway to reserve a sticky IP/port pair. In the UDP request is the local IP and port assigned by the real bind() call, as retrieved via the real getsockname() call. If the library does not receive an affirmative response containing the socket's sticky address and port within a timeout (currently 500ms), the library returns -1 and sets errno to EADDRINUSE. If the library receives an affirmative response from the gateway, it returns 0. To ensure that peer to peer applications that wish to announce their presence can do so, we intercept getsockname(). If the gateway allowed the allocation of a sticky address, then we possess the socket's externally-visible IP address/port combination, and return it to the application. When the application calls listen(), we acknowledge the setup of the sticky address in a second UDP packet to the gateway; the packet serves a similar purpose to a DHCP lease, and must be renewed periodically (we do not implement periodic renewal; how often to renew is a matter of policy) to maintain the public address. In addition, we add the socket to a table of active server sockets. Finally, when the application calls accept(), we return the result of the real accept() call, but also add the newly returned socket to the list of sockets with the given sticky address.

5   Analysis

We have already analyzed several aspects of AHP's security in-line in Section 4. In addition we study specific aspects of AHP's design—including collision likelihood and forwarding performance—that warrant further exploration. We consider the length of the key rotation interval in Appendix C.

5.1   Forwarding Performance

Any in-network system such as AHP must be capable of high line rates. While we expect that a real deployment would involve a hardware implementation of the AHP gateway, we measured our software prototype as an indication of the efficiency of the design itself. Our prototype of AHP runs as a daemon process under Linux 2.6 and handles all AHP gateway functionality. The prototype captures packets using superuser-specified IPTables rules that divert packets to the daemon via userspace queueing. Packets are then translated appropriately and transmitted via a raw socket. The prototype supports configuration of the size of the IP prefix in question, of its memory usage, and of its key rotation interval.

We forwarded data via an ordinary TCP socket from a host to itself over the system's loopback network interface, to test the performance of the core of the algorithm. We perform the test on a 1-Ghz Pentium M laptop running Linux 2.6.22. We find, not surprisingly, that other packet handling costs are greater than the cost of AHP's processing, and thus, as the packet size increases, so does the forwarding rate. At its peak, the system forwards at 408 Mbps. We find that although our AHP gateway is somewhat slower than native Linux forwarding, which peaks at 506 Mbps on the same hardware, the precise forwarding rates themselves are not of primary importance, since the overhead of AHP processing is a fixed per-packet cost that is small relative to other overheads.

5.2   Collisions

In the operation of an AHP gateway, "collisions" can occur wherein two distinct local IP/port tuples going to different IP/port tuples are mapped to the same external IP/port tuple. Since tweakable block ciphers represent a family of permutations parametrized by both the tweak and the key, key rotation yields a different, specific permutation that may collide with mappings under past or future keys. Here, the collision probability is governed not by the birthday paradox, as arriving flows with the same key cannot collide with one another. We compute the likelihood of collision as follows: the collision of a newly arriving flow is related only to the number of flows that exist in the flow sets for old keys. Thus, by selecting an appropriate key rotation interval—one that balances privacy and collisions—the problem can be mitigated. A recent study by Lee and Brownlee [14] indicates that only about 10% of flows last over ten seconds, and the fraction that lasts for 1,000 seconds is vanishingly small—less than 0.1%. Assuming a key rotation period of 1,000 seconds, which is well under that which is needed for maintaining key rotation privacy (indeed, with a 1,000-second key-rotation period, the probability of a birthday collision of the local port on a host is less than 0.003), less than 0.1% of flows will remain in flow sets for old keys. Assuming these flows all remain for a long time (conservatively, one day), and the gateway services ten million flows per day, that yields, conservatively, 10,000 old flows. Given a /16 IP prefix, the space of possible address/port pairs is roughly 2^{32}, and thus the probability that any single flow arrival will collide with an old flow is 2.3×10^{-6}, which we believe to be small enough for practical purposes—about one out of every half-million flows will collide.

To rest our analysis upon firmer ground, we perform a trace-based simulation of collision rates. Our goal is to better understand the collision probability that governs the rate of TCP RSTs being sent to hosts. We use a real day-long cross-Pacific trace from March 3, 2006 of a 100-Mbps backbone link provided by the Japanese WIDE project [33]. A summary of our results is shown in Table 2. While the sources and destinations of the packets in the trace are not all from one particular ISP or IP prefix, we use the trace to get a better understanding of not only how many flows occur over the one-day period, but also how many persist long enough that they would have caused collisions if they had been hidden by an AHP gateway. We begin our trace-based simulation by preprocessing the input trace: since we have 32-bits of IP address and 16-bits of port for each packet source by hashing them together to produce a single 32-bit identifier for them. (This preprocessing step may cause extra collisions that would not occur in practice, which will mean our results are on the safe-side.) After this step, we apply our ordinary AHP address hiding to the resulting packet headers and store them appropriately in their flow sets. We rotate keys every 300 seconds and use a 30-second grace period before rotation; we did not carefully choose these durations, but found the results were not sensitive to them. We use only two sets—a current flow set and a recent flow set. We keep an exact old-flow set for those flows that last more than two rotations (600 seconds).

What we find, as shown in Table 2, is that since the vast majority of flows are short-lived, the tables for older flows do not gather many flows, and remain small over time. As a result, the collision rate (and thus, the RST rate) is low. However, we were initially puzzled that the collision rate was even as high as it was. Upon careful examination of the packet traces, we found that the vast majority of the collisions in our count appear to be due to TCP SYN flood attacks—if such a packet is unlucky enough to collide once, then each duplicate SYN in the flood similarly collides[12]. Legitimate senders, on the other hand, do not send many duplicate SYNs for each flow.

6   Related Work

AHP belongs to a different class of privacy-preserving network protocols, but resembles prior protocols designed to provide anonymity. We note some of the

---

[12] We did not exactly quantify the impact of SYN floods on the collision rate, since there were several cases in which it was ambiguous whether a series of packets constituted an attack.

key works here, but defer to Danezis and Diaz's detailed survey of the extensive research in anonymity [4]. Prior work can be broadly classified as belonging either to *anonymity* research or *new Internet architectures*. Since Chaum's seminal work, many researchers have developed re-routing based anonymity systems, including Crowds [26], Freedom [34], Tor [7], Tarzan [10], GAP/GNUnet [2], Herbivore [30], P5 [28], Hordes [16], Slicing [13], and JAP [12]. Over time, researchers have developed attacks of ever-increasing sophistication, involving techniques such as timing analysis [15,27,29] and broad spectrum traffic analysis [22,25], and have found weaknesses in systems designed to enable forensic support [5]. From a design perspective, AHP bears closest resemblance to CPP, a system that hierarchically encrypts IPv6 addresses to obtain privacy [32], and Anonymizer [1] and Proxify [24], which provide commercial application-level anonymization proxying. However, the design goals of AHP are different; critically, AHP is easily composable with other anonymity systems (including Anonymizer.com and Proxify) and operates at the network layer. As a result of our different goals, the architecture AHP differs significantly from that of either of these commercial services. While not designed explicitly with anonymity or address hiding in mind, a separate thread of research in the networking community lends itself to address hiding. In particular, four projects—IPnl [8], ROFL [3], HIP [21], and i3 [31]—describe fundamentally new Internet architectures that could accommodate additions to provide AHP-like functionality.

7   Conclusions

Today's Internet does not adequately protect the privacy of users. Indeed, even with strong end-to-end cryptographic mechanisms like SSL and the emergence of privacy controls within applications, such as the private browsing modes of Safari and Firefox, the Internet architecture—almost by definition—violates the privacy of Internet users by assigning unique identifiers (IP addresses) to users' machines. Dingledine and Mathewson's [6] observation—that a little bit of anonymity for everyone by default is valuable—captures the essence of the goal in this research, while also striving for a system that is is both incrementally deployable *and* appropriately incentivized for those responsible for deployment: ISPs. If our approach were adopted, the privacy of network communications would not be decreased from that to today's, even *if* ISPs chose to invoke AHP's forensic capabilities—and indeed users could layer Tor or other stronger mechanisms on top of AHP. In addition, we argue that the average Internet user's privacy would be improved by AHP. Our results show that today's ISPs can be treated as a crowd to provide users identity privacy. Our prototype shows that AHP induces negligible overhead. In addition to benchmarks, we ran ordinary Internet applications as case studies—Firefox, BitTorrent, and Tor—on top of AHP and anecdotally observed no negative impact. We believe that AHP could be integrated into existing ISP infrastructures, and is appropriately incentivized with forensic capabilities for regulatory and policy compliance, high performance, and the ability to provide address hiding as a service to one's customers.

References

1. Anonymizer, http://www.anonymizer.com/
2. Bennett, K., Grothoff, C.: Gap – practical anonymous networking. In: Proceedings of Workshop on Privacy Enhancing Technologies (2003)
3. Caesar, M., Condie, T., Kannan, J., Lakshminarayanan, K., Stoica, I.: ROFL: routing on flat labels. In: Proceedings of ACM SIGCOMM (2006)
4. Danezis, G., Diaz, C.: A survey of anonymous communication channels. Technical Report MSR-TR-2008-35, Microsoft Research (January 2008)
5. Danezis, G., Sassaman, L.: How to bypass two anonymity revocation schemes. In: Borisov, N., Goldberg, I. (eds.) PETS 2008. LNCS, vol. 5134, pp. 187–201. Springer, Heidelberg (2008)
6. Dingledine, R., Mathewson, N.: Anonymity loves company: Usability and the network effect. In: Proceedings of WEIS (2006)
7. Dingledine, R., Mathewson, N., Syverson, P.: Tor: The second-generation onion router. In: Proceedings of the USENIX Security Symposium (2004)
8. Francis, P., Gummadi, R.: IPNL: A nat-extended internet architecture. In: Proceedings of ACM SIGCOMM (2001)
9. Freedman, M.J., Lakshminarayanan, K., Mazières, D.: OASIS: Anycast for any service. In: Proceedings of USENIX/ACM NSDI (2006)
10. Freedman, M.J., Morris, R.: Tarzan: a peer-to-peer anonymizing network layer. In: Proceedings of ACM CCS (2002)
11. Granboulan, L., Pornin, T.: Perfect block ciphers with small blocks. In: Biryukov, A. (ed.) FSE 2007. LNCS, vol. 4593, pp. 452–465. Springer, Heidelberg (2007)
12. Java Anon Proxy, http://anon.inf.tu-dresden.de/
13. Katti, S., Cohen, J., Katabi, D.: Information slicing: Anonymity using unreliable overlays. In: Proceedings of USENIX NSDI (2007)
14. Lee, D., Brownlee, N.: Passive measurement of one-way and two-way flow lifetimes. SIGCOMM Comput. Commun. Rev. 37(3) (2007)
15. Levine, B.N., Reiter, M.K., Wang, C., Wright, M.K.: Timing attacks in low-latency mix-based systems. In: Juels, A. (ed.) FC 2004. LNCS, vol. 3110, pp. 251–265. Springer, Heidelberg (2004)
16. Levine, B.N., Shields, C.: Hordes — A Multicast Based Protocol for Anonymity. Journal of Computer Security 10(3) (2002)
17. Liskov, M., Rivest, R.L., Wagner, D.: Tweakable block ciphers. In: Yung, M. (ed.) CRYPTO 2002. LNCS, vol. 2442, p. 31. Springer, Heidelberg (2002)
18. McCoy, D., Bauer, K., Grunwald, D., Kohno, T., Sicker, D.: Shining light in dark places: Understanding the Tor network. In: Borisov, N., Goldberg, I. (eds.) PETS 2008. LNCS, vol. 5134, pp. 63–76. Springer, Heidelberg (2008)
19. Meyer, D.: Route Views Project. http://antc.uoregon.edu/route-views
20. Moore, D., Periakaruppan, R., Donohoe, J., Claffy, K.: Where in the world is netgeo. caida.org? In: Proceedings of INET (2000)
21. Moskowitz, R.: Host identity payload. Internet Draft, IETF (Feburary 2001), draft-moskowitz-hip-arch-02.txt (expired)
22. Murdoch, S.J., Danezis, G.: Low-cost traffic analysis of tor. In: Proceedings of the IEEE Symposium on Security and Privacy, pp. 183–195 (2005)
23. Privoxy, http://www.privoxy.org/
24. Proxify, http://proxify.com/
25. Raymond, J.-F.: Traffic analysis: Protocols, attacks, design issues and open problems. In: Federrath, H. (ed.) Designing Privacy Enhancing Technologies. LNCS, vol. 2009, pp. 10–29. Springer, Heidelberg (2001)

26. Reiter, M.K., Rubin, A.D.: Anonymous web transactions with crowds. Commun. ACM 42(2), 32–48 (1999)
27. Serjantov, A., Sewell, P.: Passive attack analysis for connection-based anonymity systems. In: Snekkenes, E., Gollmann, D. (eds.) ESORICS 2003. LNCS, vol. 2808, pp. 116–131. Springer, Heidelberg (2003)
28. Sherwood, R., Bhattacharjee, B.: P5: A protocol for scalable anonymous communication. In: Proceedings of IEEE Symposium on Security and Privacy (2002)
29. Shmatikov, V., Wang, M.-H.: Timing analysis in low-latency mix networks: Attacks and defenses. In: Gollmann, D., Meier, J., Sabelfeld, A. (eds.) ESORICS 2006. LNCS, vol. 4189, pp. 18–33. Springer, Heidelberg (2006)
30. Sirer, E.G., Goel, S., Robson, M., Engin, D.: Eluding carnivores: file sharing with strong anonymity. In: Proceedings of the ACM SIGOPS European workshop (2004)
31. Stoica, I., Adkins, D., Zhuang, S., Shenker, S., Surana, S.: Internet indirection infrastructure. In: Proceedings of ACM SIGCOMM (2002)
32. Trostle, J., Way, B., Matsuoka, H., Tariq, M.M.B., Kempf, J., Kawahara, T., Jain, R.: Cryptographically protected prefixes for location privacy in ipv6. In: Proceedings of the Privacy Enhancing Technologies Symposium (2004)
33. WIDE Project, http://www.wide.ad.jp/
34. Zero Knowledge Systems Freedom Network, http://www.zks.net/

A   Case Studies

In this section, we briefly discuss the use of AHP with common applications, and in post-hoc forensic analysis. To provide anecdotal evidence that use of AHP presents no user-perceived changes in application behavior or performance degradation, one of the authors of this paper spent an afternoon using several ordinary applications that were on a network segment behind our prototype AHP gateway. We used several typical network applications—Mozilla Firefox, BitTorrent, SSH, and XChat—and an existing anonymity system—Tor[13].

Firefox and XChat. Firefox ran normally, as did XChat—both only open ordinary HTTP connections and perform DNS queries, which are translated properly by AHP in hidden mode. There was no noticeable slowdown in browsing performance. While this is only anecdotal, we found no cases in which a Web page failed to load as usual.

Tor. Though Tor opens a listening socket on the local machine (which is the port on which it accepts SOCKS connections), since all connections are local, AHP does not interfere. As recommended, we used Tor with Privoxy [23] which presents an HTTP proxy interface to Tor and performs application-level privacy

---

[13] To accommodate for the fact that when connecting to the Internet, our broadband Internet service only has a single IP address assigned to it, we set up a small local network within which to perform address hiding before routing to the Internet. We connected the user's machine directly (over Ethernet) to a second machine which served as the AHP gateway. Given the constraint of only one public IP address, we performed address hiding within the local subnet and then performed NAT (which was needed since the public IP address space is much smaller than the private address space in this scenario) before actually sending packets out to the public Internet.

filtering. We were able to browse the Web as usual via Tor with no interference from AHP. As a result, those Internet users who desire additional privacy beyond the capabilities provided by AHP will still be able to enjoy the benefits of Tor and similar overlay anonymity services.

BitTorrent. BitTorrent performs best when it can make outgoing connections to other peers *and* accept incoming connections. To enable inbound connections, we ran the official BitTorrent client in sticky mode using expose. While this did require one additional step—adding expose to the command line—we believe this step is not onerous, and furthermore, we believe the changes required here are even less than those to support transition to NATs (for which many applications had to be updated). *No* code needed to be changed in the BitTorrent application itself. Regardless, our main observation is that Internet users can continue to use peer-to-peer applications if their ISPs offer AHP to them as a service. One concern is that sticky mode incurs overhead at the AHP gateway, as the gateway has to process and store requests on behalf of applications that wish to accept inbound connections. To discover whether BitTorrent requires repeated or burdensome communication with the AHP gateway when in sticky mode, we logged its system calls while downloading the top ranked torrent from a popular BitTorrent website. We left all application settings at their defaults. Over the course of the approximately 30 minute download, BitTorrent accepted 2,034 inbound TCP connections, made 3,980 outbound TCP connections, and yet only needed to bind() a listening TCP socket exactly once. (That one call to bind() initialized a sticky IP/port pair in the AHP gateway.)

Forensic recovery. Recall that one of the principal goals of AHP is to enlist ISPs to help improve users' Internet privacy while also still allowing ISPs to be consistent with existing or emerging government legislation and internal corporate policies. AHP thus, for example, enables ISPs to easily respond to requests. We built a simple forensic tool that performs the same operation as an AHP gateway to Unhide the address and port of a given packet—the packet is read in from a user-specified file. The only remaining information—the timestamp and which side initiated the flow—must be provided to the tool so it can select the key for that timestamp. Though collisions can occur, they only occur across different remote IP/port tuples. For a given (remote) destination IP address and port, there exists only one permutation at a given gateway, and thus a unique mapping for each hidden address that is communicating with that IP/port pair.

B   Flexible Hiding Sets

A fundamental property of in-network, directed-routed anonymity or address hiding systems is that their hiding sets are firmly tied to route advertisements. Thus, if an ISP only advertises small IP prefixes, and cannot or does not aggregate them with adjacent prefixes, then the address space within which a user hides is small, leaving the user open to a host of de-anonymization attacks. At the other extreme, a large ISP with a large IP prefix (such as a /8) can leverage the expansive IP space to hide all its customers even across continents. This tension between presenting larger hiding sets for users and enabling fine grained route control is not a new one—network engineers in ISPs try to optimize their routing advertisements to maximize routing flexibility (by advertising small prefixes) while also considering route stability, convergence, and update overhead (by advertising large prefixes). Thus the consideration of selecting the appropriate size IP prefix to advertise to aid in user address hiding is not a new, undue burden upon network administrators and engineers.

B.1 Variable Prefix Sizes

Due to the lack of variable block-size block ciphers to use as the underlying PRP, the span of IP prefix sizes we can support using the exact techniques we describe above directly using the block cipher are limited. In our prototype implementation, we first built support for 16 bit externally visible IP prefixes, which, along with a 16-bit port field, are appropriate for a cipher with a 32-bit block width.

However, to provide ISPs greater flexibility, a deployment implementation would need to support a variety of IP prefix lengths. The shuffle-based random permutation design of Granboulan and Pornin [11] lets us select arbitrary size prefixes, though their algorithm is computationally expensive. In hardware, a table-based permutation is appropriate for small IP prefixes.

We extended our prototype to cope both with IP prefixes larger than and smaller than a /16 prefix. For those smaller, we were required to perform a slight layer violation, and include the high-order bits of the TCP timestamp field in the block permuted by the cipher (to pad the IP/port pair up to the 32-bit mark). For those prefixes larger than /16, we restrict ourselves to even bitlength IP prefixes, and build a Luby-Rackoff cipher using a larger block-size primitive—in our case AES—as a PRF; such a design comes with the corresponding loss of security due to the PRF to PRP transformation.

B.2 Disjoint Prefix Aggregation

A fundamental problem with operating strictly on IP prefixes is that an ISP may not use strictly neighboring address spaces, and thus, may be forced to advertise them separately. Instead, we suggest that with a slightly modified version of AHP, we can aggregate multiple smaller, disjoint prefixes into one IP address space over which AHP can anonymize clients. Our primary approach is to revisit the notion of permuting addresses as opposed to encrypting them. By permuting addresses, we eliminate the need for strict, IP prefix-based partitioning.

The following simple technique would allow the aggregation of disjoin prefixes: given n prefixes $(p_1, \ldots, p_n)$, we map the addresses via a bijection to $\mathbb{Z}_k^+$ where $k = |p_1| + \cdots + |p_n|$. We then apply a permutation such as that of Granboulan and Pornin [11] to $\mathbb{Z}_k^+$ and remap the result back to the original prefixes.

As a result of this approach, anonymity sets can be made as large an ISP's entire address space. We leave a thorough study of disjoint prefix aggregation to future work.

C   Key Rotation

In AHP we must rotate keys if we are to protect the unlinkability of flows originating from the same true source address to the same destination address over time. How often should key rotation occur? The epoch length, which we define to be the period of key rotation, constrains the maximum length of a flow. Too short an epoch will unduly constrain flow durations—too long and it may allow port reuse at end hosts and thus privacy loss.

Suppose a client creates a new socket to the same port on a server repeatedly. Though most server applications typically set the SO_REUSEADDR socket option, thereby allowing port reuse even before TCP fully flushes its state for a particular port, most client applications allow the operating system to select a random port. Under that assumption, and with the additional constraint that client applications do not have the necessary rights to use the first 1024 port numbers, $k = 64512$ ports are available. Allowing the full 2 minutes for each port to become available again after use, we can compute the time required to reuse a port with probability 0.5 using the Taylor series approximation of the birthday paradox: $p(n) = 1 - e^{-\frac{n(n-1)}{2k}}$. Substituting, we compute n to be 299 attempts, which indicates that we should expect a port collision to occur after 35886 seconds, or roughly 10 hours. Naturally, then, we would like for the counter value that we use to increment in 10 hours or less. We discuss selection of a specific key rotation interval later in the context of collision analysis.

Privacy-Preserving Policy-Based Information Transfer

Emiliano De Cristofaro[1], Stanislaw Jarecki[1], Jihye Kim[2], and Gene Tsudik[1]

[1] Computer Science Department, University of California, Irvine
[2] Department of Mathematical Sciences, Seoul National University

Abstract. As the global society becomes more interconnected and more privacy-conscious, communication protocols must balance access control with protecting participants' privacy. A common current scenario involves an authorized party (client) who needs to retrieve sensitive information held by another party (server) such that: (1) the former only gets the information for which it is duly authorized, (2) the latter does not learn what information information is retrieved. To address this scenario, in this paper, we introduce and explore the concept of Privacy-preserving Policy-based Information Transfer (PPIT). We construct three PPIT schemes based, respectively, on: RSA, Schnorr and IBE techniques. We then investigate various performance improvements and demonstrate the practicality of proposed PPIT schemes.

1 Introduction

There are many scenarios where sensitive information is requested by some authority due to some legitimate need. The challenge for the information owner (server) is to allow access to only duly authorized information, whereas, the challenge for the information requester (client) is to obtain needed information without divulging what is being requested. We refer to this concept as *Privacy-preserving Policy-based Information Transfer* or PPIT. To motivate it, we begin with two envisaged scenarios:

Scenario 1. University of Lower Vermont (ULoVe) is confronted with an FBI investigation focused on one of its faculty members (Alice). The university is understandably reluctant to allow FBI unlimited access to its employee records. For its part, FBI is unwilling to disclose that Alice is the target of investigation. There might be several reasons for FBI's stance: (1) Concern about unwarranted rumors and tarnishing Alice's reputation, e.g. leaked information might cause legal action and result in bad PR for the FBI; (2) The need to keep the investigation secret, i.e., preventing malicious insiders (ULoVe employees) from forewarning Alice about the investigation.

Ultimately, ULoVe must comply with FBI's demands, especially, if the latter is armed with appropriate authorization (e.g., a court order) from, say, the US Attorney General's office. However, the authorization presumably applies only to Alice. Assuming all communication between ULoVe and FBI is electronic, there seems to be an impasse.

I. Goldberg and M. Atallah (Eds.): PETS 2009, LNCS 5672, pp. 164–184, 2009.

An additional nuance is that, even if ULoVe is willing to provide FBI unrestricted access to all its employee records, FBI may not want the associated liability. This is because mere possession of ULoVe sensitive employee information would require FBI to demonstrate that the information is/was treated appropriately and disposed of when no longer needed. Considering a number of recent incidents of massive losses of sensitive government and commercial employees' records, FBI might be unwilling to assume additional risk.

An ideal solution would be as follows: ULoVe learns that FBI is most likely investigating someone who might be an employee of ULoVe. No one outside FBI learns who is being investigated. This holds even if someone in ULoVe tries to manipulate the process attempting to learn more information. For its part, FBI learns nothing about any ULoVe employee who does not meet the exact criteria specified in its court order.

Scenario 2. An international airline (VultureAir) has daily flights transiting the United States. US Department of Homeland Security (DHS) maintains a **secret** terrorist watch-list and needs to determine whether any names on the watch-list match those on the passenger manifest of each VultureAir flight. Bound by some international privacy treaty (or its own policy), VultureAir is unwilling to disclose its passenger list to DHS. However, as ULoVe in Scenario 1, VultureAir is ready to comply with DHS's request as long as each entry on the DHS's watch-list is individually and duly authorized by the independent Judicial Branch.

Ideally, VultureAir transfers information to DHS only about those passengers for which DHS has valid authorizations. In the process, VultureAir does not learn whether DHS has an authorization on any of its passengers. In particular, VultureAir can learn nothing about the DHS watch-list by manipulating its own passenger lists. More generally, no party learns any material it should not have, either by law or because of liability. Nonetheless, DHS retrieves all information to which it is entitled.

What is PPIT? Privacy-preserving Policy-based Information Transfer (PPIT) is applicable to any scenario with a need to transfer information – and, more generally, perform some data-centric task – between parties who:

1. Are willing and/or obligated to transfer information in an accountable and policy-guided (*authorized*) manner.
2. Need to ensure privacy of server's data by preventing unauthorized access.
3. Need to ensure privacy of client's *authorization(s)* which grant it access to server's data.

PPIT vs Prior Techniques. As evident from the remainder of this paper, PPIT's main technical challenge is how to enable the server to efficiently and *obliviously* compute proper authorization decisions. This might sound similar to the goals of certain other concepts, which are overviewed in this section.

Of course, PPIT could be trivially implemented with the aid of on-line trusted third party (TTP) which could take data from both parties and perform necessary operations. However, on-line TTPs are generally unrealistic, for a number of well-known reasons. As any two-party security problem, PPIT could be implemented using generic secure computation techniques [22]. However, such generic techniques are unlikely to yield protocols efficient enough to be used in practice.

PPIT has some features in common with Private Information Retrieval (PIR) [7]. Although PIR aims to ensure privacy of client's query target(s) from the server, a PIR server is willing to unconditionally release any and all of its data to the client. In *symmetric* PIR [11,16], the server releases to the client exactly one data item per query. However, there is no provision for ensuring that the client is authorized by some trusted authority to retrieve the requested item. Also, a PIR protocol must communicate strictly fewer bits than the the server's database size. Whereas, PPIT involves no such requirements; indeed, PPIT protocols presented in this paper have linear communication complexity.

PPIT can be thought of a variant of secure set intersection [10,12,13]. For example, in Scenario 2, a secure set intersection protocol would allow DHS and VultureAir to *privately* compute an intersection of their respective lists (terror watch-list and passenger manifest). However, note that both parties could inject arbitrary data into the protocol. In contrast, in PPIT, the client is forced to request data for which it has valid authorization obtained from appropriate authorities. Thus, PPIT is a strictly stronger *policy-based* version of the secure set intersection problem: its privacy guarantees are the same, but the client's input is controlled by well-defined access policies, e.g., authorization certificates.

PPIT is also related to *Public Encryption with Keyword Search* (PEKS) [2] or searchable encrypted logs [21]. The server could use a PEKS scheme to attach encryptions of keywords to encrypted database entries, which can be tested by the client only using a corresponding trapdoor. Although this can be used to implement PPIT, it is unclear how to make the resulting protocols efficient using existing PEKS schemes in the setting where the client has multiple credentials. However, as shown in this paper, one can indeed construct an efficient PPIT scheme following this approach using Anonymous Identity-Based Encryption: the server encrypts each entry under its keyword, and the client decrypts it using the decryption key corresponding to the same keyword.

Finally, another closely related construction is *Oblivious Signature-Based Envelope* (OSBE) [14]. Like PPIT, OSBE allows the server to release some information to the client conditional upon the latter's possession of a signature (on a message known to both parties, e.g. a keyword) by a trusted authority, while the server learns nothing about the signatures held by the client. This can be implemented using Identity-Based Encryption, or using standard signature schemes, such as RSA, Schnorr, and DSS [14,17]. However, unlike PPIT, an OSBE scheme does not guarantee privacy of *all* information about the client's authorization. Nevertheless, as shown in this paper, OSBE schemes can be adapted to obtain efficient PPIT instantiations.

Contributions. This paper makes several contributions: (1) it defines a new cryptographic notion, PPIT, motivated by certain practical scenarios, (2) it shows that PPIT can be resolved under a variety of standard assumptions, (3) it constructs several efficient PPIT protocols for the case of the client with multiple authorizations, and (4) it demonstrates feasibility of proposed PPIT instantiations with experimental results obtained from prototype implementations.

2   Privacy-Preserving Policy-Based Information Transfer

This section describes out notation as well as the participants and the components of a PPIT scheme.

Notation. A function $f(\tau)$ is *negligible* in the security parameter τ if, for every polynomial p, $f(\tau) < 1/|p(t)|$ for large enough t. Throughout this paper, we use semantically secure symmetric encryption and we assume the key space to be τ_1-bit strings, where τ_1 is a (polynomial) function of a security parameter τ. We use $Enc_k(\cdot)$ and $Dec_k(\cdot)$ to denote symmetric-key encryption and decryption (both under key k), respectively. We also use public key signature schemes, where each scheme is a tuple of algorithms: $DSIG = [INIT, SIG, VER]$, representing key set-up, signature generation and verification, respectively. $DSIG.INIT(\tau_2)$ returns a public/private key-pair, where τ_2 is a polynomial function of τ. $DSIG.SIG(SK, m)$ returns a signature σ on message m, whereas, $DSIG.VER(PK, \sigma, m)$ returns 1 or 0 indicating that σ is valid or invalid signature on m, under PK. Finally, we use $a \leftarrow A$ to designate that variable a is chosen uniformly at random from set A.

Players/Entities. A PPIT scheme involves three players:

(1) Server (S): stores the set $I = \{(ID, D_{ID}) \mid ID \in \{0,1\}^l\}$. ID uniquely identifies a record and D_{ID} denotes the associated information.
(2) Client (C): has a pair (σ, ID_C), where σ is authorization for ID_C issued by the court and ID_C is an l-bit string.
(3) Court: a trusted third party, which issues authorizations for accessing a record identified by a given string ID.

Components. Without loss of generality, we assume that an authorization σ for record with identifier ID is a signature under CA's key on ID. Therefore we define a PPIT scheme as a tuple of the following three algorithms:

(1) Setup(τ): It is an algorithm executed by the court. Given a security parameter τ, it generates – via $DSIG.INIT$ – a key-pair (SK, PK) for the signature scheme $DSIG$. The court then publishes the public key PK.
(2) Authorize(SK, ID): It is an algorithm executed by the court to issue an authorization $\sigma = DSIG.SIG(SK, ID)$ on an identifier string ID. Note that if $\sigma = $ Authorize(SK,ID) then $DSIG.VER(PK, \sigma, ID) = 1$.
(3) Transfer: It is an interactive algorithm (protocol) executed between server S and client C, on public input PK, on S's private input (ID_S, D) and C's private input (ID_C, σ). At the end of transfer, S has no outputs and C outputs D if $ID_S = ID_C$ and $DSIG.VER(PK, ID_C, \sigma) = 1$.

3   Security Requirements

We now describe PPIT security requirements.

Correctness. A PPIT scheme is *correct* if, at the end of transfer, C outputs D, given that:

(1) $(SK, PK) \leftarrow$ Setup(1^τ) and $\sigma =$ Authorize(ID) for some ID,
(2) S and C respectively run the transfer protocol on input (ID, D) and (ID, σ).

Security. Informally, security of a PPIT scheme means that only clients authorized to access data D can learn any information about D. Formally, we say that a PPIT scheme is *secure* if any polynomially bounded adversary $\mathcal{A}$ cannot win the following game, with probability non-negligibly over $1/2$. The game is between $\mathcal{A}$ and a challenger Ch:

1. Ch runs $(PK, SK) \leftarrow$ Setup(1^τ)
2. $\mathcal{A}$, on input PK, adaptively queries Ch a number n of times on a set of strings $Q = \{ID_i | ID_i \in \{0, 1\}^l, i = 1, \cdots, n\}$. For every ID_i, Ch responds by giving $\mathcal{A}$ a signature $\sigma_i \leftarrow DSIG.SIG(SK, ID_i)$
3. $\mathcal{A}$ announces a new identifier string, $ID^* \notin Q$, and generates two equal-length data record $(D_0{}^*, D_1{}^*)$
4. Ch picks one record by selecting a random bit $b \leftarrow \{0, 1\}$, and executes the server's part of the transfer protocol on public input PK and private inputs $(ID^*, D_b{}^*)$. We denote the protocol transcript by T^*.
5. $\mathcal{A}$ outputs b' (and wins if $b' = b$).

Server Privacy. Informally, a PPIT scheme is server-private if only an authorized client learns any information about ID_S which S inputs into the transfer protocol with C. Formally, we say that a PPIT scheme is *server-private* if no polynomially bounded adversary $\mathcal{A}$ can win the following game with probability non-negligibly over $1/2$. The game is between $\mathcal{A}$ and Ch:

1. Ch runs $(PK, SK) \leftarrow$ Setup(1^τ)
2. $\mathcal{A}$, on input PK, adaptively queries Ch a number n of times on a set of strings $Q = \{ID_i | ID_i \in \{0, 1\}^l, i = 1, \cdots, n\}$. For every ID_i, Ch responds by giving $\mathcal{A}$ a signature $\sigma_i \leftarrow DSIG.SIG(SK, ID_i)$
3. $\mathcal{A}$ announces two new identifier strings, $(ID_0{}^*, ID_1{}^*) \notin Q$, and generates a data record D^*
4. Ch picks one identifier by selecting a random bit $b \leftarrow \{0, 1\}$, and executes the server's part of transfer on public input PK and private inputs $(ID_b{}^*, D^*)$. We denote the protocol transcript by T^*.
5. $\mathcal{A}$ outputs b' (and wins if $b' = b$).

We note that security and server-privacy games could be merged into one. It is possible to modify $\mathcal{A}$ to announce two pairs $(ID_0{}^*, D_0{}^*), (ID_1{}^*, D_1{}^*)$ and let Ch pick a random bit b and execute the server's part of transfer on input $(ID_b{}^*, D_b{}^*)$. The *security* property alone is obtained by restricting $\mathcal{A}$'s challenge query so that $(ID_0{}^* = ID_1{}^*)$, while *server-privacy* alone is obtained if $(D_0{}^* = D_1{}^*)$.

Client Privacy. Informally, client privacy means no information is leaked about client's authorization and ID to a malicious server. Formally, a PPIT scheme is *client-private* if no polynomially bounded adversary $\mathcal{A}$ can win the following game with the probability non-negligibly over $1/2$. The game is between $\mathcal{A}$ and Ch:

1. Ch executes $(PK, SK) \leftarrow \mathsf{Setup}(1^\tau)$
2. $\mathcal{A}$, on input SK, chooses two strings $ID_0{}^*$, $ID_1{}^*$ and two strings $\sigma_0{}^*, \sigma_1{}^*$
3. Ch picks a random bit $b \leftarrow \{0,1\}$ and interacts with $\mathcal{A}$ by following transfer on behalf of client on public input PK and private inputs $(ID_b{}^*, \sigma_b{}^*)$
4. $\mathcal{A}$ outputs b' (and wins if $b' = b$).

For the sake of simplicity, we say that a PPIT scheme is **private** if it is both server- and client-private.

Client Unlinkability. Informally, client unlinkability means that a malicious server cannot tell if any two instances of the transfer protocol are related, i.e., executed on the the same inputs ID_C and/or σ. Formally, we say that a PPIT is *client-unlinkable* if no polynomially bounded adversary $\mathcal{A}$ can win the following game with probability non-negligibly over $1/2$. The game is between $\mathcal{A}$ and Ch:

1) Ch executes $(PK, SK) \leftarrow \mathsf{Setup}(1^\tau)$
2) $\mathcal{A}$, on input SK, chooses two strings $ID_0{}^*$, $ID_1{}^*$ (where it could be that $ID_0{}^* = ID_1{}^*$) and two strings $\sigma_0{}^*, \sigma_1{}^*$
3a) Ch interacts with $\mathcal{A}$ by following transfer on behalf of client on public input PK and private inputs $(ID_0{}^*, \sigma_0{}^*)$
3b) Ch picks a random bit $b \leftarrow \{0,1\}$ and interacts with $\mathcal{A}$ by following transfer on behalf of client on public input PK and private inputs $(ID_b{}^*, \sigma_b{}^*)$.
4) $\mathcal{A}$ outputs b' (and wins if $b' = b$).

In other words, observing transfer does not give $\mathcal{A}$ any advantage in the game described for client privacy.

4   Building Blocks

In this section, we present three PPIT variants, based on RSA signatures scheme [19], Schnorr signature scheme [20], and Anonymous Identity-Based Encryption (IBE) [3]. For ease of presentation, we assume that S stores just one pair: (ID_S, D_{ID_S}). The full versions of these schemes, described in Section 5, work with multiple records on S and/or multiple authorizations on C.

4.1   RSA-PPIT

We show how to obtain PPIT by adapting the RSA-based Oblivious Signature Based Envelope (OSBE) scheme of [14].

Setup. On input of security parameter τ, generate a safe RSA modulus $N = pq$, where $p = 2p' + 1$, $q = 2q' + 1$, and p, q, p', q' are primes. The set of all quadratic residues mod N is denoted as QR_N. The algorithm picks a random element g which is a generator of QR_N. RSA exponents (e, d) are chosen in the standard way. The secret key is $SK = (p, q, d)$ and the public key $PK = (N, g, e)$. The algorithm also fixes a full-domain hash function $H : \{0, 1\}^* \to \mathbb{Z}_N$, $H' : \{0, 1\}^* \to \{0, 1\}^{\tau_1}$.

Authorize. To issue an authorization on ID to C court computes an RSA signature on ID, $\sigma = (h_{ID})^d \pmod{N}$, where $h_{ID} = H(ID)$. (The signature on ID is verified by checking if $\sigma^e = H(ID)$.)

Transfer. This is a protocol between C and S where public input is $PK = (N, e, g)$, and C's private input is (ID_C, σ), where $\sigma^e = H(ID_C) \bmod N$ and S's private input is (ID_S, D). The protocol is shown in Figure 1.

$\underline{\mathbf{C}}$ on input: $ID_C, \sigma, PK = (N, g, e)$
    where $\sigma^e = H(ID_C)$

$\underline{\mathbf{S}}$ on input: $ID_S, D, PK = (N, g, e)$

$r \leftarrow \mathbb{Z}_{N/4}$, $\mu = \sigma^2 \cdot g^r \bmod N$ $\xrightarrow{\;\;\mu\;\;}$ If $\mu \notin \mathbb{Z}_N^*$ then abort.
                                                        $R = g^{ez} \bmod N$, for $z \leftarrow \mathbb{Z}_{N/4}$
                                                        $K_S = (\mu)^{ez} \cdot (H_{ID_S})^{-2z} \bmod N$
                                                        $k_S = H'(K_S)$

$K_C = R^r \bmod N$, $k_C = H'(K_C)$ $\xleftarrow{\;\langle R, C \rangle\;}$ $C = Enc_{k_S}(D)$
$D' = Dec_{k_C}(C)$

Fig. 1. RSA-PPIT

To see that RSA-PPIT is *correct*, observe that, when $ID_C = ID_S$:

$$K_S = (\mu)^{ez} \cdot H(ID_S)^{-2z} = (H(ID_C))^{2z} \cdot g^{rez} \cdot H(ID_S)^{-2z} = g^{erz} = R^r = K_C.$$

Recall that this scheme is based on RSA-OSBE from [14]. However, in the first step of the transfer, C picks $\mu = \sigma^2 \cdot g^r$ instead of $\sigma \cdot h^r$. The use of g – instead of $h = H(ID)$ – allows C to batch computation in case it has multiple authorizations. (For more details, see Section 5). Also, we square σ to guarantee that μ is in QR_N, as shown in the proof in Appendix C, where we present the complete proof of security, privacy, and client-unlinkability for RSA-PPIT.

4.2 Schnorr-PPIT

We show here a PPIT construction using Schnorr-OSBE scheme [6]. It's proof of security, privacy, and client-unlinkability is in Appendix C.

Setup. On input of a security parameter τ, this algorithm creates a Schnorr key: (p, q, g, a, y), where p, q are primes, s.t. q divides $p - 1$ but q^2 does not divide $p - 1$, g is a generator of a subgroup in $\mathbb{Z}_p^*$ of order q, a is picked randomly in

$\mathbb{Z}_q^*$, and $y = g^a \bmod p$. The public key is $PK = (p, q, g, y)$ and the secret key is $SK = a$. The algorithm also defines hash functions $H : \{0,1\}^* \rightarrow \in \mathbb{Z}_q^*$, and $H' : \{0,1\}^n \rightarrow \in \{0,1\}^{\tau_1}$.

Authorize. To issue authorization on string ID, court computes a Schnorr signature on ID, $\sigma = (X, s)$ where $X = g^k \bmod p$ and $s = k + a \cdot H(ID, X) \bmod q$ for random $k \leftarrow \mathbb{Z}_q^*$. The signature on ID is verified by checking whether $g^s = X \cdot y^{H(ID,X)} \bmod p$.

Transfer. This protocol (see Figure 2) is between C and S, where public input is $PK = (p, q, g, y)$, and C's private input is $(ID_C, \sigma = (X, s))$ s.t. $g^s = X \cdot y^{H(ID_C,X)} \bmod p$ and S's private input is (ID_S, D).

C on input: $ID_C, \sigma = (X, s)$ $\qquad$ $PK = (p, q, g, y)$	**S** on input: $ID_S, D, PK = (p, q, g, y)$
$g^s = X \cdot y^{H(ID_C,X)} \bmod p$ $\quad\xrightarrow{\quad X \quad}$	If $X^{(p-1)/q} \neq 1 \bmod p$ then abort. $R = g^z \bmod p$, for $z \leftarrow \mathbb{Z}_q^*$ $K_S = (y^{H(ID_S,X)} X)^z \bmod p$, $k_S = H'(K_S)$
$K_C = R^s \bmod p$, $k_C = H'(K_C)$ $\quad\xleftarrow{\langle R, C \rangle}\quad$ $C = Enc_{k_S}(D)$	
$D' = Dec_{k_C}(C)$	

Fig. 2. Schnorr-PPIT

To show that Schnorr-PPIT is *correct*, we observe that, when $ID_C = ID_S$:
$$K_S = \left(y^{H(ID_S,X)} X\right)^z = (g^{aH(ID_S,X)} g^k)^z = (g^{aH(ID_C,X)+k})^z = g^{sz} = R^s = K_C$$

4.3   IBE-PPIT

Here we show a PPIT construction using any anonymous Identity-Based Encryption (IBE) scheme, e.g. [3,4]. Recall that IBE is a form of public key encryption where any string can be used as a public key. A trusted third party, called a Key Distribution Center (KDC), has a master key, which is used to generate the private key corresponding to any public key string.

Setup. On input of a security parameter τ, the Court runs the setup algorithm of the IBE system to generate the KDC master key and global IBE system parameters, denoted as PK.

Authorize. As shown in [3], selective-ID semantically secure IBE implies CMA-secure signatures. The authorization on ID is thus simply σ – the IBE private key corresponding to the public key ID. The verification tests that the private key corresponds to the given ID.

Transfer. IBE implies a non-interactive PPIT scheme: S encrypts D under the identifier string ID_S and C decrypts it using its authorization σ, which is an IBE private key identifier corresponding to C's string ID_C.

We observe that this is similar to the IBE-based Signature Based Envelope (OSBE) scheme previously explored in [14]. However, in IBE-based OSBE, the use of anonymous IBE to achieve key-privacy (in the sense of [1]) is optional. Whereas, this is a fundamental requirement in our scheme: an adversary who correctly guesses the encryption key used to generate a ciphertext would immediately break server privacy.

To see that IBE-PPIT is *correct*, observe that, when $ID_C = ID_S$, C has the corresponding authorization from the court, i.e. the private decryption key, and hence will successfully decrypt data D. The complete proof of security, privacy, and client-unlinkability for IBE-PPIT are in Appendix C.

5   Extensions

Thus far, we considered solutions for a simple scenario where client is authorized to access at most one record and server stores at most one record. We now consider the case of multiple authorizations/records.

Multiple Records. Consider a setting where server stores a set of n records, denoted by by $I = \{(ID_i, D_i)|ID_i \in \{0,1\}^l\}$, with $|I| = n$. Since one of the PPIT requirements prevents server to know which record is requested, server has to send all of its records. A naïve solution would be to reiterate the interaction presented in the previous section n times. Specifically, the PPIT transfer protocol would require: (i) server to perform and send n encryptions under n different Diffie-Hellman [8] keys, and (ii) client to try decrypting *all* received encryptions to output the authorized record. This would result in $O(n)$ encryptions, bandwidth utilization, and decryptions.

Hence, we aim to speed up the computation by using a two-pronged approach:

1. We let server use same random values, z, across all records, so that encryptions can be batched.
2. We let server accompany every encryption with a tag, i.e. a hash function of each Diffie-Hellman key, K_{s_i}. In turn, client computes the tag on its own Diffie-Hellman key, K_C so that it decrypts only the record accompanied by the matching the tag.

Fast decryption in RSA-PPIT. We assume that in the setup algorithm, an additional cryptographic hash function H'' is chosen. The protocol is shown in Figure 3. As a result, the computation for client is reduced to $O(1)$. However, we cannot speed up server-side computation without violating client-privacy. (See Appendix C for proofs.)

Fast decryption in Schnorr-PPIT. We assume that in the setup algorithm, an additional cryptographic hash function H'' is chosen. The protocol is shown in Figure 4. Similar to RSA-PPIT, client's computation cost becomes constant, but there does not seem to be way to speed up server-side computation without violating client-privacy. (The proofs are deferred to Appendix C.)

$\underline{\mathbf{C}}$ on input $(ID_C, \sigma, PK = (N, g, e))$ $\underline{\mathbf{S}}$ on input $(\{ID_i, D_i\}, PK = (N, g, e))$
where $\sigma^e = H(ID_C)$

$r \leftarrow \mathbb{Z}_{N/4}, \mu = \sigma^2 \cdot g^r \bmod N \qquad \xrightarrow{\mu}$ If $\mu \notin \mathbb{Z}_N^*$ then abort.
$R = g^{ez} \bmod N$, for $z \leftarrow \mathbb{Z}_{N/4}$
For every i compute:
$\quad K_{S_i} = (\mu)^{ez} \cdot (H_{ID_i})^{-2z} \bmod N$
$\quad k_{S_i} = H'(K_{S_i})$
$\quad C_i = Enc_{k_{S_i}}(D_i), t_i = H''(K_{S_i})$

$K_C = R^r \bmod N, k_C = H'(K_C) \qquad \xleftarrow{\langle R, \vec{C}, \vec{T} \rangle} \quad \vec{C} = \{C_i\}$ and $\vec{T} = \{t_i\}$
$t^* = H''(K_C)$
If $\exists i \in \{1, ..., n\}$, s.t. $t_i = t^*$
$\quad$ Output $D' = Dec_{k_C}(C_i)$.

Fig. 3. RSA-PPIT with multiple records

$\underline{\mathbf{C}}$ on input: $(ID_C, \sigma = (X, s)$ $\underline{\mathbf{S}}$ on input: $(\{ID_i, D_i\}, PK = (p, q, g, y))$
$\qquad PK = (p, q, g, y))$
for $g^s = X \cdot y^{H(ID_C, X)} \bmod p \quad \xrightarrow{X}$ If $X^{(p-1)/q} \neq 1 \bmod p$ then abort.
$R = g^z \bmod p$, for $z \leftarrow \mathbb{Z}_q^*$
For every i compute:
$\quad K_{S_i} = (y^{H(ID_i, X)} \cdot X)^z \bmod p$
$\quad k_{S_i} = H'(K_{S_i})$
$\quad C_i = Enc_{k_{S_i}}(D_i), t_i = H''(K_{S_i})$

$K_C = R^s \bmod p, k_C = H'(K_C) \xleftarrow{\langle R, \vec{C}, \vec{T} \rangle} \quad \vec{C} = \{C_i\}$ and $\vec{T} = \{t_i\}$
$t^* = H''(K_C)$
If $\exists i \in \{1, ..., n\}$, s.t. $t_i = t^*$
$\quad$ Output $D' = Dec_{k_C}(C_i)$.

Fig. 4. Schnorr-PPIT with multiple records

Fast decryption in IBE-PPIT. Similarly to RSA-PPIT and Schnorr-PPIT extensions above, we label each encrypted record with a tag based on the corresponding encryption keys. Then client quickly retrieves and decrypts the record for which it has the decryption key.

As described in Section 4.3, PPIT can be instantiated using any efficient anonymous IBE scheme. We now describe how to compute key tags using Boneh-Franklin's IBE [3], presented in Appendix A. To support multiple records, we add key tagging, where tags are computed using BF-IBE, as we show in Figure 5. We assume that two cryptographic hash function H, H' are chosen during setup. Recall that, in BF-IBE, s is the master private key and $(P, Q = sP)$ are public parameters. We modify the Authorize so that, when the court issues to client an authorization for ID, client also receives a signature $\sigma' = s \cdot H(ID)$. Note that

PK_i^{IBE} is the IBE private key corresponding to public key ID_i and SK^{IBE} is the IBE private key corresponding to public key ID^* for which client holds a court-issued authorization.

C on input: $(ID_C, \sigma, \sigma', P, Q)$ for $\sigma = SK^{IBE}, \sigma' = s \cdot H(ID)$	**S** on input: $(\{ID_i, D_i\}, \{PK_i^{Ibe}\}, P, Q)$

	$R = zP$, for random $z \leftarrow \mathbb{G}_1$
	For every i compute:
	  $C_i = \text{IBE-Encrypt}(PK_i^{IBE}, D_i)$
	  $t_i = H'(e(Q, H(ID_i))^z)$

Compute $t^* = H'(e(R, \sigma'))$ $\xleftarrow{\langle R, \overrightarrow{C}, \overrightarrow{T}\rangle}$ $\overrightarrow{C} = \{C_i\}$ and $\overrightarrow{T} = \{t_i\}$	
If $\exists i \in \{1, ..., n\}$, s.t. $t_i = t^*$, output $D' = \text{IBE-Decrypt}(SK^{IBE}, C_i)$	

Fig. 5. IBE-PPIT with multiple records

We emphasize, that re-use of randomness z for each tag in the IBE scheme is similar to [5]. However, our approach provides multi-encryption (i.e., encryption of different messages) instead of broadcast encryption [9]. Moreover, we embed the tags to reduce the number of decryptions to $O(1)$. Proofs appear in Appendix C.

Multiple Authorizations. We now consider the scenario where client receives multiple authorizations, allowing access to multiple records with only one instance of PPIT. We say that client stores $\Sigma = \{(ID_j, \sigma_j)|ID_j \in \{0,1\}^l\}$, with $|\Sigma| = n'$, the set of n' pairs defining a record identifier along with the court's authorization. For completeness, we consider server to store the set I of pairs (ID_i, D_i) with $|I| = n$.

As discussed above, server has to send all of its records during the transfer. RSA-PPIT and Schnorr-PPIT require a different Diffie-Hellman key for each record. In these interactive instantiations, each key depends on some partial information of client's alleged authorization. For this reason, in the RSA-PPIT transfer protocol client should send $\mu_j = \sigma_j^2 \cdot g^{r_j}$ for every j. In the Schnorr-PPIT, client should send $X_j = g^{s_j} \cdot y^{-e_j}$ for every j. This implies that server should compute and send $n' \cdot n$ encryptions under $n' \cdot n$ different Diffie-Hellman keys, resulting in $O(n \cdot n')$ computation time for both entities, as well as $O(n \cdot n')$ bandwidth utilization. Using the tag extensions presented above, the number of decryptions will be reduced to the linear $O(n')$.

Specifically, the computation on server is burdened by performing $O(n \cdot n')$ exponentiations needed to compute $n \cdot n'$ Diffie-Hellman keys. However, in RSA-PPIT the number of exponentiations can be easily reduced to $O(n + n')$. In fact, it is possible to separately compute: (i) n' different exponentiations for the received μ_j, for $j = 1, ...n'$, (ii) n different exponentiations for $H_{ID_i}^{-2z}$, for $i = 1, ..., n$. Then for each Diffie-Hellman key computation, server should only perform a multiplication, thus resulting in $O(n \cdot n')$ total multiplications.

In contrast, the IBE-based extension presented for multiple records can be applied unaltered to the scenario with client's multiple authorizations.. Therefore, the server computation and the bandwidth utilization remains $O(n)$, as well as the client computation remains linear in the number of authorizations, i.e. $O(n')$. This is possible because the transfer protocol in IBE-PPIT is a one-round interaction and no information is sent from client to server. Hence, the encryption keys do not depend on any information sent by client.

6   Discussion

We now evaluate and compares the proposed schemes for the case of S with n records and C with n' authorizations.

Performance Analysis. Table 1 summarizes the performance of the proposed PPIT schemes. Both S's and C's run-times are measured in terms of public key operations, **ops**, i.e., exponentiations in case of RSA-PPIT and Schnorr-PPIT (exponent sizes are, respectively, 1024 and 160 bits), and bilinear map operations in case of IBE-PPIT. However, for server operations in RSA-PPIT, we distinguish between exponentiations, **exp**, and multiplications **mul**. Recall that n is the number of records stored by S, and n' – the number of authorizations held by the C.

Table 1. Performance Comparison for scenarios where $n' \gg 1$

	RSA	**Schnorr**	**IBE**
Transfer Rounds	2	2	1
Server ops	$O(n + n')$ **exp** $O(n \cdot n')$ **mul**	$O(n \cdot n')$	$O(n)$
Client ops	$O(n')$	$O(n')$	$O(n')$
Bandwidth	$O(n \cdot n')$	$O(n \cdot n')$	$O(n)$

IBE-PPIT is the most efficient by all counts, since it: (1) takes one round, (2) requires a linear number of public key operations for both S and C, and (3) consumes linear amount of bandwidth. Whereas, both Schnorr-PPIT and RSA-PPIT are two-round protocols. Schnorr-PPIT has quadratic – $O(n \cdot n')$ – computation and bandwidth overheads, while RSA-PPIT requires $O(n + n')$ exponentiations and $O(n \cdot n')$ multiplication on S. However, for small n' values the Schnorr-PPIT and the RSA-PPIT protocols might be faster because they use less expensive operations (modular exponentiations versus bilinear maps).

The dominant cost factor varies with the scheme: (1) in RSA-PPIT it is a 1024-bit exponentiation mod N, (2) in Schnorr-PPIT, it is a 160-bit exponentiation mod 1024-bit prime p, and (3) in IBE-PPIT, it is the bilinear map function.

Experimental Results. To assess the performance of proposed schemes, we now present some experimental results. All tests were performed on S with two quad-core CPUs Intel Xeon at 1.60 GHz with 8GB RAM. All schemes were implemented in ANSI C, using the well-known OpenSSL toolkit [23], except pairing operations in IBE-PPIT for which we used the PBC Library [15]. We used 1024-bit moduli for RSA-PPIT, 1024- and 160-bit primes for Schnorr-PPIT, and 512-bit group elements and 160-bit primes for IBE-PPIT [1]. We note that all our tests measured total computation time for PPIT transfer, i.e. the sum of client's and server's computation times. We did not measure time for setup or authorization, since these algorithms are performed only once, at initialization time. We also note that both client and server were running on the same machine; thus, measurements do not take into account the transmission time.

Multiple records and one authorization. In the first test, we timed the performance of the transfer protocol between S storing an increasing number of records and C holding a single authorization. Figure 6(a) shows that Schnorr-PPIT is the fastest, while IBE-PPIT is (not surprisingly) the slowest one.

Multiple records and multiple authorizations. In the second test, we experimented with the case of C holding 100 **authorizations** and S having an increasing number of records. Figure 6(b) shows that IBE-PPIT becomes faster than Schnorr-PPIT, yet, remains slower that RSA-PPIT.

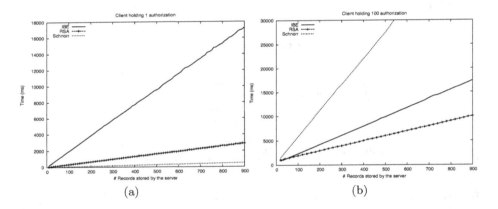

Fig. 6. Total Computation time for PPIT-Transfer for 1 (100) client authorization(s) and increasing server records

We also timed the case where S has a fixed number of records (**100 records**) and C holds an increasing number of authorizations. Figure 7 shows that IBE-PPIT is clearly faster than RSA-PPIT when C has more than 200 authorizations.

However, note that, in this scenario, transmission time can be a relevant factor. In IBE-PPIT, this is linear in the number of S's records. Whereas, in

---

[1] Details on the curves we used can be found in PBC library documentation at `http://crypto.stanford.edu/pbc/manual/ch06s01.html` and `http://crypto.stanford.edu/pbc/manual/ch10s03.html`

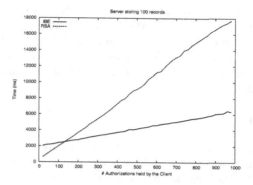

Fig. 7. Total Computation time for PPIT-Transfer for increasing client authorizations and 100 server records

Schnorr-PPIT and RSA-PPIT, the bandwidth is proportional to the product of S's records and C's authorizations. For instance, if S has $1,000$ records, C holds 100 authorizations, and each record is $1,000$ bits, the bandwidth for RSA-PPIT and Schnorr-PPIT would be on the order of 100Mb but only 1Mb for IBE-PPIT.

Observation. Experimental results yield several observations:

1. Schnorr- and RSA-PPIT are preferred over IBE-PPIT in settings where C holds a few authorizations (e.g., Scenario 1 in Section 1.). As shown in Figure 6(a), IBE-PPIT is much slower than others and the speed gap grows linearly with the number of records. In particular, Schnorr-PPIT is efficient enough for quite large databases.
2. IBE-PPIT is preferred for settings where C holds many authorizations (e.g., Scenario 2 in Section 1). IBE allows us to avoid interaction, which saves a lot of computation and bandwidth, especially, if C holds many authorizations.

Unlinkability and Forward Security. We now discuss some differences in terms of security features provided by the three schemes.

First, note that, unlike RSA-PPIT, Schnorr-PPIT does not offer *client-unlinkability*, since the value $X = g^k$ sent by C stays fixed for a given ID. IBE-PPIT is trivially unlinkable.

Whenever multiple transfers take place, *forward security* becomes important. We say that a PPIT scheme *forward-secure* if:

1. Adversary who learns all of S's data (ID-s and records) cannot violate client-privacy of prior transfer interactions.
2. Adversary who learns C's authorization(s) cannot violate security and server-privacy of past transfer interactions.

Note that the first part of the forward-security requirement is already achieved through the notion of *client-privacy*. The second part is not obvious.

RSA-PPIT provides built-in forward security due to the use of g^r in computing each μ. Schnorr-PPIT and IBE-PPIT schemes do not provide forward security, but this can be easily added by requiring both C and S to establish an ephemeral Diffie-Hellman key [8]. This modification increases the computation cost by adding an extra exponentiation. In addition, it makes the IBE-PPIT transfer protocol interactive.

7   Conclusion

This paper introduced a new cryptographic notion of Privacy-preserving Policy-based Information Transfer (PPIT). We constructed and compared three different PPIT instantiations, based, respectively, on: RSA, Schnorr and IBE techniques. We also proposed simple techniques for improving server and/or client performance for cases where either or both parties have multiple records and authorizations, respectively. In our future work, we plan to investigate other solutions to obtain linear complexity using standard digital signatures.

References

1. Bellare, M., Boldyreva, A., Desai, A., Pointcheval, D.: Key-Privacy in Public-Key Encryption. In: Boyd, C. (ed.) ASIACRYPT 2001. LNCS, vol. 2248, pp. 566–582. Springer, Heidelberg (2001)
2. Boneh, D., Di Crescenzo, G., Ostrovsky, R., Persiano, G.: Public key Encryption with Keyword Search. In: Cachin, C., Camenisch, J.L. (eds.) EUROCRYPT 2004. LNCS, vol. 3027, pp. 506–522. Springer, Heidelberg (2004)
3. Boneh, D., Franklin, M.K.: Identity-based encryption from the weil pairing. SIAM Journal of Computing 32(3), 586–615 (2003)
4. Boyen, X., Waters, B.: Anonymous Hierarchical Identity-Based Encryption (Without Random Oracles). In: Dwork, C. (ed.) CRYPTO 2006. LNCS, vol. 4117, pp. 290–307. Springer, Heidelberg (2006)
5. Bradshaw, R., Holt, J., Seamons, K.: Concealing complex policies with hidden credentials. In: CCS 2004, pp. 146–157 (2004)
6. Castelluccia, C., Jarecki, S., Tsudik, G.: Secret Handshakes from CA-Oblivious Encryption. In: Lee, P.J. (ed.) ASIACRYPT 2004. LNCS, vol. 3329, pp. 293–307. Springer, Heidelberg (2004)
7. Chor, B., Kushilevitz, E., Goldreich, O., Sudan, M.: Private information retrieval. Journal of the ACM (JACM) 45(6), 965–981 (1998)
8. Diffie, W., Hellman, M.: New directions in cryptography. IEEE Transactions on Information Theory 22(6), 644–654 (1976)
9. Fiat, A., Naor, M.: Broadcast Encryption. In: Stinson, D.R. (ed.) CRYPTO 1993. LNCS, vol. 773, pp. 480–491. Springer, Heidelberg (1994)
10. Freedman, M.J., Nissim, K., Pinkas, B.: Efficient private matching and set intersection. In: Cachin, C., Camenisch, J.L. (eds.) EUROCRYPT 2004. LNCS, vol. 3027, pp. 1–19. Springer, Heidelberg (2004)
11. Gertner, Y., Ishai, Y., Kushilevitz, E., Malkin, T.: Protecting data privacy in private information retrieval schemes. In: STOC 1998, pp. 151–160 (1998)
12. Hazay, C., Lindell, Y.: Efficient protocols for set intersection and pattern matching with security against malicious and covert adversaries. In: Canetti, R. (ed.) TCC 2008. LNCS, vol. 4948, pp. 155–175. Springer, Heidelberg (2008)

13. Jarecki, S., Liu, X.: Efficient Oblivious Pseudorandom Function with Applications to Adaptive OT and Secure Computation of Set Intersection. In: Reingold, O. (ed.) TCC 2009. LNCS, vol. 5444, pp. 577–594. Springer, Heidelberg (2009)
14. Li, N., Du, W., Boneh, D.: Oblivious signature-based envelope. Distributed Computing 17(4), 293–302 (2005)
15. Lynn, B.: PBC: The Pairing-Based Cryptography Library, http://crypto.stanford.edu/pbc/
16. Naor, M., Pinkas, B.: Oblivious Transfer and Polynomial Evaluation. In: STOC 1999, pp. 245–254 (1999)
17. Nasserian, S., Tsudik, G.: Revisiting oblivious signature-based envelopes. In: Financial Cryptography 2006, pp. 221–235 (2006)
18. Pointcheval, D., Stern, J.: Security proofs for signature schemes. In: Maurer, U.M. (ed.) EUROCRYPT 1996. LNCS, vol. 1070, pp. 387–398. Springer, Heidelberg (1996)
19. Rivest, R., Shamir, A., Adleman, L.: A method for obtaining digital signatures and public-key cryptosystems. Communications of the ACM 21(2), 120–126 (1978)
20. Schnorr, C.: Efficient signature generation by smart cards. Journal of Cryptology 4(3), 161–174 (1991)
21. Waters, B., Balfanz, D., Durfee, G., Smetters, D.: Building an encrypted and searchable audit log. In: NDSS 2004 (2004)
22. Yao, A.: Protocols for secure computations. In: FOCS 1982, pp. 160–164 (1982)
23. Young, E., Hudson, T.: OpenSSL: The Open Source toolkit for SSL/TLS, http://www.openssl.org

A   Boneh and Franklin's IBE

We recall that the BF-IBE scheme is composed by four algorithms: *setup, extract, encrypt, decrypt.*

Setup, given a security parameter k, is used to generate a prime q, two groups $\mathbb{G}_1, \mathbb{G}_2$ of order q, a bilinear map $e : \mathbb{G}_1 \times \mathbb{G}_1 \to \mathbb{G}_2$. Then a random $s \in \mathbb{Z}_q^*$, a random generator $P \in \mathbb{G}_1$, P are chosen and Q is set such that $Q = sP$. (P, Q) are public parameters. s is the private master key. Finally, two cryptographic hash function, $H_1 : \{0,1\}^* \to \mathbb{G}_1$ and $H_2 : \{0,1\}^n \to \mathbb{G}_2$ for some n, are chosen.

Extract, given a string $ID \in \{0,1\}^*$, is used to compute the corresponding private key $s \cdot H(ID)$.

Encrypt is used to encrypt a message M under a public key ID: for a picked random $r \in Z_q^*$ the ciphertext is set to be $C = \langle rP, M \oplus H_2(e(Q, H_1(ID)^r)) \rangle$.

Decrypt is used to decrypt a ciphertext $C = \langle U, V \rangle$, by computing $M = V \oplus H_2(e(U, sH(ID))$.

B   Cryptographic Assumptions

RSA assumption. Let $RSASetup(\tau)$ be an algorithm that outputs so-called safe RSA instances, i.e. pairs (N, e) where $N = pq$, e is a small prime that satisfies $gcd(e, \phi(N)) = 1$, and p, q are randomly generated τ-bit primes subject to the constraint that $p = 2p' + 1$, $q = 2q' + 1$ for prime p', q', $p' \neq q'$. We say that the RSA problem is (τ, t)-hard on 2τ-bit safe RSA moduli, if for every algorithm $\mathcal{A}$ that runs in time t we have

$$Pr[(N, e) \leftarrow RSASetup(\tau), \alpha \leftarrow \mathbb{Z}_N^* : \mathcal{A}(n, e, \alpha) = \beta \text{ s.t. } \beta^e = \alpha \pmod{N}] \leq \tau.$$

CDH Assumption. Let G be a cyclic group of prime order q with a generator g. We say that the Computational Diffie-Hellman Problem (CDH) in G is (ϵ, t)-hard if for every algorithm $\mathcal{A}$ running in time t we have

$$\Pr[x \leftarrow \mathbb{Z}_q : \mathcal{A}(g, g^x, g^y) = g^{xy}] \leq \epsilon.$$

DDH oracle. A DDH oracle in group G is an algorithm that returns 1 on queries of the form (g, g^x, g^y, g^z) where $z = xy \bmod q$, and 0 on queries of the form (g, g^x, g^y, g^z) where $z \neq xy \bmod q$.

GDH Assumption. We say that the Gap Diffie-Hellman Problem (GDH) in group G is (ϵ, t)-hard if for every algorithm $\mathcal{A}$ running in time t on access to the DDH oracle $\mathsf{DDH_G}$ in group G we have

$$\Pr[x \leftarrow \mathbb{Z}_q : \mathcal{A}^{\mathsf{DDH_G}}(g, g^x, g^y) = g^{xy}] \leq \epsilon.$$

C   Proofs

Basic RSA-PPIT. RSA-PPIT is *secure, private, and client-unlinkable* under the RSA assumption described in Appendix B on safe RSA moduli and the GDH assumption in the Random Oracle Model, given semantically secure symmetric encryption.

Proof. We first prove the security and server-privacy by demonstrating that no efficient $\mathcal{A}$ (acting as a client) has a *non-negligible* advantage over $1/2$ against Ch in the following game:

1. Ch executes $(PK, SK) \leftarrow \mathsf{Setup}(1^\tau)$ and gives PK to $\mathcal{A}$.
2. $\mathcal{A}$ invokes Authorize on ID_j of its choice and obtains the corresponding signature σ_j.
3. $\mathcal{A}$ generates ID_0^*, ID_1^* and two equal-length data records D_0^*, D_1^*.
4. $\mathcal{A}$ participates in transfer as a client with message μ^*.
5. Ch selects one record pair by selecting a random bit b and executes the server's part of the transfer protocol on public input PK and private inputs (ID_b^*, D_b^*) with message (R, C).
6. $\mathcal{A}$ outputs b' and wins if $b = b'$.

Let HQuery be an event that $\mathcal{A}$ ever queries H' on input K^*, where K^* is defined (as the combination of message μ^* sent by $\mathcal{A}$ and message C sent by Ch), as follows: $K^* = (\mu^*)^{ez} \cdot (h^*)^{-2z} \bmod N$, where $R = (g)^{ez}$ and $h^* = H(ID^*)$. In other words, HQuery is an event that $\mathcal{A}$ computes (and enters into hash function H') the key-material K^* for the challenging protocol.

[Claim 1]: Unless HQuery happens, $\mathcal{A}$'s view of interaction with Ch on bit $b = 0$ is indistinguishable from $\mathcal{A}$'s view of the interaction with Ch on bit $b = 1$.

Since the distribution of $R = g^{ez}$ is independent from (ID_b, D_b), it reveals no information about which of (ID_b, D_b) is related in the protocol. Since PPIT uses a semantically secure symmetric encryption, the distribution with $b = 0$ is indistinguishable from that with $b = 1$, unless $\mathcal{A}$ computes $k^* = H'(K^*)$, in the random oracle model, by querying H', i.e., HQuery.

[Claim 2]: If event HQuery happens with non-negligible probability, then $\mathcal{A}$ can be used to violate the RSA assumption.

We describe a reduction algorithm called RCh using a modified challenger algorithm. Given the RSA challenge (N, e, α), RCh sets the public key as (N, e, g) where g is a generator of QR_N. RCh simulates signatures on each ID_j by assigning $H(ID_j)$ as $\sigma_j^e \bmod N$ for some random value σ_j. In this way RCh can present the certificate of ID_j as σ_j. RCh embeds α to each H query, by setting $H(ID_i) = \alpha(a_i)^e$ for random $a_i \in \mathbb{Z}_N$. Note that given $(H(ID_i))^d$ for any ID_i the simulator can extract $\alpha^d = (H(ID_i))^d / a_i$.

We describe how RCh responds to $\mathcal{A}$ in the transfer protocol and how RCh computes $(H(ID_i))^d$ for certain ID_i. On $\mathcal{A}$'s input message μ^*, RCh picks a random $m \leftarrow \mathbb{Z}_{N/4}$, computes $R = g^{(1+em)}$, and sends C and a random encryption C to $\mathcal{A}$. We remark that $g^{1+em} = g^{e(d+m)}$. On the HQuery event, RCh gets $K^* = (\mu^*)^{e(d+m)}(h^*)^{-2(d+m)}$ from $\mathcal{A}$. Since RCh knows μ^*, h^*, e, and m, RCh can compute $(h^*)^{2d}$. Since $gcd(2, e) = 1$, computing $(h^*)^{2d}$ leads to computing $(h^*)^d$.

We prove client-privacy and unlinkability. In the following description, we use $U \approx_S V$ to denote that distribution U is statistically close to V in the sense that the difference between these distributions is at most $O(2^\tau)$. We show that $\{h^{2d}g^x\}_{x \leftarrow \mathbb{Z}_{N/4}} \approx_S QR_N$. Take any $h \in \mathbb{Z}_N^*$ and compute $\sigma = h^d \bmod N$. (Note that since $N - (p'q')$ is on the order of $\sqrt{N}$, which is negligible compared to N, the distribution of h chosen in $\mathbb{Z}_N$ is statistically close to uniform in $\mathbb{Z}_N^*$.) Since multiplication by h^{2d} is a permutation in QR_N, we have

$$\{h^{2d}g^x\}_{x \leftarrow \mathbb{Z}_{p'q'}} \equiv QR_N.$$

Since $\mathbb{Z}_{N/4} \approx_S \mathbb{Z}_{p'q'}$, the above implies that

$$\{h^{2d}g^x\}_{x \leftarrow \mathbb{Z}_{N/4}} \approx_S QR_N.$$

Since client selects a random value for each protocol instance, it is easy to know that RSA-PPIT scheme also provides client-unlinkability. □

Basic Schnorr-PPIT. Schnorr-PPIT is *secure, private* (but *not* client-unlinkable) under the GDH assumption (described in Appendix B) in the Random Oracle Model, given semantically secure symmetric encryption.

Proof. Client-privacy is easy to know since $X = g^k$ for random k is independent from the ID value. We now prove security and server privacy. For the security and privacy, we use the same game as in RSA-PPIT security and server-privacy, except $\mathcal{A}$ sends X^* instead of μ^*.

Let HQuery be an event that $\mathcal{A}$ ever queries H' on input K^*, where K^* is defined via the combination of the message X^* sent by $\mathcal{A}$ and message R sent by Ch, as follows: $K^* = (X^*)^z \cdot (y)^{cz} \bmod p$, where $R = g^z$ and $c = H(i, X^*)$.

[Claim 3]: Unless HQuery happens, $\mathcal{A}$'s view of the interaction with the challenger on bit $b = 0$ is indistinguishable from $\mathcal{A}$'s view of the interaction with the challenger on bit $b = 1$.

[Claim 4]: If event HQuery happens with non-negligible probability, then $\mathcal{A}$ can be used to break the CDH assumption (described in Appendix B).

We describe a reduction algorithm called RCh using a modified challenger algorithm. The goal of a CDH problem on $(p, q, g, y = g^a, R = g^z)$ is to compute $g^{az} \bmod p$. RCh takes $(p, q, g, y = g^a)$ as its public key and simulates the signatures (X_j, s_j) on each ID j by taking random s_j, e_j and computing $X_j = g^{s_j} \cdot y^{e_j}$ and assigning $H(j, X_j)$ to e_j. Since the verification equation is satisfied and s_j, e_j are picked at random, this is indistinguishable from receiving real signatures. In the protocol on $\mathcal{A}$'s input X^*, RCh responds with $R = g^z$ and random encryption C.

Assume that HQuery happens, which can be detected by querying to DDH oracle on $(g, X^* \cdot y^e, g^z, Q_H)$ for every query input Q_H to H. Then, as in the forking lemma argument of [18], we know that $\mathcal{A}$ can be executed twice in a row with the same value $X = g^k \bmod p$ and different hash values such that $(e \neq e')$ and $\mathcal{A}$ wins both games with non-negligible probability of at least $\frac{\epsilon^2}{q_h}$, where q_H is the number of queries $\mathcal{A}$ makes to the hash function. This means, $\mathcal{A}$ can compute with non-negligible probability the values $K = g^{z(ea+k)} \bmod p$ and $K' = g^{z(e'a+k)} \bmod p$ with $e \neq e'$. Consequently, $\mathcal{A}$ can also efficiently compute g^{az}: $(K/K')^{(e-e')^{-1}} = (g^{zea-ze'a})^{(e-e')^{-1}} = (g^{za(e-e')})^{(e-e')^{-1}} = g^{az} \bmod p$. $\square$

Basic IBE-PPIT. IBE-PPIT is *secure, private and client-unlinkable* if IBE is semantically secure and key-private under selective ID attack.

Proof. Providing client-privacy and unlinkability is trivial since server does not receive any information from client in the transfer.

Assuming an underlying IBE system semantically secure under a chosen ciphertext attack and key-private, the resulting PPIT scheme is trivially *secure* and *server-private* against a malicious client. We prove this claim by contradiction. Assuming our claim is not true, then there exists a polynomial-bounded adversary $\mathcal{A}$ that wins the security game in Section 2. $\mathcal{A}$ is given the PK = "$\mathcal{A}$ is authorized to access the record ID" and the IBE-encryption of D_{ID} under the key PK but not the corresponding SK. If $\mathcal{A}$ decrypts D_{ID} with non-negligible probability, then we can construct a polynomial-bounded adversary $\mathcal{B}$ which uses $\mathcal{A}$ to break the CCA-security of IBE. This contradicts our assumption.

Finally, server-privacy is trivially achieved if the underlying IBE scheme is key-private. $\square$

RSA-PPIT Extension. RSA-PPIT extension in Figure 3 is *secure, private, and client-unlinkable* under the RSA assumption on safe RSA moduli in the Random Oracle Model, given semantically secure symmetric encryption.

Proof. The proof for the client-privacy and unlinkability is the same as shown in the proof for Theorem 1.

We now prove the security and server-privacy. The game for the extended scheme is the same as for the basic scheme, except the adversary challenges the protocol on two pairs of input vectors $(\overrightarrow{ID_0^*}, \overrightarrow{D_0^*})$, $(\overrightarrow{ID_1^*}, \overrightarrow{D_1^*})$, instead of (ID_0^*, D_0^*), (ID_1^*, D_1^*). Namely, we demonstrate that no efficient $\mathcal{A}$ (acting as a client) has a *non-negligible* advantage over $1/2$ against Ch in the following game:

1. Ch executes $(PK, SK) \leftarrow \mathsf{Setup}(1^\tau)$ and gives PK to $\mathcal{A}$.
2. $\mathcal{A}$ invokes Authorize on ID_j of its choice and obtains the corresponding signature σ_j.
3. $\mathcal{A}$ generates two ID vectors:
   $\overrightarrow{ID_0^*} = \{ID_{0i}\}_{i=1,\dots,n}$, $\overrightarrow{ID_1^*} = \{ID_{1i}\}_{i=1,\dots,n}$,
   and two corresponding record vectors
   $\overrightarrow{D_0^*} = \{D_{0i}\}_{i=1,\dots,n}$, $\overrightarrow{D_1^*} = \{D_{1i}\}_{i=1,\dots,n}$.
4. $\mathcal{A}$ participates in transfer as a client with message μ^*.
5. Ch selects one record pair by selecting a random bit b and executes the server's part of the transfer protocol on public input PK and private inputs $(\overrightarrow{ID_b^*}, \overrightarrow{D_b^*})$ with message (R, C).
6. $\mathcal{A}$ outputs b' and wins if $b = b'$.

We define HQuery the same event as in the proof for RSA-PPIT. By the hybrid argument, if the adversary wins the above game with a non-negligible advantage over $1/2$, HQuery happens on at least one pair (ID_{bj}^*, D_{bj}^*) out of $(\overrightarrow{ID_b^*}, \overrightarrow{D_b^*})$. Using this adversary, we can build a reduction algorithm to break the RSA assumption, by the same argument as described in the proof for Theorem 1. $\square$

Schnorr-PPIT Extension. Schnorr-PPIT extension in Figure 4 is *secure, private* (but *not* client-unlinkable) under the GDH assumption in the Random Oracle Model, given semantically secure symmetric encryption.

Proof. Again, as in the basic Schnorr-PPIT scheme, client-privacy is easy to know since $X = g^k$ for random k is independent from the ID value.

For the security and privacy, we use the same game used for Schnorr-PPIT security and server-privacy, except A selects two pairs of vectors $(\overrightarrow{ID_0^*}, \overrightarrow{D_0^*})$, $(\overrightarrow{ID_1^*}, \overrightarrow{D_1^*})$, instead of (ID_0^*, D_0^*), (ID_1^*, D_1^*). We define HQuery the same event as in the proof for Schnorr-PPIT. By the hybrid argument, if the adversary wins the above game with a non-negligible advantage over $1/2$, HQuery happens on at least one pair (ID_{bj}^*, D_{bj}^*) out of $(\overrightarrow{ID_b^*}, \overrightarrow{D_b^*})$. Using this adversary, we can build a reduction algorithm to break the GDH assumption, by the same argument as described in the proof for Theorem 2. $\square$

IBE-PPIT Extension. IBE-PPIT extension in Figure 5 is *secure, private and client-unlinkable* if IBE is semantically secure and key-private under selective ID attack.

Proof. Again, providing client-privacy and unlinkability is trivial since server does not receive any information from client in the transfer.

Assuming an underlying IBE system semantically secure under a chosen ciphertext attack, the resulting PPIT scheme is trivially *secure* and *server-private* against malicious C. This claim is true in the case of multiple records. The proof is similar to that described in Appendix C. Assuming our claim is not true then there exists a polynomial-bounded adversary A that wins the game on vectors $(\overrightarrow{ID_0^*}, \overrightarrow{D_0^*})$, $(\overrightarrow{ID_1^*}, \overrightarrow{D_1^*})$. By the hybrid argument, A decrypts at least one encrypted record out of $\overrightarrow{D_b^*}$ with $b \leftarrow \{0, 1\}$ without the corresponding secret key. This adversary can be used to construct an algorithm to break the CCA-security of IBE. This contradicts our assumption.

Furthermore, we argue that the use of key tags to reduce the number of client's decryptions do not affect the security and privacy of the scheme under the assumption that Boneh and Franklin's IBE instantiation [3]. Indeed, the key tags are bilinear maps operations as in BF-IBE. Hence, we claim that if the tags are not secure then there exists a polynomial-bounded adversary A that breaks the security of BF-IBE, contradicting our assumption. Finally, the re-use of randomness z (as described in Figure 5) has been proved to be CPA-secure in [5], thus we skip the entire proof for space limitation. □

Privacy-Preserving Computation and Verification of Aggregate Queries on Outsourced Databases[*]

Brian Thompson[1], Stuart Haber[2], William G. Horne[2],
Tomas Sander[2], and Danfeng Yao[1]

[1] Department of Computer Science
Rutgers University
Piscataway, NJ 08854, USA
{bthom,danfeng}@cs.rutgers.edu
[2] Hewlett-Packard Labs
5 Vaughn Drive, Suite 301
Princeton, NJ 08540, USA
{stuart.haber,william.horne,tomas.sander}@hp.com

Abstract. Outsourced databases provide a solution for data owners who want to delegate the task of answering database queries to third-party service providers. However, distrustful users may desire a means of verifying the integrity of responses to their database queries. Simultaneously, for privacy or security reasons, the data owner may want to keep the database hidden from service providers. This security property is particularly relevant for aggregate databases, where data is sensitive, and results should only be revealed for queries that are aggregate in nature. In such a scenario, using simple signature schemes for verification does not suffice. We present a solution in which service providers can collaboratively compute aggregate queries without gaining knowledge of intermediate results, and users can verify the results of their queries, relying only on their trust of the data owner. Our protocols are secure under reasonable cryptographic assumptions, and are robust to collusion among k dishonest service providers.

Keywords: Aggregate query, outsource, privacy, integrity, secret sharing, verification.

---

[*] This work has been supported in part by NSF grant CCF-0728937, CNS-0831186, and the Rutgers University Computing Coordination Council Pervasive Computing Initiative Grant. This material is also based upon work supported by the U.S. Department of Homeland Security under grant number 2008-ST-104-000016. The views and conclusions contained in this document are those of the authors and should not be interpreted as necessarily representing the official policies, either expressed or implied, of the U.S. Department of Homeland Security.

I. Goldberg and M. Atallah (Eds.): PETS 2009, LNCS 5672, pp. 185–201, 2009.

1   Introduction

Privacy concerns are still a major obstacle that makes sensitive data inaccessible to data mining researchers and prevents collaborative data analysis and filtering among multiple organizations from becoming a reality. Many databases contain sensitive information, and the data owner may not want to share it in full with untrusted entities. Thus, the data owner may only want to allow queries of a statistical or aggregate nature. This privacy requirement has become a common issue for large collections of sensitive data, with applications to census data, medical research, and educational testing [19]. For example, aggregate medical information about a group of patients may be accessible for research purposes. However, medical records of individual patients are confidential and should be kept hidden from all parties except for the hospital maintaining them [17].

An increasing trend in today's organizational data management is data outsourcing and cloud computing. An owner may choose to outsource the data, that is, to allow the data to be hosted by third-party service providers. The data hosts would be given the ability to store full or partial information from the database, and the capability to answer queries of a certain type. Data outsourcing alleviates the workload of the data owner in answering queries by delegating the tasks to powerful third-party servers with large computational and network resources.

However, data outsourcing poses additional privacy risks to the sensitive contents. The outsourcing service providers may not be fully trusted by the data owner, or may be susceptible to attacks by malicious parties (both internal and external). Studies have shown that in an outsourced setting it is extremely easy for malicious employees at the service provider organization to access the passwords of business owners and thus their customer data [5]. Security breaches at providers caused by outside adversaries may expose sensitive hosted information.

However, existing database-as-a-service (DAS) models are unable to support sophisticated queries such as aggregation while simultaneously maintaining the secrecy of microdata (i.e., individual data entries). Existing approaches based on the encryption of outsourced contents [1,31] apply to models where the user who queries the encrypted outsourced data is the data owner herself. We consider a more general setting where the database can be queried by anyone. Thus, there is a gap between the security guarantees provided by existing data outsourcing systems and the privacy needs of the data owners. To protect sensitive data from these threats, it is desirable to outsource the data in such a way that *aggregate queries can be computed without revealing microdata to service providers*. This paper presents a solution that realizes this goal.

Cross-domain collaborative data analysis is another application that motivates our work. For example, multiple regional hospitals collaborate to discover the most frequently occurring flu strain of the season in that area. Existing solutions that support multi-party privacy-preserving data mining require either a trusted or semi-trusted third-party to moderate the computation [28] or the active online participation of players in order to complete the computation [6,33]. Neither approach provides a practical solution that can be deployed and operated in a completely decentralized fashion. As it will soon become clear, we aim to realize a more practical model without any trusted party, where each data owner may preprocess their data once, independently, and then a (qualified) user can have aggregate query responses computed on the entire collection of data coming from heterogeneous data sources. The privacy-preserving requirement specifies that neither the user nor the service providers learn any microdata—just the aggregation results.

Aside from the aforementioned privacy requirements, an outsourcing framework should also address the clients' need for assurnace of the *integrity of query results*. Here, clients are individual customers of the data owner who queries the data. For example, a client may not trust a third-party service provider to accurately represent the data in the outsourced database. Suppose the client submits an aggregate query and receives an answer from the service provider. How can he be sure that the value was calculated correctly and completely without being permitted to see the individual data entries involved in the computation? Aggregate query integrity has been largely ignored in the current literature. By contrast, we present a comprehensive solution to the problem of securely computing and verifying aggregate queries on outsourced databases, as we describe next in more detail.

Our Contributions. In this paper, we formalize a model called PDAS (for Privacy-preserving Database-As-a-Service) for preserving privacy and integrity of aggregate query results. We describe a distributed architecture that supports querying outsourced data in a multi-player setting, in which a data owner delegates to third-party service providers the task of answering queries from users.

We construct lightweight cryptographic protocols for privacy-preserving computation and verification of the aggregate queries SUM and AVERAGE. We describe the handling of aggregate queries with SELECT clauses as an extension. Our protocols allow a user to verify correctness of aggregate results while the individual data values contributing to the results are kept secret from both the user and the service providers. The user interacts with a single service provider to obtain aggregate results, and can verify whether or not the service provider returns the correct results. Our solutions utilize simple cryptographic primitives such as threshold secret-sharing.

Our algorithms are efficient. Let n be the size of the data set, and let m be the number of service providers available to host the data. Let k be the threshold value, i.e. k data hosts must cooperate to compute a query. Then the setup cost is $O(nmk)$ time and $O(n)$ space for the data owner, plus a communication cost of $O(n)$ between the data owner and each of the m service providers. Each service provider requires $O(n)$ space but no additional setup time. The time complexity for computing a query over a subset of size s is only $O(s)$ for each of the k servers participating (done in parallel); the service provider responding to the query needs $O(k^2)$ time to compute the result, with a total communication complexity of $O(k)$ between the responder and the other servers. Verifying the result requires $O\left(\min(s \log n, n)\right)$ communication cost and run-time for the user.

2   Preliminaries

In this section, we provide background on the cryptographic building blocks we use to construct our solution.

2.1   Shamir's Secret-Sharing Scheme

In a k-out-of-n secret-sharing scheme, the data owner distributes *shares*, or parts, of the secret to n servers in such a way that any k of them can cooperate and recover the entire secret, but any smaller group cannot [29,4].

Shamir's secret-sharing scheme [29] is based on polynomial interpolation. Suppose there are m participants, and any k of them should be able to recover the secret S. Let q be a large prime. The distributor chooses a random $(k-1)$-degree polynomial P over the field $\mathbf{F}_q$ such that $P(0) = S$. That is, he chooses $a_1, \ldots, a_{k-1}$ independently and uniformly at random from $[0, q-1]$, and lets $a_0 = S$, where S is interpreted as an element of $\mathbf{F}_q$. The corresponding polynomial will be

$$P = a_{k-1}x^{k-1} + \ldots + a_1 x + a_0.$$

The share for each participant is a distinct point on P, but obviously not $P(0)$. If any k participants share their knowledge, they collectively will have k distinct points on the curve, from which they can determine P using polynomial interpolation, and thus recover the secret $S = P(0)$. If only $k-1$ participants cooperate, however, they will be unable to recover the polynomial. Furthermore, each different value of S would yield a different polynomial that agrees with their $k-1$ points, so they have gained no knowledge about the secret S.

2.2   Pedersen's Commitment Scheme

A commitment scheme is a protocol for committing to a value without revealing it to observers, so that knowledge of the value may later be proven, but the value to which the commitment was made cannot be changed. There are many different schemes; here, we will use the Pedersen commitment scheme [25] because of its homomorphic properties.

There are two parties involved, a Prover and a Verifier. The Prover would like to commit to a value x, and only reveal it at a later time. The Verifier wants to ensure that the Prover cannot modify the value of x during the protocol. Both parties first agree on a group G_p of prime order p, and choose two generators g, h for which the discrete log problem is believed to be difficult and $\log_g h$ is unknown. The Prover generates a random exponent r, and publishes the commitment $c = C_r(x) = g^x h^r \in G_p$. Due to the use of randomness, the Verifier cannot determine anything about x. Later the Prover may prove his knowledge of x by revealing both x and r to the Verifier, who then checks that $g^x h^r = c$ in G_p. Because of the presumed difficulty of finding, discrete logs, the Prover could not have changed his commitment to y because he would have had to find $r' = \log_h(c \cdot g^{-y})$. Thus the commitment scheme is computationally binding and unconditionally hiding.

The Pedersen scheme enjoys a convenient homomorphic property: Given commitments $c_i = C_{r_i}(x_i) \in G_p$ for $i = 1, \ldots, m$, it is easy to compute a commitment to the sum of the unknown values $X = \sum_{i=1}^{m} x_i \pmod{p}$ simply by computing the product of the individual commitments: $\prod_{i=1}^{m} c_i = C_R(X) \in G_p$, where $R = \sum_{i=1}^{m} r_i \pmod{p}$.

3   Models and Definitions

There are three types of players in our model. A *data owner* is the creator or maintainer of a database. The data owner delegates to a set of *service providers* the responsibility of answering queries. A *user* obtains query responses from a single service provider and does not interact directly with the data owner. The basic interaction model is as follows: The data owner gives the service providers partial information about each entry in the database, along with auxiliary information that enables the verification of query results. Upon receiving a query, a service provider seeks the cooperation of $k - 1$ other service providers, who may then jointly reconstruct the result of the query. The result is then passed back to the user, along with sufficient information for the user to verify its correctness.

Here we describe our **trust model** among the players. Our model is similar to the trust assumptions of existing literature on outsourced databases [13,21].

- *Between data owner and service provider:* The data owner trusts an honest service provider to follow the protocol. Honest service providers are expected not to disclose their data directly to others, but rather only to provide information as dictated by the protocol. Dishonest service providers may collude in order to attempt to reconstruct data entries in the database from their shares, or may not follow the protocol. For example, they may reveal their shares to others or replace their shares with arbitrary values when answering queries.
- *Between service provider and user:* The service provider is not necessarily trusted to answer queries correctly, since it may be malicious or compromised by outside attacks. Therefore, the user should be able to verify that responses from the service provider are correct and complete.
- *Between data owner and user:* The user must trust the data owner in the sense that the user trusts any messages signed with respect to the data owner's public key.

Adversarial Model. There are three types of adversaries in our model.

- A curious player (user or service provider) who wants to infer the individual data entries from the response to an aggregate query.
- A compromised service provider who may provide untruthful aggregate results or not follow the protocol.
- An adversary who may intercept and tamper with the protocol communication, e.g., modifying query results, inserting or deleting messages.

Operations. At setup, the data owner takes as input a security parameter, computes a public-key/private-key pair (PK, SK) for a digital signature system, and public parameters *params*. The data owner keeps SK secret. We define the following operations: COMMIT, DISTRIBUTE, QUERY, RESPOND, and VERIFY.

COMMIT: The data owner takes as input a data set $D = (x_1, \ldots, x_n)$. It generates auxiliary information *aux*, computes a digital signature Sig, and publishes (aux, Sig) to m service providers.

DISTRIBUTE: The data owner splits database entries among the m service providers in such a way that it requires at least k providers to jointly retrieve the original values.

QUERY: The user sends to a service provider SP_j a request for an aggregate query Q over a selection of data set D.

RESPOND: SP_j and $k - 1$ other service providers jointly compute the aggregate answer *ans*. SP_j prepares the correctness and integrity proofs *pf*, and returns the tuple (ans, pf, Sig) to the user.

VERIFY: The user takes as input $(params, ans, pf, Sig)$. It verifies that the answer *ans* satisfies correctness and integrity properties using proofs *pf*, signature Sig, and the public key PK of the data owner (that is obtained from a trusted source). The answer is accepted if the verification passes.

Security properties. *Secrecy, correctness, integrity,* and *collusion-resistance* are the four required security properties in our protocol.

Intuitively, *secrecy* requires that no entity besides the data owner should learn more about the data set D than is implied by (Q, ans). *Correctness* requires that *ans* is the correct response to query Q. *Integrity* requires that *ans* is computed based on authentic (outsourced) data set D that has not been tampered with. *Collusion-resistance* requires that $k - 1$ or less dishonest service providers cannot collude to break the secrecy requirement.

We address the property of correctness in Section 4, and the other three properties in our formal definition of security, which is given in Section 5.

4   Our Protocol

For the simplicity of description, we consider a database D with n rows and one column, with each cell containing a positive integer.[1] All of our protocols can easily be generalized to accommodate multiple attributes (i.e., columns). Let $D = x_1, \ldots, x_n$. The data owner would like to outsource his database to m different servers, but with an important security requirement: *any k servers can cooperate to determine the answer to an aggregate query, but $k - 1$ cooperating servers cannot.* To achieve this requirement, our approach is to have the

---

[1] Our computation can also be applied to strings or multimedia data, which first need to be converted into numerical values using an encoding or transformation mechanism.

Table 1. Notation used in our protocol

D	A database
S	A subset of D
x	A database entry (or cell)
n	Number of rows
m	Number of service providers (SPs)
P	A polynomial
$P_i(j)$	SP_j's share of value x_i
k	Threshold for secret-sharing scheme
c_i	Commitment to x_i with random seed r_i
X	An aggregate query result

data owner distribute the original entries among multiple service providers via a simple threshold secret-sharing scheme. In a naive solution, a service provider SP_j asks $k-1$ other providers for their secret shares of the data entries relevant to the query, and then combines the values to compute the aggregate for the user. Unfortunately, this naive approach fails because SP_j reconstructs the individual data entries as an intermediate result, which violates our privacy requirement.

To solve this problem, we leverage a nice and simple feature of polynomials that allows service providers to first aggregate or *blend* their shares associated with the distinct data entries, and then send the blended values to SP_j. The data leakage problem is eliminated as the service provider SP_j is unable to retrieve individual data shares. Yet, it can still interpolate the polynomial based on the blended shares to obtain the final aggregate result. A more detailed description is given next.

Furthermore, to verify the correctness of the aggregate computation, we use a special type of commitment scheme, namely a homomorphic commitment scheme, which allows anyone to verify the query result without knowing the data. PDAS also achieves the integrity requirement by cleverly utilizing existing authentication data structures over commitment values. As a result, the tampering of data entries during the computation process can be detected while the secrecy of data is safely protected.

PDAS Protocol

The PDAS protocol is run between the data owner, the service providers, and the user. Let $N = \sum_{i=1}^{n} x_i$. For the setup, the data owner chooses a large prime $q \gg N$. This will avoid potential problems with overflow later. The computation associated with aggregate queries is performed in the field $\mathbf{F}_q$. The computation with Pedersen's commitment is in group G_p. The operations in PDAS include COMMIT, DISTRIBUTE, QUERY, RESPOND, and VERIFY.

COMMIT The data owner chooses parameters (G_p, g, h) and computes commitments for the data entries using the Pedersen commitment scheme described in Section 2.2:

$$c_1 = C_{r_1}(x_1), \ldots, c_n = C_{r_n}(x_n).$$

The data owner then generates a Merkle hash tree [20] on the commitment values, and signs on the root hash of the tree.

DISTRIBUTE The data owner distributes each database entry x_i, along with its corresponding random seed r_i, according to Shamir's secret-sharing protocol (Section 2.1) as follows. He chooses random polynomials P_i and Q_i with $P_i(0) = x_i$ and $Q_i(0) = r_i$, and to service provider SP_j for $1 \le j \le m$, he gives the share $(j, P_i(j), Q_i(j))$. Thus, SP_j has the values $(j, P_1(j), Q_1(j)), \ldots, (j, P_n(j), Q_n(j))$. Shares $P_i(j)$ are for answering aggregate queries, and shares $Q_i(j)$ are for integrity and correctness verification. The data owner also gives both the entire Merkle hash tree and his signature on the root hash to all m service providers. The data owner can delete the intermediate values from storage.

QUERY A user submits an aggregate query to a service provider, say SP_1. Let us assume the query is for the SUM $X^S = \sum_{i \in S} x_i$ over the values in a subset $S \subseteq D$. (See Section 6 for more discussion on SELECT queries.) SP_1 then sends messages requesting cooperation from $k - 1$ other service providers.

RESPOND The k service providers now jointly compute the aggregate query result X^S. Note that they simultaneously compute the corresponding value R^S for the purpose of verification.

1. Each of the k service providers computes its *share of the aggregate result* as follows. Provider SP_j computes $X_j^S = \sum_{i \in S} P_i(j)$, where $P_i(j)$ is the SP_j's share of value x_i. Similarly, SP_j calculates its *share of the random seed* $R_j^S = \sum_{i \in S} Q_i(j)$. Both X_j^S and R_j^S are returned to SP_1.
2. Provider SP_1 collects all $k - 1$ shares (j, X_j^S), plus its own sum of relevant shares. Using polynomial interpolation, SP_1 determines the unique polynomial P of degree $k - 1$ passing though these k coordinates. It computes $X = P(0)$ as the aggregate result.
3. Again using polynomial interpolation, SP_1 determines the unique polynomial Q of degree $k-1$ passing through the k points (j, R_j^S) from the $k-1$ assisting providers and itself, and computes $R = Q(0)$.
4. SP_1 finally sends the following information to the user: $(X, R, \{c_i\}_{i \in S}, Proof)$, where c_i is the commitment for value x_i, and the *Proof* contains the values of all sibling nodes along paths from the commitments to the root in the Merkle hash tree, and the data owner's signature on the root hash. The *Proof* is provided to the user to verify the integrity of x_i and correctness of computation without revealing the microdata.

VERIFY Upon receiving response $(X, R, \{c_i\}_{i \in S}, Proof)$, the user verifies that the obtained sum X is *correctly computed on the original data*.

1. Using the publicly-known hash function, the user re-computes the root hash of the Merkle hash tree from the commitments $\{c_i\}_{i \in S}$ and their sibling

values, which are in *Proof*. He verifies the signature of the root hash using the public key of the data owner, and therefore knows that he has the *authentic* commitment values.[2]

2. With value R and the public parameters g and h, the user calculates the corresponding commitment $C_R(X) = g^X h^R$.

3. The user checks whether the SUM is computed correctly by verifying that the obtained SUM is consistent with the individual commitments. If $\prod_{i \in S} c_i = C_R(X)$, then the delivered answer is accepted.

Correctness of PDAS

The correctness of our algorithm is based on the additive property of polynomials over a field F. If $P = P_1 + P_2$, then $P(x) = P_1(x) + P_2(x)$ for all $x \in F$. We state this claim concisely that, *the sum of the shares is a share of the sum*.

When the data owner distributes the data, he creates a polynomial P_i for each data item x_i. Each service provider SP_j gets a share that is the point $(j, P_i(j))$ along the curve. When a service provider receives a request for a SUM $X^S = \sum_{i \in S} x_i$ over the subset S, it returns the sum of its relevant shares, $X_j^S = \sum_{i \in S} P_i(j)$.

Consider the polynomial $\hat{P} = \sum_{i \in S} P_i$. The summed value returned by service provider SP_j in our protocol is $X_j^S = \sum_{i \in S} P_i(j) = \hat{P}(j)$. When the responding service provider interpolates the polynomial from these k values, it derives the summation polynomial $\hat{P}$. Therefore, the value $\hat{P}(0)$ returned to the user is equal to the desired aggregate value:

$$\hat{P}(0) = \sum_{i \in S} P_i(0) = \sum_{i \in S} x_i = X^S.$$

AVERAGE can be easily computed and verified by dividing SUM by the size of the subset $s = |S|$. Similarly, the above protocol can be generalized to compute any linear combination on the selected entries. Just as $(P+Q)(x) = P(x)+Q(x)$, we also have $(aP)(x) = a \cdot P(x)$, where a is an element of the field $\mathbf{F}_q$. For example, a user can query for the sum $3x_1 + 5x_2 + 12x_3 + \ldots$. To that end, each service provider simply needs to multiply their shares by the appropriate scalars.

The above description completes the basic operations in our PDAS protocol. In Section 6, we describe several important extensions to PDAS, including how SELECT can be realized, support for multiple data owners, and how to accommodate dynamic databases.

5 Security and Efficiency

In this section, we analyze the adversary model and prove the security of PDAS. We also give the complexity analysis of our protocols. We provide security definitions, and prove that PDAS satisfies those security requirements.

---

[2] As in many security protocols, we assume that the user has an authenticated copy of the data owner's public key.

We consider an attacker who can access *all commitment and signature values*, and can *adaptively choose a sequence of aggregate queries*, i.e., queries for aggregate results and their proofs. The adversary's goal is to have a non-negligible probability of success in violating one of the security properties of our protocol: *secrecy*, *integrity*, or *collusion-resistance*.

We consider three types of attacks: using intermediate or aggregate results to deduce sensitive information about individual entries (*inference attack*), computing a new incorrect query-response pair that passes the VERIFY algorithm (*spoofing attack*), or disrupting the computation of an aggregate query (*disruption attack*). We give security proofs for the inference and spoofing attacks, reducing the existence of a successful polynomially bounded adversary to the existence of an adversary that successfully breaks one or more of the signature scheme, the Pedersen commitment scheme, or the one-way hash function. We then explain how PDAS can easily deal with disruption attacks.

An adversary may act as a user, a service provider, or have a network of colluding service providers. Note that a SP can simulate a user's query request, and thus has at least as much discerning power as a user. Under our security assumptions, the value of k is chosen to be greater than the number of dishonest or compromised service providers. For the rest of this discussion, we assume the worst case: a *network adversary* that has a network of $k-1$ colluding service providers.

Theorem 1. *The PDAS protocol provides information theoretic security against an inference attack by a computationally unbounded adversary. No information is leaked beyond that which can be deduced from the aggregate query results alone.*

Proof. Consider a network adversary who requests aggregate queries over l subsets of the data $S_1, \ldots, S_l$, yielding sums $X^{S_1}, \ldots, X^{S_l}$. To determine each sum X^{S_i}, he may request the corresponding shares from any of the m service providers: $X_1^{S_i}, \ldots, X_m^{S_i}$. In addition, he has access to all data shares from the $k-1$ service providers $SP_{\alpha_1}, \ldots, SP_{\alpha_{k-1}}$ in his adversarial network.

Suppose the adversary has an algorithm A that takes as input $\{X_1^{S_i}, \ldots, X_m^{S_i} | i = 1, \ldots, l\}$ and returns some sensitive information about the database (e.g., one of the individual data entries). Let O_A be an oracle for algorithm A. We construct an algorithm A^* that computes the same output as A but using only the l aggregate query results as input.

1. Input the aggregate query results $X^{S_1}, \ldots, X^{S_l}$.
2. Compute the aggregate shares $X_{\alpha_j}^{S_1}, \ldots, X_{\alpha_j}^{S_l}$ for each service provider SP_{α_j} in the adversarial network.
3. The aggregate query result X^{S_1} and the $k-1$ shares $X_{\alpha_1}^{S_1}, \ldots, X_{\alpha_{k-1}}^{S_1}$ are in total k points along the polynomial P_{S_1}; similarly for $P_{S_2}, \ldots, P_{S_l}$. Derive $P_{S_1}, \ldots, P_{S_l}$ using polynomial interpolation.
4. Query the oracle O_A using input $\{P_{S_i}(1), \ldots, P_{S_i}(m) | i = 1, \ldots, l\}$, and return the result.

Therefore no information about the data is leaked that cannot be gained from the query results alone, and so we have guaranteed the security properties of *secrecy* and *collusion-resistance*. The question of whether sensitive information can be inferred from the combination of multiple aggregate query results is an orthogonal issue known as *inference control* [9,17], and privacy guarantees pertaining to that are beyond the scope of this paper.

Note that an adversary may also try to recover individual data entries using the published commitment values. However, a similar argument to that above shows that the individual random seeds involved in the commitment protocol are protected by the same means as for data entries. Since the random seeds are not disclosed, the Pedersen commitment scheme enjoys unconditional hiding of committed values (see Section 2.2).

Theorem 2. *The PDAS protocol is secure against a spoofing attack by a polynomially-bounded adversary. An adversary with access to the committed database values and signature on the root hash of the data owner's Merkle hash tree cannot spoof the data owner's signature on commitments to a set of incorrect data entries in polynomial time with non-negligible probability.*

Proof. Suppose an adversary computes a new incorrect query-response pair that passes the VERIFY algorithm. Since the VERIFY algorithm checks the commitments against a signed root hash, the adversary must have achieved one of the following:

1. Generated a new pair (x_i', r_i') such that $C_{r_i'}(x_i') = C_{r_i}(x_i)$.
2. Generated a commitment to a new value (x_i'', r_i'') such that $H(C_{r_i''}(x_i'')) = H(C_{r_i}(x_i))$, where H is the collision-resistant hash function used in constructing the Merkle hash tree.
3. Forged the data owner's signature for the resulting new root hash.

In case (1), the adversary has broken the computationally binding property of the Pedersen commitment scheme. Case (2) is equivalent to finding a collision in the collision-resistant hash function. In case (3), the adversary has broken the signature scheme. By the respective security guarantees of these cryptographic tools, these tasks cannot be achieved with non-negligible probability in polynomial time. Thus we have preserved the *integrity* of the data.

Claim: *PDAS can effectively counter disruption attacks.*

Note that under our security assumptions, a service provider who gives an incorrect share value for a query can be detected. In this case, we would like to guarantee that the user can still retrieve the correct results of a query. This fault-tolerance property can be achieved using a publicly verifiable secret-sharing scheme [26], even if there are $k - 1$ dishonest service providers disrupting the procedure. Due to space limitations, discussion is omitted in this paper.

Furthermore, in the PDAS model, service providers can easily be held accountable for their actions. That is, if a service provider gives several faulty values, it can be reported to the data owner, who can then disregard the bad SP and redistribute the data to the remaining $m - 1$ service providers.

Table 2. Summary of computation and space complexities for PDAS, not including communication costs. DISTRIBUTE and QUERY are omitted because they incur no computation cost. Here, s is the size of the subset over which the query is performed.

	COMMIT	RESPOND	VERIFY	Storage
Data Owner	$O(nmk)$	——	——	$O(n)$
Primary SP	——	$O(k^2)$	——	$O(n)$
Helper SP	——	$O(s)$	——	
User	——	——	$O(\min(s\log n, n))$	——

Table 3. Communication complexity of operations in PDAS. There is no communication cost associated with the COMMIT or VERIFY operations.

	DISTRIBUTE	QUERY	RESPOND
Data Owner	$O(nm)$	——	
Primary SP	$O(n)$	$O(ks\log n)$	$O(k)$
Helper SP		$O(s\log n)$	$O(\min(s\log n, n))$
User	——	$O(s\log n)$	$O(\min(s\log n, n))$

Efficiency of PDAS The run-time, space, and communication complexities of operations by each entity in PDAS are summarized in Tables 2 and 3. We note that the amount of storage required at the data owner is $O(n)$ instead of $O(nk)$, since the data owner does not need to store all the secret shares. The shares are erased by the data owner after they are distributed to service providers.

6   Extensions

Our PDAS protocol provides a general framework for managing the privacy and security of outsourced databases. In this section, we describe several important extensions of PDAS, including the handling of dynamic insertions and deletions, selection queries, and multiple data owners.

While some real databases remain largely unchanged over time, many other applications require a database system to allow for the addition or deletion of database entries. The first question to ask, then, is how well our infrastructure for outsourced databases can deal with dynamic data. Similarly to before, we assume that honest service providers follow the protocol specification.

Additions. When a new entry is added to the database, the data owner generates a random polynomial for the entry and distributes shares according to our protocol (Section 4). The shares of other database entries were independently generated and are not affected. The data owner must also update the Merkle hash tree and broadcast the update to all service providers. However, because of the tree structure, this only incurs an additional $O(\log n)$ cost.

Deletions. In the case of a deletion, the data owner simply needs to broadcast to the service providers that they must delete their shares of that entry. There is

User ID	age	state	[weight]
00159265	16	NJ	122
00173094	35	NJ	168
00298216	18	CA	145

```
SELECT AVG weight WHERE age > 15 AND age < 19 AND state = 'NJ'
```

Fig. 1. An aggregate query for the sensitive attribute 'weight', computed over a selection based on insensitive attributes

no need to remove the commitment value from the Merkle hash tree - the value will just never be used again during verification.

Since all secret-sharing polynomials are independently and randomly chosen, these additional operations introduced to the PDAS protocol do not affect our security guarantees. In conclusion, our protocol can accommodate dynamic databases both efficiently and securely.

Our database system can also handle multi-attribute data and answer complex aggregate queries. Consider a database with one attribute containing sensitive data, and also several insensitive attributes, such as the example given in Figure 1. Values for the sensitive attribute will be distributed according to our secret-sharing protocol, whereas values for the insensitive attributes can be sent to the service providers in plaintext. When a user poses a complex query, the responding service provider first determines the subset over which to aggregate using the selection conditions on the insensitive data, and then computes the aggregate query according the PDAS protocol.

Consider an environment in which several data owners have disjoint sets of data with the same attributes, and are willing to collaborate to allow aggregate queries over the union of their data. However, they still want to protect the privacy of their own constituents, so are not willing to reveal their data to the other parties.

This scenario fits in perfectly with our PDAS protocol. The collaborating parties must first agree on choosing several parameters: the field $\mathbf{F}_q$, the m service providers, the security parameter k, and the parameters for the commitment scheme (G_p, g, h). From then on, their contributions are independent of each other. Each data owner distributes his data and signs on the root hash of his Merkle hash tree. A service provider may then take aggregates over all the data regardless of its origin. When verifying a query result, the service provider simply sends the commitment values from the appropriate data owners.

7 Related Work

A substantial amount of research has been done on how to verify outsourced data and computation [3,7,14,13,15,21,22,23,18], including the verification of both correctness and completeness of relational database queries. Existing literature on database query verification has focused on non-aggregate queries such as select, project, join, set union, and set intersect. Merkle hash trees have been used extensively for authentication of data elements [20]. Aggregate signatures are another approach for data authentication, where each data tuple is signed by the data owner [23]. The privacy issue of verifying non-aggregate queries was addressed in [24], which gave an elegant solution using hashing for proving the completeness of selection queries without revealing neighboring entries.

The aggregate query verification problem has been studied in the DAS model [14,15,22], an instantiation of the computing model involving clients who store their data at an untrusted server, which is administrated by a third-party service provider. The clients have limited computational power and storage, and thus rely on the service provider for its large computational resources. The challenge is to make it impossible for the service provider to correctly interpret the data, but still allow it to compute and return aggregate queries. The data is owned by the clients, and only they are permitted to perform queries on the database.

The paper by Hacigümüs, Iyer, and Mehrotra addresses the execution of aggregate queries over encrypted data using a homomorphic encryption scheme [15]. Their model has two parties: the data owner and the untrusted service provider. Mykletun and Tsudik propose an alternative approach where the data owner pre-computes and encrypts the aggregate results and stores them at the service provider [22]. Hohenberger and Lysyanskaya were the first to give formal security definitions for outsourced computation, and probabilistic solutions for checking failures in outsourced exponentiation and the Cramer-Shoup cryptosystem [16]. However, these solutions are only applicable to the two-party model, where the querier is also the data owner. In comparison, our PDAS protocol works in the more general three-party model, where the client who queries the service provider may not be the same as the data owner.

In the data mining literature, one approach to protecting data privacy is to publish modified versions of database tables so that each individual entry enjoys a certain degree of anonymity [2,27,30,32]. This imposes no restrictions on queries that may be performed on the data, but the anonymization process necessarily introduces some loss of integrity in the accuracy of the data. Our solutions differ from these efforts in that we support authenticated data analysis without releasing any data to the public. Because the aggregate is computed over exact data instead of anonymized data, there is no loss of data accuracy in the aggregation results.

A new approach to providing anonymity when sharing data has appeared with the recent stream of research on *differential privacy* [8,11,12,10], in which noise is added to query results to prevent the querier from inferring information about individuals. Our work, on the other hand, is concerned with adding proofs of integrity to exact responses to queries to the database, and so our protocols are vulnerable to the privacy attacks studied in the differential privacy literature—as are all protocols whose responses to queries are close to exact. It is a challenging open problem to design protocols that resist the differential-privacy attacks while still providing integrity guarantees for the protocol's responses compared to the original data.

8 Conclusions

In this paper, we proposed a simple privacy-preserving protocol PDAS for computing and verifying queries in outsourced databases. We focused on computing aggregate queries including SUM and AVERAGE with SELECT clauses. The main goal of PDAS is to prevent microdata (i.e., individual data entries) from being accessed by users or any of the third-party service providers who are delegated by the data owner to answer queries. Existing DAS models are unable to support sophisticated queries such as aggregation while maintaining secrecy of microdata simultaneously. We overcame this challenge and introduced two main techniques:

- **A distributed architecture** is introduced for outsourcing databases using multiple service providers. We extended threshold secret sharing schemes to support sophisticated aggregation operations by leveraging the additive property of polynomials over a field.
- **A verification protocol** is developed for the user to verify that the outsourced computation is indeed computed correctly, *without* leaking any microdata.

We provided security analysis that our protocol achieves secrecy, integrity, correctness, and collusion-resistance properties. We also discussed possible variants of our PDAS model, including handling of dynamic databases, multiple data owners, and inference control.

References

1. Abdalla, M., Bellare, M., Catalano, D., Kiltz, E., Kohno, T., Lange, T., Lee, J.M., Neven, G., Paillier, P., Shi, H.: Searchable encryption revisited: Consistency properties, relation to anonymous IBE, and extensions. In: Shoup, V. (ed.) CRYPTO 2005. LNCS, vol. 3621, pp. 205–222. Springer, Heidelberg (2005)
2. Agrawal, R., Srikant, R.: Privacy-preserving data mining. In: Proceedings of the ACM SIGMOD International Conference on Management of Data (May 2000)
3. Bertino, E., Ooi, B.C., Yang, Y., Deng, R.H.: Privacy and ownership preserving of outsourced medical data. In: Proceedings of the 21st International Conference on Data Engineering (ICDE), pp. 521–532 (2005)
4. Blakley, G.: Safeguarding cryptographic keys. In: Proceedings of AFIPS National Computer Conference, pp. 313–317 (1979)
5. Chumash, T., Yao, D.: Detection and prevention of insider threats in database driven web services. In: Proceedings of The Third IFIP WG 11.11 International Conference on Trust Management (IFIPTM) (June 2009)
6. Cruz, I.F., Tamassia, R., Yao, D.: Privacy-preserving schema matching using mutual information. In: Barker, S., Ahn, G.-J. (eds.) Data and Applications Security 2007. LNCS, vol. 4602, pp. 93–94. Springer, Heidelberg (2007)

7. Devanbu, P., Gertz, M., Martel, C., Stubblebine, S.: Authentic third-party data publication. Journal of Computer Security 11(3) (2003)

8. Dinur, I., Nissim, K.: Revealing information while preserving privacy. In: PODS, pp. 202–210 (2003)

9. Domingo-Ferrer, J. (ed.): Inference Control in Statistical Databases. LNCS, vol. 2316. Springer, Heidelberg (2002)

10. Dwork, C.: Differential privacy: A survey of results. In: Agrawal, M., Du, D.-Z., Duan, Z., Li, A. (eds.) TAMC 2008. LNCS, vol. 4978, pp. 1–19. Springer, Heidelberg (2008)

11. Dwork, C., McSherry, F., Nissim, K., Smith, A.: Calibrating noise to sensitivity in private data analysis. In: Halevi, S., Rabin, T. (eds.) TCC 2006. LNCS, vol. 3876, pp. 265–284. Springer, Heidelberg (2006)

12. Ganta, S.R., Kasiviswanathan, S.P., Smith, A.: Composition attacks and auxiliary information in data privacy. CoRR, abs/0803.0032 (2008)

13. Hacigümüs, H., Iyer, B., Li, C., Mehrotra, S.: Executing SQL over encrypted data in the database-service provider model. In: Proceedings of ACM SIGMOD Conference on Management of Data, pp. 216–227. ACM Press, New York (2002)

14. Hacigümüs, H., Iyer, B., Mehrotra, S.: Providing database as a service. In: Proceedings of International Conference on Data Engineering (ICDE) (March 2002)

15. Hacigümüs, H., Iyer, B., Mehrotra, S.: Efficient execution of aggregation queries over encrypted databases. In: Proceedings of International Conference on Database Systems for Advanced Applications (DASFAA) (2004)

16. Hohenberger, S., Lysyanskaya, A.: How to securely outsource cryptographic computations. In: Kilian, J. (ed.) TCC 2005. LNCS, vol. 3378, pp. 264–282. Springer, Heidelberg (2005)

17. Jagannathan, G., Wright, R.N.: Private inference control for aggregate database queries. In: ICDM Workshops, pp. 711–716. IEEE Computer Society, Los Alamitos (2007)

18. Li, F., Hadjieleftheriou, M., Kollios, G., Reyzin, L.: Dynamic authenticated index structures for outsourced databases. In: Chaudhuri, S., Hristidis, V., Polyzotis, N. (eds.) SIGMOD Conference, pp. 121–132. ACM, New York (2006)

19. Massell, P., Zayatz, L., Funk, J.: Protecting the confidentiality of survey tabular data by adding noise to the underlying microdata: Application to the commodity flow survey. In: Domingo-Ferrer, J., Franconi, L. (eds.) PSD 2006. LNCS, vol. 4302, pp. 304–317. Springer, Heidelberg (2006)

20. Merkle, R.: Protocols for public key cryptosystems. In: Proceedings of the 1980 Symposium on Security and Privacy, pp. 122–133. IEEE Computer Society Press, Los Alamitos (1980)

21. Mykletun, E., Narasimha, M., Tsudik, G.: Authentication and integrity in outsourced databases. In: Proceedings of Symposium on Network and Distributed Systems Security (NDSS) (February 2004)

22. Mykletun, E., Tsudik, G.: Aggregation queries in the database-as-a-service model. In: IFIP WG 11.3 Working Conference on Data and Applications Security (DBSec) (July 2006)

23. Narasimha, M., Tsudik, G.: Authentication of outsourced databases using signature aggregation and chaining. In: International Conference on Database Systems for Advanced Applications (DASFAA) (April 2006)

24. Pang, H., Jain, A., Ramamritham, K., Tan, K.-L.: Verifying completeness of relational query results in data publishing. In: Proceedings of the ACM SIGMOD International Conference on Management of Data (SIGMOD), pp. 407–418 (2005)

25. Pedersen, T.P.: Non-interactive and information-theoretic secure verifiable secret sharing. In: Feigenbaum, J. (ed.) CRYPTO 1991. LNCS, vol. 576, pp. 129–140. Springer, Heidelberg (1992)
26. Pedersen, T.P.: Non-interactive and information-theoretic secure verifiable secret sharing. In: Feigenbaum, J. (ed.) CRYPTO 1991. LNCS, vol. 576, pp. 129–140. Springer, Heidelberg (1992)
27. Samarati, P.: Protecting respondent's privacy in microdata release. IEEE Transactions on Knowledge and Data Engineering 13(6), 1010–1027 (2001)
28. Scannapieco, M., Figotin, I., Bertino, E., Elmagarmid, A.K.: Privacy preserving schema and data matching. In: Proceedings of the ACM SIGMOD International Conference on Management of Data, pp. 653–664 (2007)
29. Shamir, A.: How to share a secret. Communications of the ACM 22(11), 612–613 (1979)
30. Sweeney, L.: k-Anonymity, a model for protecting privacy. International Journal on Uncertainty, Fuzziness and Knowledge-based Systems 10(5), 557–570 (2002)
31. Waters, B.R., Balfanz, D., Durfee, G., Smetters, D.K.: Building an encrypted and searchable audit log. In: Proceedings of Symposium on Network and Distributed Systems Security (NDSS 2004) (2004)
32. Xiao, X., Tao, Y.: Anatomy: Simple and effective privacy preservation. In: Proceedings of the 32nd Very Large Data Bases (VLDB) (2006)
33. Yao, D., Frikken, K.B., Atallah, M.J., Tamassia, R.: Private information: To reveal or not to reveal. ACM Trans. Inf. Syst. Secur. 12(1) (2008)

APOD: Anonymous Physical Object Delivery

Elli Androulaki and Steven Bellovin

Columbia University
{elli,smb}@cs.columbia.edu

Abstract. Delivery of products bought online can violate consumers' privacy, although not in a straightforward way. In particular, delivery companies that have contracted with a website know the company selling the product, as well as the name and address of the online customer. To make matters worse, if the same delivery company has contracted with many websites, aggregated information per address may be used to profile customers' transaction activities. In this paper, we present a fair delivery service system with guaranteed customer anonymity and merchant-customer unlinkability, with reasonable assumptions about the threat model.

1 Introduction

A lot of work has been done over the last 25–30 years on privacy for networking and paying for products. Here, we address privacy concerns from the delivery of products to the buyers. Delivery of purchases made online is usually performed by a courier company who has contracted with the website selling the product (merchant). Based on the current product delivery infrastructure and a plausible threat model, we propose a privacy-preserving product system.

Privacy Concerns. Product delivery raises many privacy concerns, primarily deriving from information the delivery company acquires from the merchant. As noted, the delivery company is usually under contract to the seller. Given the (usually) long-term monetary relationship between the two, the delivery company knows the following: *(a)* the type of products the merchants sell; *(b)* the name and shipping address of the person the product is for. This person may or may not be the one who bought the product; *(c)* the exact object shipped, if it is fragile or of great value.

Certainly, the courier company knows the person to whom the product is delivered, as well as the type of the product. In addition, since the same delivery company may serve a variety of other websites, the former may obtain a very good approximation of the transaction profile of consumers who often make purchases online.

Our Contribution. In this paper, we will introduce a privacy-preserving delivery system based on package-routing through multiple courier companies, where,

- the courier company knows at most the merchant or the type of the product shipped, but not the recipient.
- there is no way for the merchant to recover the address of the intended recipient without collaborating with more than one courier company.

I. Goldberg and M. Atallah (Eds.): PETS 2009, LNCS 5672, pp. 202–215, 2009.

We emphasize on the fact that our system is deployable. Our threat model is based on the powers of any current real-world delivery system entities. For the purposes of our protocols, we made use of blind ([C81], [CL02], [O06]) and group ([CS97]) signatures as well as of blind group signature schemes ([LR98]).

Organization. In the following section we provide a brief overview of our system entities and requirements with a particular focus on privacy definition and threat model. Sections 3 and 4 present in detail our delivery protocol and discuss many deployability and security issues related to it.

2   System Architecture

As in all currently-deployed e-commerce systems, the most important entities are:

- **Merchants**, who are the entities who maintain a website selling a particular product or series of products. A broader definition of merchants may include websites like Amazon or EBay, where a large variety of products is sold.
- **Customers**, who buy one more products from merchants.
- **Delivery Companies** (DCs), which are the courier companies paid by a merchant to deliver the product to an address specified by the customer. Delivery companies maintain a number of *mail stations* (MSs) on their own, while (if necessary) making use of the mail stations of other DCs. Although affiliated with DCs, in the following sections MSs will constitute separate entities.

For anonymity purposes, we extend the current delivery system with a central **Anonymous Physical Object Delivery Administration** (APODA), which is the manager of our Anonymous Physical Object Delivery (APOD) system. It authorizes the DCs and their mail stations to participate in the APOD, maintains the APOD website, etc. Merchants who need to send something anonymously may do it through any of the DCs which have contracted with APOD. As we will show in a later section, a part of the DC's payment goes to the APODA, who then distributes the payments among the rest of the nodes in the system according to the services they provided.

2.1   System Requirements

Privacy is the main focus in our system and defining it is critical. According to a general privacy definition [SS07], *Privacy is the right of an entity (normally a person), acting on its own behalf, to determine the degree to which it will interact with its environment, including the degree to which the entity is willing to share information about itself with others.* In the context of product delivery service (and assuming that no identity is revealed through the online payment procedure), privacy requires that the merchant should not be able to learn his customer's address, unless authorized by the latter. In addition, the DC should not be able to link any particular package destination address to the merchant who authorized the package's shipment.

Other requirements of our system, which basically derive from the nature of the system we want to enhance, are the following:

- *Package Delivery to Intended Recipients.* We require that the package shipped is delivered to the legal recipient of the package.
- *Package Tracing.* We require that a customer who has requested anonymous delivery of her online purchases is able to trace her packages without any information related to her or the item shipped being leaked. In addition, we require that merchant is able to trace the status of the delivery of the product, without acquiring any information regarding the intended package recipient. Tracing the package from both merchant and customer is especially important when the package has not been delivered within the estimated time.
- *Fairness.* Delivery Companies and mail stations involved are only paid when they perform their service correctly.
- *Proof of Delivery/Accountability.* We require that there can exist an undeniable proof of receipt issued by the anonymous recipient when she receives the package. Although unforgeable, this "receipt" should carry no identification or location-related information. In addition, in case of delivery failure, there should be possible to trace the misbehaving party.

2.2 Adversarial Model

Our goal is to create a realizable system. Thus, we require that our entities have the abilities and powers of the corresponding entities in real systems.

Each **Merchant** is interested in maintaining his clientele, which implies that he is trusted to perform his functional operations correctly. However, we assume that he is "curious", namely he may try to combine information he possesses to reveal his customers' identities. A merchant may also collaborate with the DC he has paid to learn the recipient's address.

We make similar assumptions regarding **Delivery Companies'** powers . In particular, although "honest" in their functional operations, it is likely that a DC would collaborate with a merchant it has contracted with to reveal the recipient of a particular package[1]. The reason for the latter assumption is the following: the DC's primary concern is to maximize its profit and thus to get paid for the services it has provided. Because of this strong monetary DC-dependence on the merchant, DCs are motivated — if requested — to provide the latter with all the recipient-related information its *mail stations* possess. Collusion between two DCs, however, is considered to be highly unlikely.

Anonymous Physical Object Delivery System(APOD) consists of several independent or semi-dependent *mail stations* (MSs) which are associated with one of the DCs as well as affiliated with an administration authority (APODA). We generally assume that MSs are independent if they belong to a different DC, while there is a chance of sharing the information they possess when they are part of the same company. More specifically, each MS: *(a)* possesses its own secret authorization/identification information (digital and group membership signature keys), *(b)* forwards mail towards their

---

[1] It is easy to see how this model is applied in real world if we consider the fact the employees in a DC may not trick any client directly, since they will lose their job, while they may try to combine information the company has obtained legally to draw their own conclusions.

destination by contacting at most the MS the package came from and the MS the mail is forwarded to, and, *(c)* may provide the information it possesses to the central authority of the same DC.

As mentioned before, for practical purposes we include in the design of the DC system an central administration station APODA, which handles payment and authorization matters. As such, it provides a valid MS with certificates (keys etc.). In our threat model, only the payment section of APODA is online and obtains no further information regarding the system unless compelled by a privileged authority such as a judge.

2.3 Payments for Anonymous Routing vs. Anonymous Product Delivery

Our anonymous delivery system has many similarities with PAR [ARS+08], a payment system specially designed for the Tor anonymity network [DMS04]. In particular, APODand PAR are similar in terms of threat models and goals.

1. (Goals) In both cases the goal is accountable and fair packet/package delivery through a group of nodes/MSs with guaranteed sender/merchant - receiver/recipient unlinkability. Another similar goal is the user-anonymity w.r.t. the other communication party: PAR (Tor) requires *sender anonymity w.r.t. the receiver*, while in APOD we require *recipient anonymity w.r.t. the merchant*.
2. (Adversarial Model) In both cases we deal with a local adversary, i.e. an adversary that may not control all the nodes/MSs in a user-chosen[2] delivery path. As in PAR (Tor), path nodes can only observe the traffic of their path neighbors and collaborate with other nodes which may or may not be part of the same path. Similarly, in our APOD MSs may observe the package-flow from/to their path neighbors and collaborate only with mail stations of the same DC which may or may not be part of the path of a particular package. For APOD, we explicitly rule out "active attacks" such as attaching a GPS-based tracking device to the packages.

3 Privacy Preserving Delivery Systems

In what follows, we will assume that each customer has completed her transactions with the merchants anonymously, i.e., no identification information has leaked through product browsing or payment procedure.

As mentioned before, APOD is coordinated by an offline administration authority, the APODA. Delivery companies (DCs) which participate in the APOD obtain membership credentials from the APODA. In a similar way, APODA issues authorization credentials to the *mail stations* (MSs) that offer their services to the APOD. Therefore, the APODA is the coordinator of two groups: (a) the DC group (APODA-DC) and (b) the MS group (APODA-MS) of the participating DCs and MSs respectively. We need to emphasize that, although DC group members may own some or all of the MSs in the APODA-MS group, no package may be provided anonymous delivery unless authorized by a DC group member.

---

[2] *User* for PAR (Tor) is the sender, while for the APOD *user* is the recipient.

Each Merchant is in agreement with one or more DCs. In particular, each merchant is a member of the Mgroup (DC-M) of one or more DCs.

The customer chooses one among the DCs that have contracted with the merchant and are part of the APODA-DC group. Then, the merchant uses his DC membership credentials to issue a blind ticket T to the customer. The customer uses T to log in to APOD's website anonymously and to choose the MSs she wants her package to go through. She then collaborates with the APODA to issue one blind *package-coin* (pcoin) per MS in the path with serial numbers of her choice. Serial numbers in this case serve as package tracking numbers. The client uses the information contained in the website to encrypt triplets of

(package-coin, tracing-info, next-destination)

with each path station's public key. She then interacts with the merchant to get a proof-receipt of the final form of the label which the latter will attach to the product.

Within the delivery process, each path MS decrypts the part of the package-label corresponding to it, revealing the package coins (pcoins) as well as the MS to forward the package to. In addition, each MS uploads the tracing information to the APODA site, so that both the merchant and the client are informed of the package delivery status. We note that no piece of label-information provided to each path MS carries merchant/client identification information.

To assure that only the intended recipient of the product may receive the package, the customer and the merchant agree on a secret PIN number whose endorsed hash is added to the overall packet label. The endorsement is basically created by the DC in collaboration with the merchant in a way that it reveals no information regarding which exactly DC of the APODA-DC group has produced it.

To enforce that each station forwards the packet towards the right direction, package-coins (pcoins) are accompanied by receipts which MSs will only get from the next path station after the latter receives the package. As pcoins with their receipts will later be used for the distribution of payments among the path MSs, there is a strong motivation for MSs to do their job properly.

3.1 Building Blocks

In this section, we describe the definition and security of the group, blind, and blind group signatures. See [CL02], [JLO97], [KY05] and [LR98] respectively.

Group Signature Schemes (GSS). In a typical GSS, there is a group manager (GM), the group-members, who act as signers (let each be S) and produce signatures on behalf of the group. The procedures supported are the following:

- $(gpk, gsk) \leftarrow GS.Setup(1^k)$. This algorithm generates a group public key gpk and the GM's secret group information gsk .
- $\langle usk_S, JLog_S \rangle \leftarrow GS.Join(gpk)[S, GM(gsk)]$. When this interactive join procedure ends, an S obtains a secret signing key usk_S, and the GM (group manager) logs the join transcript in the database D.
- $\sigma \leftarrow GS.Sign(gpk, usk_S, m)$. This algorithm generates a group signature on a message m.

- $\langle \top / \bot \rangle \leftarrow$ GS.Verify(gpk, m, σ). This is a verification algorithm.
- MS $\leftarrow$ GS.Open(gsk, σ, D). With this algorithm the GM determines the identity of the group member who generated the signature σ.

Security Properties: (a) Anonymity. Given a signature and two members, one of whom is the originator, the adversary can identify its originator among the group members no better than randomly. *(b) Unforgeability.* The adversary cannot produce a valid group signature without owning group membership information. *(c)Non-framability.* The adversary cannot create a valid group signature that opens to another group member.

Blind Signature Scheme (BSS). In a typical BSS, there are signers (let each be S) who produce blind signatures on messages of users (let each be U). The procedures supported are the following:

- $(pk_S, sk_S) \leftarrow$ BS.KeyGen(1^k). This is a key-generation algorithm that outputs a public/secret key-pair (pk_S, sk_S).
- $\langle \top / \bot, \ \sigma / \bot \rangle \leftarrow$ BS.Sign(pk_S)[S(sk_S), C(m)]. At the end of this interactive procedure, the output of the S is either *completed* or *not-completed* and the output of U is either the signature (σ) or a failure sign $(\bot)$.
- $\langle \top / \bot \rangle \leftarrow$ BS.Verify(m, σ, pk_S) is a verification algorithm.

Security Properties: Apart from *Unforgeability*, *Blindness* is the most important security property of blind signature schemes: S does not learn any information about the message m on which it generates a signature σ.

We make use of GSS to instantiate the APODA-MS group, where the APODA is the group manager and the MSs who participate in the APOD are the group members.

Blind Group Signature Scheme (BGS). In a typical group signature scheme we can identify the group manager(GM), who maintains the BGS group administration information, the group-members who produce group signatures on users' messages. For now we will assume that a user U, has requested group member S to produce a signature on message m. The procedures supported are the following:

- (bgpk, bgsk) $\leftarrow$ BGS.Setup(1^k). This algorithm generates a group public key bgpk and the GM's secret administration information bgsk .
- $\langle usk_S, bcert_S, \text{BJLog}_S \rangle \leftarrow$ BGS.Join(bgpk)[S, GM(bgsk)]. When this interactive join procedure ends, S obtains her secret signing key usk_S, her membership certificate $bcert_S$, and the GM logs the join transcript in the database D.
- $\sigma \leftarrow$ BGS.Sign(bgpk)[S(usk_S), U(m)], where U obtains a signature on m.
- $\langle \top / \bot \rangle \leftarrow$ BGS.Verify(bgpk, m, σ). This is a verification algorithm run by a verifier.
- S $\leftarrow$ BGS.Open(bgsk, σ, D). This algorithm is run only by GM and determines the identity of the S which generated the signature σ.

Security Properties: They combine the properties of group and blind signature schemes: *Anonymity, Unforgeability, Non-framability, Undeniable Signer Identity* towards the group manager, *Signatures' Unlinkability* and *Blindness*.

We make use of BGS in two cases: to instantiate the APODA-DC group — where APODA is the GM and the DCs participating in APOD are the group members — and to instantiate the M-group — where a DC is the GM and the merchants-clients of that DC are the group members.

Notation: We will use BSig_y (BSig_y^x) for blind (group x) signatures and Sig_y (Sig_y^x) for regular (group x) digital signatures of y.

3.2 Protocol Description

Anonymous Delivery System's Administration (APODA) makes the required setup (if any) for the two groups it manages (see subsection 3.1 for preliminaries):

- the APODA-DC group, which is instantiated through a blind group signature scheme and
- the APODA-MS group, which is realized through a plain group signature scheme.

Therefore, the APODA executes BGS.Setup and GS.Setup to obtain:

$$(\mathsf{bgpk}^{\mathsf{APODA-DC}}, \mathsf{bgsk}^{\mathsf{APODA-DC}}) \text{ and } (\mathsf{gpk}^{\mathsf{APODA-MS}}, \mathsf{gsk}^{\mathsf{APODA-MS}}).$$

In addition, for payment purposes, APODA executes BS.KeyGen to generate a blind signature key pair ($\mathsf{pk}_{\mathsf{APODA}}, \mathsf{sk}_{\mathsf{APODA}}$) and defines two hashes: a pcoin(H_{pcoin}) and a PIN (H_{PIN}) - related. The APODA publishes her public keys and the hashes:

$$\mathsf{bgpk}^{\mathsf{APODA-DC}}, \mathsf{gpk}^{\mathsf{APODA-MS}}, \mathsf{pk}_{\mathsf{APODA}}, H_{\mathsf{pcoin}} \text{ and } H_{\mathsf{PIN}}.$$

Delivery Companies (DCs) acquire membership in the group of companies participating in the APOD. More specifically, each delivery company DC_i collaborates with the APODA in a BGS.Join procedure to issue a blind group signature key-pair ($\mathsf{bgpk}_{DC_i}^{\mathsf{APODA-DC}}, \mathsf{bgsk}_{DC_i}^{\mathsf{APODA-DC}}$).

To manage all of its participating merchants, DC_i groups them together in a blind group signature group (see subsection 3.1), the $DC_i - M$. Therefore, DC_i performs the appropriate setup (BGS.Setup) to generate the corresponding blind group signature administration information:

$$\mathsf{bgpk}^{DC_i - M}, \mathsf{bgsk}^{DC_i - M}. \quad DC_i \text{ publishes } \mathsf{bgpk}^{DC_i - M}.$$

Mail stations (MSs) acquire membership in the APODA-MS group by interacting with the APODA in GS.Join protocol to issue ($\mathsf{gpk}_{MS_i}^{\mathsf{APODA-MS}}, \mathsf{gsk}_{MS_i}^{\mathsf{APODA-MS}}$), which enables each MS MS_i to sign a quantity on behalf of the APODA-MS group in an indistinguishable way. Each MS_i also runs EC.UKeyGen procedure to issue a public encryption key pair ($pk_{MS_i}^e, sk_{MS_i}^e$).

Each *Merchant* M_j is a member of the group of clients (M-group) of one or more DCs he has contracted with. Let DC_i be one of these DCs. To obtain membership, M_j collaborates with the DC_i's central authority in BGS.Join protocol to issue a blind group signature key-pair ($\mathsf{bgpk}_{M_j}^{DC_i - M}, \mathsf{bgsk}_{M_j}^{DC_i - M}$). M_j also runs EC.UKeyGen protocol to create a public encryption key pair (pk_M^e, sk_M^e).

Customer C has preestablished a pseudonymous account with the merchant, which we assume carries no C-identification information ($P_C, \mathsf{secret}_{P_C}$). Although out of the scope of this paper, we may consider P_C as a pseudonym such as the ones introduced in [LRSW99].

In what follows we will assume that a customer C collaborates anonymously with a merchant M_j, while M_j has contracted with the Delivery Company DC_i.

Package Label Preparation Procedure. There are four main phases in preparing the label which will be attached to each package sent anonymously: merchant-client interaction, DC-client interaction, APOD-client interaction and merchant client interaction:

Merchant-Client Interaction. M_j and C agree on a number PIN , which will serve as an authentication code between the two. M_j hashes the PIN into

$$PIN_h = H_{PIN}(PIN \| date)$$

in order to use it later as part of the barcode on top of the product. Final MS will only hand out the package to a person who demonstrates knowledge of PIN . Finally, M_j interacts with C — through P_C — such that the latter obtains a blind credential from M_j, $cred_b$. $cred_b$ is a blind signature of M_j on a random number N_r of C's choice

$$cred_b = BSig_{M_j}^{DC_i - M}(N_r),$$

where $DC_i - M$ denotes the M-group of DC_i. M_j does not know the final form of $cred_b$. However, anyone can confirm $cred_b$'s validity as having derived by a valid DC_i's customer.

Client-Delivery Company Interaction. C uses $cred_b$ to enter DC_i's website anonymously. DC_i's M-group administrator evaluates $cred_b$ (BGS.Verify) and updates the statistics regarding merchant M_j. Here we need to note that according to the group signature attributes (see 3.1) DC_i, as the M-group administrator is the only entity, who using BGS.Open procedure, can identify the merchant who produced a $DC_i - M$ group signature. C — through her $cred_b$ — collaborates with DC_i to obtain a blind endorsement on PIN_h:

$$\sigma_{PIN_h} = BSig_{DC_i}^{APODA-DC}(PIN_h),$$

where $APODA - DC$ denotes the DC group of APODA. In addition, C establishes a one time use anonymous account with DC_i to enter APOD's website

$$A_C = (BSig_{DC_i}^{APODA-DC}(N_A), N_A).$$

Client-APODA Interaction. Customer C logs in to APOD's website using A_C. The APODA verifies A_C's validity (BGS.Verify), updates DC_i's statistics (BGS.Open) and allows C to browse in APOD's website to choose the route of her package. For each intermediate stop of the path she chooses, C:

1. collaborates with APOD to issue:

$$(pc_1, r_1), (pc_2, r_2), \ldots, (pc_m, r_m),$$

where $pc_k = BSig_{APODA}(H_{pcoin}(r_k)), k = 1 \ldots m$ are the receipt enabled package-coins (pcoins). Receipt parts (r_k) are chosen by C and their hashes will serve as packet tracking numbers.

2. creates merchant-related package tracing parts: $mt_1, mt_2, \ldots, mt_m$, where

$$mt_k = Enc_{M_j}(K)||Enc_K\{1||Sig_{P_C}(N_k)\}, i = 1, \ldots, m.$$

Namely mt_k are pseudonym-signed random numbers(N_k), encrypted under M_j's public key. "1" is used for merchant to realize whether an uploaded tracing number is referring to him.

3. combines the pcoins, their receipts and merchant package-tracing parts in groups of

$$Msg_k = \{pcoin(stop_k), receipt(stop_{k-1}), mt(stop_k), stop_{k+1}\}$$

where

$$receipt(stop_{k-1}) = Enc_{pk^e_{stop_{k-1}}}(K)||Enc_K(r_{k-1})$$

is encrypted with (k-1)-stop's public key. The Msg for the last stop f, contains, additionally, pcoin($stop_f$)'s receipt in a PIN -encrypted form: $Enc_{PIN}(receipt(stop_f))$. All Msg-s are encrypted with the public encryption keys each MS acquires from APOD's administration authority into $barcode_{stop_k} = Enc_{pk^e_{stop_k}}(Msg_k)$.

Merchant-Client Interaction. C, as P_C, sends all barcodes and σ_{PIN_h} to the merchant M_j. M_j hashes and digitally signs (S.Sign) the entire barcode sequence into

$$\sigma_{barcodes} = Sig_{M_j}(H_{proof}(barcodes, \sigma_{PIN_h}))$$

and sends it to C (P_C) as a proof of what the former attaches to the packet to be sent out. C verifies the $\sigma_{barcodes}$'s validity and sends a verification response email with a notification of the first mail stop of the path: $Sig_{P_C}(stop_1, date)$.

Shipment. Merchant M_j prints out stickers for each of the barcodes as well as for the σ_{PIN}, which he attaches to the package to be sent anonymously. He then delivers the package to the first station of the path. For label integrity purposes, both parties, M_j and $stop_1$, exchange signed hashes of the encrypted route of the packet sent out:

$$Sig_{M_j}(H(barcodes, \sigma_{PIN_h})) \text{ and } Sig_{stop_1}^{APODA-MS}(H(barcodes, \sigma_{PIN_h})).$$

While the package moves from one MS to the other, each MS decrypts the barcode which corresponds to it. In this way, the next package destination is revealed along with the pcoin. Pcoins(pc_k-s) contained in each barcode are checked for validity (BS.Verify), while their serial is uploaded in the database of the APOD along with the merchant tracing parts (mt-s). In this way, C may track her package delivery status (by checking whether each serial number has been uploaded and thus reached its destination). At the same time, receipt parts of each barcode are sent back to the path predecessors of each station as a proof that the package was properly delivered. Merchant tracing parts (mt-s) are uploaded on APOD's website; M_j may then attempt to decrypt them using his secret decryption key. We note that M_j can only see the tracing numbers uploaded on the APOD website and not the particular MSs who uploaded them. To avoid any path recovery attacks based on the time each mt-s are uploaded, path MSs may randomize the time interval between the package arrival time and the corresponding mt-upload.

When the package reaches the final stop — where C picks her package up the last pcoin serial is uploaded. To obtain the package, C should provide the PIN agreed upon with the merchant. Non invertibility property of hash functions guarantees that only C is able to provide that number. A value different from H_{PIN} and a pre-agreed hash of the PIN ($H_{PIN\_received}$) is then signed with MS's MS group signature uploaded to APOD's website:

$$\mathsf{Rec_{Del}} = \mathsf{Sig}_{MS_k}^{APODA-MS}(H_{PIN\_received}(PIN)).$$

M_j records $\mathsf{Rec_{Del}}$ as proof that the package was properly delivered. At the same time, PIN reveals the receipt for the pcoin provided in the last stop. If no one comes to pick the package up within 10 days of its arrival at the last stop, the latter returns the packet to the MS it received it from.

Payment. The merchant charges the customer for the anonymous delivery service. The price may include the services of the upper bound of number of MSs that can be included in the anonymous path. DC_i charges the merchant in proportion to the merchant-signed endorsements the former receives from customers in the client-DC_i interaction phase. In a similar vein, the APODA charges the DC_i at each valid client-APODA interaction. The aggregated payments the APODA receives are distributed among the different MSs in proportion to the valid pcoins and receipts they present to the APODA.

4 System Considerations

In this section we will provide a brief presentation of how our requirements are satisfied.

Privacy. Privacy in our system consists of two parts: (a) *Recipient Anonymity* against the merchant and the delivery companies the latter has contracted with, and (b) *Sender-Recipient Unlinkability* against any delivery company or the APODA.

During the label preparation procedure, *Recipient Anonymity* is preserved through the combination of the anonymity provided by P_C and the unlinkability property guaranteed by the *Blindness* property of blind (group) signatures. In particular, a customer C uses her P_C pseudonym to browse the merchant's website, an (unlinkable to P_C) anonymous account $cred_b$ to browse to the DC's website and an (unlinkable to $cred_b$) account A_C to visit APODA's website. The information each entity possesses at the stage of the label preparation is the following:

- the *merchant* M knows P_C, the product P_C wants to have anonymously delivered, and that he provided P_C a blind $cred_b$.
- the *delivery company* DC_i (as the manager of its M-group) knows that $cred_b$ has interacted with M and that it provided $cred_b$ with a blind A_C.
- the APODA knows that that A_C has interacted with DC_i and the MSs A_C has requested info for, which may finally be added to the delivery path or not. However, APODA has no information regarding M.

It is obvious that there is no recipient (customer) identification information known to any of the entities participating in the label preparation procedure. *Sender-Recipient*

Unlinkability is also satisfied at this stage. Since timing is not an issue here, the merchant can not be linked to a particular A_C.

Customer Anonymity is preserved throughout the package delivery procedure. No C-identification information is contained in the label attached to the product. For the delivery of the product at the final stop, C only needs to demonstrate knowledge of PIN.

As far as the *Sender-Recipient Unlinkability* requirement is concerned, the information attached to the package, $(\sigma_{PIN}||barcode_1||\dots||barcode_m)$, has been created by the customer and cannot be linked to any of $cred_b/A_C$ accounts the latter used to create the label. However, each MS in the path knows both the exact form of the label attached to the package and its delivery path neighbors. In our threat model, MSs from the same DC may collaborate by comparing package labels, so they recover a package's path. Although we consider this case highly unlikely as it is not cost effective, the severity of this attack is considerably decreased by the following:

- M_j may attach the barcodes in any order. Although this would require extra computation power in each stop, as each MS will have to go through the entire label to detect the barcode which refers to it, no MS — except for the first and the last — will be able to find its place in the path.
- C is the one choosing the entire path. She can easily choose the first and final stops[3] to be from different DCs.

Even in cases where the aforementioned scenario cannot be avoided, the most a DC may learn is the location of the final stop of a particular package without knowing the corresponding it to particular merchant or recipient. For completeness, we will refer to different types of collaborations between entities in our system. Although collaborations involving APODA or more than one DCs are not included in our threat model — since there is no direct monetary dependence between the merchant and APODA or other DCs — we refer to them as they may occur in the extreme case where a Judge has requested information about the recipient of a particular package.

a. M-DC_i (or DC_i-APODA): Because of $cred_b$ (A_C) blindness, M-DC_i (DC_i-APODA) collaboration will reveal nothing more than what DC_i (APODA) knows.

b. any M-APODA collaboration: The APODA knows the MS − (mt-s/Rec$_{Del}$) uploads correspondence, while M knows the (mt-s/Rec$_{Del}$) − P_C correspondence. Thus M-APODA collusion may lead to complete package path recovery.

Depending on the privacy level we need to enforce, one way to avoid this attack scenario is via authorized-anonymous MS-logins(uploads) to APODA's website, using unlinkable-blind credentials ([SSG97]). Payments can be made through another type of blind coins, issued in response to each valid pcoin-receipt upload; these may be deposited unlinkably by MSs in person. Delivery proofs Rec$_{del}$s may have the form of

$$Rec_{del} = BSig_{APODA}(H_{PIN\_received}(PIN)),$$

---

[3] We refer to the stops of these path positions, since they would link the sender (merchant) to a particular recipient (location wise).

where the signature is produced blindly by the MS-APODA collaboration and uploaded anonymously by the final path MS. In this way, M-APODA attempts at package path recovery will fail.

Package Delivery to Intended Recipients. It is satisfied through the non-invertibility attribute of hash functions. In this way, only the legal recipient of the package, i.e., the one who interacted with the merchant, is able to demonstrate knowledge of PIN . To avoid any attack on any party's behalf to link a package to a particular Rec_{del} upload, the final path MS uploads a pre-agreed hash of the PIN as opposed to the PIN itself.

Package Tracing. Package tracing is satisfied through the uploads of the pcoins' serials and the mt-s to the APOD's website. A merchant may visit that site anytime to collect the mt-s which refer to him. The customer may trace her package delivery status by checking on the serial numbers uploaded.

Fairness-Accountability. Fairness is satisfied in our system since, if a MS does not forward the package towards the right direction, it will never receive his pcoin receipt and will thus not be paid. pcoin receipts serve accountability as well, as they provide a proof of proper delivery of the package to the next path MS. Invalid pcoin-receipt pairs may be resolved through APODA, which will request the cooperation of all nodes to recover the full path corresponding to a package label and, thus, the misbehaving MS.

We note that we assume a customer does not deliberately provide invalid pcoin-receipt pairs, as it would only affect the payment distribution within the MSs, while she — having already paid the merchant — will have no monetary motive. On the other hand, the PIN requirement for the final package delivery guarantees that no customer can falsily claim failure of the delivery process.

5 Related Work

As mail service is not a new concept, anonymous package delivery has been addressed in the past by several companies.

iPrivacy [s01] guarantees anonymous ecommerce activity, including anonymous delivery service. However, in iPrivacy the delivery company already knows the address of the recipient. The consumer provides the merchant with a special code number which corresponds to his address in iPrivacy's databases. iPrivacy then uses extra physical boxes, each with different address for the package to be sent to different locations prior to its final destination. Recipient anonymity in this case is physically vulnerable, while the iPrivacy company may link a merchant to a particular address.

ContinentalRelay [CON07] is another company guarranteing anonymous package delivery. However, in this case anonymity is guarranteed from the merchant (sender) but not from the delivery company itself: customers pay a monthly fee to maintain a fake Australian address. Every package sent to this imaginary mailbox is then forwarded to the customer's real address. However, this solution may be more expensive and inconvenient, as some mail carrier services will not deliver to a mailbox.

Kushik Chatterjee in [C08] has also suggested a patent for efficient anonymous package delivery service. In particular, Chatterjee suggested a system where the physical address of the recipient is identified within the delivery system with an identification number, which is what sender attaches to the mail sent. Thus recipient's physical address is concealed from the sender but not from the delivery company.

Tor[DMS04] and other onion routing protocols[SGR97] as well as PAR[ARS+08] can also be considered as part of the related work in this paper as described in section2.3.

6 Conclusion

In this paper, we presented a real-world applicable delivery service protocol for online purchases with guaranteed merchant-customer unlinkability and recipient anonymity w.r.t. the merchant and/or the delivery companies involved. Our protocols utilise similar techniques to the Tor[DMS04] anonymity network and support package tracing and mail delivery proof. As opposed to currently deployed anonymous delivery techniques, recipient's address is concealed even from the company paid to perform the delivery.

Acknowledgment

The authors would like to thank the anonymous referees for their valuable comments and suggestions and Google Inc. for subsidizing this work.

References

[ARS+08] Androulaki, E., Raykova, M., Srivatsan, S., Stavrou, A., Bellovin, S.M.: PAR: Payment for anonymous routing. In: Borisov, N., Goldberg, I. (eds.) PETS 2008. LNCS, vol. 5134, pp. 219–236. Springer, Heidelberg (2008)

[C81] Chaum, D.L.: Untraceable electronic mail, return addresses, and digital psuedonyms. Communications of the ACM (1981)

[C08] Chatterjee, K.: System and method for anonymous mail delivery services (2008)

[CL02] Camenisch, J., Lysyanskaya, A.: A signature scheme with efficient protocols. In: Cimato, S., Galdi, C., Persiano, G. (eds.) SCN 2002. LNCS, vol. 2576, pp. 268–289. Springer, Heidelberg (2003)

[CON07] Protect your privacy with your own offshore private maildrop (1999-2007)

[CS97] Camenisch, J., Stadler, M.: Effcient group signature schemes for large groups. In: Kaliski Jr., B.S. (ed.) CRYPTO 1997. LNCS, vol. 1294, pp. 410–424. Springer, Heidelberg (1997)

[DMS04] Dingledine, R., Mathewson, N., Syverson, P.: Tor: The second-generation onion router. In: Proceedings of the 13th USENIX Security Symposium (August 2004)

[JLO97] Juels, A., Luby, M., Ostrovsky, R.: Security of blind digital signatures (extended abstract). In: Kaliski Jr., B.S. (ed.) CRYPTO 1997. LNCS, vol. 1294, pp. 150–164. Springer, Heidelberg (1997)

[KY05] Kiayias, A., Yung, M.: Group signatures: Provable security, efficient constructions and anonymity from trapdoor-holders. In: Dawson, E., Vaudenay, S. (eds.) Mycrypt 2005. LNCS, vol. 3715, pp. 151–170. Springer, Heidelberg (2005)

[LR98] Lysyanskaya, A., Ramzan, Z.: Group blind digital signatures: A scalable solution to electronic cash. In: Hirschfeld, R. (ed.) FC 1998. LNCS, vol. 1465, pp. 184–197. Springer, Heidelberg (1998)

[LRSW99] Lysyanskaya, A., Rivest, R., Sahai, A., Wolf, S.: Pseudonym systems (Extended abstract). In: Heys, H.M., Adams, C.M. (eds.) SAC 1999. LNCS, vol. 1758, pp. 184–199. Springer, Heidelberg (2000)

[O06] Okamoto, T.: Efficient blind and partially blind signatures without random oracles. In: Halevi, S., Rabin, T. (eds.) TCC 2006. LNCS, vol. 3876, pp. 80–99. Springer, Heidelberg (2006)

[S01] Smith, J.M.: Iprivacy white paper (2001)

[SGR97] Syverson, P.F., Goldschlag, D.M., Reed, M.G.: Anonymous connections and onion routing. In: IEEE Symposium on Security and Privacy, Oakland, California, pp. 44–54, 4–7 (1997)

[SS07] Smith, R., Shao, J.: Privacy and e-commerce: a consumer-centric perspective. Electronic Commerce Research 7(2), 89–116 (2007)

[SSG97] Syverson, P.F., Stubblebine, S.G., Goldschlag, D.M.: Unlinkable serial transactions. In: Proceedings of Financial Cryptography, pp. 39–55. Springer, Heidelberg (1997)

On the Optimal Placement of Mix Zones

Julien Freudiger, Reza Shokri, and Jean-Pierre Hubaux

LCA1, EPFL, Switzerland
firstname.lastname@epfl.ch

Abstract. In mobile wireless networks, third parties can track the location of mobile nodes by monitoring the pseudonyms used for identification. A frequently proposed solution to protect the location privacy of mobile nodes suggests changing pseudonyms in regions called mix zones. In this paper, we propose a novel metric based on the mobility profiles of mobile nodes in order to evaluate the mixing effectiveness of possible mix zone locations. Then, as the location privacy achieved with mix zones depends on their placement in the network, we analyze the optimal placement of mix zones with combinatorial optimization techniques. The proposed algorithm maximizes the achieved location privacy in the system and takes into account the cost induced by mix zones to mobile nodes. By means of simulations, we show that the placement recommended by our algorithm significantly reduces the tracking success of the adversary.

1 Introduction

Modern mobile devices are increasingly equipped with peer-to-peer communication technologies, such as WiFi or Bluetooth, thus allowing them to directly exchange information with other devices in proximity. Such peer-to-peer communications enable *context-aware* applications. For example, vehicular networks provide safer and more efficient road transportation [23,47]. Similarly, mobile social networks allow users to automatically detect and exchange information with their friends [1,2,3,4]. In practice, mobile nodes detect each others' presence by periodically broadcasting messages and use *pseudonyms* instead of their actual identity (i.e., MAC/IP address, public key) to identify/authenticate each other.

However, much to the detriment of privacy, external parties eavesdropping on communications can monitor pseudonyms to learn mobile nodes' locations. Previous works [7,27,34] show that if the *spatial* and *temporal* correlation between successive locations of mobile nodes is not carefully eliminated, an external party (i.e., an adversary) can compromise the *location privacy* of mobile nodes and obtain the real identity of mobile nodes' owners. For example, using location traces collected in an office environment from the Active Bat system, Beresford and Stajano [7] correctly identified all participants by simply examining where the participants spent most of their time. Similarly, using GPS traces from vehicles, two studies by Hoh *et al.* [27] and Krumm [34] found the home addresses (and thus the identity) of most drivers. Hence, pseudonyms are not sufficient to protect the location privacy of mobile nodes.

I. Goldberg and M. Atallah (Eds.): PETS 2009, LNCS 5672, pp. 216–234, 2009.

One popular technique for achieving location privacy consists in using *multiple pseudonyms* [7,22,46] that are changed over time to impede traceability. As a pseudonym changed by an isolated node can be trivially guessed by an external party, pseudonym changes are coordinated among mobile nodes in regions called *mix zones* [8]. But even if location traces of mobile nodes are completely anonymized (i.e., do not contain any identifier), Hoh and Gruteser [25] were able to reconstruct the tracks of mobile nodes using a multiple target tracking (MTT) algorithm. Hence, to protect against the spatial correlation of location traces, location traces should also be altered *spatially*. To do this, mix zones can also conceal the trajectory of mobile nodes to the external adversary by using: (i) Silent/encrypted periods [17,28,37], (ii) a mobile proxy [42], or (iii) regions where the adversary has no coverage [12]. The effectiveness of a mix zone, in terms of the location privacy it provides, depends on the adversary's ability to relate mobile nodes that enter and exit the mix zone [7]. Hence, mix zones should be placed in locations with high node density and unpredictable mobility [8,29].

While traversing a given area, mobile nodes go through a *sequence of mix zones* and "accumulate" untraceability [12,30]. Unlike wired mix networks such as Tor [16] where packets can be freely routed, the sequence of mix zones traversed by mobile nodes depends on the mobility of each node. In other words, the flow of mobile nodes cannot be controlled to maximize location privacy. Instead, we propose to control the *placement* of mix zones to impede the adversary from tracking the nodes' location. However, similarly to the delay introduced by mix nodes on packets, mix zones induce a cost for mobile nodes: With silent mix zones, mobile nodes cannot communicate while they are in the mix zone, and with a mobile proxy, all messages have to transit through the same mobile node. Hence, the number of mix zones to be deployed over a given area must be kept small.

We consider a trusted central authority that is responsible for the establishment of security and privacy in the network (e.g., in vehicular networks, the vehicle registration authority [23]). This authority deploys a limited number of mix zones in a given area to protect the location privacy of mobiles nodes. In order to help the authority evaluate the mixing effectiveness of mix zones prior to network operation, we first propose a metric based on mobility profiles. To do so, we model the strategy of the adversary in assigning exiting to entering flows as a decision problem [9]. We propose to use the Jensen-Shannon divergence [38] to measure the probability of error of the adversary. Then, we model the problem of placing mix zones as an optimization problem: We propose an algorithm to find the optimal placement of mix zones by maximizing the mixing effectiveness of the system at an acceptable cost for mobile nodes. The algorithm offers minimum location privacy guarantees by enforcing a maximum distance between traversed mix zones. Finally, we compare the optimal mix zones deployment to other deployments by using a realistic mobility simulator [33]. To the best of our knowledge, this paper is the first to investigate deployment strategies of mix zones in mobile networks.

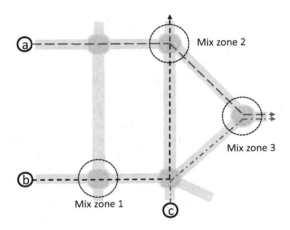

Fig. 1. Example of system model. Nodes move on plane (x, y) according to trajectories defined by flows a, b, and c. To achieve location privacy, nodes change pseudonyms in mix zones.

2   Preliminaries

2.1   System Model

We study a network where mobile nodes are autonomous entities equipped with WiFi or Bluetooth-enabled devices that communicate with each other upon coming in radio range. In other words, we consider a mobile wireless system such as a vehicular network or a network of directly communicating hand-held devices. Without loss of generality, we assume that each user in the system has a single mobile device and thus corresponds to a single node in the network.

As commonly assumed in such networks, we consider an offline central authority (CA) run by an independent trusted third party that manages, among other things, the security and privacy of the network. In vehicular networks for example, the vehicle registration authority could take this role. In line with the multiple pseudonym approach, we assume that prior to joining the network, every mobile node s registers with the CA that preloads a finite set of *pseudonyms* [40] (e.g., certified public/private key pairs, MAC addresses). Mobile nodes change pseudonyms in mix zones in order to achieve location privacy (Fig. 1). Upon changing pseudonyms, we consider for simplicity that the old pseudonym expires and is removed from the node's memory. Once a mobile node has used all its pseudonyms, it contacts the CA to obtain a new set of pseudonyms.

We assume that mobile nodes automatically exchange information (unbeknownst to their users) as soon as they are in communication range of each other. Note that our evaluation is independent of the communication protocol. Without loss of generality, we assume that mobile nodes advertise their presence by periodically broadcasting proximity beacons containing the node's identifying/authenticating information (i.e., the sender attaches its pseudonym to its messages). Due to the broadcast nature of wireless communications, beacons enable mobile nodes to discover their neighbors. For example, when a node s receives an authenticated beacon, it controls the legitimacy of the sender by checking the certificate of the public key of the sender. After that, s verifies the signature of the beacon message.

We consider a discrete time system with initial time $t = 0$. At each time step t_s, mobile nodes can move on a plane (Fig. 1) in the considered area. As shown by Gonzalez, Hidalgo and Barabasi [19], mobile users tend to return regularly to certain locations (e.g., home and workplace), indicating that despite the diversity of their travel locations, humans follow simple reproducible patterns. Hence, we consider a *flow-based* mobility model [33]: Based on real trajectories of mobile nodes in the network (e.g., pedestrian or vehicular), we construct $f \in F$ flows of nodes in the network between the few highly frequented locations of mobile nodes, where F is the set of all flows. In practice, such real trajectories could be provided, for example, by city authorities in charge of road traffic optimization. Thus, each flow f defines a trajectory shared by several mobile nodes in the network during a period of time. For example in Fig. 1, each node is assigned to one of the three flows a, b, or c and follows the trajectory defined by the flow during the traversal of the plane. In stationary regime, a flow is characterized by its average number of nodes, λ. Note that during the course of the day, flows usually vary. For simplicity, we consider one of the possible stationary regimes of the system. Flows are defined over the road segments in the considered area. The mobility of the nodes is thus bound to the road segments.

2.2 Threat Model

An adversary $\mathcal{A}$ aims at tracking the location of some mobile nodes. In practice, the adversary can be a rogue individual, a set of malicious mobile nodes, or might even deploy its own infrastructure (e.g., by placing eavesdropping devices in the considered area). We consider that the adversary is *passive* and simply eavesdrops on communications. In the worst case, $\mathcal{A}$ obtains complete coverage and tracks mobile nodes throughout the entire area. We characterize the latter type of adversary as *global*.

$\mathcal{A}$ collects identifying information (e.g., the MAC address or the public keys used to sign messages) from the entire network and obtains *location traces* that allow him to track the location of mobile nodes. Hence, the problem we tackle in this paper consists in protecting the *location privacy* of mobile nodes, that is, to prevent other parties from learning a node's past and current location [8]. It must be noted that, at the physical layer, the wireless transceiver has a wireless fingerprint that the adversary could use to identify it [41]. However, because this requires a costly installation for the adversary and stringent conditions on the wireless medium, it remains unclear how much identifying information can be extracted in practice from the physical layer and we do not consider this threat.

3   Mix Zones

As described in the Introduction, location privacy is achieved by changing pseudonyms in regions called *mix zones* [7]. Mix zones are *effective* in anonymizing the trajectory of mobile nodes if the adversary is unable to predict with high certainty the relation between mobile nodes entering and exiting mix zones. In this section, we first give a description of mix zones and then evaluate their effectiveness using an information-theoretic divergence measure.

3.1   Mix Zones Description

A mix zone $i \in Z$ is defined by a triplet (x_i, y_i, R_i), where Z is the set of all mix zones in the considered area. The x_i and y_i coordinates are the center of the mix zone i and determine the location of the mix zone in the network. R_i is the radius of mix zone i, which we assume constant over all mix zones, $R_i = R$. In other words, a mix zone is a region of pre-determined shape and size that can be established anywhere in the considered area. We consider that the location of mix zones is determined centrally and communicated to the mobile nodes prior to their joining the network.

Each mix zone i is traversed by flows $f_j \in F_i \subseteq F$ of mobile nodes. Mobile nodes traversing a mix zone create entering and exiting *events* of the mix zone. Each node in a flow takes a certain amount of time, called the *sojourn time*, to traverse the mix zone. The sojourn time models the speed diversity of mobile nodes traversing mix zones. Speed differences are caused, for example, by a higher density of nodes on specific flows or by traffic lights. Each mix zone i has a set of entry/exit points L_i typically corresponding to the road network. Consider the example in Fig. 1: Mix zone 3 has three entry/exit points that are all traversed by some flows. Based on the flows traversing a mix zone, we can evaluate the different *trajectories* of mobile nodes in each mix zone. The *mobility profile* of a mix zone captures the typical behavior of mobile nodes traversing the mix zone (i.e., their sojourn time and trajectory). In practice, city authorities in charge of traffic lights optimization could provide the measured sojourn time distributions as well as typical trajectories over the course of the day.

There are several techniques for obtaining a mix zone: (i) Turning off the transceiver of mobile nodes [28,31,37], (ii) encrypting messages [17], (iii) relaying all wireless communications through a proxy [42], or (iv) exploiting regions where the adversary has no coverage [12]. In all cases, the adversary cannot observe the movements of the nodes within the mix zone. For example in Fig. 1, three mix zones have been established encompassing the entire intersection.

3.2   Mix Zones Effectiveness

In order to efficiently place mix zones in the network, we need to know - prior to their deployment - their mixing effectiveness. As the previously proposed entropy metric [7] depends on entering/exiting events of mix zones (after deployment), we propose a new metric based exclusively on the mobility profile of mix zones (before deployment).

Event-Based Metric. As presented by Beresford and Stajano [7] for mobile networks and by Diaz *et al.* [15] and Serjantov and Danezis [43] for mix networks, the uncertainty of the adversary (i.e. entropy) is a measure of the location privacy/anonymity achieved by a node. Assuming that $\mathcal{A}$ knows the *mobility profile* of the nodes within each mix zone, the adversary can predict their future direction from their past behavior. Consider a sequence of entering/exiting nodes traversing a mix zone i over a period of T time steps, the uncertainty of the adversary is:

$$H_T(i) = -\sum_v^I p_v \log_2(p_v) \tag{1}$$

where p_v is the probability of different assignments of entering nodes to exiting nodes and I is the total number of such hypothesized assignments. Each value p_v depends on the entering/exiting nodes and the mobility profile. In other words, the anonymity provided by mix zones mostly depends on factors beyond the control of the nodes. It is thus interesting to compute the average location privacy provided by a mix zone to evaluate its *mixing effectiveness*. The entropy measure is bound to the set of events happening in an interval of T time steps and does not capture the average mixing of a mix zone. The average mixing effectiveness of a mix zone i can be computed by taking the average entropy over n successive periods of T time steps: $E[H(i)] = \frac{1}{n} \sum_{v=1}^{n} H_{T_v}(i)$.

Flow-Based Metric. We propose a new method to theoretically evaluate the mixing effectiveness provided by mix zones. The proposed metric relies on the statistics of the mix zone, i.e., the mobility flows and the mobility profile, to compute the mixing effectiveness of the mix zone. The advantage of the proposed metric is that the mixing effectiveness can be computed prior to the operation of the mobile network as it does not rely on a particular set of events.

The metric is generic and independent of the nature of traffic. However, to simplify the treatment, we model each flow f_j as a homogeneous Poisson process with intensity λ_j. The distribution $Pois(b; \lambda_j)$ denotes the probability that b nodes enter the flow f_j during a time step t_s. Each flow f_j that traverses a mix zone i is subject to a sojourn time distribution $h_{i,j}(\Delta t)$, where Δt is the time spent in the mix zone. Observing the exit of a mix zone i, the adversary is confronted to a classical *decision-theory problem*: $\mathcal{A}$ must classify each exit event $x \in X$ happening at time t_x as coming from one of the F_i possible entering flows.

Let $m = |F_i|$ be the number of flows in mix zone i. Assume that $m = 2$ flows $\{f_1, f_2\}$ converge to the same mix zone exit l. The probability that the adversary misclassifies x depends on the number of nodes that can potentially correspond to it. This is related to the time spent in the mix zone and the inter-arrival time. We focus on a simple scenario where one mobile node from each flow enters the mix zone. Without loss of generality, we assume that the first mobile node arrives at time $t = 0$ from f_1 and that the second node arrives with a time difference δ from f_2. Figure 2 shows the exiting time probability distribution time for a given δ. We first compute the error probability with a fixed value of δ and then generalize our model by considering different values of δ.

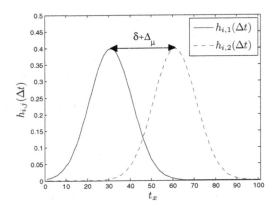

Fig. 2. Example of exiting time distribution of two flows with $h_{i,j}(\Delta t) \sim \mathcal{N}(\mu_j, \sigma_j)$, $j = 1, 2$. In this example, $(\mu_1, \sigma_1) = (2, 1)$, $(\mu_2, \sigma_2) = (4, 1)$, $\Delta_\mu = \mu_2 - \mu_1$, and δ is the arrival time difference between events of two flows (i.e., the first node arrives at time $t = 0$, and the second one arrives at time δ).

To compute the location privacy generated by a mix zone, we are interested in computing the probability that an adversary misclassifies an event. In other words, for one exit l, a successful mixing occurs whenever the adversary makes an error, i.e., assigns an exit event to the wrong flow. It is well known that the decision rule that minimizes the probability of error is the Bayes decision rule (i.e., choosing the hypothesis with the largest a posteriori probability). According to Bayes' theorem, the *a posteriori* probability that an observed event x belongs to flow f_j is

$$p(f_j|x) = \frac{p_j(x)\pi_j}{\sum_v p_v(x)\pi_v}, j = 1, 2 \tag{2}$$

where $p_j(x) = p(x|f_j)$ is the conditional probability of observing x knowing that x belongs to f_j and $\pi_j = p(f_j)$ is the a priori probability that an observed exit event belongs to flow f_j. The Bayes probability of error [24] is then given by:

$$p_e(p_1, p_2) = \sum_{x \in X} \min(\pi_1 p_1(x), \pi_2 p_2(x)) \tag{3}$$

The a priori probabilities depend on the intensity of the flows and are equal to: $\pi_j = \lambda_j/(\sum_{v:f_v \in F_i} \lambda_v)$. The conditional probabilities $p_1(x)$, $p_2(x)$ are equal to the probability that f_j generates an exit event at time t_x: $p_1(x) = \int_{t_x}^{t_x+t_s} h_{i,1}(t)dt$ and $p_2(x) = \int_{t_x}^{t_x+t_s} h_{i,2}(t - \delta)dt$.

A large body of research has focused on minimizing the probability of error. For example, the MTT algorithm minimizes the probability of error when tracking multiple moving objects. In the location privacy context, it is used to measure the effectiveness of path perturbation techniques by Hoh and Gruteser [25]. In our case, we evaluate the probability of error in order to find mix zones with

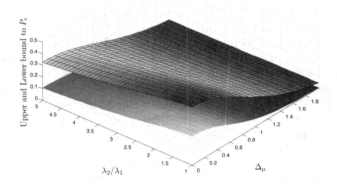

Fig. 3. Lower and upper bounds of the probability of error with $Pois(b; \lambda_j)$, $h_{i,j}(\Delta t) = \mathcal{N}(\mu_j, \sigma_j = 0.5)$, $j = 1, 2$, $\lambda_1 = 0.2$, $\lambda_2 \in [0.2, 2]$, $\mu_1 = 2s$, and $\mu_2 \in [2, 4]s$. As λ_2/λ_1 increases, the difference between the two probability functions increases as well and it becomes easier to classify the events (p_e becomes smaller). The decrease in p_e is faster if Δ_μ increases as well.

high mixing effectiveness, i.e., that maximize the probability of error. Because computing the probability of error is most of the time impractical [32] (when $m > 2$), we consider the *distance* between the two probability distributions p_1, p_2 to compute bounds on the error probability. Intuitively, the further apart these two distributions are, the smaller the probability of mistaking one for the other should be. The *Jensen-Shannon divergence* [38] (JS) is an information-theoretic distance measure that is particularly suitable for the study of decision problems as the one considered here. It provides both a lower and an upper bound for the Bayes probability of error.

$$JS_\pi(p_1, p_2) = H(\pi_1 p_1(x) + \pi_2 p_2(x)) - \pi_1 H(p_1(x)) - \pi_2 H(p_2(x)) \qquad (4)$$

The JS divergence (4) provides a simple way to estimate the misclassification error of the adversary over a mix zone. The Bayes probability of error is lower/upper bounded as follows [38]:

$$\frac{1}{4}(H(\pi_1, \pi_2) - JS_\pi(p_1, p_2))^2 \le p_e(p_1, p_2) \le \frac{1}{2}(H(\pi_1, \pi_2) - JS_\pi(p_1, p_2)) \qquad (5)$$

where $H(\pi_1, \pi_2)$ is the entropy of the a priori probabilities. The JS divergence is thus particularly useful in order to select mix zones with a high mixing effectiveness. In addition, the JS divergence can be extended to a larger number of flows [38]:

$$JS_\pi(p_1, ..., p_m) = H(\sum_{i=1}^{m} \pi_i p_i(x)) - \sum_{i=1}^{m} \pi_i H(p_i(x)) \qquad (6)$$

Consider the following example: Two flows f_1, f_2 with equal input Poisson intensities $\lambda_j = 0.2$ share an exit l of mix zone i. The sojourn times are distributed according to a Normal distribution $h_{i,j}(\Delta t) = \mathcal{N}(\mu_j = 2, \sigma_j = 0.5)$, $j = 1, 2$, and $\delta = 0$. Figure 3 shows how the lower and upper bounds on the probability of error are influenced by a difference Δ_μ of the sojourn time distributions ($\Delta_\mu = \mu_2 - \mu_1$) and by the ratio λ_2/λ_1 of flows' intensities. We observe that if Δ_μ increases and $\lambda_2/\lambda_1 = 1$, p_e decreases, showing that, with a fixed δ, a difference in the sojourn time distributions alone helps distinguish between the two distributions. We also observe that if λ_2/λ_1 increases and $\Delta_\mu = 0$, the probability of error decreases. The intuition is that as the difference between the flows' intensities increases, the flow with higher intensity dominates the exit of the considered mix zone. In addition, we observe that if both λ_2/λ_1 and Δ_μ increase, p_e decreases faster. The mixing effectiveness is maximal when both flows have the same intensity and sojourn time distribution.

Until now, we focused on scenarios with one mobile node entering from each flow, and a fixed δ. We generalize our model by considering the average difference in arrival time of nodes in flows. More specifically, based on the average arrival rate λ_j, we compute the average difference in arrival time between flows and the average number of nodes that can potentially correspond to an exit event x. The average difference in arrival time between any two flows depends on the flow intensities. The average number of nodes that can be confused with an event x depends on the maximum sojourn time window $\omega_{i,l} = \max_{f_j \in F_{i,l}}(\Delta t_{f_j})$, where Δt_{f_j} is the time spent in the mix zone by nodes in flow f_j and $F_{i,l}$ is the set of flows in F_i that exit at l. For each flow $f_j \in F_{i,l}$, there is a set of possible entering events with average arrival time differences in a time window $\omega_{i,l}$ with respect to beginning of the window: $\zeta^i_{j,l} = \{\delta_{j,v}: v/\lambda_j \le \omega_{i,l}, v \in \mathbb{N}\}$, where $\delta_{j,v} = v/\lambda_j$. We compute the probability of error of the adversary at exit l as follows:

$$p^i_{e,l} = \frac{\sum\limits_{f_j \in F_{i,l}} p_e\Big(p_j(x,0), p_{\kappa_1}(x, \delta_{\kappa_1, v_1}), p_{\kappa_1}(x, \delta_{\kappa_1, v_2}), ..., p_{\kappa_2}(x, \delta_{\kappa_2, v_1}), ...\Big)}{|F_{i,l}|} \tag{7}$$

where $p_j(x,0)$ is the conditional probability $p_j(x)$ with $\delta = 0$, $p_{\kappa_1}(x, \delta_{\kappa_1, v_1})$ corresponds to the conditional probability $p_{\kappa_1}(x)$ with $\delta_{\kappa_1, v_1} \in \zeta^i_{\kappa_1, l}$, and κ_1, κ_2, ..., κ_{m-1} are not equal to j. In other words, we evaluate the confusion of the adversary for each flow with respect to other flows. Finally, we compute the average probability of error caused by a mix zone i by considering the error created by each exit $l \in L_i$ of mix zone i:

$$\bar{p}^i_e = \frac{\sum_{L_i} p^i_{e,l}}{|L_i|} \tag{8}$$

With this model, we consider the average arrival rate of the nodes and can thus compute the mixing effectiveness prior to network operation. Note that we assumed for simplicity that the sojourn time distribution is independent of the flows' intensity. The model can be extended to capture the interactions between nodes in the mix zone and their effect on the sojourn time distributions [18].

4   Placement of Mix Zones

In principle, mix zones can be placed anywhere in the considered area. Their placement determines the accumulated location privacy provided by each mix zone. Thus, the optimal solution consists in placing mix zones on the entire surface of the considered area. However, mix zones have a cost because they impose limits on the services available to mobile users and require a pseudonym change. Hence, the total number of mix zones deployed in the network should be limited to minimize the disruptions caused to mobile nodes. We assume that a central authority, responsible for the establishment of security and privacy in the system, is confronted with the problem of organizing mix zones in the network. Thus, users must trust that the central authority will protect their privacy. We propose a solution based on combinatorial optimization techniques that relies on the divergence metric introduced in Sect. 3 to select appropriate mix zones. Our paper, by making a possible algorithm public, increases the trustworthiness of the authority as it provides a basis for comparison.

4.1   Mix Zones Placement

After Chaum's seminal work on *mixes* [13], there have been multiple proposals on the way mixes should be connected and organized to maximize the provided anonymity [11]. This led to a classification of different organization concepts. For example, the choice of the sequence of mixes is either distributed (i.e., *mix networks*) or centrally controlled (i.e., *mix cascades*).

The system considered in this paper, namely mix zones deployed over a considered area, presents three different characteristics: (i) The organization of mixes depends on the placement of mix zones in the area, (ii) mobile nodes move in the considered area according to flows constrained by the underlying road network, and (iii) the road network is a connected network with a restricted number of routes. Hence, we must characterize mix zones placements that maximize the achievable location privacy.

In order to evaluate the location privacy provided by mix zones deployed over a mobile network, one solution consists in computing the uncertainty accumulated by the adversary with the joint entropy [43]. However, the complexity of the formulation increases as the number of mix zones increases, making it hard to evaluate. Instead, to compute the overall location privacy, we maximize the total probability of error of the adversary by considering the sum of error probabilities over each deployed mix zone and we guarantee that the distance over which the adversary can successfully track mobile nodes is upper-bounded, i.e., the average *distance-to-confusion* (dtc). A mix zone is a *confusion point* if the error probability of the adversary is larger than a given threshold θ [26].

However, mix zones induce a cost on mobile nodes that must be taken into account in the mix zone deployment phase. The cost associated to each mix zone depends on the considered application. For example, with silent periods, the cost is typically directly proportional to the duration of the imposed silent period (i.e., the size of the mix zone). Similarly, the cost also depends on the number of used pseudonyms. Pseudonyms are costly to use because they are a limited resource that requires contacting the CA for refill.

4.2   Placement Optimization

In this section, we model the problem of mix zones placement as an optimization problem. Formally, consider a finite set Z of all possible mix zones' locations, a set F of mobility flows in the system, and a mobility profile for each potential mix zone in the considered area. The goal is to optimize the placement of mix zones to maximize the overall probability of error of an adversary tracking mobile nodes in the considered area while respecting the cost and distance-to-confusion constraints. We select a subset $\widehat{Z} \subseteq Z$ of $active$ mix zones, which is a solution of the following combinatorial optimization problem:

$$\max_{\widehat{Z}} \sum_{i \in Z} \bar{p}_e^i \cdot z_i \tag{9}$$

$$\text{subject to } \sum_{i \in f_j} w_i z_i \leq W_{max}, \forall f_j \tag{10}$$

$$E[dtc(f_j, \widehat{Z})] \leq C_{max}, \forall f_j \tag{11}$$

where $z_i \in \{0, 1\}, \forall i \in Z$ indicates if a mix zone is active (i.e., $z_i = 1$), $\widehat{Z}$ is the set of active mix zones, $\bar{p}_e^i$ captures the error introduced by mix zone i, w_i is the cost associated with mix zone i, W_{max} is the maximum tolerable cost, $E[dtc(f_j, \widehat{Z})]$ is the average distance-to-confusion of flow f_j with the set of active mix zones $\widehat{Z}$, and C_{max} is the maximum tolerable distance-to-confusion. We compute the probability of error $\bar{p}_e^i$ by using the lower bound obtained with the Jensen-Shannon divergence in the previous section. The first constraint limits the number of mix zones that can be deployed per flow by taking into account the cost associated with each mix zone. The second constraint ensures that the average distance-to-confusion is upper bounded, i.e., C_{max} defines a maximal distance over which mobile nodes can be tracked on average.

5   Application Example

To test the relevance of our approach, we implemented a simulator in Java that evaluates the tracking efficiency of the adversary.[1] The simulator takes as input a mobility trace on a map and a set of locations for mix zones. It first computes the mobility profile of mix zones and then attempts to predict the trajectory of mobile nodes.

5.1   Simulation Setup

We simulate mobility traces with Sumo [33], a urban mobility simulator, over a cropped map [5] of Manhattan of 6 km^2. Sumo features the creation of routes

---

[1] The code is available at: http://icapeople.epfl.ch/freudiger

for mobile nodes using mobility flows: Each flow is defined by a source, a destination and a traffic intensity. Each mobile node belongs to a single flow and is
routed from source to destination over the shortest path. Roads have one lane
in each direction, and road intersections are modeled with yields. Some roads
(e.g., highways) have higher priority and do not have to yield.

In this application example, the constraints of the optimization algorithm are
defined as follows. The cost of mix zones w_i is proportional to the cost of a
pseudonym change γ. We assume that the cost of a pseudonym change is fixed
and the same for all nodes, $\gamma = 1$. We set $W_{max} = 3$, meaning that each node
can traverse a maximum of three mix zones. Similarly, we set $C_{max} = 2000m$,
i.e., the adversary cannot track nodes over more than two kilometers. A total of
40 flows were deployed over the area, generating 1210 nodes in a fluid scenario
($\lambda_j \sim 0.02$) and 2000 nodes in a congested scenario ($\lambda_j \sim 0.04$). The radius of
mix zones is a constant $R = 100m$. We simulate a mobile network for 20 minutes
with nodes moving at a maximum speed of 50km/h and with an average trip
time of 6 minutes. Finally, a mix zone is considered as a confusion point if the
introduced error is larger than zero, i.e., $\theta = 0$.

Mobility Profiles. We consider a powerful (worst-case) adversary that can
construct a mobility profile of each mix zone i by measuring the time at which
nodes enter/exit mix zones. We denote with Q the measuring precision of the
adversary, and assume $Q = 1$ second. Hence, $\mathcal{A}$ knows for each mix zone: (i)
The distribution of nodes' trajectories, and (ii) the sojourn time distributions.
The distribution of nodes' trajectories is captured in a matrix of directions D_i:
For each entering/exiting points (k, l), the matrix contains the probability of
the trajectory: $D_i^{k,l} = Pr(\text{" Enter at } k \text{ and exit at } l \text{ ")}$. The sojourn time distribution is captured in a matrix of sojourn times J_i: For each entering/exiting
points (k, l), the matrix contains the probability distribution of the sojourn time:
$J_i^{k,l}(\Delta t) = Pr(\text{"Enter at } k \text{ and spend } \Delta t \text{ before exiting at } l\text{")}$.

Attack. Based on the mobility profiles, the adversary $\mathcal{A}$ predicts the most
probable assignment of entering/exiting mobile nodes for each mix zone. To do
so, the attacker can model entering/exiting events with a weighted bipartite
graph as suggested by Beresford in [6]. Each edge is weighted according to the
a priori probability of linking an exiting event at l to an entering event at k:
$D_i^{k,l} \cdot J_i^{k,l}(\Delta t)$. Then, the maximum weight matching of the bipartite graph corresponds to the optimal guess of the adversary. As discussed in [45], a more
elaborate attack consists in computing all perfect matchings of the bipartite
graph to weight edges, according to the a posteriori probability of linking en-
tering/exiting events. However, this attack has a large complexity, increasing
exponentially with the number of entering/exiting pairs and its scalability remains an open problem.

Metrics. Assume that Z_s is the set of mix zones traversed by node s and let
$G_s \subseteq Z_s$ be the set of mix zones successfully matched by the adversary. $\mathcal{A}$ is
successful in tracking the location of node s in a mix zone if the real trajectory

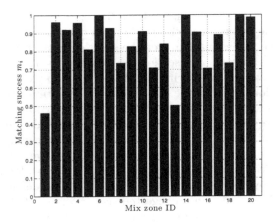

Fig. 4. Matching success m_i of the 20 potential mix zone locations

of node s is correctly guessed. For example, $G_s = \{z_3, z_5, z_{10}\}$ means that node s was successfully tracked in three mix zones.

For each mix zone i, the mixing effectiveness is $m_i = \frac{u_i}{N_i}$ where u_i is the number of successful matches in mix zone i and N_i is the total number of nodes that entered mix zone i over the course of the simulation. This metric reflects the mixing effectiveness of mix zones. The tracking success of the adversary is defined as the percentage of nodes that can be tracked over k consecutive mix zones: $ts(k) = \frac{N_{suc}(k)}{N(k)}$, where $N_{suc}(k)$ is the number of nodes successfully tracked over k consecutive mix zones, and $N(k)$ is the total number of nodes traversing k consecutive mix zones. This metric reflects the distance over which nodes can be tracked before confusing the adversary.

5.2   Results

Mix Zone Performance. Figure 4 shows the histogram of mixing effectiveness for the 20 potential mix zone locations. We observe that the mixing effectiveness can vary significantly across mix zones and hence some nodes might experience a poor mixing while traversing a mix zone. This affects the optimal deployment, because mix zones with a low mixing effectiveness are sometimes chosen to fulfill the distance-to-confusion constraint. Other than that, the optimization algorithm will tend to choose mix zones that offer the lowest tracking success to the adversary, e.g., mix zones 1 and 13 are particularly effective.

Mix Zone Placement. We consider a total of 20 possible mix zone locations and test four deployments of mix zones: (i) The *optimal* mix zone deployment computed according to Sect. 4.2 resulting in 6 deployed mix zones, (ii) a *random* mix zone deployment of 10 mix zones selected uniformly at random, (iii) a *bad* mix zone deployment of 6 mix zones with poor mixing effectiveness, and (iv)

Table 1. Percentage of mobile nodes traversing a certain number of mix zones for various mix zone deployments. The avg column gives the average number of traversed mix zones. The last column gives the percentage of nodes that were successfully tracked over all mix zones in the considered area.

# of traversed mix zones	0	1	2	3	4	5	6	7	8	avg	Tracked (%)
Bad (6 mix zones)	68	20	7	5	0	0	0	0	0	0.48	98
Random (10 mix zones)	14	43	24	10	9	0	0	0	0	1.56	78
Optimal (6 mix zones)	14	33	37	16	0	0	0	0	0	1.55	53
Full (20 mix zones)	0	8	24	24	16	14	8	4	2	3.56	48

a *full* mix zone deployment where the 20 mix zones are in use. We observe in Table 1 that in the optimal deployment, the majority of the nodes traverses at least one mix zone and none exceeds the tolerable cost of three mix zones. The random and optimal deployment perform relatively close in terms of the number of traversed mix zones, but with the optimal deployment, less nodes are tracked (53%) approaching the performance of the full deployment (48%). As expected, the bad mix zone deployment performs the worst.

The average number of traversed mix zones in Table 1 also reflects the total cost. We observe that the optimal deployment has a higher cost than the bad deployment for the same number of deployed mix zones. However, compared to the full deployment, the optimal deployment achieves a tolerable cost and approaches the same mixing effectiveness.

Tracking Success. We compare the tracking success of the adversary for the optimal, random, bad and full deployment of mix zones. We observe in Fig. 5 (a) that in general the probability of success of the adversary decreases as mobile nodes traverse more mix zones. The optimal deployment of mix zones is more effective at anonymizing flows than other deployments and complies with the cost constraint. In particular, the optimal deployment is superior to the full deployment because it avoids the bad placement of mix zones.

Note that in the case of the full deployment, traversing more mix zones does not necessarily increase (and actually decreases) the location privacy. The reason is that the majority of the flows traversing more than five mix zones actually go through a sequence of ineffective mix zones. Hence, all flows are not equal in terms of the achievable location privacy.

In Fig. 5 (b), we observe the effect of an increase in the flow intensity λ_j (leading to a congested scenario). The optimal deployment is not affected by the change of intensity because it places mix zones in regions with high traffic density anyway. The random deployment significantly improves its mixing effectiveness and approaches the performance of the optimal deployment.

In Fig. 5 (c), we observe that as the tracking precision Q of the adversary diminishes, so does its ability to track nodes. A reduction of the tracking precision of the adversary reflects scenarios where the knowledge of the adversary about mobility profiles is noisy.

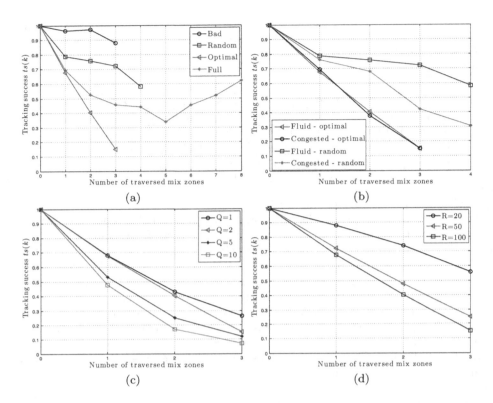

Fig. 5. Tracking success of adversary $ts(k)$, i.e., the fraction of nodes that can be tracked over k consecutive mix zones. (a) Tracking success for various mix zones' deployments. (b) Tracking success in a fluid and congested scenario. (c) Tracking success with various adversary's precision. (d) Tracking success for various sizes of mix zone.

In Fig. 5 (d), we observe that increasing the mix zone radius R from 50 to 100 does not increase much the mixing effectiveness, whereas a small radius $R = 20$ dramatically reduces the achieved location privacy. One reason is that changes in speed and direction occur mostly at the center of mix zones. Another reason is that with $R = 20$, the size of mix zones tends to be smaller than the size of crossroads of the considered map. On one hand, it is thus important to choose mix zones that are not too small. On another hand, large mix zones are inappropriate because they do not significantly increase location privacy and have a high cost.

We also vary the parameters of the optimization problem. The cost w_i, associated with mix zones, changes the optimal placement of mix zones. As we increase the cost, fewer mix zones are deployed and the achievable location privacy decreases compared to the full deployment. Instead, if the tolerable cost increases, the optimal deployment performs closer to the full deployment in terms of the achieved location privacy. Finally, if the tolerable distance-to-confusion is lowered, the optimization problem might not have a solution. If there is a solution, it will require more mix zones and will increase the cost per node.

Discussion. Our results show the limitations of mix zones, but also exhibit the importance of optimizing their placement. In particular, the optimal deployment prevents bad placement of mix zones. Another interesting result is that traversing more mix zones is not necessarily an advantage. It must be noted that the relatively high success rate of the adversary is also due to the application example. First, we consider a worst-case adversary with global coverage and access to precise mobility profiles ($Q = 1$). Second, we consider a relatively small map with a simple road intersection model.

6 Related Work

There are several techniques for achieving location privacy besides the multiple pseudonyms approach [36]. Mobile nodes can also intentionally add noise to their location [21], or report their location as a region instead of a point [44]. However, in mobile wireless networks, the peer-to-peer wireless communications between mobile nodes unveil their locations. Hence, obfuscating the location data contained in messages is insufficient to protect the location privacy of mobile nodes. In other words, the use of multiple pseudonyms is required for achieving location privacy in such networks. To anonymize pseudonyms such as the MAC address, one approach [22] consists in changing the MAC address over time between connections with WiFi access points. Another possibility [20] is to obscure the MAC address and use an identifier-free link layer protocol. However, in peer-to-peer wireless networks, mobile nodes continuously broadcast messages and cannot be anonymized only with respect to WiFi access points. Similarly, mobile nodes must be identifiable on several layers of the protocol stack. Hence, we propose to change pseudonyms in optimally placed mix zones.

Huang *et al.* suggest in [30] the use of cascading mix zones. Mix zones are created by repeatedly turning off the transceivers of mobile nodes. They evaluate the quality of service implications on real-time applications of users traversing several mix zones, but do not evaluate strategies of mix zones deployments. In [12], Buttyan *et al.* evaluate the performance of sequences of mix zones for vehicular networks. The locations of mix zones correspond to regions where the adversary has no coverage. In their system, the adversary has a high tracking success because of the insufficient mixing of vehicles. In this paper, we provide a theoretical framework for the analysis of the mixing effectiveness of mix zones and of their optimal placement in a considered area.

Note that in wired mix networks, the disadvantages of free routes were studied in [10,14] showing the importance of route selection and network connectivity. In this paper, we study an equivalent problem for mobile networks considering the optimal positioning of mix zones and its effect on the achievable location privacy.

7   Conclusion

We have considered the problem of constructing a network of mix zones in a mobile network. We first showed how to evaluate the mixing effectiveness of mix zones prior to network operation by using the Jensen-Shannon divergence measure. The proposed metric relies on statistical information about the mobility of nodes in mix zones. Then, we modeled the problem of placing mix zones as an optimization problem by taking into account the distance-to-confusion and the cost induced by mix zones on mobile nodes. By means of simulations, we investigated the importance of the mix zone deployment strategy and observed that the optimal algorithm prevents bad placement of mix zones. In addition, we measured the benefit brought by the optimal placement of mix zones, i.e., a 30% increase of location privacy compared to a random deployment of mix zones, in our considered example. We also noticed that the optimal mix zone placement performs comparatively well to the full deployment scenario, but at a lower cost. This work is a first step towards a deeper understanding of the advantages and limitations of mix zones.

Future Work. We intend to extend the simulations by using real mobility traces. In order to allow for location privacy at specific locations (i.e., nodes might want to hide the fact that they traversed a particular location), we also plan to weigh the importance of specific locations in the placement strategy. Finally, it would be interesting to consider other attacks [35,39] and how an active adversary would affect the performance of the system.

Acknowledgements

We would like to thank Mathias Humbert, Maxim Raya, Marcin Poturalski, and Michal Piorkowski for their insights and suggestions on earlier versions of this work, and the anonymous reviewers for their helpful feedback. Special thanks go to Carmela Troncoso and Claudia Diaz for shepherding the paper.

References

1. http://en.wikipedia.org/wiki/Bluedating
2. http://www.aka-aki.com
3. http://csg.ethz.ch/research/projects/Blue_star
4. http://reality.media.mit/serendipity.php
5. TIGER maps, http://www.census.gov/geo/www/tiger/
6. Beresford, A.R.: Location privacy in ubiquitous computing. In: Ph.D. Thesis (2005)
7. Beresford, A.R., Stajano, F.: Location privacy in pervasive computing. IEEE Pervasive Computing 2(1), 46–55 (2003)
8. Beresford, A.R., Stajano, F.: Mix zones: user privacy in location-aware services. In: Pervasive Computing and Communications Workshops, pp. 127–131 (2004)
9. Berger, J.O.: Statistical Decision Theory and Bayesian Analysis. Springer, Heidelberg (1993)

10. Berthold, O., Pfitzmann, A., Standtke, R.: The disadvantages of free MIX routes and how to overcome them. In: Federrath, H. (ed.) Designing Privacy Enhancing Technologies. LNCS, vol. 2009, pp. 30–45. Springer, Heidelberg (2001)
11. Bohme, R., Danezis, G., Diaz, C., Kopsell, S., Pfitzmann, A.: Mix cascades vs. peer-to-peer: Is one concept superior? In: PET (2004)
12. Buttyán, L., Holczer, T., Vajda, I.: On the effectiveness of changing pseudonyms to provide location privacy in VANETs. In: Stajano, F., Meadows, C., Capkun, S., Moore, T. (eds.) ESAS 2007. LNCS, vol. 4572, pp. 129–141. Springer, Heidelberg (2007)
13. Chaum, D.: Untraceable electronic mail, return addresses, and digital pseudonyms. Communications of the ACM 24(2), 84–90 (1981)
14. Danezis, G.: Mix-networks with restricted routes. In: Dingledine, R. (ed.) PET 2003. LNCS, vol. 2760, pp. 1–17. Springer, Heidelberg (2003)
15. Díaz, C., Seys, S., Claessens, J., Preneel, B.: Towards measuring anonymity. In: Dingledine, R., Syverson, P.F. (eds.) PET 2002. LNCS, vol. 2482, pp. 54–68. Springer, Heidelberg (2003)
16. Dingledine, R., Mathewson, N., Syverson, P.: Tor: the second-generation onion router. In: USENIX Security Symposium, pp. 21–21 (2004)
17. Freudiger, J., Raya, M., Felegyhazi, M., Papadimitratos, P., Hubaux, J.-P.: Mix zones for location privacy in vehicular networks. In: WiN-ITS (2007)
18. Gazis, D.C.: Traffic Theory. Kluwer Academic Publishers, Dordrecht (2002)
19. Gonzalez, M.C., Hidalgo, C.A., Barabasi, A.-L.: Understanding individual human mobility patterns. Nature 453(7196), 779–782 (2008)
20. Greenstein, B., McCoy, D., Pang, J., Kohno, T., Seshan, S., Wetherall, D.: Improving wireless privacy with an identifier-free link layer protocol. In: MobiSys, pp. 40–53 (2008)
21. Gruteser, M., Grunwald, D.: Anonymous usage of location-based services through spatial and temporal cloaking. In: MobiSys, pp. 31–42 (2003)
22. Gruteser, M., Grunwald, D.: Enhancing location privacy in wireless LAN through disposable interface identifiers: a quantitative analysis. Mobile Networks and Applications 10(3), 315–325 (2005)
23. Hartenstein, H., Laberteaux, K.: A tutorial survey on vehicular ad hoc networks. IEEE Communications Magazine 46(6) (June 2008)
24. Hellman, M., Raviv, J.: Probability of error, equivocation, and the Chernoff bound. IEEE Transactions on Information Theory 16(4), 368–372 (1970)
25. Hoh, B., Gruteser, M.: Protecting location privacy through path confusion. In: SECURECOMM, pp. 194–205 (2005)
26. Hoh, B., Gruteser, M., Herring, R., Ban, J., Work, D., Herrera, J.-C., Bayen, A.M., Annavaram, M., Jacobson, Q.: Virtual trip lines for distributed privacy-preserving traffic monitoring. In: MobiSys, pp. 15–28 (2008)
27. Hoh, B., Gruteser, M., Xiong, H., Alrabady, A.: Enhancing security and privacy in traffic-monitoring systems. IEEE Pervasive Computing 5(4), 38–46 (2006)
28. Huang, L., Matsuura, K., Yamane, H., Sezaki, K.: Enhancing wireless location privacy using silent period. In: WCNC, pp. 1187–1192 (2005)
29. Huang, L., Yamane, H., Matsuura, K., Sezaki, K.: Towards modeling wireless location privacy. In: Danezis, G., Martin, D. (eds.) PET 2005. LNCS, vol. 3856, pp. 59–77. Springer, Heidelberg (2006)
30. Huang, L., Yamane, H., Matsuura, K., Sezaki, K.: Silent cascade: Enhancing location privacy without communication QoS degradation. In: Clark, J.A., Paige, R.F., Polack, F.A.C., Brooke, P.J. (eds.) SPC 2006. LNCS, vol. 3934, pp. 165–180. Springer, Heidelberg (2006)

31. Jiang, T., Wang, H.J., Hu, Y.-C.: Preserving location privacy in wireless LANs. In: MobiSys, pp. 246–257 (2007)
32. Kailath, T.: The divergence and Bhattacharyya distance measures in signal selection. IEEE Transactions on Communication Technology 15(1), 52–60 (1967)
33. Krajzewicz, D., Hertkorn, G., Rossel, C., Wagner, P.: SUMO (Simulation of Urban MObility) - an open-source traffic simulation. In: MESM (2002)
34. Krumm, J.: Inference attacks on location tracks. In: LaMarca, A., Langheinrich, M., Truong, K.N. (eds.) Pervasive 2007. LNCS, vol. 4480, pp. 127–143. Springer, Heidelberg (2007)
35. Krumm, J.: A Markov model for driver route prediction. In: SAE World Congress (2008)
36. Krumm, J.: A survey of computational location privacy. In: Personal and Ubiquitous Computing (2008)
37. Li, M., Sampigethaya, K., Huang, L., Poovendran, R.: Swing & swap: user-centric approaches towards maximizing location privacy. In: WPES, pp. 19–28 (2006)
38. Lin, J.: Divergence measures based on the Shannon entropy. IEEE Transactions on Information theory 37, 145–151 (1991)
39. De Mulder, Y., Danezis, G., Batina, L., Preneel, B.: Identification via location-profiling in GSM networks. In: WPES, pp. 23–32 (2008)
40. Pfitzmann, A., Köhntopp, M.: Anonymity, unobservability, and pseudonymity – a proposal for terminology. In: Designing Privacy Enhancing Technologies, pp. 1–9 (2001)
41. Rasmussen, B., Capkun, S.: Implications of radio fingerprinting on the security of sensor networks. In: SECURECOMM, pp. 331–340 (2007)
42. Sampigethaya, K., Huang, L., Li, M., Poovendran, R., Matsuura, K., Sezaki, K.: CARAVAN: Providing location privacy for VANET. In: ESCAR (2005)
43. Serjantov, A., Danezis, G.: Towards an information theoretic metric for anonymity. In: Dingledine, R., Syverson, P.F. (eds.) PET 2002. LNCS, vol. 2482, pp. 41–53. Springer, Heidelberg (2003)
44. Sweeney, L.: k-anonymity: a model for protecting privacy. International Journal of Uncertainty, Fuzziness and Knowledge-Based Systems 10, 557–570 (2002)
45. Tóth, G., Hornák, Z.: Measuring anonymity in a non-adaptive, real-time system. In: Martin, D., Serjantov, A. (eds.) PET 2004. LNCS, vol. 3424, pp. 226–241. Springer, Heidelberg (2005)
46. Wong, F.-L., Stajano, F.: Location privacy in Bluetooth. In: Molva, R., Tsudik, G., Westhoff, D. (eds.) ESAS 2005. LNCS, vol. 3813, pp. 176–188. Springer, Heidelberg (2005)
47. Xu, Q., Mak, T., Ko, J., Sengupta, R.: Vehicle-to-vehicle safety messaging in DSRC. In: VANET, pp. 19–28 (2004)

Privacy-Preserving Face Recognition[*]

Zekeriya Erkin[1], Martin Franz[2], Jorge Guajardo[3],
Stefan Katzenbeisser[2], Inald Lagendijk[1], and Tomas Toft[4]

[1] Technische Universiteit Delft
[2] Technische Universität Darmstadt
[3] Philips Research Europe
[4] Aarhus University

Abstract. Face recognition is increasingly deployed as a means to unobtrusively verify the identity of people. The widespread use of biometrics raises important privacy concerns, in particular if the biometric matching process is performed at a central or untrusted server, and calls for the implementation of Privacy-Enhancing Technologies. In this paper we propose for the first time a strongly privacy-enhanced face recognition system, which allows to efficiently hide both the biometrics and the result from the server that performs the matching operation, by using techniques from secure multiparty computation. We consider a scenario where one party provides a face image, while another party has access to a database of facial templates. Our protocol allows to jointly run the standard Eigenfaces recognition algorithm in such a way that the first party cannot learn from the execution of the protocol more than basic parameters of the database, while the second party does not learn the input image or the result of the recognition process. At the core of our protocol lies an efficient protocol for securely comparing two Paillier-encrypted numbers. We show through extensive experiments that the system can be run efficiently on conventional hardware.

1 Introduction

Biometric techniques have advanced over the past years to a reliable means of authentication, which are increasingly deployed in various application domains. In particular, face recognition has been a focus of the research community due to its unobtrusiveness and ease of use: no special sensors are necessary and readily available images of good quality can be used for biometric authentication. The development of new biometric face-recognition systems was mainly driven by two application scenarios:

- To reduce the risk of counterfeiting, modern electronic passports and identification cards contain a chip that stores information about the owner, as well as biometric data in the form of a fingerprint and a photo. While this

---

[*] Supported in part by the European Commission through the IST Programme under Contract IST-2006-034238 SPEED and by CASED (www.cased.de).

I. Goldberg and M. Atallah (Eds.): PETS 2009, LNCS 5672, pp. 235–253, 2009.

biometric data is not widely used at the moment, it is anticipated that the digitized photo will allow to automatize identity checks at border crossings or even perform cross-matching against lists of terrorism suspects (for a recent Interpol initiative to use face recognition to mass-screen passengers see [5]).
- The increasing deployment of surveillance cameras in public places (e.g. [18] estimates that 4.2 million surveillance cameras monitor the public in the UK) sparked interest in the use of face recognition technologies to automatically match faces of people shown on surveillance images against a database of known suspects. Despite massive technical problems that render this application currently infeasible, automatic biometric face recognition systems are still high on the agenda of policy makers [25,19].

The ubiquitous use of face biometrics raises important privacy concerns; particularly problematic are scenarios where a face image is automatically matched against a database without the explicit consent of a person (for example in the above-mentioned surveillance scenario), as this allows to trace people against their will. The widespread use of biometrics calls for a careful policy, specifying to which party biometric data is revealed, in particular if biometric matching is performed at a central server or in partly untrusted environments.

In this paper we propose for the first time strong cryptographic Privacy-Enhancing Technologies for biometric face recognition; the techniques allow to hide the biometric data as well as the authentication result from the server that performs the matching. The proposed scheme can thus assure the privacy of individuals in scenarios where face recognition is beneficial for society but too privacy intrusive.

In particular, we provide a solution to the following two-party problem. Alice and Bob want to privately execute a standard biometric face recognition algorithm. Alice owns a face image, whereas Bob owns a database containing a collection of face images (or corresponding feature vectors) from individuals. Alice and Bob want to jointly run a face recognition algorithm in order to determine whether the picture owned by Alice shows a person whose biometric data is in Bob's database. While Bob accepts that Alice might learn basic parameters of the face recognition system (including the size of the database), he considers the content of his database as private data that he is not willing to reveal. In contrast, Alice trusts Bob to execute the algorithm correctly, but is neither willing to share the image nor the detection result with Bob. After termination, Alice will only learn if a match occurred; alternatively, an ID of the identified person may be returned.

In a real world scenario Bob might be a police organization, whereas Alice could be some private organization running an airport or a train station. While it may be common interest to use face recognition to identify certain people, it is generally considered too privacy intrusive to use Bob's central server directly for identification, as this allows him to create profiles of travelers. Thus, the two parties may decide for a privacy-friendly version where the detection result is not available to the central party. As the reputation of both parties is high and because both parties are interested in computing a correct result, it is reasonable to assume that they will behave in a semi-honest manner.

We provide a complete implementation of the above-mentioned two-party problem using the standard Eigenface [34] recognition system, working on encrypted images. At the heart of our privacy-enhanced face recognition system lies a highly optimized cryptographic protocol for comparing two Pailler-encrypted values. The system is very efficient and allows matching of an encrypted face image of size 92×112 pixels against a database of 320 facial templates in approximately 40 seconds on a conventional workstation. This is achieved despite the huge computational complexity of the underlying cryptographic primitives. Using pre-computations for intermediate values which do not depend on the input image, recognition only takes 18 seconds. While there is a small constant overhead when performing a face-recognition, the time to perform the recognition is linear in the size of the database. For a large database containing M facial templates, time for one recognition increases only slowly and requieres approximately $0.054M$ seconds for the conventional approach and $0.031M$ seconds when using pre-computations.

2   Cryptographic Tools

As a central cryptographic tool, we use two semantically secure additively homomorphic public-key encryption schemes, namely the Paillier and the DGK cryptosystem. In an additively homomorphic cryptosystem, given encryptions $[a]$ and $[b]$, an encryption $[a + b]$ can be computed by $[a + b] = [a][b]$, where all operations are performed in the algebra of the message or ciphertext space. Furthermore, messages can be multiplied with constants under encryption, i.e., given an encrypted message $[a]$ and a constant b in the clear, it is possible to compute $[ab]$ by $[ab] = [a]^b$.

Paillier cryptosystem. Introduced by Paillier in [29], its security is based on the decisional composite residuosity problem. Let $n = pq$ of size k, with p, q prime numbers and k from the range 1000-2048. Also let $g = n + 1$ [10]. To encrypt a message $m \in \mathbb{Z}_n$, the user selects a random value $r \in \mathbb{Z}_n$ and computes the ciphertext $c = g^m r^n \bmod n^2$. Note that due to our choice of g, encryption requires only one modular exponentiation and two modular multiplications, as $c = (mn + 1)r^n \bmod n^2$. We will write the encryption of a message m in the Paillier cryptosystem as $[m]$. Since all encryptions in the proposed protocol will be computed using one fixed public key, we do not specify the key explicitly. It is easy to see that Paillier is additively homomorphic and that for an encryption $[m]$ we can compute a new probabilistic encryption of m without knowing the private key (this will be referred to as *re-randomization*). We refer the reader to [29] for a description of the decryption operation and further details on the cryptosystem.

Damgård, Geisler and Krøigaard cryptosystem (DGK). For efficiency reasons we use at a key point in our protocol another homomorphic cryptosystem, which was proposed by Damgård, Geisler and Krøigaard [8,9]. As in Paillier, let $n = pq$ be a k-bit integer (with k chosen from the range 1000-2048), with p, q primes. The ciphertext c corresponding to a message $m \in \mathbb{Z}_u$ is computed as $c = g^m h^r \bmod n$, where u is a prime number and r is a randomly chosen integer. In practice (and more importantly in our application) u is from a very small range, say 8-bit values, which results in a very small plaintext space $\mathbb{Z}_u$. Similarly to Paillier, DGK is also additively homomorphic and it is possible to re-randomize existing ciphertexts. Compared to Paillier, the scheme has substantially smaller ciphertexts and the smaller plaintext space results in a large performance gain. To note the difference between Paillier and DGK ciphertexts we will denote the encryption of m in the DGK cryptosystem as $[\![m]\!]$.

3   Face Recognition

In 1991, Matthew Turk and Alex Pentland proposed an efficient approach to identify human faces [34,35]. This approach transforms face images into characteristic feature vectors of a low-dimensional vector space (the face space), whose basis is composed of *eigenfaces*. The eigenfaces are determined through Principal Component Analysis (PCA) from a set of training images; every face image is succinctly represented as a vector in the face space by projecting the face image onto the subspace spanned by the eigenfaces. Recognition of a face is done by first projecting the face image to the face space and subsequently locating the closest feature vector. A more detailed description of the enrollment and recognition processes is given below.

During enrollment, a set of M training images $\Theta_1, \Theta_2, \ldots, \Theta_M$, which can be represented as vectors of length N, is used to determine the optimal low-dimensional face space, in which face images will be represented as points. To do this, the average of the training images is first computed as $\Psi = \frac{1}{M} \sum_{i=1}^{M} \Theta_i$. Then, this average is subtracted from each face vector to form difference vectors $\Phi_i = \Theta_i - \Psi$. Next, PCA is applied to the covariance matrix of these vectors $C = \frac{1}{M} \sum_{i=1}^{M} \Phi_i \Phi_i^T = \frac{1}{M} A A^T$ to obtain orthonormal eigenvectors and corresponding eigenvalues where A is the matrix where each column corresponds to the image Θ_i for $i = 1$ to M. (As the size of C makes it computationally infeasible to directly run PCA, the eigenvectors are usually obtained by applying PCA to the much smaller matrix $A^T A$ and appropriate post-processing). At most M of the eigenvalues will be nonzero. To determine the face space, we select $K \ll M$ eigenvectors $u_1, \ldots, u_K$ that correspond to the K largest eigenvalues. Subsequently, images $\Theta_1, \Theta_2, \ldots, \Theta_M$ showing faces to be recognized (not necessarily the training images) are projected onto the subspace spanned by the basis $u_1, \ldots, u_K$ to obtain their feature vector representation $\Omega_1, \ldots, \Omega_M$.

During recognition, a new face image Γ is projected onto the face space by calculating weights $\bar{\omega}_i = u_i^T (\Gamma - \Psi)$ for $i = 1, \ldots, K$. These weights form a feature vector $\bar{\Omega} = (\bar{\omega}_1, \bar{\omega}_2, \ldots, \bar{\omega}_K)^T$ that represents the new image in the face space. Subsequently, the distances between the obtained vector $\bar{\Omega}$ and all feature vectors $\Omega_1, \ldots, \Omega_M$ present in the database are computed,

$$D_i = \|(\bar{\Omega} - \Omega_i)\|.$$

A match is reported if the smallest distance $D_{min} = \min\{D_1, \ldots, D_M\}$ is smaller than a given threshold value T. Note that this basic recognition algorithm can be augmented with additional checks that reduce the number of false positives and negatives during recognition; for the sake of simplicity, we stick to the basic eigenface recognition algorithm presented above.

4   Privacy-Preserving Eigenfaces

In this section, we present a privacy preserving realization of the Eigenface recognition algorithm which operates on encrypted images. We work in the two-party setting in the semi-honest attacker model. Informally, this assumes that the parties involved in the protocol follow it properly but keep a log of all the messages that have been exchanged (including their own) and try to learn as much information as possible from them. Alice's privacy is ensured against a computationally bounded attacker, while Bob's is unconditional—even a computationally unbounded Alice cannot compromise it. It is also assumed that the parties communicate over an authenticated channel (this can be achieved by standard mechanisms and is thus outside the scope of this paper).

4.1   Setup and Key Generation

Two parties Alice and Bob jointly run the recognition algorithm. We assume that Bob has already set up the face recognition system by running the enrollment process (in the clear) on all available training images to obtain the basis $u_1, \ldots, u_K$ of the face space and feature vectors $\Omega_1, \ldots, \Omega_M$ of faces to be recognized. Furthermore, we assume that all coordinates of the eigenfaces and feature vectors are represented as integers; this can always be achieved by appropriate quantization: non-integer values are first scaled by a fixed scale factor S and rounded to the nearest integer. This is necessary, as all values need to be integers in order to encrypt them with Paillier and process them using homomorphic operations. The effects of this quantization step on the detection reliability are experimentally analyzed in Section 6. Each feature vector in the database is further accompanied by a string Id_i that contains the identity of the person the feature vector belongs to; we assume that the identity is encoded as a *non-zero* element of the message space of the chosen encryption scheme.

During the interactive recognition protocol, Alice provides an encrypted face image $[\Gamma]$ as input. At the end of the protocol, Alice learns whether the face shown on her image matches one of the feature vectors $\Omega_1, \ldots, \Omega_M$ owned by Bob: Depending on the application, Alice either receives the identity Id_i of the best matching feature vector or only a binary answer (i.e. whether there was a match or not). Apart from this answer (and the number M), Bob keeps the database content secret. Bob learns nothing from the interaction, i.e. neither the face image Γ, nor its representation in the face space, nor the result of the matching process.

Note that the vectors u_i are directly computed from the set of training images; thus, they *do* carry information on the faces stored in Bob's database.

Even though it is hard to quantify the exact amount of data leakage through the knowledge of the basis $u_1, \ldots, u_K$, our solution will treat it as sensitive data that will not be disclosed to Alice. In an alternative implementation, the basis $u_1, \ldots, u_K$ can be derived from a sufficiently large public face database so that they do not carry personal information; the proposed system can easily be changed to take advantage of public basis vectors, see Section 6 for details. Since Alice is the only party who receives an output, we can construct the protocol using any standard homomorphic public-key encryption algorithm; as stated in Section 2 we choose Paillier encryption for the implementation. In particular, we do *not* need a threshold homomorphic scheme, as it is widely employed in the construction of secure multiparty protocols. Before the interaction starts, Alice generates a pair of public and private keys and sends her public key to Bob over an authenticated channel. In the first step of the protocol, Alice encrypts all pixels of the image Γ separately with her public key and sends the result to Bob, who is unable to decrypt them. However, Bob can use the homomorphic property of the cipher to perform linear operations on the ciphertexts; for some operations (such as computing distances between vectors or finding a minumum), he will require assistance from Alice in the form of an interactive protocol. At the end of the protocol, Alice receives back an encryption containing the result of the biometric matching operation, which only Alice can decrypt. Appendix A gives a sketch of the security of our system in the semi-honest attacker model.

4.2   Private Recognition Algorithm

To match a face image against feature vectors in a database, three steps need to be performed. First, the image needs to be projected onto the face space in order to obtain its corresponding feature vector representation. Subsequently, distances between the obtained vector and all feature vectors in Bob's database need to be computed. Finally, the one with minimum distance is selected; if this distance is smaller than a threshold, a match is reported. In the following, we show how these three steps can be realized in a privacy preserving manner. Figure 1 shows an outline of the private face recognition protocol; the gray area denotes operations that need to be performed on encrypted values.

Projection. As a first step, the input image Γ has to be projected onto the low dimensional face space spanned by the eigenfaces $u_1, \ldots, u_K$. This can be performed by computing the scalar product of

$$\Phi = \Gamma - \Psi = \begin{pmatrix} \Gamma_1 - \Psi_1 \\ \vdots \\ \Gamma_N - \Psi_N \end{pmatrix}$$

and each eigenface vector u_i to obtain

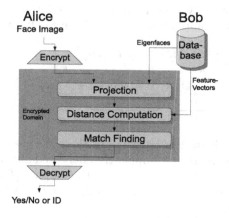

Fig. 1. Privacy-Preserving Face Recognition

$$\bar{\omega}_i = \Phi_1 \cdot u_{i1} + \ldots + \Phi_N \cdot u_{iN}$$

for each $i \in \{1, \ldots, K\}$.

These operations have to be performed in the encrypted domain by Bob, who receives the encrypted face image $[\Gamma]$ from Alice. As Bob knows the vector Ψ in plain, he can easily compute $-\Psi = (-1) \cdot \Psi$ and then encrypt each of its components. These encryptions can be pairwise multiplied with the encrypted components of $[\Gamma]$ in order to perform the componentwise subtraction of the vectors Γ and Ψ. Thus Bob computes

$$[\Phi] = [\Gamma - \Psi] = \begin{pmatrix} [\Gamma_1] \cdot [-\Psi_1] \\ \vdots \\ [\Gamma_N] \cdot [-\Psi_N] \end{pmatrix}.$$

Subsequently Bob performs the projection

$$[\bar{\omega}_i] = [\Phi_1 \cdot u_{i1} + \ldots + \Phi_N \cdot u_{iN}] = [\Phi_1]^{u_{i1}} \cdot \ldots \cdot [\Phi_N]^{u_{iN}}$$

for each $i \in \{1, \ldots, K\}$. This is done as follows. As Bob knows the vector u_i in plain, he can perform the required multiplications using the homomorphic property. For example, in order to multiply the first components of both vectors Bob has to compute $[\Phi_1]^{u_{i1}}$. To obtain the sum of all these products he just multiplies the encryptions with each other. Doing this for all $1 \leq i \leq K$, Bob obtains an encrypted feature vector description of the face image as $[\bar{\Omega}] := ([\bar{\omega}_1], \ldots, [\bar{\omega}_K])^T$. Note that every computation in the projection operation can be performed by Bob without interacting with Alice.

Calculating distances. After having obtained the encrypted feature vector $[\bar{\Omega}]$, encryptions of the distances $D_1, \ldots, D_M$ between $\bar{\Omega}$ and all feature vectors $\Omega \in \{\Omega_1, \ldots, \Omega_M\}$ from the database have to be computed. Since in the remainder of the protocol we are only concerned with the relative order of the obtained distances, it suffices to compute the square of the Euclidean distance,

$$D(\Omega, \bar{\Omega}) = \|\Omega - \bar{\Omega}\|^2 = (\omega_1 - \bar{\omega}_1)^2 + \ldots + (\omega_K - \bar{\omega}_K)^2$$

$$= \underbrace{\sum_{i=1}^{K} \omega_i^2}_{S_1} + \underbrace{\sum_{i=1}^{K} (-2\omega_i \bar{\omega}_i)}_{S_2} + \underbrace{\sum_{i=1}^{K} \bar{\omega}_i^2}_{S_3}. \tag{1}$$

Again, we need to evaluate this equation in the encrypted domain: Bob knows the encryption $[\bar{\Omega}]$ and needs to compute the encrypted distance $[D(\Omega, \bar{\Omega})]$, while he knows the feature vector Ω in the clear. To compute $[D(\Omega, \bar{\Omega})]$ it suffices to compute encryptions of the three sums S_1, S_2 and S_3, as by the homomorphic property and Eq. (1),

$$[D(\Omega, \bar{\Omega})] = [S_1] \cdot [S_2] \cdot [S_3].$$

The term S_1 is the sum over the components of Ω known in the clear. Thus, Bob can compute S_1 directly and encrypt it to obtain $[S_1]$. S_2 consists of the products $\omega_i \bar{\omega}_i$, where Bob knows ω_i in the clear and has $[\bar{\omega}_i]$ in encrypted form. In a first step the values ω_i can be multiplied with -2. The term $[(-2\omega_i)\bar{\omega}_i]$ can be computed by raising $[\bar{\omega}_i]$ to the power of $(-2\omega_i)$, using the homomorphic property. To obtain an encryption of S_2, Bob finally computes $[S_2] = \prod_{j=1}^{K} [(-2\omega_i)\bar{\omega}_i]$. Thus, the value $[S_2]$ can again be computed by Bob without interacting with Alice. The term S_3 consists of the squares of the encrypted values $[\bar{\omega}_i]$. Unfortunately, Bob cannot perform the required multiplication without help from Alice. Thus, Bob additively blinds the value $\bar{\omega}_i$ with an uniformly random element r_i from the plaintext space to obtain $[x_i] = [\bar{\omega}_i + r_i] = [\bar{\omega}_i] \cdot [r_i]$. Note that for every component $\bar{\omega}_i$ of the vector $\bar{\Omega}$ a fresh random value must be generated. Finally, he sends the elements $[x_i]$ to Alice who decrypts. Alice can now compute the values x_i^2 in plain as the square of the plaintext x_i and compute the value $S_3' = \sum_{j=1}^{K} x_i^2$. She encrypts this value and sends $[S_3']$ back to Bob, who computes

$$[S_3] = [S_3'] \cdot \prod_{j=1}^{K} ([\bar{\omega}_i]^{(-2r_i)} \cdot [-r_i^2]),$$

which yields the desired result because

$$[x_i^2] \cdot [\bar{\omega}_i]^{(-2r_i)} \cdot [-r_i^2] = [(\bar{\omega}_i + r_i)^2 - 2r_i\bar{\omega}_i - r_i^2] = [\bar{\omega}_i^2].$$

Note that this interactive protocol to compute the value $[S_3]$ needs to be run only once. The value $[S_3]$ depends only on the encrypted feature vector $[\bar{\Omega}]$ and can be used for computation of all distances $[D_1], \ldots, [D_M]$. Note further that due to the blinding factors, Alice does not learn the values $\bar{\omega}_i$.

Match finding. In the last step of the recognition algorithm, the feature vector from the database that is closest to $\bar{\Omega}$ must be found. This distance is finally compared to a threshold value T; if the distance is smaller, a match is reported and an encryption of the identity Id which corresponds to the best matching feature vector is returned to Alice.

As a result of the last step we obtained encrypted distances $[D_1], \ldots, [D_M]$, where D_i denotes the distance between $\bar{\Omega}$ and the i-th feature vector $\Omega_i \in \{\Omega_1, \ldots, \Omega_M\}$ from the database. To find the minimum we employ a straightforward recursive procedure: in the first step, we compare the $k = \lfloor \frac{M}{2} \rfloor$ encrypted distances $[D_{2i+1}]$ and $[D_{2i+2}]$ for $0 \leq i \leq k - 1$ with each other, by using a cryptographic protocol that compares two encrypted values; a re-randomized encryption of the smaller distance is retained (re-randomization is necessary to prevent Bob from determining the outcome of the comparison by inspecting the ciphertexts). After this step, there will be $\lceil \frac{M}{2} \rceil$ encryptions left. In a second run we repeat this procedure for the remaining encryptions, and so forth. After $\lceil \log_2(M) \rceil$ iterations there will only be one encryption left, the minimum.

As we need to return the identity of the best matching feature vector, we also have to keep track of the IDs during the minimum computation. This is done by working with pairs $([D_i], [Id_i])$ of distances and their corresponding identities, where the recursive minimum finding algorithm is applied to the distances only, but re-randomized encryptions of both the smaller distance and its identity are retained for the next round. An efficient implementation of the required comparison protocol is described in Section 5.

To check if the minimum distance is smaller than a threshold T, we can treat the value T as one additional distance that has the special identity 0. Together with the distances $D_1, \ldots, D_M$ we run the algorithm to find the minimum as described above. After $\lceil \log_2(M + 1) \rceil$ iterations, Bob receives the minimum distance and the corresponding identity $([D], [Id])$, where $D \in \{T, D_1, \ldots, D_M\}$ and $Id \in \{0, Id_1, \ldots, Id_M\}$. Thus, if a face image could be recognized the value Id contains the corresponding identity. If no match could be found Id is equal to 0. The value $[Id]$ is finally sent to Alice as the result of the private face recognition protocol.

Note that there is an easy way to modify the protocol to make it terminate only with a binary output: rather than using actual IDs, Bob may assign a second special identity, the integer 1, to all images. In this case Alice will either receive a 1 or a 0, with the former indicating that a match was found.

5   Comparison Protocol

The only missing block is a protocol for selecting the minimum of two encrypted ℓ-bit values $[a]$ and $[b]$ along with the encrypted ID of the minimum. (Note that the bit-length ℓ can be determined by knowing the bit-length of the input data and the scale factor S used to quantize eigenfaces).

At the core of our protocol is a comparison protocol due to Damgård, Geisler and Krøigaard [8,9]. Their setting differs from ours as follows: one input is public while the other is held (bitwise) in encrypted form by one party; moreover the output is public. They note several variations, but in order to provide a solution for the present setting some tweaking is needed. This section presents the protocol in a top-down fashion.

5.1   A High-Level View of the Protocol

Initially Bob, who has access to both $[a]$ and $[b]$, computes

$$[z] = [2^\ell + a - b] = [2^\ell] \cdot [a] \cdot [b]^{-1}.$$

As $0 \le a, b < 2^\ell$, z is a positive $(\ell+1)$-bit value. Moreover, z_ℓ, the most significant bit of z, is exactly the answer we are looking for:

$$z_\ell = 0 \Leftrightarrow a < b.$$

If Bob had an encryption of $z \bmod 2^\ell$, the result would be immediate: z_ℓ could be computed as

$$z_\ell = 2^{-\ell} \cdot (z - (z \bmod 2^\ell)).$$

Correctness is easily verified; the subtraction sets the least significant bits to zero, while the multiplication shifts the interesting bit down. As only z and $z \bmod 2^\ell$ are encrypted, this is a linear combination in the encrypted domain, which can be computed by Bob.

Once Bob has an encryption of the outcome $[z_\ell] = [a < b]$, an encryption of the minimum m, is easily obtained using arithmetic, as $m = (a < b) \cdot (a - b) + b$. The multiplication requires assistance of Alice, but is easily performed through a (short) interactive protocol. Determining an encryption of the ID is analogous, $(a < b) \cdot (Id_a - Id_b) + Id_b$. Thus, it remains to describe how Bob obtains the encryption of $z \bmod 2^\ell$.

5.2   Computing $[z \bmod 2^\ell]$

The value z is available to Bob only in encrypted form, so the modulo reduction cannot easily be performed. The solution is to engage in a protocol with Alice, transforming the problem back to a comparison.

First, Bob generates a uniformly random $(\kappa + \ell + 1)$-bit value r, where κ is a security parameter, say 100, and $\kappa + \ell + 1 \ll \log_2(n)$. This will be used to additively blind z,

$$[d] = [z + r] = [z] \cdot [r];$$

$[d]$ is then re-randomized and sent to Alice who decrypts it and reduces d modulo 2^ℓ. The obtained value is then encrypted, and returned to Bob.

Due to the restriction on the bit-length of r, Bob can now *almost* compute the desired encryption $[z \bmod 2^\ell]$. The masking can be viewed as occurring over the integers, thus we have $d \equiv z + r \bmod 2^\ell$ and

$$(z \bmod 2^\ell) = ((d \bmod 2^\ell) - (r \bmod 2^\ell)) \bmod 2^\ell.$$

Alice has just provided $[d \bmod 2^\ell]$ and r is known to Bob. Thus, he can compute

$$[\tilde{z}] = [(d \bmod 2^\ell) - (r \bmod 2^\ell)] = [d \bmod 2^\ell] \cdot [(r \bmod 2^\ell)]^{-1}.$$

Had the secure subtraction occurred modulo 2^ℓ, $\tilde{z}$ would be the right result; however, it occurs modulo n. Note, though, that if $d \bmod 2^\ell \ge r \bmod 2^\ell$, $\tilde{z}$ is the right result. On the other hand, if $r \bmod 2^\ell$ is larger, an underflow has occurred; adding 2^ℓ in this case gives the right result. So, if Bob had an encryption $[\lambda]$ of a binary value indicating whether $r \bmod 2^\ell > d \bmod 2^\ell$, he could simply compute

$$[z \bmod 2^\ell] = [\tilde{z} + \lambda 2^\ell] = [\tilde{z}] \cdot [\lambda]^{2^\ell},$$

which adds 2^ℓ exactly when $r \bmod 2^\ell$ is the larger value. This leaves us with a variant of Yao's millionaires problem: Bob must obtain an encryption $[\lambda]$ of a binary value containing the result of the comparison of two private inputs: $\hat{d} = d \bmod 2^\ell$ held by Alice and $\hat{r} = r \bmod 2^\ell$ held by Bob.

5.3   Comparing Private Inputs

The problem of comparing private inputs $\hat{d}$ and $\hat{r}$ is a fundamental one, which has been studied intensively (see e.g. [38,28,14,3,4,15,8]). For efficiency reasons, we solve this problem using a *different* homomorphic encryption scheme, namely the one proposed by Damgård et al. [8,9], which has a very small plaintext space $\mathbb{Z}_u$ for some prime u. This allows very efficient multiplicative masking; in contrast to the Paillier scheme, the exponents are small.

Though the basic setting of Damgård et al. considers one public and one secret value, they note how to construct a solution for private inputs. They also note how to obtain a secret output. However, they obtain this output as an additive secret sharing, while in our setting Bob must receive a *Paillier encryption* $[\lambda]$ at the end of the protocol. Naturally Alice must not see this encryption as she knows the secret key.

We assume that Alice has run the DGK key-generation algorithm and has sent the public key to Bob. This key pair can be re-used whenever the comparison protocol will be run. Inertially, Alice sends Bob encryptions of the bits of her input, $[\![\hat{d}_{\ell-1}]\!], \ldots, [\![\hat{d}_0]\!]$. Bob then chooses $s \in_R \{1, -1\}$ and computes

$$[\![c_i]\!] = [\![\hat{d}_i - \hat{r}_i + s + 3 \sum_{j=i+1}^{\ell-1} w_j]\!] = [\![\hat{d}_i]\!] \cdot [\![-\hat{r}_i]\!] \cdot [\![s]\!] \cdot \left(\prod_{j=i+1}^{\ell-1} [\![w_j]\!] \right)^3, \quad (2)$$

where $[\![w_j]\!] = [\![\hat{d}_j \oplus \hat{r}_j]\!]$, which he can compute as Bob knows $\hat{r}_j$. For technical reasons (to avoid the case $\hat{d} = \hat{r}$), we append differing bits to both $\hat{d}$ and $\hat{r}$, i.e., we compare the values $2\hat{d} + 1$ and $2\hat{r}$ instead.

Equation (2) differs from the one proposed by Damgård et al. in order to efficiently hide the output, but the core idea remains. Consider the case of $s = 1$; if $\hat{d}$ is larger, then all c_i will be non-zero. (The modulus u is chosen such that there is no overflow.) However, if $\hat{r}$ is larger, then exactly one c_i will equal zero, the one at the most significant differing bit-position. Both claims are easily verified. For $s = -1$ we have exactly the same situation, except that the zero occurs if $\hat{d}$ is larger. The factor of 3 ensures that the values are non-zero once even a single w_j is set.

Bob now multiplicatively masks the $[\![c_i]\!]$ with a uniformly random $r_i \in \mathbb{Z}_u^*$

$$[\![e_i]\!] = [\![c_i \cdot r_i]\!] = [\![c_i]\!]^{r_i},$$

re-randomizes and permutes the encryptions $[\![e_i]\!]$ and sends them to Alice. Note that e_i is uniformly random in $\mathbb{Z}_u^*$ except when $c_i = 0$, in which case e_i also equals zero, i.e. the existence of a zero is preserved.

Alice now decrypts all e_i and checks whether one of them is zero. She then encrypts a bit $\tilde{\lambda}$, stating if this is the case. At this point she switches back to Paillier encryptions, i.e. Alice sends $[\tilde{\lambda}]$ to Bob. Given the knowledge of s, Bob can compute the desired encryption $[\lambda]$: while $[\tilde{\lambda}]$ only states whether there was a zero among the values decrypted by Alice, s explains how to interpret the result, i.e. whether the occurrence of a zero means that $\hat{r} > \hat{d}$ or $\hat{d} \geq \hat{r}$. In the former case, Bob negates the result $[\tilde{\lambda}]$ under encryption, otherwise he directly takes $[\tilde{\lambda}]$ as output $[\lambda]$.

6   Implementation

The privacy-preserving face recognition system, as described in this paper, has been implemented in C++ using the GNU GMP library version 4.2.4, in order to determine its performance and reliability. Tests were performed on a computer with a 2.4 GHz AMD Opteron dual-core processor and 4GB of RAM running Linux. Both sender and receiver were modeled as different threads of one program, which pass messages to each other; thus, the reported performance data does not include network latency.

For testing purposes, we used the "ORL Database of Faces" from AT&T Laboratories Cambridge [1], which is widely used for experiments and contains 10 images of 40 distinct subjects, thus 400 images in total. All images in this database have a dark background with the subject in upright, frontal position. The size of each image is 92×112 pixels with 256 grey levels per pixel (thus $N = 92 \cdot 112 = 10304$). We use 5-fold cross validation for the experiments such that for each subject we use 8 images in the enrollment phase and 2 images for testing (thus, the database consists of 320 feature vectors). The security parameter k for both Paillier- and DGK-cryptosystem was set to 1024 bits (see Section 2 for details). Furthermore we set $\ell = 50$ (see Section 5 for details).

Reliability. During reliability testing, we assured that our privacy-preserving implementation of the Eigenface algorithm does not degrade the reliability when compared to a standard implementation which achieves approximately 96% correct classification rate. Reliability losses may occur due to the use of scaled and quantized feature vectors and eigenfaces. This scale factor has both an influence on the accuracy of the result and the performance of the scheme. Figure 2 shows the detection rates of the implementation for different scale factors, plotted on a logarithmic scale. It can be seen that scale factors below the value 1000 significantly degrade detection performance, while scale factors larger than 1000 do not improve the results. Hence, it suffices to set $S = 1000$ to achieve the same reliability as a reference implementation operating on floating point values. Another

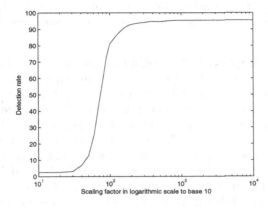

Fig. 2. Relation between scale factor and detection rate

parameter that influences both the detection rate and the performance is the number K. Turk and Pentland [34] advised to set $K = 10$; experiments with our implementation demonstrate that values of $K > 12$ do not yield a significant gain in the detection rate; thus we set $K = 12$ in subsequent tests.

Computational complexity. We measure the computational complexity of the full recognition protocol, thus the efforts of both Alice and Bob. Table 1 depicts the average runtime of a single query (wall clock time) with respect to the size of the database M (second column) in seconds. Thus, matching an image against a database of size 320 takes roughly 40 seconds; this time includes all steps of the protocol of Section 4: computing the encrypted face image by Alice, projecting it into the face space, computing distances and selecting the minimum.

One can note that a major part of the computation efforts comes from computing encryptions, since they require one rather complex modular exponentiation. The time required to run the protocol can be largely reduced if these computationally expensive operations, which do *not* depend on the input image of Alice, can be computed in advance, during idle times of a processor or on a separate processor dedicated to this task. With this optimization in place, computing one encryption requires only two modular multiplications. The third column of Table 1 shows the execution time of the recognition algorithm under the assumption that *all* randomization factors r^n (Paillier) and h^r (DGK) can be pre-computed for free during idle times. In this case, matching an image against 320 feature vectors takes only 18 seconds; furthermore, the computations performed by Alice become much more lightweight, as nearly all of Alice's efforts is spent in computing encryptions.

In a third test we assume that Alice knows the eigenfaces u_i. As noted in Section 4.1, this might be the case if a (sufficiently large) public database of faces can be used to compute the eigenfaces, or if Bob explicitly decides to reveal these values to Alice. In this case Alice performs the projection and distance computation steps and sends an encrypted feature vector to Bob. The results of this experiment are depicted in the fourth column of Table 1. Observe that compared to a standard query (second column) only a small constant factor can be saved.

Communication complexity. The communication complexity highly depends on the size of Paillier and DGK encryptions; in our implementation, the size of a Paillier ciphertext is 2048 bits, whereas a DGK encryption requires only 1024 bits. Sending the encrypted image and performing the distance computations requires communication efforts independent of M; in particular, this part of the protocol requires transmission of $N + K + 1$ Paillier encrypted values (roughly 2580 kilobytes). The rest of the communication is linear in M: more precisely, the minimum searching step requires transmission of $6M$ Pailler and $M(2\ell+1)$ DGK encryptions, which in our setting amounts to roughly 14.5 kilobytes per feature vector in the database. Table 2 shows the average amount of data in kilobytes transmitted in one run of the privacy-preserving face recognition protocol for several database sizes M (second column) and the communication complexity in case that a public basis of Eigenfaces can be used (third column). The overall communication complexity for matching an image against 320 feature vectors is thus approximately 7.25 MB.

Table 1. Computational complexity (sec.)

M	Query	With pre-computations	Public Eigenfaces
10	24	8.5	1.6
50	26	10	3.4
100	29	11.5	6
150	31.6	13	8.6
200	34.2	14.5	11.4
250	36.6	16	14.4
300	39.6	17.5	18
320	40	18	18.2

Table 2. Communication Complexity(kB)

M	Full Query	Public Eigenfaces
10	2725	149
50	3310	734
100	4038	1461
150	4765	2189
200	5497	2921
250	6228	3652
300	6959	4382
320	7249	4674

Round complexity. The round complexity of our protocol is very low. Sending the face image and receiving the result of the protocol takes one round. Another round is spent for distance computation. As the comparison protocol (see Section 5) runs in three rounds, finding the minimum of $M + 1$ values takes at most $3\lceil \log_2(M + 1) \rceil$ rounds. Therefore the round complexity of our protocol is $\mathcal{O}(\log_2(M))$.

7   Related Work

The problem considered in this paper is an instance of a secure two-party problem; thus standard methods of Secure Multiparty Computation [38,7] can be applied. Basic concepts for secure computations were introduced by Yao [38].

Subsequently, various approaches to securely evaluating a function have been developed for different function representations, namely combinatorial circuits [17,20], ordered binary decision diagrams [24], branching programs [27,26], or one-dimensional look-up tables [26]. Nevertheless, these solutions tend to be impractical due to their high computational complexity for functions as the biometric matching process considered in this paper. Thus, specific protocols must be developed.

Recently there has been an increasing interest in the use of SMC for data-intensive problems, like clustering [16,21], filtering [6] or statistical analysis [11] of sensitive private data. Furthermore, the combination of signal processing with cryptographic techniques in order to protect privacy is an active area of research [13]; among others, solutions for recognizing speech on encrypted signals [33] or image classification and object recognition on encrypted images [37,2] have been proposed. The latter work describes a solution to a problem that is complementary to the one discussed in the present paper (and can be used in conjunction with our solution): locating rectangular regions on an encrypted image that show human faces.

Some authors have proposed different complementary techniques for making surveillance cameras more privacy friendly, e.g. [32,12,39]. However, they do not consider face recognition. These approaches use methods from signal processing and pattern recognition to wipe out sensitive regions of a surveillance video automatically, based on access permissions of the surveillance personnel.

There were a few attempts to make other biometric modalities privacy-preserving, most notably fingerprints and iris codes [36,30,23]. However, these works consider a different setting, where the biometric measurement is matched against a hashed template stored on a server. The server that performs the matching gets to know both the biometric and the detection result (the aim is only to secure storage of templates). In contrast, our scenario even allows to hide this information. There are only a few works that apply cryptographic secure multiparty computation to the problem of securing iris codes and fingerprint templates (most notably [22,31]); to the best of our knowledge there is no prior solution to the much more data-intensive problem of securing face biometrics.

8   Conclusions and Future Work

In this paper we have presented for the first time strong cryptographic Privacy-Enhancing Technologies for biometric face recognition systems. In particular, we provided an efficient protocol that allows to match an encrypted image showing a face against a database of facial templates in such a way that the biometric itself and the detection result is hidden from the server that performs the matching. Through extensive tests, we showed that our privacy-preserving algorithm is as reliable as a reference implementation in the clear, and that the execution of the protocol is feasible on current hardware platforms.

In this paper we used Eigenfaces, which provides a detection rate of about 96%, as core face recognition algorithm. Biometric algorithms that achieve better detection rates are known in the literature; however, these schemes are much more complex and thus more difficult to implement on encrypted images. We leave this, as well as further optimizations, as future work.

Acknowledgments. We would like to thank Berry Schoenmakers and Thijs Veugen for helpful discussions and the anonymous reviewers of PETS 2009 for their comments and suggestions. Work performed by Martin Franz while at Philips Research Europe. Work by Tomas Toft performed at CWI Amsterdam and TU Eindhoven and supported by the research program Sentinels (http://www.sentinels.nl).

References

1. The Database of Faces, (formerly 'The ORL Database of Faces') AT&T Laboratories Cambridge,
   http://www.cl.cam.ac.uk/research/dtg/attarchive/facedatabase.html
2. Avidan, S., Butman, M.: Blind vision. In: Leonardis, A., Bischof, H., Pinz, A. (eds.) ECCV 2006. LNCS, vol. 3953, pp. 1–13. Springer, Heidelberg (2006)
3. Blake, I.F., Kolesnikov, V.: Strong Conditional Oblivious Transfer and Computing on Intervals. In: Lee, P.J. (ed.) ASIACRYPT 2004. LNCS, vol. 3329, pp. 515–529. Springer, Heidelberg (2004)
4. Blake, I.F., Kolesnikov, V.: Conditional Encrypted Mapping and Comparing Encrypted Numbers. In: Di Crescenzo, G., Rubin, A. (eds.) FC 2006. LNCS, vol. 4107, pp. 206–220. Springer, Heidelberg (2006)
5. Bowcott, O.: Interpol wants facial recognition database to catch suspects. Guardian (October 20, 2008),
   http://www.guardian.co.uk/world/2008/oct/20/interpol-facial-recognition
6. Canny, J.F.: Collaborative filtering with privacy. In: IEEE Symposium on Security and Privacy, pp. 45–57 (2002)
7. Cramer, R., Damgård, I., Nielsen, J.B.: Multiparty Computation from Threshold Homomorphic Encryption. In: Pfitzmann, B. (ed.) EUROCRYPT 2001. LNCS, vol. 2045, pp. 280–299. Springer, Heidelberg (2001)
8. Damgård, I., Geisler, M., Krøigaard, M.: Efficient and Secure Comparison for On-Line Auctions. In: Pieprzyk, J., Ghodosi, H., Dawson, E. (eds.) ACISP 2007. LNCS, vol. 4586, pp. 416–430. Springer, Heidelberg (2007)
9. Damgård, I., Geisler, M., Krøigaard, M.: A correction to Efficient and secure comparison for on-line auctions. Cryptology ePrint Archive, Report 2008/321 (2008),
   http://eprint.iacr.org/
10. Damgård, I., Jurik, M.: A Generalization, a Simplification and some Applications of Paillier's Probabilistic Public-Key System. Technical report, Department of Computer Science, University of Aarhus (2000)
11. Du, W., Han, Y.S., Chen, S.: Privacy-preserving multivariate statistical analysis: Linear regression and classification. In: Proceedings of the Fourth SIAM International Conference on Data Mining, Lake Buena Vista, Florida, USA, April 22-24, pp. 222–233. SIAM, Philadelphia (2004)
12. Dufaux, F., Ebrahimi, T.: Scrambling for video surveillance with privacy. In: 2006 Conference on Computer Vision and Pattern Recognition Workshop (CVPRW 2006). IEEE Press, Los Alamitos (2006)

13. Erkin, Z., Piva, A., Katzenbeisser, S., et al.: Protection and retrieval of encrypted multimedia content: When cryptography meets signal processing. EURASIP Journal on Information Security, Article ID 78943 (2007)
14. Fischlin, M.: A Cost-Effective Pay-Per-Multiplication Comparison Method for Millionaires. In: Naccache, D. (ed.) CT-RSA 2001. LNCS, vol. 2020, pp. 457–472. Springer, Heidelberg (2001)
15. Garay, J.A., Schoenmakers, B., Villegas, J.: Practical and Secure Solutions for Integer Comparison. In: Okamoto, T., Wang, X. (eds.) PKC 2007. LNCS, vol. 4450, pp. 330–342. Springer, Heidelberg (2007)
16. Goethals, B., Laur, S., Lipmaa, H., Mielikainen, T.: On secure scalar product computation for privacy-preserving data mining. In: Park, C.-s., Chee, S. (eds.) ICISC 2004. LNCS, vol. 3506, pp. 104–120. Springer, Heidelberg (2005)
17. Goldreich, O., Micali, S., Wigderson, A.: How to Play any Mental Game or A Completeness Theorem for Protocols with Honest Majority. In: ACM Symposium on Theory of Computing – STOC 1987, May 25-27, pp. 218–229. ACM Press, New York (1987)
18. Grose, T.: When surveillance cameras talk. Time Magazine (February 11, 2008), http://www.time.com/time/world/article/0,8599,1711972,00.html
19. Interpol wants facial recognition database to catch suspects. Heise Online UK (March 20, 2008), http://www.heise-online.co.uk/news/British-police-build-a-database-of-portrait-photos-for-facial--recognition--110363
20. Jacobsson, M., Juels, A.: Mix and match: Secure function evaluation via ciphertexts. In: Okamoto, T. (ed.) ASIACRYPT 2000. LNCS, vol. 1976, pp. 162–177. Springer, Heidelberg (2000)
21. Jagannathan, G., Wright, R.N.: Privacy-preserving distributed k-means clustering over arbitrarily partitioned data. In: KDD 2005: Proceeding of the eleventh ACM SIGKDD international conference on Knowledge discovery in data mining, pp. 593–599. ACM Press, New York (2005)
22. Kerschbaum, F., Atallah, M.J., M'Raïhi, D., Rice, J.R.: Private fingerprint verification without local storage. In: Zhang, D., Jain, A.K. (eds.) ICBA 2004. LNCS, vol. 3072, pp. 387–394. Springer, Heidelberg (2004)
23. Kevenaar, T.: Protection of Biometric Information. In: Security with Noisy Data, pp. 169–193. Springer, Heidelberg (2007)
24. Kruger, L., Jha, S., Goh, E.-J., Boneh, D.: Secure function evaluation with ordered binary decision diagrams. In: Proceedings of the 13th ACM conference on Computer and communications security CCS 2006, Virginia, U.S.A, pp. 410–420. ACM Press, New York (2006)
25. Magnier, M.: Many eyes will watch visitors. Los Angeles Times (August 07, 2008), http://articles.latimes.com/2008/aug/07/world/fg-snoop7
26. Naor, M., Nissim, K.: Communication complexity and secure function evaluation. Electronic Colloquium on Computational Complexity (ECCC), 8(062) (2001)
27. Naor, M., Nissim, K.: Communication preserving protocols for secure function evaluation. In: ACM Symposium on Theory of Computing, pp. 590–599 (2001)
28. Naor, M., Pinkas, B., Sumner, R.: Privacy preserving auctions and mechanism design. In: ACM Conference on Electronic Commerce, pp. 129–139 (1999)
29. Paillier, P.: Public-Key Cryptosystems Based on Composite Degree Residuosity Classes. In: Stern, J. (ed.) EUROCRYPT 1999. LNCS, vol. 1592, pp. 223–238. Springer, Heidelberg (1999)

30. Ratha, N., Connell, J., Bolle, R., Chikkerur, S.: Cancelable biometrics: A case study in fingerprints. In: Proceedings of the 18th International Conference on Pattern Recognition (ICPR), vol. IV, pp. 370–373. IEEE Press, Los Alamitos (2006)
31. Schoenmakers, B., Tuyls, P.: Computationally Secure Authentication with Noisy Data. In: Security with Noisy Data, pp. 141–149. Springer, Heidelberg (2007)
32. Senior, A., Oankanti, A., Hampapur, A., et al.: Enabling video privacy through computer vision. IEEE Security and Privacy Magazine 3(3), 50–57 (2005)
33. Smaragdis, P., Shashanka, M.: A framwork for secure speech recognition. IEEE Transactions on Audio, Speech and Language Processing 15(4), 1404–1413 (2007)
34. Turk, M.A., Pentland, A.P.: Eigenfaces for Recognition. Journal of Cognitive Neuroscience 3(1), 71–86 (1991)
35. Turk, M.A., Pentland, A.P.: Face recognition using eigenfaces. In: IEEE Computer Society Conference on Computer Vision and Pattern Recognition, pp. 586–591 (1991)
36. Tuyls, P., Akkermans, A.H.M., Kevenaar, T.A.M., Schrijen, G.-J., Bazen, A.M., Veldhuis, R.N.J.: Practical biometric authentication with template protection. In: Kanade, T., Jain, A., Ratha, N.K. (eds.) AVBPA 2005. LNCS, vol. 3546, pp. 436–446. Springer, Heidelberg (2005)
37. Vaidya, J., Tulpule, B.: Enabling better medical image classification through secure collaboration. In: Proc. IEEE International Conference on Image Processing (ICIP), pp. IV–461–IV–464 (2007)
38. Yao, A.C.-C.: Protocols for Secure Computations (Extended Abstract). In: Annual Symposium on Foundations of Computer Science – FOCS 1982, November 3-5, pp. 160–164. IEEE Computer Society Press, Los Alamitos (1982)
39. Yu, X., Chinomi, K., Koshimizu, et al.: Privacy protecting visual processing for secure video surveillance. In: IEEE International Conference on Image Processing (ICIP 2008). IEEE Computer Society Press, Los Alamitos (2008)

A   Security (Sketch)

In this appendix we sketch why the face recognition protocol is privacy preserving. For semi-honest Alice and Bob, neither learns anything on the other's input—the database and the image—except the database size and what can be inferred from the output. As the parties are honest-but-curious, it suffices to demonstrate that no information is leaked by the messages seen.

Comparison protocol. The comparison protocol allows Bob to obtain a new encryption of the minimum of two encryptions he already possesses. On the intuitive level, security towards Bob is simple. All messages received are encrypted under Alice's public keys, and Bob cannot learn anything from these without breaking the semantic security of one of those schemes.

Alice on the other hand has access to the secret key. It must therefore be argued that no information is learned from the *contents* of the encryptions sent. But this is the case, as Alice only receives values that Bob has masked: this includes the messages sent for the secure selection of the minimal and ID, as well as $[d] = [z + r]$, which is statistically indistinguishable from a uniformly random $(\kappa + \ell + 1)$-bit value.

Treatment of the permuted $\llbracket e_i \rrbracket$ of Section 5.3 is only slightly more difficult. Alice either sees a list of uniformly random non-zero values, or an equivalent list, where one entry is replaced by a zero. A list of random values provides no information. Similarly, the zero does not cause any problems: Its position is random due to the permutation, and its existence also reveals nothing as it occurs with probability $1/2$; s can be viewed as a one-time-pad for the outcome. Thus, neither Alice nor Bob learn anything from the comparison protocol.

Complete Recognition Protocol. The proof of security of the full protocol is similar to that of the comparison. In addition to the comparisons, interaction is only needed to compute the distances $D_1, \ldots, D_M$. As above, the values $x_1, \ldots, x_K$ that Alice receives are masked, in this case they are uniformly random over the whole plaintext space. Bob again receives only semantically secure encryptions, so he also learns nothing. This is also true when he receives Alice's input.

Based on the above intuition, a formal simulator proof is easily constructed. Given one party's input and the output, simulation of the other party is easy: Alice must be handed encryptions of random values, while Bob can be handed encryptions of 0, which are indistinguishable due to the semantic security.

Author Index